👎| *The Reasoning Voter* |👍

The Reasoning Voter

Communication and Persuasion
in Presidential Campaigns

Samuel L. Popkin

Second Edition

The University of Chicago Press

Chicago and London

The University of Chicago Press, Chicago 60637
The University of Chicago Press, Ltd., London
© 1991, 1994 by The University of Chicago
All rights reserved. Originally published 1991
Paperback edition 1994
Printed in the United States of America
12 11 10 09 08 07 06 05 04 03   9 8 7 6 5

ISBN 0-226-67545-9

Library of Congress Cataloging-in-Publication Data

Popkin, Samuel L.
    The reasoning voter : communication and persuasion in
presidential campaigns / Samuel L. Popkin. — 2nd ed.
        p.   cm.
    Includes bibliographical references and index.
        1. Presidents—United States—Election.   2. Voting—United
States.   3. Electioneering—United States.   I. Title.
    JK524.P64   1994
    324.973—dc20   93-43845
                                                        CIP

To Ithiel de Sola Pool
and Jean MacKenzie Pool

". . . to learn, to teach, to do."

Contents

Acknowledgments

This book reflects my experiences doing survey research about presidential campaigns since my undergraduate days at MIT, when I began to work with Ithiel de Sola Pool. He introduced me to campaign research and to the field of communications research. More important, he taught me that scholarship knows no boundaries, that economics, sociology, psychology, and psychoanalysis all have important insights for the study of political communications. Above all, he and Jean were my family away from home and role models for what marriage, family, and career together could be.

Ithiel introduced me to Robert Abelson, who has been a source of stimulation for three decades. In every campaign in which I have participated he has been a sounding board and a source of insight. Writing questionnaires and devising campaign strategy with Bob provided me a master class in modern psychology.

John Gorman and Pat Caddell made it possible for me to be both an academic and a campaign researcher and strategist. As their utility infielder and survey analyst, I was able to be part of three presidential campaigns. John has also been a demanding critic of my attempts to be rigorous and readable.

From 1983 until 1990 I served as a consultant to Warren Mitofsky of CBS News. While working on current elections Warren encouraged me to explore the CBS News/*New York Times* survey archive, and without that encouragement this would have been a lesser book. I hope that my book, by introducing other scholars to this rich and valuable data source, increases appreciation for the work he did and the research unit he created. At CBS, Kathy Frankovic was a fount of empirical knowledge about past elections and a valued colleague. Warren and Kathy made it possible for me to keep my hand in presidential campaigns while maintaining the semblance of family life that is otherwise impossible with children and two careers.

Gary Cox and Don Kinder were brutally helpful with their ongoing readings of various drafts of this book. Don was particularly helpful with my attempts to absorb contemporary voting research. Knowing that anytime he found serious fault with logic or exposition, I would be back for another reading, Gary still maintained his standards. Larry Bartels and Henry Brady were good-natured and tolerant about my attempts to deal with their research and explain verbally the nuances of primary dynamics. Their help exceeded reasonable expectations and gave me momentum. John Aldrich, Michael Alvarez, Dick Brody, Paul Chan, James S. Coleman, Norman Frohlich, Gary Jacobson, Shanto Iyengar, Sam Kernell, Jon Krosnick, Sandy Lakoff, Simon Lazarus, Skip Lupia, Mat McCubbins, Joe Oppenheimer, Nathan J. Winograd, Aaron Wildavsky, and Ken Williams all provided me readings which helped me sharpen my arguments and clarify their relations to existing voting studies. That means they all found things I had left out or done poorly; none of them made it easier, but they all helped me make it better.

Chuck Nathanson pushed me time and again to clarify the links between my research and larger questions about American politics. Alan Houston, Victor Magagna, and Tracy Strong suggested implications of my analysis for democratic theory. David Laitin and Michael Schudson helped me connect the research to larger questions of social theory. Jay McClelland introduced me to Daniel Kahneman, who was a patient tutor on the nuances of his work. James Morris and Robert Tyson introduced me to relevant psychoanalytic insights and helped me think through their implications.

Reuben Rosen and Judy McTigue helped with research; Reuben was also a great help with organization. Gene Tanke was an exacting copyeditor and Joan Brun patiently kept track of the many drafts and revisions. John Tryneski helped, from the earliest drafts, to structure and focus the book, to make it focus on the future instead of the past. I am grateful to him for his faith in this project. Salena Fuller Krug edited the final copy and Robert Krug clarified the tables.

My children, Lucy and David Popkin, were encouraging throughout, cheering every milestone and reminding me why I care about the state of American government and the outcome of our campaigns. My aunt Jeanette Popkin spent countless Saturday and Sunday mornings with them so my wife and I could simultaneously finish books. That we did so with so little strain speaks to her good cheer and to the special qualities of our nanny-of-all-trades, Mary Tschosik. Finally, Susan Shirk, my wife, has been my partner through this all.

Prologue

AFTER President Gerald Ford lost the presidential election to Jimmy Carter, he was asked to name the most important lesson he had learned from his campaign. He answered, "Always shuck your tamales."[1]

During the 1976 primary campaign, President Ford was attacked by challenger Ronald Reagan on the issue of negotiations with the government of Panama, begun by President Carter, to turn over management and control of the canal to the Panamanian government. Reagan's assault was clear and direct: "We built it, we paid for it, and we're gonna keep it." The Ford campaign countered this attack with John Wayne, who was featured prominently in commercials supporting the canal negotiations. Still, Reagan's use of the canal issue was proving effective. Before the Texas primary, he was ahead of the president in the polls, and since Texas was too important to concede to Reagan, Ford was making an energetic effort to win enough delegates to derail him. Ford's campaign targeted the city of San Antonio, where, his strategists reasoned, Mexican-American voters were more likely to support negotiations with Panama. With roots in Mexico, they would not believe that the canal negotiations were either humiliating or a giveaway, or that a canal treaty was just one more setback for post-Vietnam, post-Watergate America.

Predictably enough, the San Antonio rally for President Ford featured Mexican food, and so the President of the United States was served his first tamale, a food not common in Grand Rapids, Michigan, or even in Washington, D.C. While reporters and television cameras recorded the scene, Ford proceeded with gusto to bite into the tamale, corn husk and all.

Videotapes and still photos of this gastronomic gaffe were used throughout the country and on network news broadcasts. The *New York Times* found it news fit to print on the front page. The accompanying photo showed Ford as he put the tamale in his mouth, with this caption: "CAMPAIGNING IN TEXAS: President Ford starting to eat a hot tamale during a visit to the Alamo yesterday. The snack was interrupted after the first bite so that his hosts could remove the corn shucks which serve as a wrapper and are not supposed to be consumed."[2]

Ford was not the first candidate to encounter trouble with unfamiliar food. In 1972, during the New York primaries, Senator George McGovern of South Dakota was courting the Jewish vote, trying to demonstrate his sympathy for Israel. As Richard Reeves wrote for *New York* magazine in August,

> During one of McGovern's first trips into the city he was walked through Queens by City Councilman Matthew Troy and one of their first stops was a hot dog stand. "Kosher?" said the guy behind the counter, and the prairie politician looked even blanker than he usually does in big cities. "Kosher!" Troy coached him in a husky whisper. "Kosher and a glass of milk," said McGovern.[3]

Worse yet, McGovern and his staff decided that he should make his Israel speech in a synagogue on a Friday night. It took New York Democrats three days to explain to them why a political speech could not be given in a synagogue on the Jewish Sabbath.[4]

Would a Mexican-American voter who saw President Ford bite into an unshucked tamale be wrong to conclude that the president had little experience with Mexican-American culture, little feel for it? Would a Jewish voter who saw George McGovern order a kosher hot dog and a glass of milk, and plan to talk politics in a synagogue on a Friday night, be wrong to conclude that the good senator knew little about Jews and Jewish concerns?

There is a wonderful treatise to be written someday about the role of food in American political campaigns. No serious candidate for president can rest secure in his knowledge of the intricacies of Iowa agriculture or New Hampshire environmentalism; he must master ethnic food as well. At the minimum, he (or she) must know how to use chopsticks; how to shuck tamales; how to open a lobster; how to eat ribs; how to eat pasta standing up without getting sauce on his tie (or her blouse); and when it is permissible to drink milk in a kosher deli. And failing a plausible defense of abstinence for reasons of religion or health, the candidate must be able to drink green beer, dark beer, sweet kosher wine, wine spritzers, retsina, and sake. The candidate also must show familiarity with deli food, Chinese food, soul food and barbecue, corned beef and cabbage, sauerkraut and wurst, souvlaki and baklava, pizza, sushi, quiche, and—of course—tamales and tacos.

In a multiethnic, polyglot society, with its inevitable bigotries and prejudices, showing familiarity with a voter's culture is an obvious and easy test of ability to relate to the problems and sensibilities of the ethnic group and to understand and care about them. Incidents involving such tests illustrate the kinds of *cues* that voters use to make judgments on the fly—judgments, I will argue, that need to be taken seriously in order to understand voters and campaigns.

Tamale shucking is not, of course, the best test of a candidate's policy stands on income redistribution, nuclear disarmament, and foreign trade. But neither is it merely symbolism, devoid of content and without meaning for the political process. The effects a president has on the benefits enjoyed by the citizenry go far beyond policies: a president provides moral and social cues to the country. American presidential elections integrate the country and provide the common symbols which inform public discourse. A president who understands and is familiar with an ethnic group is more likely to help ease that group's way into the American mainstream, and will make open disparagement of that group less acceptable. A president with friends from such a group is more likely to understand its sensibilities and the ways that presidential behavior affects them than one who doesn't even know how to cope with their foods.[5] Such cues are taken seriously enough in other contexts; when the Senate considers a candidate for the Supreme Court, membership in exclusionary country clubs or lodges is often given as much serious consideration as are the judge's opinions.

In 1988, when Michael Dukakis, governor of Massachusetts, picked Senator Lloyd Bentsen of Texas as his vice-presidential nominee, there were more than a few ruffled feathers between Dukakis and Jesse Jackson. Jackson, Dukakis, and a few top aides met to clear the air and negotiate a role for Jackson at the convention and in the fall campaign. Senator Bentsen joined the group, and, according to Jackson, "saved the meeting." He did so, Jackson said, because "he understands coalitions and constituencies. . . . He can go from biscuits to tacos to caviar real fast, knowing that's just the cultural diversity that makes up America." Bentsen, Jackson noted, "knew instinctively if you go and campaign among Hispanics, [you] talk Spanish and eat tacos, or [you] go over to the Black side of town and do a soul shake or some cultural expression, eat a biscuit." Jackson also noted that these things could be done without losing support elsewhere in the electorate. As these comments implied, a politician like McGovern, who lacked such skills, would have to try to demonstrate familiarity and commitment with awkward promises that would cost him support elsewhere.[6]

Ford's admonition to "always shuck your tamales" shows how concerned campaigners can be with media emphasis on personal behavior. Of course, it shows only that candidates perceive such incidents to be important; it does not demonstrate that they actually affect any votes or even affect attitudes about the candidate. As I will show, however, campaigners are right to be concerned; campaign incidents like these sometimes do have large electoral effects. A book about campaigns ought to be able, along the way, to analyze this concern and provide a way for understanding and evaluating when and why such incidents will matter.

In a postmortem of the 1980 election, Gerald Rafshoon, who had done most of the advertising for Jimmy Carter in 1976 and 1980, and who had been on the White House staff as a senior adviser to improve the president's "communications" (image), was asked about the effectiveness of the Carter advertising he had done in 1980. He answered, "If we had it to do all over again, we would take the 30 million dollars we spent in the campaign and get three more helicopters for the Iran rescue mission."[7] He was referring, of course, to the effort to rescue the fifty-five Americans held hostage in the American embassy in Teheran, Iran. The rescue attempt was aborted when defective helicopters forced the mission to turn back from its desert rendezvous outside Teheran.

Rafshoon's comment about the relative value of an abortive rescue mission and an entire year's advertising is an important reminder of the possible limits of image-making in the face of "political reality." Thirty million dollars' worth of political advertising was more than offset in his mind by the negative effect on the Carter campaign of the failed rescue mission and the ongoing hostage crisis.

Although Rafshoon's comment about the hostage crisis specifically emphasizes only the limits of television *advertising,* the crisis also provides a powerful example of the effect television news can have on a campaign. The first anniversary of the seizure by Iranian students of fifty-five hostages in the American embassy in Teheran coincided with the Sunday before the 1980 presidential election. As the hostage-crisis focus of recent television news reached a peak, reminding Americans of a yearlong humiliation, Sunday's NFL games were interrupted for news bulletins on the hostage anniversary and the possibilities for imminent release. Voters began thinking more about the failings of the Carter administration and less about the risks of Ronald Reagan, whose economic, social, and military policies had worried many voters. A choice between two futures became, for many, a referendum on the past four years, and Carter fell 10 points behind Reagan in forty-eight hours. What had been a close campaign became a major electoral rout for Carter and the Democratic party.[8]

Rafshoon's comparison of the relative value of campaign advertising and presidential accomplishments probably reveals more than he intended. His offhanded equation of campaign events and international military missions emphasizes how political campaigns and governance merge in the minds of some of the key players in a campaign; foreign policy is seen as part and parcel of a reelection effort—no different from campaign speeches, patronage, and pork barrel. Indeed, in recent history we have seen many small rescue raids that in retrospect appear more related to domestic politics than to any international concerns. Under President Ford, forty-one men were killed or missing in action as a result of the rescue of crewmen from the freighter *Mayaguez*.[9] Under President Nixon, the military raided an empty North Vietnamese prisoner-of-war camp at Son Tay. Under President Reagan, American medical students were "rescued" from Grenada. Perhaps most notably, the Reagan White House and National Security Council staffers such as Oliver North were obsessed with obtaining the release of American hostages held in Lebanon, and were even willing to trade arms—that is, pay ransom—to Iran in order to do so. A theory of voting and campaigning must be able to explain the electoral rationale for such raids and the role they play in campaigns.

Should incidents involving tamales and helicopters even be relevant to choosing the leader of "the greatest show on earth"? Should the Panama Canal and hostages in Lebanon, instead of energy crises and OPEC or domestic issues, be at the center of a presidential campaign? In the 1976 Republican primary, the Panama Canal treaty was discussed more than any domestic issue or any other foreign-policy topic except the Soviet Union and détente.[10] What is more important, substance or style?

The routine answer used to be that issue assessments were a more substantial basis for judging presidents than character or style. But if concern with personal style and competence can turn into an ethnic-food contest, concern with policy choices can lead to demagoguery over a Panama Canal treaty. As Richard Fenno trenchantly notes, issue voting can be corrupted just as easily as voting on character and style:

> Normative theorists . . . have a tendency to think of policy congruence as the only legitimate basis for representation, and to denigrate extrapolicy bases of representation as "symbolic." . . . It may be objected that a search for support that stresses stylistic compatibilities . . . easily degenerates

into pure image selling. And, of course, it may. But the
search for support that emphasizes policy compatibil-
ities . . . easily degenerates into pure position taking. . . .
Position taking is just as misleading to constituents and as
manipulative of their desires as image selling. It may be just
as symbolic as any form of candidate advertising.[11]

As we study campaigns, we cannot equate the divide between fluff and
substance with the divide between the personal character of the candidate
and the public importance of issues. When a George Wallace crowns a
beauty queen who is black, or a Rockefeller eats a knish, each man is communicating important changes in his relations with and attitudes about
ethnic or religious minorities. When the southern governor who promised
"segregation forever" congratulates a homecoming queen who is black,
does this have less significant implications for policy than posturing about
gun control or drug control?

Failed missions to rescue hostages and failed attempts to eat tamales are
similar: the same basic principles drawn from economics and psychology
can help us understand both the concern with tamales and the campaign
temptations to conduct rescue missions and covert activities.

In this book I use some basic principles of economics and psychology to
reexamine most of our conventional wisdom about campaigns, and most
of our academic ideas about them as well. I have tried to steer a theoretical
course between the approaches of campaigners and journalists on one
hand and those of political scientists and media scholars on the other. The
contributions of each have been valuable, and I hope this book will encourage them to continue this dialogue.

O N E

The Reasoning Voter

THIS BOOK has two main purposes. The first is to construct a general theory of voting that incorporates academic research of recent decades into a framework built from cognitive psychology, economics, and sociology. The second is to demonstrate the utility of that theory for analyzing political campaigns with three case studies.

I use the term *reasoning voter* because my theory recognizes that voters actually do reason about parties, candidates, and issues. They have premises, and they use those premises to make inferences from their observations of the world around them. They think about who and what political parties stand for; they think about the meaning of political endorsements; they think about what government can and should do. And the performance of government, parties, and candidates affects their assessments and preferences.

The term *low-information rationality*—popularly known as "gut" reasoning—best describes the kind of practical thinking about government and politics in which people actually engage. It is a method of combining, in an economical way, learning and information from past experiences, daily life, the media, and political campaigns.

This reasoning draws on various information shortcuts and rules of thumb that voters use to obtain and evaluate information and to simplify the process of choosing between candidates. People use shortcuts which incorporate much political information; they triangulate and validate their opinions in conversations with people they trust and according to the opinions of national figures whose judgments and positions they have come to know. With these shortcuts, they learn to "read" politicians and their positions.

The better we understand voters and how they reason, the more sense campaigns make and the more we see how campaigns matter in a democracy. Academic studies of voting have begun to reveal more and more about the substance of voting decisions and the limits to manipulation of voters. Directly and indirectly, these studies refer to campaigning. Collectively, they show that voters do learn from campaigns, and that what they learn concerns policies and character and competence. They can do this because they know how to "read" the media and the politicians—that is, because they reason about what they see and hear.

There is something rather miraculous about the fact that citizens believe that leaders selected by balloting are legitimate—that they are entitled to govern. Part of the reason for this belief is that campaigns are able to reach people and involve them in the election. It is worth remembering that the term *campaign* is derived from the French word for "open country" and brings to politics some of its original military use: in a military campaign, an army left its barracks in the capital city for operations in the field, or open country. This is an apt metaphor for politics, because campaigns bring politicians out of the capital into the open country, where they must engage their political opponents in a series of battles conducted in full view of their countrymen, who will judge each contest. To arouse public opinion and generate support for their cause, they must defend their old policies, sell new policies, and justify their rule.

These contests are commonly criticized as tawdry and pointless affairs, full of dirty politics, dirty tricks, and mudslinging, which ought to be cleaned up, if not eliminated from the system. In their use of sanitary metaphors, however, many of these critiques confuse judgments of American culture with aesthetic criticisms of American politicians. They do not look closely at how voters respond to what they learn from campaigns, and they do not look closely at the people they wish to sanitize. If campaigns are vulgar, it is because Americans are vulgar.

Not surprisingly, most suggestions for reforming the campaigns have no basis in any sustained argument about how proposed reforms would affect voters or improve the system. Voters have a limited amount of information about politics, a limited knowledge of how government works, and a limited understanding of how governmental actions are connected to consequences of immediate concern to them. Campaigns give them much of the information they reason from as they deal with their uncertainty about these matters. Somehow, candidates manage to get a large proportion of the citizenry sorted into opposing camps, each of which is convinced that the positions and interests of the other side add up to a less desirable package of benefits. Thus campaigns, to the extent that they are successful, temporarily change the basis of political involvement from citizenship to partisanship, and in the process attract interest and votes from people who generally find politics uninteresting or remote.

Campaigns reach most people through the media. Besides attracting attention to the campaign "horse race," the media play a critical role in shaping voters' limited information about the world, their limited knowledge about the links between issues and offices, their limited understanding of the connections between public policy and its immediate consequences for themselves, and their views about what kind of person a president should be. The campaigns and media, in other words, influence the voter's frame of reference, and can thereby change his or her vote.

Low-Information Rationality

My theory of how voters reason is a theory of low-information rationality which emphasizes the sources of information voters have about politics, as well as their beliefs about how government works. The theory, as I develop it, is drawn from three main sources: the voting studies done at Columbia University in the 1940s; the theoretical contributions to the economics of information made by Anthony Downs; and certain ideas from modern cognitive psychology, as exemplified in the works of Jerome Bruner, Amos Tversky, and Daniel Kahneman. I must emphasize at the outset that I am attempting to provide a theoretical basis upon which future studies can build, not to demonstrate or test every relevant proposition. Some parts of my argument have been demonstrated by others; other parts are demonstrated in this book; still other parts are theoretically grounded conjecture, not yet tested.

Social psychologists—notably Hilde Himmelweit and the coauthors of *How Voters Decide*—are beginning to emphasize that the vote is a choice, and that "the act of voting, like the purchase of goods, is . . . simply one instance of decision making, no different in kind from the process whereby other decisions are reached."[1] The final act of voting, they argue, is a consumer choice like any other, regardless of whether the voter's information gathering is "searching or superficial" and whether the voter's beliefs are "accurate or misleading," "transient or stable."

As far back as Aristotle, analysts have used metaphors based on choice or commerce to describe voting. Aristotle wrote about citizens directly involved in political deliberations; he assumed that citizens making public choices were like consumers making vital private choices. He argued, therefore, that political oratory needed little flourish or emotional appeal: "In a political debate the man who is forming a judgment is making a deci-

sion about his own vital interests. There is no need, therefore, to prove anything except that the facts are what the supporter of a measure maintains
they are."[2] However, the choice terminology appropriate in a mass democracy is different from that appropriate to deliberations in Athens.

Behind every voting theory there is a metaphor or an analogy, either implicit or explicit, about the process of choice. If the analogy is successful, it
helps to generate hypotheses and explain voting. I propose to view the
voter as an investor and the vote as a reasoned investment in collective
goods, made with costly and imperfect information under conditions of
uncertainty. This analogy is appropriate because the voter expends time
and effort in the expectation of some later return, a return that will depend
in large part on what others do. The investor analogy, as I will use it, does
something the consumer analogy cannot. It draws attention to the difference between public and private goods and allows us to begin to predict
several things: when information gathering will be searching and when it
will be superficial; when voter beliefs will be accurate and when they will
be misleading; and, to a lesser extent, when those beliefs will be transient
and when they will be stable.

In fact, voting is not like buying a television set. Voters are public investors, not private consumers. They expend effort voting in the *expectation* of
gaining future satisfaction. They are investors in future benefits to be derived from government, not purchasers of goods to be consumed immediately. This investment, furthermore, must be made in situations in which
the likelihood of different outcomes is not easily calculated, for want of either data or theory to guide the decision-making process. Many consumer
decisions involve clear alternatives and immediate results, but a decision
about voting always involves uncertainty and the prospects of a long-term
payoff.[3]

Public choices differ from private choices because the incentives to
gather information are different in each instance. The resources expended
to gather and process information before making personal consumption
decisions have a direct effect on the quality of the outcome for the consumer, whereas time and money spent gathering information about
candidates leads to a better vote, not necessarily a better outcome. The
wrong economic policy or the wrong approach to arms control may in fact
have a bigger effect on a voter's life than the wrong choice of home or college, but the expected gains from being an informed consumer remain
higher than the gains from being an informed voter. Voters are thus not
particularly well informed about the details of public policy and government activities. Everybody's business is nobody's business. If everyone

spends an additional hour evaluating the candidates, we all benefit from a better-informed electorate. If everyone but me spends the hour evaluating the candidates and I spend it choosing where to invest my savings, I will get a better return on my investment as well as a better government.

Public choices also differ from private choices because voting is a form of collective action; elections are won only when enough people vote together. Voters focus not only on their own concerns and preferences but on those of others as well. Therefore, in deciding which issues to focus on and which candidates to vote for, voters will be affected by information about what other voters are doing. Information about the preferences and votes of others will help them decide whether there are enough people with the same concerns or preferences to make a critical mass. Learning what government is doing and what government is capable of doing can also affect the issues a citizen will focus on in an election. Information will affect my perception of whether a problem is mine alone or common to many; whether a problem common to many is an individual or a collective problem; and whether a collective problem is "our" problem or our government's problem.

Public choices also differ from some private choices because they involve the provision of services. A politician is promising to deliver a future product about which the voter may have limited understanding, so the vote involves uncertainty about whether the product can be delivered, and, if so, whether it will perform as promised. Thus the voter has to assess the politician's ability to accomplish what he or she promises. Private consumers also face uncertainty in making certain decisions—such as choosing a surgeon to perform a life-threatening operation—but choosing a political leader can be even more complex. To deliver promised benefits, a politician must do more than attract enough votes; he or she must attract the support of other politicians as well. For this reason, voters consider not only the personal characteristics of their candidate, but also the other politicians with whom he or she is affiliated.

Every voting theory begins, implicitly or explicitly, from a question which voters ask as they cast their votes. I suggest that the voter behaves as if asking, "What have you done for me lately?" *What have you done?* stresses feedback from government performance and the need to specify how that performance affects attitudes and expectations. *Lately* raises the issue of time horizons—how voters can discount older information when presented with new claims. In *for me,* however, there is an inherent ambiguity, a tension that cannot be resolved. Doing some things for the voter includes doing the same things for everybody, like reducing pollution. It

includes doing things for specific groups, like feeding or housing the home-
less. And it involves doing things that protect the voter against future
possibilities, like improving Medicare or supporting research into a cure for
AIDS. This is an unresolvable ambiguity. In 1952, campaign buttons said "I
like Ike," but at rallies people said "*We* like Ike." The very ambiguity in the
meaning of *for me*, however, stresses that political leaders seek to create political identities and to forge links between individual and group concerns.

The transformation of "What have you done for me lately?" into "What
have you done for *us* lately?" is the essence of campaigning. Transforming
unstructured and diverse interests into a single coalition, making a single
cleavage dominant, requires the creation of new constituencies and political identities. It requires the aggregation of countless *I*'s into a few *we*'s.
Behind the *we*'s, however, are people who are still reasoning about the
ways in which their lives and government policies are related. The single
most important lesson I have learned from campaigning is never to tell
people they are selfish, and never to assume that they aren't.

Communications and Persuasion: The Columbia School

I begin with the original studies of presidential campaigns done at Columbia University's Bureau of Applied Social Research in the 1940s.[4] The
Columbia studies took the social reasoning of voters seriously and focused
on the relation of the campaign to the final vote. These studies also had a
relevant normative concern: the manipulative potential of the media. Today there is widespread concern about the impact of the newest medium,
television, on the electoral process. People worry that television is leading
to a politics of "spinmasters" and admen who manipulate voters and create
"Teflon" presidents. When the first Columbia study was done, there was
even more reason to be concerned about the power of radio: Hitler had
used it with seeming brilliance to manipulate his countrymen.

The Columbia studies were designed to assess the communication and
persuasion effects of campaigns at a time when these effects were generally
much smaller than today. Today, in an environment of diminished party
loyalty, campaigns and candidates exert a greater influence on voters than
they did in the elections of 1940 and 1948. However, the theoretical insights of the Columbia researchers are still illuminating for the study of
politics in the 1990s. Their research on party identification, misperception,
and interpersonal influence, as well as their insights into campaign dynamics, are still the foundation for modern election studies.

The central insight of the Columbia voting studies is captured in one sen-
tence: "The people vote in the same election, but not all of them vote *on*

it."[5] This statement recognizes the importance of party identification, of public communication and persuasion, and of the role of issues in elections. It suggests that voters in any one election are being moved not only by new issues of which they are aware but also by old issues that have influenced their party identification. It also stresses that voters are not tabulae rasae when they are exposed to the media barrages of the campaigns; to the contrary, they already have some firm beliefs, so are often not moved at all by campaign propaganda. Finally, the Columbia studies also showed that the effect of the mass media on voters is not direct, but mediated by discussion with others.

In beginning with the older Columbia studies, I am presenting an alternative to the theories and standards developed at the University of Michigan's Survey Research Center (SRC), which have dominated the study of voting since the 1950s. *The American Voter* developed a theoretical view of party identification and the role of issues in elections which has been central to voting studies for decades.[6] The SRC's quadrennial national election surveys have made possible numerous important studies, but its theories about voting and party identification have not held up well.[7]

Information Shortcuts: The Contributions of Anthony Downs

The central insight of Anthony Downs's pioneering book, *An Economic Theory of Democracy,* is that voters will rely on information shortcuts because they do not have much incentive to gather information about politics solely in order to improve their voting choices.[8] Downs builds on the Columbia studies' findings that voters lack knowledge about the government: "Voters are not always aware of what the government is or could be doing, and often they do not know the relationship between government actions and their own utility incomes." Given the many gaps in voters' information about government, and their lack of theory with which to make connections between government actions and their benefits, governments concerned primarily with gaining as many votes as possible have little incentive to maximize benefits to voters. "Government is motivated by voters' opinions, not their welfare, since their opinions about their welfare are what influence voting."[9]

Somehow, in a manner that I will leave to a sociologist of knowledge to explain, the word *rational,* which conjured up images of sophistication, materialism, and narrow self-interest, became a fighting word to many students of voting who had been raised on social psychology and sociology. Properly understood, however, the main emphasis of the economic approach is on choice, information, uncertainty, and the way voters link their votes with the votes of others and with the output of their government. When elaborated, it also crosses the divide between the work of scholars following the economic approach to the study of voting and the work of scholars of a more psychological bent, and provides a synthesis which is the ideal starting place for the study of campaigns and political change.

Downs's application of the economics of information to politics complements the Columbia studies. Indeed, Downs's central insight about information shortcuts is a generalization of the Columbia findings about the roles of party identification and informal opinion leaders. Party identification, viewed from the perspective of low-information rationality, is an informational shortcut or default value, a substitute for more complete information about parties and candidates. This is a key insight for building a model of the voter that can be used to study the role of campaigns and issues in presidential elections. Party identification is a standing decision; even so, it is affected by voters' beliefs about how government works, by the information they obtain in their daily lives and connect with government policies, and by the information they absorb simply because it is interesting or entertaining.[10]

I elaborate Downs's ideas about information costs and uncertainty, apply them to the ways voters evaluate candidates and parties, and also take account of how voters connect the state of the world with the actions of government and the benefits they desire. Downs is an economist, but he is not assuming that voters care only about money, or only about benefits for themselves. He assumes only that they base their votes on the benefits they may receive from government action. As he puts it,

> [It is] possible for a citizen to receive utility from events that are only remotely connected to his own material income. For example, some citizens would regard their utility incomes as raised if the government increased taxes upon them in order to distribute free food to starving Chinese. There can be no simple identification of "acting for one's greatest benefit" with selfishness in the narrow sense because self-denying charity is often a great source of benefits.[11]

Extending Downs, I explore how voters' understanding of government and candidates helps determine which issues and benefits they will connect with particular offices—which benefits, in other words, are *attributable*. It is not the importance of a policy, nor even the extent to which parties or candidates differ on it, that determines when an issue will become central to voter decision making. What make an issue central are the voters' motivations to gather information about it, the conditions under which they will get that information, and the beliefs by which they connect the issue to their own lives and to the office for which they are voting. Further, by stressing not just the limited information about issues but also the limited understanding voters have of the way government works, we can begin to evaluate the effects of television—the prime information medium, as well as one of the usual suspects in any investigation into the quality of the electoral process or electoral outcomes in the United States.

The notion of attributable benefits, furthermore, can lead us to a new understanding of the many ways campaigns influence voters. The Columbia studies correctly noted that a campaign can affect the salience of an issue by increasing its perceived importance to voters. It follows from my elaborations on the Columbia and Downs findings that a campaign can change the salience of an issue in two other ways: by providing better connections between an issue and an office, and by increasing the perceived difference between candidates on an issue.

My emphasis on voters' incentives for gathering information leads me to consider not only voters' demand for information but also the supply and cost of that information. Political campaigns and party conventions are particularly important sources of relevant information. In using information about candidates and their supporters, voters extrapolate from personal characteristics to policy preferences, and from campaign performance to governmental competence. They also gather information about the candidate's place in the party and the credibility of his or her platform from two other sources: the party convention, and party leaders they have learned about in the past.

Framing and Reasoning: Cognitive Psychology

Contemporary research into the psychology of cognition fills the theoretical gaps left by the original Columbia voting studies and Downs's theoretical reformulation of them. Without cognitive psychology there is no satisfactory way to answer important questions about how people assess meaning and use information. My analysis of campaigns requires an understanding of the role of symbols and stories; to understand people not as naive statisticians, but as symbol processors and naive theorists, requires cognitive psychology. Cognitive psychology's findings about meaning and information usage go beyond cues and information shortcuts to describe modes of reasoning, processing aids, and calculation aids, all of which can be applied to the analysis of reasoning voters' decisions.[12]

Each of the three sources from which I draw provides crucial insights about information and political reasoning. From the Columbia studies, we know that people do not absorb all the information to which they are exposed. From Downs, we know that this happens because people do not have incentives to acquire and absorb much of that information. From cognitive psychology, we know that people do not use all the information they have received, and—paradoxically—that people have not received from outside all the information they use. That is, people take the information they have received and use previous experience to complete the picture.

To study the cues, or informational shortcuts, that people use in voting is to study how people supply themselves with information that fills in their pictures of candidates and governments. Cues enable voters to call on beliefs about people and government from which they can generate or recall scenarios, or "scripts," as they are called in psychology. A little information can go a long way because people have so many scenarios and ideas that they can generate from their cues. They can absorb a few cues and then complete their picture with the help of their "default values."[13]

Downs never explicitly considered just how voters combine new and old information, or how recent events affect their ongoing assessment of parties, but his work generally leads to what can be called neo-Bayesian assumptions. In Bayesian statistical analysis, decisions are based not solely on old information or solely on new information, but on a weighted combination of the two, with the weights assigned to reflect the quantity of each type. The cognitive literature, in contrast, shows that there are instances when a small amount of new information is given more weight than a large amount of equivalent old information, as well as cases when a small amount of old information is given more weight than a large amount of equivalent new information.

One reason that people do not behave like naive statisticians is that data presented in an emotionally compelling way may be given greater consideration and more weight than data that is statistically more valid, but emotionally neutral. This is not a new insight; as Bertrand Russell noted in 1927, "popular induction depends upon the emotional interest of the instances, not upon their number."[14] The ramifications of this insight for decision making are only now being fully explored by psychologists. Campaign analysis must begin to explain what kinds of data are compelling to voters and how they combine old and new data.[15] This means, in particular, learning why some forms of information are more easily used than others, and why not all information is necessarily informative:

> Some kinds of information that the scientist regards as high-
> ly pertinent and logically compelling are habitually ignored
> by people. Other kinds of information, logically much weak-

er, trigger strong inferences and action tendencies. We can think of no more useful activity for psychologists who study information processing than to discover what information their subjects regard as information worthy of processing.[16]

There is another reason why people do not act like crude statisticians: they cannot easily integrate all their political information about parties or candidates into a single yardstick, or "prior," as a statistician would call such a measure. In particular, they do not always integrate personal and political data about candidates.

The cognitive literature also leads researchers beyond information shortcuts to the calculation shortcuts people use when choosing one favorite from an array of candidates. Since people cannot easily integrate all their information, their choices are context-sensitive: "Preferences are not simply read off from some master list; they are actually constructed in the elicitation process. Furthermore, choice is contingent or context sensitive. . . . An adequate account of choice, therefore, requires a psychological analysis of the elicitation process and its effect on the observed response."[17]

Plan of the Book

The next five chapters cover the essential theoretical issues that must be addressed in order to understand campaigns from the perspective of the voter.

Chapter 2 outlines the process of acquiring information—how voters become informed through daily-life experiences and their monitoring of the news. Voters obtain a good deal of information during their daily lives which they connect to government policies, whether correctly or not; meat and gas shortages change opinions about presidents as surely as "Communist gains" once did. Senior citizens whose only livelihood is Social Security pay close attention to debates on this issue—not in order to be better citizens, but because they need to know how to budget their money, and sometimes to decide whether they can afford to eat three meals a day or two. The use of this information depends upon reasoning about government, incorporates campaign information, and is not reflexive.

Chapter 3 examines the information shortcuts that voters use when they have little information about, or an incomplete understanding of, the political choices before them—an examination that involves reevaluating the concept of party identification and identifying the shortcuts voters use to assess candidates. These shortcuts include assessing a candidate's policy stands from his demographic characteristics; using overall estimates of a candidate's competence and of his integrity or sincerity; and judging political integrity from personal morality. These shortcuts also incorporate information from political campaigns, while at the same time limiting the extent to which campaigns can manipulate voters.

Chapter 4 describes how voters process information about candidates, and go beyond their information, when they form images of their candidacies. By understanding how voters incorporate information, and by understanding how they combine new and old information, we see how campaigns can affect which information will actually be used. The chapter also describes how voters use calculation shortcuts and how they compare and choose among candidates.

Chapter 5 elaborates the concept of attributable benefits, and then shows that voters' ideas about government can affect politicians' actions and the issues they choose to emphasize in campaigns, and can also help determine which issues will matter whether the politicians mention them or not.

In chapter 6 I turn to the formation of new constituencies in presidential primaries and examine the contrast between the theories I develop here and theories about primary voting which have emphasized the role of momentum or "bandwagon" effects.

Chapters 7, 8, and 9 examine three presidential primary campaigns in which hitherto unknown candidates suddenly emerged to challenge for, or even to win, their party's nomination for president: Jimmy Carter in the Democratic primaries of 1976; George Bush in the Republican primaries of 1980; and Gary Hart in the Democratic primaries of 1984. Ironically, it is by analyzing the campaigns of these once-unknown candidates that I can most effectively demonstrate the value of the theory I am developing, for the analysis enables me to show politics and political reasoning at work in precisely the place where other theories would least expect it.

I realize that, because all three case studies involve primary campaigns, some people may draw the inference that the theory I am developing is only for primaries. I emphasize that I am doing case studies of primaries because primaries are more difficult for voters and have been harder to explain for scholars. In primaries, voters face a multitude of candidates, with less prior information about candidates than they have in general elections; they also receive less exposure to campaign information, and have no party cues to guide them. Therefore, primaries place greater demands on the voters to quickly absorb information and to reason with incomplete information. I believe, to paraphrase Sinatra, that if a theory can make it there, it can make it anywhere. Most of the examples in chapters 2 through

5 are taken from general elections, which is where I have had most of my practical campaign experience.

In an age when voting is increasingly centered on candidates, political primaries are part of the process of renewing and updating party identification.[18] Primary candidates create and mobilize constituencies within parties, and they respond to public beliefs about the past performance of the party and the perceived relevance of its approach to government. Thus in analyzing primaries I can demonstrate the many forms of information about their political parties that voters gather, as well as the forms of feedback from government performance that shape their ideas about parties.

The three primaries analyzed here demonstrate just how sensitive voters are to the direction their party is taking, and how their views of their party are affected by its past performance. In other words, these three primaries exhibit the kinds of feedback about parties that voters receive, and show how voters translate this feedback into preferences. These fights over the direction a party should take—including arguments about whether the party's traditional ways are adequate both to win the presidency and to deal with the future problems of the country—show just how policy-oriented party identification can be.

Indeed, these three case studies, taken together, show the tremendous changes in political thinking which have occurred in this country since the 1960s. The Democratic primary of 1976 demonstrates how conflicts over race, Vietnam, and the role of unions, among other issues, eroded the credibility of the party's Washington elite and left its best-known representatives unable to compete against outsiders like Jimmy Carter, George Wallace, and Jerry Brown. Carter's emergence, furthermore, prefigured the emergence of the religious fundamentalist movement in this country and the inability of traditional Democratic leaders to compete against Republicans for the presidency. The fights between Mondale, Hart, and Jackson in 1984 were in fact clear continuations of the same unresolved battles between black, blue-collar, and educated Democrats over the role of government and the direction the party should take.

The 1980 fights in the Republican party between Bush supporters and Reagan supporters were a continuation of the 1976 fights between Reagan and Ford supporters over the direction of the Republican party and whether it should repudiate the moderation of the Nixon years. The 1980 battles, and the Republican repudiation of the ERA that year, were part of the continuing battle over abortion policy, which was already creating a "gender gap" between parties.

Recent studies of primaries have focused on the role of momentum, and the ways in which lesser-known candidates could win primaries because of "bandwagon" effects—where people are directly influenced to vote for a candidate by that candidate's earlier victories. By demonstrating that there are clear issue effects even when the least-known candidates first become known, I support my argument that there is a substantive basis for voting decisions.

The claim of political savants and insiders that the right commercials and the right consultants can win any election, particularly any primary, is fed by the self-serving myth that certain "magic moments" on television have turned elections around. I will show that there is no evidence at all for the supposed effects of many of these "magic moments," and that the dramatic effects of many others occurred only because they symbolized changes of opinion that had been developing for some time and which had far more complex causes. I object to media critics who simply infer from commercials and speeches that voters were manipulated.

I also object to studies of primaries which suggest that when large numbers of voters suddenly shift their support to new candidates, they are simply jumping on a bandwagon. These jumps to new candidates are in fact attempts to change the direction of the party, or to protest against the established order, and they reflect information that voters use about the issue differences between the new and the old candidates.

I challenge the related fantasies of Democrats who believe that campaign faux pas explain the Republicans' near-monopoly on the White House. Democrats do not lose the presidency because Republicans have better admen. They lose because they have less popular policies on the issues that voters connect to the presidency, notably inflation, national defense, and the role of government in society. Nor do Democrats lose because a controversial candidate (like Jesse Jackson) is visible in their primaries; they lose because they do not have convincing responses to such a candidate that they can give in both primary and general elections.

I also challenge the terms of the traditional assessment of voter information. It is certainly true that most citizens do not know many of the basic facts about their government, but assessing voters by civics exams misses the many things that voters *do* know, and the many ways in which they can do without the facts that the civics tradition assumes they should know. Further, the focus on voters' lack of textbook information about many political issues underestimates just how much information they pick up during campaigns and from conventions. This misinformation approach is a red herring. It focuses on what voters don't know instead of on what they do know, who they take their cues from, and how they read candidates.

I also challenge the idea that voter self-interest is either entirely selfish or simplistic. Voters do care about their economic well-being, of course, but they also care about the welfare of others, and when they reason about economic benefits and economic performance, they do not make simplistic connections between their bank balances and the performance of the government.

By bringing the economics of information and the recent developments in cognitive science to bear on the normative agenda of the Columbia studies, I hope to prompt a rethinking of the role of democratic citizenship. I believe my theory redeems the voter from some of the blame heaped upon him or her by contemporary criticism of the electoral process. My theory also addresses "loopholes" in voter reasoning that candidates can exploit. However, I hope to show that, in the mixture of trivial and profound issues that will always be found in campaigns, there is more meaning to voting, and less manipulation of voters, than either media-centered analyses or the traditional civics-information focus would have us believe.

T W O

Acquiring Data: The Process of Becoming Informed

THIS CHAPTER focuses on what voters know, when they know it, and how they relate their knowledge to voting decisions. They may have few incentives to gather information simply for the purpose of becoming good citizens, and may thus be uninformed about politics, but they can and do apply to political decision making a great deal of information they have acquired in their daily lives. This is the by-product theory of political information: the information that people acquire to negotiate their daily lives is later applied to their political judgments and choices. The specific connections that voters make between personal information, personal problems, and personal experiences with government, on one hand, and their political evaluations and choices, on the other, will depend upon several variables: what they believe government can do; what they know about what government is doing; what they know about what other people want from government; and what they are told by the media and political campaigns.

The By-Product Theory of Information

In economic terms, the process of procuring, analyzing, and evaluating information carries a cost—the investment of time and energy. Further, the expected return from time invested in reaching political decisions is small compared to the expected return from other uses of the same time—far smaller, certainly, than with decisions about personal consumption. For example, the health of the national economy may in fact have a greater effect on voters than whether their next vacation is fabulous or merely good; but time spent deciding where to travel leads to better vacations, whereas time spent evaluating economic policies leads not to better policies but only to a better-informed vote. Similarly, the ultimate economic well-being of a college senior may be affected more by America's economic future than by where the student goes to law school; but a week spent deciding where to attend law school has a higher return for the student than a week spent evaluating alternate approaches to trade imbalances or deficits. Some people, of course, find politics so fascinating that they inform themselves even when they have no personal stake in political outcomes. But in general, voters do not devote much time or energy directly to their votes. This does *not* imply either that voters are uninformed about general conditions or that they have no knowledge of specific government programs. What it means is that most of the information voters use when they vote is acquired as a *by-product* of activities they pursue as part of their daily lives. In that sense, political uses of this information are free.[1]

Daily-Life Information

A good deal of information is obtained in daily life about the economy and the community in which people live. Two-thirds of the country own their own homes and 55 percent have a mortgage; 84 percent have checking accounts and 81 percent have savings accounts; and 30 percent own stock. Three-quarters purchase items on credit, three-quarters go grocery shopping, and 78 percent have auto insurance. One in twelve adults is self-employed, and about the same number are actively looking for a new job at any one time.[2] In a typical year, 30 percent of all households will contain someone who is unemployed and actively looking for work. Some 95 percent of the people in the country file income-tax returns, and 55 percent pay someone to complete their income-tax forms.[3] One in five Americans knows someone who cheats on income taxes, and one in four takes steps specifically to reduce the amount owed in income taxes.[4]

One need not be an economist to see which way the economy is going. Generally, half the electorate knows the current unemployment rate within 1 or 2 percentage points, and about the same number have a good idea of what the inflation rate is.[5] These numbers, however, understate sensitivity to economic shocks. Most of the electorate buys gasoline; when gas prices rose in 1977, 40 percent of the citizenry nationwide reduced the miles they drove, and 25 percent used car pools.[6] When the price of gas rose faster and higher after the Shah of Iran was overthrown in 1979, 80 percent of the country cut back on gasoline consumption. As inflation rose to 21 percent, 52 percent cut back on the kinds of groceries they bought, two-thirds scaled back on vacations, and four-fifths lowered their thermostats. Not surprisingly, inflation was considered a more important problem than unemployment by five to one. Even less surprisingly, in early 1980 President Jimmy Carter received the lowest approval ratings of any president since World War II.[7]

While managing daily life, people also learn about crime and drugs. One person in four knows of a place where drugs are sold, and one in six sees them sold. Half of all Americans know someone hurt by drugs, and three-quarters know someone hurt by alcohol.[8] One in eight Americans has had a crime victim in the family within the past year, and two in five Americans have had a serious crime or felony in their neighborhood within the past year. Fifty-seven percent of all women and 28 percent of all men know a place within a mile of their home where they are afraid to walk alone at night; one in six Americans does not feel safe at home during the night.[9] Concern with crime and drugs is thus a prime example of a political issue growing out of daily life.

The public's monitoring of the news is sensitive to personally relevant information—on matters of health risks, for example. More voters know their cholesterol level than know their representative's name.[10] Health problems also generate experiences with institutions and bureaucracies. In May 1982, 47 percent of the respondents in a national health-care survey had a family member who had been in an emergency room during the last year, and 38 percent had a family member who had been hospitalized during the year. One-third of the respondents had sought a second opinion on a medical procedure, and one in five had lost health-insurance coverage for some period.[11]

Thus, political information is acquired while making individual economic decisions and navigating daily life: shoppers learn about inflation of retail prices; home buyers find out the trends in mortgage-loan interest rates; owners of stocks follow the Dow-Jones averages; people learn where it is safe to walk; and they learn about health and drugs. How and when this information is used remains to be shown.

Information about Government Programs

There are times when, in addition to this general information from daily life, information about specific government programs and policies is needed for planning and negotiating one's own life. For example, a student estimating his chances of being drafted spends time learning the draft policy. A businessman interested in selling his products overseas learns about technology transfer laws to develop sales plans. A senior citizen learns about Social Security benefits to plan the next year of his or her life. Home builders and prospective home buyers learn about interest rates to estimate the cost of homes.

The growth of government involvement in social and economic regulation and the extension of entitlement programs mean that whether the electorate is better educated or not, there will be more "issue publics" (subsets of the overall public that care a great deal about particular issues; discussed below) concerned with government expenditures and policies in their areas. For example, 15 percent of the households in the country contain a government employee; 25 percent contain someone receiving Social Security old-age benefits; and 23 percent contain someone receiving Medicaid or Medicare.[12] One in five households has received welfare benefits at some time.[13]

News Media

Other main sources of information for the electorate are the news media—television, newspapers, radio, and magazines; some of this information comes directly from the media and some comes from discussions with friends, neighbors, and fellow workers.

Most Americans watch some network television news and scan newspapers several times every week. In May 1983, at a time when there were no political campaigns or major crises or political events, a general set of questions about media use was asked on a CBS News poll. The poll found that in a typical week, 80 percent of Americans see at least one network news show, and half the country sees three or more shows; that 7 percent regularly watch CNN, the Cable News Network, and another 30 percent watch it occasionally; and that over 60 percent read newspapers on a normal day.[14] All told, then, the time spent watching television news and reading newspapers averages over thirty minutes per day for all Americans over eighteen. Moreover, people also hear about the news from their friends and acquaintances; one-quarter of the respondents had talked in the past day about a story they saw on television or read in a newspaper (see table 2.1).

A great deal of news coverage caters to a strong public appetite for events that are exciting or frightening. Politicians, of course, pay careful attention to disasters because the public pays attention to them: In the May 1983 CBS poll about media usage, one-fifth of all conversations about news stories were about disasters. Congressmen and state legislators thus rush to the scenes of fires, crashes, floods, and droughts in order to be seen where the electorate is looking.[15] Steven Merksamer, the chief of staff for California governor George Deukmejian, has acknowledged this: "My biggest fear always was of not being prepared for a major disaster—and one thing about living in California is we have them. How they are handled can make or break elected officials. . . . We spent a lot of time drilling for disasters. We would have mock prison riots, mock earthquakes—eight-hour

TABLE 2.1
Education and Media Usage

	< 12th Grade (%)	H.S. Graduate (%)	Some College (%)	College Graduate (%)	All Respondents (%)
Watch network news two or more times weekly	67	68	65	61	66
Read news magazine					
Regularly	4	7	19	37	13
Once in a while	18	34	39	32	30
Read newspaper yesterday	49	62	66	77	62
Read story yesterday about foreign country	14	24	32	50	26
Read story yesterday about national government	21	32	38	50	33
Have seen or heard story about "Most important problem facing country" in last week	50	64	74	78	64
Talked about any news event today	14	25	33	45	26
Of those who talked about news event today, the news event was:					
Local	57	36	27	24	35
National	7	16	18	29	17
Foreign	0	4	18	20	12
Disaster	14	20	21	16	19
Other/Don't know	22	24	16	11	17
Total N	(389)	(555)	(236)	(208)	(1,388)

Source: CBS News Poll, "Evenews," May 1983.
Note: Number in parentheses is number of respondents in column.

drills when we would practice making decisions, several times a year."[16]

A general monitoring of the media also brings people some information about events in other countries. In 1979 and 1980, for example, 60 percent of the electorate knew of the PLO or knew who signed the Camp David accords. And when the helicopters sent to rescue the American hostages in Teheran crashed, 94 percent of the country knew about the abortive raid within twenty-four hours.[17] Less than 40 percent of the country knows whether there are any treaties between the United States and the Soviet Union, or who is involved in the SALT talks, but when Gorbachev and Reagan met, many Americans picked up enough information from the participants and the commentators to perceive a decline in tensions. While a recent poll showed that less than 4 percent of Americans know the name of the Japanese prime minister and less than one-third know what form of government Japan has, when asked which country buys more of the other country's products, 87 percent correctly said that the United States buys more, while only 6 percent thought Japan buys more.[18] Here, as in all areas of knowledge, it is clear that information considered personally relevant is more readily absorbed. For example, in 1987, only 17 percent of the general public knew that convicted spy Jonathan Pollard, an American naval officer who funneled military intelligence to Israel, had been spying for Israel; among Jews the figure was 65 percent.[19]

Media Information and Daily-Life Information

The mass media affect how voters think about government because daily-life information and media information interact. They interact because, although daily-life information may tell us how the economy and the government have performed, it takes the media to tell us what the government is actually doing. Both political evaluations and votes depend, as I will demonstrate, upon the voters' views of the national agenda—the problems they consider most important. The importance, or salience, of national problems has traditionally been measured in Gallup polls and other national polls by asking respondents, "In your opinion, what is the most important problem facing the country?" Such a question reflects the unavoidable intermingling of two different aspects of issue salience: what is important and what is conspicuous.[20]

Daily-life information can tell us that energy shortages, price rises, and increased unemployment are conspicuous at the moment, but mass-media stories about these subjects, and coverage of presidential speeches about them, still affect the national agenda. A problem may be conspicuous, but it may not necessarily be seen as "an important problem facing the country" unless it is seen as a problem *for the country,* and not just a problem many people are having. (For example, AIDS is a problem for the country; obesity is a problem for many Americans.) Information which connects a story to government also contributes to making that problem either conspicuous or important when citizens think about their government. Shanto Iyengar and Donald Kinder, investigating changes in the salience that voters assign to inflation, unemployment, and energy problems over long periods of time, found that real-world conditions which make problems more conspicuous affect the salience of these problems.[21] However, as I discuss later, their research shows that television news stories and presidential speeches also affect the salience of these problems.

In other words, the use of daily-life information in determining the national agenda—the problems a citizen wants the government to address— is not reflexive or mechanical; it is mediated by information about what the government is doing or what the president is concentrating on. A television news story or a presidential speech alerts people to the connections between the conditions of their economy and society and the actions of their government. (It is also the case, for every problem that Iyengar and Kinder investigated, that a single presidential speech was as important as twenty-five network news stories in influencing the agenda.)

Issue Publics

In considering the conditions under which voters will inform themselves, researchers in public opinion and voting behavior apply the notion of the "issue public": a subset of the overall public that cares a great deal about a particular issue, and is therefore likely to pay attention to it. Gathering and digesting details about the fate of specific bills or programs is a costly and time-consuming process; the only voters who can be expected to undertake it are those who need the details for purposes other than voting. Thus, as Jon Krosnick has noted, "only a small proportion of people are likely to be knowledgeable about and to have potent attitudes regarding any single policy option or another."[22]

Few issues are followed by most of the electorate at any one time, but many issues concern sizable minorities, and the effects of specific issues and legislation can usually be registered only by isolating specific issue publics for analysis. As Philip Converse wrote, several years after coauthoring *The American Voter,* "We have come a step closer to reality when we recognize the fragmentation of the mass public into a plethora of issue publics."[23] As considerable psychological evidence indicates, "attention and memory are indeed enhanced when information is personally relevant."[24]

In *The American Voter*, it was assumed that an issue did not matter unless *the entire public* was aware of *specific legislation* concerning it. In Angus Campbell's words, "there were no great questions of public policy which *the public* saw as dividing the two parties."[25] Thus, "an example of public indifference to an issue that was given heavy emphasis by political leaders is provided by the role of the Taft-Hartley Act in the 1948 election. . . . Almost seven out of every ten adult Americans saw the curtain fall on the Presidential election of 1948 without knowing whether Taft-Hartley was the name of a hero or a villain."[26] Given these expectations, we should not be surprised that the role of issues appeared so negligible.

In fact, what *The American Voter* demonstrates is not public indifference to Taft-Hartley, a bill designed to curb the power of labor unions, but the use of inappropriate standards for judging public opinion and inadequate survey measures for assessing public concern with unions. In 1948, voters favoring the Taft-Hartley Act voted 12 percent for Truman and 82 percent for Dewey. Voters opposing the act voted 77 percent for Truman and 14 percent for Dewey.[27] Further, when asked why they thought people voted for Truman, 24 percent of the electorate mentioned Truman's association with unions. When asked why people supported Dewey, less than one-half of 1 percent mentioned support for unions.[28] This spectrum of opinion was about the same in 1952. In that year, again according to Campbell's own data, the voters who took prolabor stands on Taft-Hartley voted 29 percent for Eisenhower; those who took antilabor stands voted 77 percent for Eisenhower.[29] Thus a third of all voters were aware of a specific piece of legislation, and their positions on it had a strong effect on their votes.

Today, if 30 percent of the electorate actually knew the name of a specific piece of legislation, it would be taken as evidence of an issue of great concern to most of the electorate, because a much higher percentage of voters would have general impressions about the issue without knowing any legislative details. There were high levels of concern with Vietnam in 1968 and 1972, tax cuts were widely discussed in 1980, and budget cuts were widely discussed yearly after 1985, but no one would argue that the importance of these issues could be measured solely by whether "the public" knew whether Cooper-Church (a bill concerning troop withdrawal from Vietnam), Kemp-Roth (a major change in tax rates), and Gramm-Rudman (a deficit-reduction act) were heroes, villains, fast-food chains, or rock groups. Likewise, concern with government spending cannot be assessed simply by asking whether people have heard of Gramm-Rudman, nor can concern with stopping abortion be measured by assessing knowledge of the Hyde amendment or the wording used by the Supreme Court in *Webster v. Reproductive Health Services,* the 1989 case that reopened many of the issues previously decided in the Court's 1973 *Roe v. Wade* ruling. We come yet another step closer to political reality when we look for *general* awareness of the positions of candidates and parties, not just detailed information about specific legislation.

The growth of government has interacted with the development of specialized communications channels to create new issue publics. The importance of this fact is emphasized by the spectacularly wrong predictions in the second Columbia study, *Voting,* about a "senior citizen's vote" or a "woman's vote." "It would be difficult in contemporary America," *Voting* argued, "to maintain strong voting differences by sex, because there are few policy issues persisting over a period of time that affect men and women differently."[30] In the last twenty years, we have seen the development of a distinctive woman's vote: more women than men have voted more Democratic in the last four presidential elections, and there are several issues on which women and men have different attitudes and different priorities. They differ, for example, in their evaluations of whether the Great Society programs were effective. The gender gap, as it is called, developed from the growth of single-parent families and an increased government role in social welfare and child care.

Voting also concluded that there could be no policy movements based on the special interests of old age, such as pensions, because such a movement could not transmit itself over time.[31] Since 1948, of course, we have seen a major migration of retired people to senior-citizens' communities throughout the Sun Belt. Along with this, there has been the growth of organizations like the American Association of Retired Persons which communicate and transmit information about Social Security and Medicare. Not surprisingly, the elderly have higher levels of knowledge of specific Social Security and Medicare legislation than do other citizens.[32]

Changes in relations between gender and vote, and between age and vote, serve to emphasize that political cleavages in the electorate respond to changes in the popular culture and are influenced by the changing nature of government. Moreover, these cleavages increasingly reflect the relation of different groups to government programs like Social Security.

Connecting Information to Government

Voters are not self-centered and reflexive in evaluating their leaders and in making voting choices. Their evaluations and voting decisions depend on whether their reasoning connects their situations to the national situation and the actions of their leaders.

The earliest voting studies, whether economic or psychological in orientation, assumed that voting would be a direct reflection of the voter's life experiences and social milieu. The first Columbia study, for example, concluded that votes could be predicted directly from knowing whether voters were urban or rural, Catholic or Protestant, blue-collar or white-collar. A combination of these factors yielded the well-known Index of Political Predisposition (IPP).[33] Although Paul Lazarsfeld was mostly right when he said that we *think* politically as we *are* socially, this index was a failure. The simplifying assumptions that the same few social characteristics could estimate at all times how a person "was socially," and that one could infer directly from how a person was socially to how he or she "thinks politically," were incorrect. Lazarsfeld did not realize how many different things we are socially, and how many different ways there are in which we can think politically.[34]

The early economic studies of voting also made simplifying assumptions about how voters connected their personal economic conditions with their votes. The economic equivalent of the IPP was "pocketbook voting"— evaluating the president's performance directly on the basis of how it affects one's personal finances. As Morris Fiorina summed up the assumptions behind it, "in order to ascertain whether the incumbents have performed poorly or well, citizens need only calculate the changes in their own welfare."[35] In fact, when voters evaluate presidential performance and choose between candidates, they do not project directly from their own social characteristics, their pocketbooks, or even their personal problems. They engage in much more reasoning than that.

Voters discriminate, first of all, between government problems and personal problems. When thinking about government, they bring to bear only those personal problems they believe are part of the political agenda, problems government should be helping with.[36] Even voters who have lost their jobs during a recession do not automatically connect their unemployment with the government and its policies: "Failing to understand their own predicament as tied to others, as produced by collective forces, the unemployed are likely to treat their own experience as *irrelevant* to social economics or to government performance."[37] People think about cause

and effect, and they are able to reason about who is responsible for a problem and who can deal with it. This is true not only for their personal
economic situations but for issues as diverse as poverty, racism, and crime
as well.[38]

Voters also distinguish between their personal performance and the performance of the government. In direct contradiction of the pocketbook-
voting hypothesis, study after study has confirmed that assessments of
national economic conditions have a bigger impact on voting than do
changes in personal economic well-being.[39] When voters evaluate presidential performance, how the national economy is doing generally matters
more than how their own pocketbooks are doing.[40] This does not mean
that voters don't care about their own economic performance; it suggests
instead that people find changes in the national economy to be better indicators of how the government is doing. Personal changes are, after all, due
to one's own efforts, to the performance of one's company, and to health
and chance. A government's economic performance is better assessed by
the performance of the whole economy. Indeed, voters connect their own
personal economic performance to the government only when they can
"connect changes in their personal financial situation[s] to broader economic trends and government policies."[41]

In other words, what matters is how voters construe their own situations. Changes in one's personal situation are seen as relevant to voting
when they are explained in collective, political terms.[42] Voters who see political reasons for changes in their pocketbooks will reward and punish
political leaders; voters with only personal explanations for their situations
will not. Of particular import in this regard is the difference between explanations for inflation and those for unemployment. Whereas people often
blame themselves for being unemployed, they are far more likely to link
inflation to government policies.[43] Voters, then, are sensitive to changes in
the economy, but they discriminate between changes in their personal condition and changes in the condition of the economy.

Voters also distinguish among changes in economic conditions, such as
inflation or unemployment, according to expected personal consequences
of these changes. However, the political effects of these economic problems
are not always the result of actions taken by those *most* affected. It is a common finding that the unemployed and other people suffering economic
setbacks spend less time with their friends and social networks and more
time trying to make ends meet; they often become anxious, depressed, and
withdrawn, and vote less than others.[44] The unemployed may drop out,
but those vulnerable to unemployment react, in their voting and in their

evaluations of the president. Blue-collar workers as a group—who are more susceptible to unemployment—are more sensitive to changes in unemployment levels than white-collar workers and retired people, whereas the retired and white-collar workers are far more sensitive to changes in the inflation rate.[45]

Voters also think ahead, taking account of both current conditions and long-term expectations. Just as there are differences between voters primarily concerned about inflation and those primarily concerned about unemployment, there are differences between voters who see storm clouds on the horizon and those who envision a sunny future. What voters want their government to do depends on what they think their country will be like several years from now.

In the 1980s, public concerns about the long-term economic future of the country were widespread. People who thought "the future of the next generation will be bogged down by problems left behind for them" had different preferences about government policies than did people who thought "the future of the next generation of Americans will be a good one." People anxious about the future are more oriented toward social programs and government action, while voters with a rosier view see less need for government programs and support a more limited role for government. People concerned about the future are also less willing to forgo services in order to cut the deficit, more willing to cut defense spending in order to fund domestic spending, more supportive of government programs to provide day care, less supportive of the use of the American military in foreign conflicts, and less supportive of government spending to finance anti-Communist forces around the world. In general, worries about the long-term future are associated with more concern about government action that will cushion that future and less concern with fiscal restraint, strong defense spending, and militant anticommunism abroad.[46] In other words, people who are pessimistic about the future are more concerned that government develop adequate insurance against hard times. The middle-aged, for example, worry the most about whether Social Security funds will be there for them when they retire. The fact that people take expectations into account when they vote emphasizes an often-ignored truth: elections test voter concern for long-term security and collective goods, not just concern for direct and immediate private benefits.

In summary, daily-life and media information are mediated by reasoning and expectations. A vote is more than a direct expression of a voter's social group, pocketbook, or personal problems; voters take account of national as well as personal conditions, and they discriminate among their own problems and problems for the government to address which are relevant to them. Further, they take into account their expectations about the long-term future and the kinds of government programs they expect will be most relevant to them in the years ahead.

Education and Civic Ignorance

Ever since the Columbia studies demonstrated low levels of textbook political knowledge in the mass electorate, scholars have been hoping for a more informed citizenry. They have assumed that an increase in years of schooling would lead to greater political knowledge and more attentiveness to the political debates that occur within government. Because the educated vote more often than the uneducated, it was also assumed that an increase in education would lead to a higher voter turnout. A well-educated electorate, it was thought, would be "attentive, knowledgeable, and participatory."[47]

Hopes for an electorate that measures up to civic ideals have not been met. Fifty years ago when the Columbia studies began, three-fourths of the electorate had not finished high school and only 10 percent had any college experience. Today, three-fourths of the electorate have finished high school and nearly 40 percent have been to college. But despite this increase in education, factual knowledge about government and current political debates is at best only marginally higher, and voter turnout is lower.[48] Indeed, within the electorate, the level of factual knowledge about the basic structure of government is so low, and the extent of information about specific legislation is so limited, that little information about *current* levels of knowledge is available on a regular basis. Survey researchers are generally reluctant to ask too many factual questions for fear of embarrassing respondents, who might terminate the interview or become too flustered to answer other questions.[49]

To directly assess the changes in levels of civics knowledge since the 1940s, Scott Keeter and Michael X. Delli Carpini recently conducted a national survey asking the same basic questions that were asked in the 1940s. They replicated questions testing knowledge of certain elementary facts, such as which party now controls the House, what the first ten amendments to the Constitution are called, the name of the vice president, the definition of a presidential veto, and how much of a majority is required for the Senate and House to override a presidential veto. Overall, they found, "the level of public knowledge of some basic facts has remained remarkably stable."[50]

Voter turnout in America is no higher today than in the 1940s, and people are no more likely now than they were then to know the name of their congressional representative. Despite all the publicity he received, Vice President Dan Quayle was only marginally better known in 1989 than Vice President Richard Nixon was in 1952; 75 percent could name Quayle, while 69 percent had been able to name Nixon.[51] Knowledge of other prominent members of government also remains low. In the week following the 1976 election, only 58 percent could name both vice-presidential nominees. In 1985, after George Shultz had been in office for more than four years, only 25 percent of the electorate could recall his name when asked, "Who is the Secretary of State?" In January 1977, when Jimmy Carter became president, only one American in four could name even a single member of the cabinet he had announced earlier.[52]

Acquaintance with the basic facts about issues being politically debated in the nation is also dismally scant, as four examples will suggest. (1) U.S.-Japanese trade issues have been in the news for years. However, less than a third of the country knows whether the Japanese form of government is a monarchy, a democracy, or a military dictatorship, and less than 4 percent can name the Japanese prime minister.[53] (2) In January 1979, only 23 percent of the public knew that the countries involved in the SALT talks were the United States and the Soviet Union. Ten months later, after the talks had been in the news for most of the year, the number had risen only to 38 percent.[54] (3) In 1987, after seven years of debate over Contra aid, only one-third of the public knew that Nicaragua is in Central America. When the USS *Stark* was hit by an Iraqi rocket in the Persian Gulf in 1987, 43 percent of the public had no opinion whose rocket it was, 25 percent thought the rocket was Iranian, and only 29 percent knew that it was Iraqi.[55] (4) For years, domestic political debate has centered on trade-offs, both implicit and explicit, involved in cutting defense spending in order to fund domestic spending, and vice versa. But in 1985 only 45 percent of the electorate knew even approximately the share of the federal budget spent on defense (just under one-third); in January 1985, 45 percent thought the share was one-quarter or one-third; 31 percent thought it was half or more, 6 percent thought it was less than one-tenth, and 20 percent had not even a guess.[56] These findings indicate that there are few, if any, national policy debates that the mass public can follow in their entirety.

The Effects of Education

Clearly, it takes more than education to bring the actual electorate into alignment with theoretical ideals. The social model of the citizen, and the role of education in increasing civic competence, need revision. Motivation to acquire and digest information must be taken into account. The Columbia insight that a person thinks politically as he is socially, as generalized by Anthony Downs to create the by-product theory of political information, indicates a wide range of knowledge and experience within the electorate. It also suggests that a voter's level of political information will vary as his or her life situation changes, and as he or she responds to new opportunities and political events. However, merely specifying daily-life experiences, familiarity with U.S. government programs, or media exposure to events in foreign countries is not sufficient to make a case that this information influences attitudes about candidates, issues, and political parties.

We need a better theory of public knowledge about politics, one that goes beyond the by-product theory to explain the differences that education *has* made, as well as the differences it hasn't made. The hoped-for "deepening" of the electorate has not occurred, because an increase in education is not synonymous with an increase in civics knowledge. Nevertheless, I contend that the changing educational level of the electorate is, in fact, changing American politics.

My hypothesis is that education affects politics not by "deepening" but by *broadening* the electorate—by increasing the number of issues that citizens see as politically relevant, and by increasing the number of connections they make between their own lives and national and international events. And therefore, given the interactions between daily-life information and media information, as noted above, any increase in the amount and kinds of information about government and the national agenda is likely to affect the ways in which voters make connections between their own lives and their government's actions. I must emphasize that this remains a hypothesis, for which I can offer only suggestive evidence.

An example of the proliferation of new concerns in a more educated public—of a widening, rather than a deepening, of politics—is the growth of concern about food additives and environmental protection. The post–World War II transformation of America into an educated, white-collar society has resulted in the growth of widespread anxiety (often approaching obsession) about toxic wastes, chemical additives, and other potential carcinogens. Tens of millions avidly followed media reports on the disasters at

Three Mile Island, Love Canal, Chernobyl, and Prince William Sound in Alaska. A new interest in health information and an age-old fascination with disasters have made ecological calamities matters of worldwide interest. Not surprisingly, then, when a few Tylenol tablets, or a few Chilean grapes, are tampered with, the news spreads rapidly. Health is only one of many topics in which symbols have proliferated because educated voters have more ability to absorb and process information than do less-educated voters.

While educational level apparently makes no difference in television news viewing, it does make a difference in newspaper reading, and an even larger difference in the reading of news magazines. According to a 1983 CBS poll, there is no difference among educational levels in exposure to television news, which is watched by 80 percent of the electorate. Educated people, however, are more likely to read newspapers and news magazines. Among those who have not been to college, only 5 percent read weekly news magazines regularly, and only 25 percent read them occasionally. Among those who have had some college, 19 percent read them regularly and 40 percent once in a while; among college graduates, 37 percent read them regularly and 32 percent occasionally (see table 2.1).

Educated people not only make more use of newspapers and news magazines; they also discuss news stories more than the less-educated do. In this same 1983 poll, 26 percent of the respondents said they had talked with others about a story that was in the news on the day they were interviewed. Among those who had never been to college, the proportion was 19 percent; among those who had been to college, 40 percent. Also, the more formal education a person has, the more likely it is that he or she reads stories about national or international news.[57] Among people who had not completed high school, only 7 percent of the news stories they discussed were national or international stories, as opposed to local stories and disaster stories. At the other extreme, college graduates reported that fully half of their discussions concerned national or international stories.[58]

That educated voters pay more attention to foreign news does not mean that they have a wealth of background civics information about the subjects they follow. In May of 1989, for example, one in five college graduates believed that the Soviet Union was a member of NATO.[59] Educated voters may know little about the actions of the Marcos regime in the Philippines, or the nuances of apartheid in South Africa, or Gorbachev's struggle with critics of *perestroika,* or Yasir Arafat's role in the PLO in Palestine. But very often they do know enough for these general subjects to influence their votes.[60]

If most citizens, in a knee-jerk manner, reflexively "voted their pocket-books," or voted to "fire the manager" after a bad season, or ignored the connections between their own lives and the national government's umbrellas and safety nets, then we would have to say that increased levels of education do not affect the electorate. However, since reasoning and information matter, changes in the amounts and kinds of information that voters acquire also matter, and education can change politics. Further, campaigns can matter as well.

Information and Campaigns

In a campaign, voters are exposed to information about the differences between the candidates or parties in the election at hand. There is, however, no assurance that they will absorb information that is new to them, for it is possible that they will misperceive the messages in ways that reinforce their preexisting ideas and commitments. Indeed, misperception has troubled observers of democracy throughout the century. As Walter Lippmann noted, "Democracy in its original form never seriously faced the problem which arises because the pictures inside people's heads do not automatically correspond with the world outside."[61] As the authors of *Voting* noted, the voter's judgments will appear more thoughtful and well-informed than they actually are because the voter's way of perceiving campaign issues "maximizes agreement with his own side and maximizes disagreement with the opposition."[62]

When voters assume that their favored candidate's issue positions are the same as their own, they are "projecting" their positions onto the candidate. The campaign that exists in the voter's mind—the "campaign as perceived"—is different from the campaign as it is carried on in the real world. Voters sometimes think they are voting consistently with their principles and positions because they are projecting—assuming that the candidate they favor takes the position they wish him or her to take.

One of the most important findings in *Voting* is that the extent of misperception, or projection, by voters is related to the political campaign. Issues discussed more often and more thoroughly in the campaign were perceived more accurately by respondents than other issues. Furthermore, misperception was inversely related to the degree of conflict, and competition, on an issue: the more the candidates talked about an issue and the greater their differences on it, the more accurately it was perceived.[63] There was more misperception at the beginning of the campaign than at the end, and there was more misperception among people who paid less attention to the campaign or who were less well educated or who were less exposed to campaign communications.[64]

Campaign communications, then, increased the accuracy of voter perceptions; misperceptions were far more likely on issues that were peripheral to the campaign. Issues at conflict between the parties received more public exposure, and the information to which voters were exposed reduced their projections. Indeed, exposure to communications was the strongest single influence on accuracy of perceptions.[65]

Projection as a "Benefit of the Doubt"

When voters identify with parties or candidates, they are giving them the benefit of the doubt. When they assume that the positions they favor are the ones their party or candidate will take, or when they assume that their favorite candidate's position is acceptable, they are *projecting* on the basis of past information in much the same way that an investor in stocks projects future earnings from past corporate performance, or assumes that a company whose new president has a record of successes will improve under his leadership. This willingness to project can be taken to mean receptivity, a tendency to give one's party the benefit of the doubt when there is no other information available—a meaning consistent with the findings in *Voting*.

If the benefit of the doubt that voters give to their party or candidates were open-ended, we would have a pure "will to believe" model of voting and campaigning. If voters had such a strong will to believe in their candidates and parties that they rejected any and all data that challenged their commitments, campaigns would be very different. Even the first Columbia study, *The People's Choice*, showed clearly the limits to the benefit of the doubt that people give to their side.[66]

In 1940, President Roosevelt sought an unprecedented third term in office. The Republican campaign hammered away at the idea of a third term, and the Democratic party countered by arguing against "changing horses in midstream"—the stream being recovery from the Great Depression. Individual Democrats, however, had a hard time accepting their party's arguments in favor of a third term and countering the Republican arguments against it: "There was hardly a Republican who did not mention the third term as a reason for his Republican vote. And there was hardly a Democrat who tried to justify the third term as such."[67] On the other side, individual Republicans were defensive about charges that their party favored business interests over those of "the people." When asked about their party, they would frequently say that Republicans were for "all the people too." They did not automatically adopt their party's claims to have policies that were best for all, and felt a need to defend themselves and their party against responsibility for causing the depression. In the 1940s, *The People's Choice* found, "The onus now rests upon a business candidate; he must somehow claim a connection with the people. No parallel obligation rests upon the candidate of the working people; he does not have to pretend to benefit business."[68]

As these examples from the 1940 campaign suggest, levels of voter projection and rationalization depend heavily on two variables: (1) how much benefit of the doubt voters give their party; and (2) how effective they judge the campaign arguments to be. Indeed, what is called "negative campaigning" is campaigning designed to provide voters with information that will break down their projections, to present "information to the contrary" that will show them issues on which they disagree with the stands of their party or candidate.[69]

Campaigns Matter

These findings about misperception still have not been completely digested within political science and democratic theory, or by critics of American political campaigns. It is critical that when a (contested) campaign focuses on an issue it leads to *less* voter misperception, not more. Psychological defenses are not so impermeable as to rule out adjustment between a voter's perceptions and "political reality." Misperception is a "psychic indulgence" that decreases when there is heated political conflict.[70] Political reality is strong enough that when the stakes are raised and more information becomes available, voters become more accurate in their perceptions. The more they care about an issue, the better they are able to understand it; the more strongly the parties differ on an issue, and the more voters hear about it, the more accurate their perceptions become. There is no denying that misperception is always present in campaigns. But it is also clear that campaign communications do affect choices, and that they generally make voters more, not less, accurate in their perceptions of candidates and issues.

Despite cries that campaigns have become less substantial in the television era, recent research has supported *Voting*'s findings that campaign communications increase the accuracy of voters' perceptions. Pamela Johnston Conover and Stanley Feldman, examining the 1976 general election, found that projection, or false consensus, vanished as learning proceeded during the campaign; misperceptions occurred "primarily when there [was an] absence both of information *and* strong feelings about the candidate."[71] In contradiction to the claim that voters' perceptions are "largely distorted by motivational forces," Jon Krosnick found that voters in the 1984 election were "remarkably accurate in their perceptions of where presidential candidates [stood] relative to one another on controversial policy issues."[72]

In addition to reducing misperception, campaign information also helps people connect issues to government and parties. In 1984, "voters who followed the presidential campaign closely were more likely to connect their personal financial situation with macroeconomic trends or government policies. . . . Attributions of responsibility for changes in economic well-being are based in part on cues received from the political environment and particularly from the mass media."[73] Thus in a world in which causal reasoning matters but voters have only limited knowledge of government, campaign communications heighten voters' awareness of how government affects their lives, while reinforcing policy differences between parties and candidates. People do not automatically grade government on net changes in personal benefits, financial or otherwise, nor do they automatically hold government accountable for "government-induced changes in well-being."[74]

Voters are ignorant of many basic facts about government, but they still pick up important information about the principal differences between candidates. In a 1976 CBS News/*New York Times* poll taken two days after the November election, respondents were asked the names of the two vice-presidential candidates, and also which task each presidential candidate was more concerned with—reducing unemployment or cutting the rate of inflation. Only 58 percent correctly recalled the names of the vice-presidential candidates. But in answering the question about the priorities of the presidential candidates, 62 percent said Ford was more concerned with inflation and 72 percent said Carter was more concerned with unemployment (see table 2.2). These answers suggest how misleading it can be to measure voters' acuity and concern simply by testing their knowledge of facts. As I demonstrate throughout this book, the low-information rationality that voters use allows them to pick up a surprising amount of information about the basic policy directions offered by opposing presidential candidates.

The authors of *The People's Choice*, the first study of an American political campaign, hoped and expected to find voters who were knowledgeable about the basics of government and voted according to their consideration of the issues. Their scholarly hopes were dashed: "The open-minded

TABLE 2.2
Education and Voter Information in the 1976 Election

	< 12th Grade (%)	H.S. Graduate (%)	Some College (%)	College Graduate (%)	All Respondents (%)
Percentage knowing names of both vice-presidential nominees	45	54	70	84	58
Does Gerald Ford care more about:					
Unemployment	14	21	15	7	16
Inflation	45	63	72	83	62
Don't know	40	16	13	8	23
Does Jimmy Carter care more about:					
Unemployment	63	73	75	83	72
Inflation	14	14	14	7	13
Don't know	23	13	11	9	15

Source: CBS News/*New York Times* postelection poll, 1976
Note: This poll was a panel, calling back 2,400 respondents who had been interviewed in the last week of the campaign. Only registered voters were asked these questions.

voters who make a sincere attempt to weigh the issues and the candidates dispassionately for the good of the country as a whole—exist mainly in deferential campaign propaganda, in textbooks on civics, in the movies and in the minds of political idealists. In real life, they are few indeed."[75]

The widespread lack of knowledge about the basic operations of government has led scholars and others to produce a voluminous literature about the "incompetent citizen," replete with concern for how democracy can survive, let alone flourish.[76] And indeed, when half of the American public cannot name the two U.S. senators from their state, and 20 percent of college graduates think Russia belongs to NATO, and a large majority of Americans do not know that Japan has a democratic system of government, there is a real basis for concern.

On the other hand, there is much that voters *do* know about government, and many ways in which they manage to consider issues without high levels of information. They need not know what Senator Moynihan and President Bush actually said in order to be affected by news reports of their debates about Social Security; they need not know how the Japanese government works in order to be concerned about U.S.-Japanese trade issues; and they need not know how many members there are in the Soviet Politburo before news about *perestroika* affects their attitudes about the U.S. defense budget. Whereas the "incompetent citizen" literature is good for telling us the many things voters do not know, it is not so good at providing clues about what they *do* know. The by-product theory, by contrast, can generate insights about where and how voters get information about government, and therefore helps describe what citizens will actually know when they vote.

In a world of pocketbook voters, education would not matter. But in a world where reasons and connections matter, education makes a difference. Though an educated electorate still will not have the basic information about legislative issues and government management that textbooks expect of ideal citizens, and no deeper understanding of older "core" issues, it *will* have limited information about a wider range of subjects, including national and international events, that are farther from daily-life experience. Political campaign communications matter precisely *because* voters do not regularly pay much attention to political news, and because they do not know many of the things that governments and candidates have done in the past.

We are now learning more about what voters know, how they reason when they vote to make sense of the many pieces of information they have. Voting is not a reflexive, mechanistic use of daily-life or media information. It involves reasoning, the connecting of some information to government performance and other information to specific government policies. People do not reason directly from personal problems to votes; they reason with ideas about governmental performance and responsibility. They consider not only economic issues but family, residential, and consumer issues as well. They think not only of their immediate needs but also of their needs for insurance against future problems; not only about private goods but also about collective goods. They think not only of how they are doing but also about how other people like themselves are doing; not just about the immediate future but also about the long term.

Somehow, without the basic civics data, voters manage to learn differences between the parties and candidates. In the next chapter, I discuss how voters use information shortcuts to keep track of the information they have—and compensate for the information they lack.

T H R E E

Going without Data: Information Shortcuts

DESPITE THE many kinds of information voters acquire in daily life, there are large gaps in their knowledge about government and politics. To overcome these limitations, they use shortcuts. In this chapter I examine how voters use shortcuts to evaluate information, maintain running tallies about political parties, and assess candidates.

At the heart of gut rationality are information shortcuts—easily obtained and used forms of information that serve as "second-best" substitutes for harder-to-obtain kinds of data. Shortcuts that voters use incorporate learning from past experiences, daily life, the media, and political campaigns. Because voters use shortcuts, low-information reasoning is by no means devoid of substantive content. The three main kinds of shortcuts voters use are shortcuts in evaluating, obtaining, and storing information.

Voters rely on the opinions of others as a shortcut in evaluating the information they have, because even when they do know about an issue, they are unaware of many relations between government and their lives.[1] They may not be able to evaluate news for relevance or veracity, and they may not have appropriate standards for assessing the performance of the government. Thus, even when they do have the facts about an issue, voters turn to others for help with evaluation because they are uncertain about the meaning of the news and want to know how others have interpreted events.

Voters use running tallies about political parties as shortcuts in storing information and as shortcuts with which to assess candidates and legislation about which they have no information. They also use shortcuts to evaluate candidates, assessing them from campaign behavior, personal characteristics, and their relations with groups and people whose general positions they know.

Whether for lack of complete information about government, lack of theory with which to evaluate policies, or lack of information about the views and reactions of others, uncertainty is pervasive when voters think about and evaluate government.[2] It follows from the pervasiveness of uncertainty that campaigns are designed to give voters new information about candidates and issues and to make new connections between specific problems and specific offices.

Interpersonal Influence as an Information Shortcut

In recent years, political campaigns have come to rely increasingly on a research tool known as the "focus group." Such a group usually consists of six to ten participants and a moderator, who uses a few general questions to steer the group into an extended discussion of the topic he or she is investigating. Whereas surveys are still heavily used to assess the state of opinion in a population at any given time, many political researchers consider focus groups, which assess the thoughts of a small number of people in depth, a better basis for predicting whether an issue will "ignite" in the larger population with exposure.[3] For example, before George Bush's 1988 campaign made an issue of Willie Horton—the murderer who was let out of a Massachusetts prison on a weekend pass, subsequently holding a couple hostage and raping the wife—the issue was tested extensively in focus groups. Indeed, tapes of two focus groups which included discussions of Dukakis's prison-furloughs program and his refusal to sign a law requiring teachers in Massachusetts public schools to lead the pledge of allegiance were shown to Bush to convince him to attack Dukakis on these issues.[4]

Of course, the fact that focus groups are more intensive than surveys is not in itself sufficient to explain why they are held in such high regard. Why hasn't the demand for more intensive research led either to very long surveys addressed to only one subject, or to long private interviews with one person at a time? The answer is that small-group discussions can do something that surveys and private interviews cannot: they can reveal inchoate attitudes that people are usually reluctant to express unless they are validated or reinforced by others.

The People's Choice, the Columbia group's first voting study, found that there were large variations in people's levels of interest in politics and political campaigns. Moreover, the concept of interest in politics was easily comprehended by everyone and had external validity. Over the course of the 1940 study, a question about political interest was asked over 5,000 times; only 1 percent of the time did respondents say they didn't know or weren't sure how interested they were in the campaign. The question "made sense to almost everyone and almost everyone had a ready answer. . . . It is not surprising that people's self-rating on interest stands up well under a series of tests of consistency and validity. For being interested is a clearly recognizable experience, as anyone knows who has been unable to put down a detective story or been bored to tears at a cocktail party."[5] People who were interested in the campaign had more opinions about politics, paid more attention to campaign events, and exposed themselves to more campaign communications. On an average day of the political campaign, the researchers found that at least 10 percent more people participated in discussions about the elections—either actively or passively—than heard or read about campaign items.[6] The two-step flow of information means that many people receive their news indirectly, and that many more validate and anchor what they have heard or read only after they have worked through the material with others: ". . . Opinion leadership is an integral part of the give-and-take of everyday personal relationships. . . . All interpersonal relations are potential networks of communications."[7] This means, above all, that campaigns matter even if many voters know little about the issues or have little interest in the campaign:

> Psychologists might say that the highly involved voters "live on" their differences with the opposition; that is, the very fact of difference provides them with a psychic energy with which they continue to engage themselves politically. And, in reverse, their deeper political engagement no doubt leads them to see and feel differences with the opposition to an unusual degree.
> But, whatever the psychological mechanisms, socially and politically the fact is that not all voters are needed to achieve a sharp polarization into two parties . . . large numbers of the latter simply "go along" with what is for them a more artificial cleavage.[8]

Uneven levels of political interest and knowledge, then, mean that an essential part of political dynamics takes place between voters. The campaign and the media only send the initial messages; until these messages have been checked with others and validated, their full effects are not felt. Focus groups, as opposed to depth interviews or surveys, capture some of this two-step flow of information. They give researchers and campaign strategists a chance to see whether discussion of an issue sparks interest in it.

Fire Alarms and Police Patrols

Downs began accepting "a priori" that people are not certain what they have learned from the media until they discuss the news with informal opinion leaders.[9] His contribution was to generalize from findings about interpersonal influence to the broader category of information shortcuts.

When a voter is unsure how to evaluate information, or doesn't have information, relying on a trusted person for validation is, in essence, a strategy for economizing on information and resolving uncertainty. Because there is a two-step flow of information, a lack of citizenship data or "textbook knowledge" understates the political impact that issues can have and understates the public's ability to make informed decisions.

There are two ways to evaluate the effects of information. One way is to ask voters directly what they know; another way is learn where voters take their cues. These two methods parallel the two approaches scholars have used to evaluate the influence of congressmen and their involvement in the affairs of government. Scholars and reporters observing the behavior of a government agency often see no congressmen observing or interfering in its affairs. If they don't detect a congressional presence they often conclude that the congressmen are not involved and are not effective. But congressmen do not patrol the entire government looking for problems to solve, like police detectives searching out criminals; they wait for constituents to set off alarms so they can race to the scene, like fire fighters.[10]

Citizens do not patrol the government looking for problems either, but they pay attention to people who do. As W. Russell Neuman, director of the Communications Research Group at MIT's Media Lab, has noted, "Most citizens don't study the details but look at the bottom line. Are we at war? Is the economy healthy? Most people entrust the rest to experts and specialists. What is important is that there are perhaps five percent who are activists and news junkies who do pay close attention. If they see that something is seriously wrong in the country, they sound the alarm and then ordinary people start paying attention."[11]

Changes in the format of television news over the last three decades also provide a two-step media flow of information. The pretelevision voting studies found that there was a two-step flow of influence in communications; the impact of the media depended on how media stories were interpreted by informal opinion leaders. There is an analogy to this two-step flow for television itself: the impact of many events and campaign activities depends not just on the viewers' interpretations of the events, but on the interpretations offered by elite opinion leaders on television. Television news provides commentary on speeches, proposals, and crises from a variety of well-known political figures from whom voters can triangulate, just as they do with local opinion leaders. The late Claude Pepper, for example, was known to senior citizens ("At my age, I don't even buy green bananas") for his defenses of Social Security, and was always asked to comment on new Social Security Insurance proposals. No coverage of an international crisis is complete without comments from Henry Kissinger and Senator Sam Nunn. Such figures become well known over time; their comments allow voters to mediate new information and watch for "fire alarms" through the media as well as through conversation.

Richard Brody has studied the effect on viewers of elite interpretation of political events.[12] Brody studied events that gave large short-term boosts to the president's popularity. Sometimes a large gain in presidential popularity appears to defy explanation. For example, the U.S.-backed invasion of Cuba in 1961 led to an ignominious defeat at the Bay of Pigs, but President Kennedy's popularity soared after the debacle, for which he took full responsibility. Brody has shown that seemingly incongruous situations like this, when a president's popularity soars after a humiliating fiasco, can be explained by the response of elite figures to the event, as featured in the media. If there is a crisis and the elite figures rally to support the president, then the president's popularity soars, fiasco or not. If the elites are divided and critical, as after the Tet Offensive in Vietnam, the president's popularity can plummet, as it did for Lyndon Johnson.

Two kinds of campaign situations wherein television coverage after an event can determine the extent of mass reaction are similar to those Brody has analyzed: (1) situations wherein challengers present their positions on issues, and (2) situations wherein ambiguous, possibly innocuous, remarks are made. When a challenger, in an attempt to demonstrate credibility and competence, releases details of his plans for defense or the budget (for example), public response depends not on an understanding of the details but on elite reaction as reported in the media. For example, in 1972 the Democratic nominee for president, George McGovern, presented his tax and defense plans to the media in an attempt to demonstrate their feasibility. When cabinet member after cabinet member in the Nixon administration attacked the plans, and no major figures in the Democratic party—neither well-known senators nor former cabinet members—stood up to denounce the attacks as unfair or partisan, McGovern's credibility suffered. Likewise, when Ronald Reagan, campaigning for the Republican nomination in 1976, presented plans for cutting the federal budget by 10 percent, and the details were attacked by many during the primaries and defended by none, there was a similar reaction. McGovern and Reagan had not organized enough elite support to counter the many cabinet members' attacks on their proposals. They had to defend against the attacks personally, which effectively precluded them from spending their precious airtime on the offensive.[13] Of course, a president with little influence cannot mobilize his office, and a challenger with elite support can fend off the attacks. Also, if the elites are discredited, it does not matter if the challenger cannot rally prominent members of the establishment to his side.

When a candidate makes careless or poorly worded statements, the public reaction often depends on whether news reports highlight these comments as significant or pass them by. In 1976, in discussing ethnic neighborhoods in a newspaper interview in New York, presidential candidate Jimmy Carter used the curious phrase "ethnic purity." Until it was featured on television several days later, there was no reaction to the phrase from voters or opposing politicians.[14] After it was widely publicized, Carter had to spend several weeks of the campaign rebuilding his links to the black community.[15] Although some remarks are so revealing when reported in the media that no elite mediation is necessary—such as Jesse Jackson's reference in a personal conversation to New York City as "Hymietown"—many statements do not register as significant to most people unless they are aware of how others evaluate the remarks as well. When citizens sample information about government, and listen to elites and "news junkies" who sound alarms, those who are most directly affected by an issue absorb the information first; for example, senior citizens pick up news about changes in Social Security before others do.[16] If the issue is one that can effectively be connected with government action and benefits that voters want, it will percolate through the public.

Just as fire alarms alert fire fighters to fires, saving them the effort of patrolling to look for smoke, so do information shortcuts save voters the effort of constantly searching for relevant facts. Since they are uncertain about the accuracy or meaning of information anyway, it makes more sense for them to act like fire fighters rather than like police—to use the information shortcuts provided by trusted local and national commentators, endorsements, and political conventions.

Whether a problem is "my problem," "our problem," "the country's problem," or a problem at all depends on information about the concerns and preferences of others, knowledge about government, and knowledge of the positions of politicians and parties.

Party Identification

The Columbia researchers began their 1940 campaign study with a view of
the voter as consumer—a person shopping for products, with price and
advertising exerting an immediate effect on choices. Their first study was
designed to assess the effects of the mass media on attitudes and behavior,
and they expected that these effects would be sizable and obvious. They
found, however, that these effects were much smaller than they had expected, in part because voters had entrenched voting habits. In 1940, there
was no inkling yet that this was an important concept: in *The People's
Choice*, people voting for Roosevelt were called Democrats and people voting for Willkie were called Republicans. The 1948 study was the first
academic research project to ask a question that separated current vote in-
tention from partisan habits and identifications: "Regardless of how you
may vote in the coming election, how have you usually thought of yourself—as a Republican, Democrat, Socialist, or what?"[17]

This general recognition that voters had standing decisions about the political parties meant that each election did not necessarily present a new
choice. "For many people, votes are not perceived as decisions to be made
in each specific election. For them, voting traditions are not changed much
more often than careers are chosen, religions drifted into or away from, or
tastes revised."[18] Party loyalties were not easily changed. They reflected
past political battles that had shaped the ways in which voters thought
about politics and government. Thus:

> In 1948 some people were, in effect, voting on the interna-
> tionalism issue of 1940, others on the depression issue of
> 1932, and some, indeed, on the slavery issues of 1860. The
> vote is thus a kind of "moving average" of reactions to the
> political past. Voters carry over to each new election rem-
> nants of issues raised in previous elections—and so there is
> always an overlapping of old and new decisions that give a
> cohesion in time to the political system.[19]

Party loyalties reduced the effects of the media. In 1940, for example, the
media were overwhelmingly Republican, but Democratic voters read and
listened to more of their own candidate's stories. The mechanism of selective exposure came into play; people chose the material listened to or read,
and the more interested and committed they were, the more likely they
were to read and listen to the material presented by their own candidate.
Availability of information plus a predisposition to consider it, rather than
availability alone, determined exposure.[20] There was more Republican

money and more Republican propaganda, but there were enough Democratic communications available to maintain the Democrats' commitment to their candidate.

It became clear over the course of the two studies that party identification was more than a voting habit; it was a worldview as well. There were major differences in the social composition of the groups supporting the two candidates, and the differences in their social philosophies were "even more pronounced than differences in their social composition."[21]

Downs pointed out that party identification, like reliance on informal opinion leaders, was an information shortcut to the vote decision. But this does not mean that the voter sacrifices his or her basic issue-orientations; he or she simply deals with them in a more economical way. This perspective emphasizes an attachment that depends on evaluations of past and future benefits from government. In a simplified Downsian perspective, parties are teams that attempt to gain elective positions through an appeal to the voters that is based on a platform composed of issue positions plus a political ideology.[22] Each voter, Downs assumes, has an ideology or "verbal image of the good society, and of the chief means of constructing such a society."[23]

This immediately raises questions: If voters care only about the benefits they receive from government, why do political parties devote so much effort to publicizing their ideologies? And why *should* voters care about party ideologies? The answer to both questions is that both parties and voters have found ideology valuable as a shortcut or cost-saving device.

If voters were not uncertain—if they were fully informed about government and could assess how their own benefits would be affected by a party's platform—they would pay no attention to the party's ideology. They would simply evaluate the party's actual performance and proposals in terms of their personal ideologies. As Downs put it, "When voters can expertly judge every detail of every stand taken and relate it directly to their own views of a great society, they are interested only in issues, not philosophies."[24]

Ideologies are, in effect, "samples of all the differentiating stands" between parties.[25] Parties use ideologies to highlight critical differences between themselves, and to remind voters of their past successes. They do this because voters do not perceive all the differences, cannot remember all the past performances, and cannot relate all future policies to their own benefits. Thus, Downs emphasizes, uncertainty is a necessary condition for ideological differences between parties: "Party ideologies can remain different only insofar as none is demonstrably more effective than the rest."[26]

When one party convinces voters that its position is demonstrably better on some issue, the other party either adapts or fails to gain votes in the future.

Ideology is thus a mark not of sophistication and education, but of uncertainty and lack of ability to connect policies with benefits. The word *ideology* is a loaded one in America, evoking the derogatory sense of *ideologues*—people who have belief systems to which they adhere steadfastly. (As Clifford Geertz has noted, "I have a social philosophy; you have public opinions; he has an ideology.")[27] Downs, however, was equating ideology not with intellectual sophistication or moral rigidity, but with simple shortcuts and loosely integrated views about what parties stand for in the minds of voters. A party's ideology and past performance matter only when the voter cannot with certainty predict its future behavior from its platform. Parties try hard to remind voters about their views of the good society and how to achieve it, because this helps voters evaluate the implications of the party's approach. This is a "default value" view of both party identification and party ideologies: when a voter has no information about current performance, or is uncertain of what the effects of a proposal are, he or she reverts to default values.

But unavailability of data is not the only reason voters revert to default values. They do this when they are so satisfied with their past choices that they see no reason to collect any data. So long as the candidates' actions appear consistent with the generalized notion the voter attaches to a particular label, the voter can avoid the effort of keeping track of all the various activities of government. As Downs put it, sometimes voters have no data because they do not expect a fair return on their investment of effort:

> Finally, some rational men habitually vote for the same party in every election. In several preceding elections, they carefully informed themselves about all the competing parties, and all the issues of the moment; yet they always came to the same decision about how to vote. Therefore they have resolved to repeat this decision without becoming well-informed, unless some catastrophe makes them realize it no longer expresses their best interests. [This habit] keeps voters from investing in information which would not alter their behavior.[28]

Since voters have limited information and different priorities, parties that seek their votes are bound to be coalitions that coordinate voter efforts to pursue a set of collective goods. Although the coalition may exhibit stability over time, the basis of each individual's attachment to it is utilitarian:

it depends on the rewards received. Thus even when there is widespread agreement within a party on general goals, there is no reason to assume that all voters have the same priorities, or that they pay attention to the same issues. This view of political parties as coalitions has two important implications for understanding voting decisions.

First, as noted earlier, the multiplicity of group and individual interests suggests that one should not expect consensus of attitudes across issues within the party. There also is no logical inconsistency in the attitudes of a black Democrat who is both pro–civil rights and anti-labor, or even any logical reason to suppose that he or she experiences any significant cross-pressure when casting a vote for a Democrat. Furthermore, seeing the parties as coalitions makes it illogical to assume that any significant number of voters should be able to locate the party on some hypothetical "continuum" that summarizes party positions for *all* issues. Given the cost of gathering information solely for the purpose of making a vote decision, we should not expect a consensus on issues within parties. Where candidates are engaged in assembling a coalition of voters interested in only one issue, or only a few issues, people in every coalition are ignorant of the candidate's stand in many areas that are not central to their primary concerns. The implication for voting research is clear: unless voters are sorted according to the importance they attach to specific issues, one cannot expect to find high levels of interest or of information.

Second, within every coalition there are people who disagree with the candidate or the party position in some area but still support the candidate or party. In 1964, for example, it was not essential for a black Democratic voter whose primary concern was civil rights to be familiar with Lyndon Johnson's Vietnam policy in order to be an issue-oriented voter. Nor would it be surprising today to find that advocates or opponents of right-to-life legislation are totally ignorant about farm price-support policy or deficit-reduction proposals. However, when there are political primaries, there are fights for control of a party between its various internal factions.

Changes in Party Identification

If party identification reflects a voter's current judgment about the political performance of the two parties, then there should be feedback from a voter's evaluations of current policies to party identification. On the other hand, if the only events that affect party identification are catastrophes on the order of the Great Depression, party identification is only a running tally of public reaction to cataclysms, and party voting is voting that is un-affected by the year-to-year turns of politics. When the authors of *The*

American Voter inferred that there were no links between party identification and normal politics, they were looking at the apparent glacial stability of party identification in America after World War II and the inheritance of partisan identification from one's parents.[29] If children inherited party identification from their parents and nothing short of a catastrophe could change it, there wasn't much political content to party voting; party voting would be merely voting based on the last catastrophe, and governments were otherwise not being held accountable at the polls for their performance.

During the 1950s, the distribution of party identification was relatively stable from survey to survey, and this was consistent with the argument that individual party identification was also stable when normal politics prevailed. However, there was one University of Michigan Survey Research Center survey in which the same respondents were interviewed in 1956, 1958, and 1960. When this "panel survey" (a study in which the same people are reinterviewed) was carefully reexamined, party identification was far less stable than had been assumed: During these four "normal" years, one of every four respondents changed positions on a Democrat–independent–Republican scale.[30]

These short-term changes in party identification (most of which are between independent and one of the two major parties) are also related to voters' evaluations of government policy performance and economic management. Morris Fiorina's analysis of data from the 1956/58/60 panel survey, and from another one covering 1972/74/76, shows that changes in the economy, domestic policy performance, and such highly publicized events as Gerald Ford's pardon of former president Nixon all affected party identification.[31] People move to and from their respective political parties in response to their evaluations of economic and political conditions and in response to their evaluations of the performance of the parties and their candidates.[32] Party identification is neither impervious to change nor devoid of political content. In other words, there is feedback from issues and performance to partisan identification. Partisanship is a running tally of current party assessment.[33]

Year-to-year changes in party identification reflect voter reaction to recent political events and have a clear and direct effect on voting. From 1956 through 1988, there is a strong correlation between changes in the distribution of the vote for Congress and changes in the distribution of party identification.[34] Changes in congressional voting prompt changes in party identification, and changes in party identification prompt changes in congressional voting. There is a mutual adjustment between political evaluations, party identification, and voting.[35]

Party Voting and Issue Voting

When do voters use their party identification as a generalized guide to voting, and when do they vote because of a particular issue? The answer depends on information and the incentives to gather it, as may be illustrated by the difference in voting patterns in the classic comparison between farm managers and urban laborers.

In *The American Voter* an analysis of farmers revealed "spectacular links between simple economic pressures and partisan choice."[36] An information-centered explanation of these "spectacular links" would follow these general lines: The collective nature of the vote means that there is low incentive for an individual to collect information solely in order to cast one vote among many millions. Farmers, however, gather the information on their own businesses in great detail—not because they are better citizens, but because they are independent managers, and the information necessary for management is directly related to government policy. What to plant, when to sell, and where to borrow are all decisions that depend on government policies at least as much as they depend on the weather.

Laborers, not being economic managers and thus having no incentive to collect such information for their daily use, would be more likely to rely on past government performance, and to use a party label as an information shortcut; thus the greater sensitivity to economic fluctuations among farmers. Further, since there was much more current information about political performance among farmers than among laborers, farmers would rely less on party identification and would have weaker generalized attachments to party ideologies, since they would always have current information on performance.

The American Voter interpreted the "spectacular links" in a reverse fashion, saying that because farmers have weaker partisan identification than laborers, they are "psychologically free to march to the polls and vote the rascals out."[37] In other words, whereas a Downsian perspective emphasizes using party as an information shortcut when no other information has been obtained, the Michigan approach emphasized that no information could be used, *even if obtained*, when voters identified with a party. When information has been obtained in daily life, voters are not psychologically barred from using it.

Despite low levels of knowledge and interest in the electorate, party identification is profoundly political.[38] And when we accept the political basis of party identification, the question is no longer whether issues matter, but whether it is new or old issues that matter.

Party Images

There are two kinds of feedback from contemporary performance, in addition to actual changes in party identification. One of them affects voters' views of how well parties represent people like themselves, and the other affects views of how well parties perform different tasks of governance—such as handling national problems like unemployment, inflation, and crime. Unfortunately, preoccupation with the argument over whether party is a purely psychological identification or a political yardstick has led academics to concentrate on changes in party identification, when Republicans or Democrats became independents or identified with the other party, and when independents began to identify with one of the parties.

Changes in voters' party identification are generally slow, often even glacial; but changes in their comparative assessments of how well parties handle different problems, or what groups the parties stand for, can be rapid. These changes in how voters judge the relative abilities of the parties to represent different groups or handle different tasks are generally based on issue-party assessments. Today, these party assessments are generally measured by asking voters questions like "Which party cares more about farmers?" or "Generally speaking, which party do you think is better at 'controlling inflation'?" I call these measures "party heats," for they directly assess the comparative advantages of parties on an issue; such questions are now a staple of public opinion research.

Responses to these questions reflect feedback from political performance to a voter's conceptions of the parties which are not immediately reflected in party identification. For example, a poor performance on inflation by a Democratic president may weaken many working-class Democrats' faith in the ability of their party to deal with inflation. This may lead them to vote for Republican presidents when inflation looms, but they may not change their minds about which party's ultimate views of the good society are most compatible with their own.

Analysis of party images shows that voters reason about the relative ability of parties to deal with different issues. They do not assume that the same party is uniformly good at representing all groups or dealing with all issues.

In 1988, for example, Americans by two to one thought Democrats were better able to protect Social Security. By two to one, they also thought Republicans were better at controlling inflation and maintaining a strong defense. In general, Democrats are considered better at protecting Social Security, lowering unemployment, ensuring minority rights, and preserving the environment; Republicans are considered better at controlling inflation, maintaining a strong national defense, and fighting crime.[39]

In chapter 2, I noted the irony of *Voting*'s spectacularly inaccurate predictions about the possibility of a "woman's vote" or a "senior citizen's vote." Moreover, the views of American adults about the relative merits of the ways parties deal with women, men, and senior citizens demonstrate just how able voters are to make discriminating judgments about the parties (see table 3.1). People may be willing to give their parties the benefit of the doubt, but there are limits to this willingness. Republicans and Democrats say that the other party is better overall only when the difference between the two parties is well established, or an incumbent of their party has failed badly; it is far more common for a partisan, when asked about a perceived party weakness, to say that he or she doesn't know which party is better. The amount of "benefit of the doubt" that people give their party varies from issue to issue and reflects reasoning about past performance.

These party heats emphasize that the benefit of the doubt that people give their own party is not open-ended; they do acknowledge poor performances by their own party and strong performances by the other party. Thus, in 1986 less than half of all Republicans believed that their party cared more about senior citizens or women, and less than half of all Democrats believed that their party cared more about men. Party assessments demonstrate information about government and reasoning about the parties. Party heats are running tallies of past performance, not wishful thinking or expressions of team loyalty. As Morris Fiorina has noted for party images on inflation and unemployment, "Expectations about the party best capable of handling inflation and unemployment in the future depend on judgments about the parties' handling of inflation and unemployment in the past."[40]

In fact, it is precisely because party images do not all move together according to an underlying level of general satisfaction, but vary so widely from issue to issue, that party candidates for office try to increase the salience of issues where their party starts out with the largest advantage. Candidates addressing an issue where their party has a strong image have

TABLE 3.1
Political Identification and Response to:
"Which political party cares more about . . ."

	Rep. (%)	Dem. (%)	Ind. (%)	All (%)
SENIOR CITIZENS				
Republicans	44	12	26	26
Democrats	35	75	48	53
Both	7	2	4	5
Neither	4	2	6	4
Don't know/no answer	9	9	15	12
WOMEN				
Republicans	47	12	21	25
Democrats	24	61	39	42
Both	9	6	7	8
Neither	6	5	9	7
Don't know/no answer	13	16	25	19
MEN				
Republicans	62	25	35	39
Democrats	11	49	23	28
Both	9	7	8	9
Neither	6	2	8	5
Don't know/no answer	13	17	26	19

Source: CBS News/*New York Times* poll, April 1986.
Note: $N = 1,601$

the wind at their backs, whereas candidates addressing an issue where their party has a weak image are running into the wind.

Changing issues changes the campaign, if not the outcome, because party images vary by issue. A particularly important change is between concern with inflation and concern with unemployment. As noted in chapter 2, blue-collar workers are more sensitive about unemployment than white-collar workers and senior citizens, while white-collar workers and the elderly are more sensitive to inflation than blue-collar workers. This makes it particularly hard in times of inflation (as in the period since 1973, when rising energy prices triggered several inflationary surges) for

Democrats campaigning for president. People know the social composition of the parties and that Democrats will be less likely to cut inflation, if doing so requires raising unemployment. While Republicans are far more sensitive to inflation than to unemployment, Democrats are equally sensitive to both. This shows a group basis for the party-heat perceptions based on knowledge of partisan preferences.[41]

Party images have also been studied by analyzing responses to open-ended questions about the parties. Since the same general questions about likes and dislikes of the two parties have been asked on the quadrennial Michigan surveys since 1952, this data can be used to study changes over time in party assessments. While the use of party heats is, I believe, preferable, the other method, because of the continuity of questions since 1952, is valuable for the insights it provides about the relations between changes in party images and changes in party identification.

Using the Michigan data, the analysis of the so-called issueless 1950s provides considerable evidence of the sort of feedback from performance that affects party images, and therefore voting patterns. The traditional associations between the Republican party and the depression, and between the Democratic party and war, were not immutable in the minds of the voters. In their study of the 1956 election, Stokes, Campbell, and Miller noted, "Four years of Republican prosperity destroyed the major part of a fourteen-to-one margin the Democrats had in the partisanship of these responses. After haunting the Republicans in every election since 1932, memories of the 'Hoover Depression' had receded at least temporarily as a direct force in American politics."[42] On the other hand, they observed that the experience of the first four years of the Eisenhower administration amplified and reinforced another set of associations: "References to war and peace in 1952 were pro-Republican or anti-Democratic by a ratio of greater than seven to one. By 1956, the virtual disappearance of comments favorable to the Democrats or hostile to the Republicans had increased the ratio five times."[43]

Changes in the images voters have of the parties are related to future changes in party identification. In analyzing the changing views of the political parties from 1952 through 1976 on the SRC surveys, and relating changes in party assessments to future changes in party identification, Richard Trilling has written, "When party images reinforce past identifications, identifications are stable. When party images conflict with past identifications, identifications are likely to be altered."[44] Trilling has also shown how changing images of the parties and the changing class structure of American society have together affected relations between the political parties.[45] In 1952 more than two-thirds of all Americans were working-class; by 1976 less than half the country was working-class. Acceptance of the New Deal by Republicans made more working-class Democrats willing to vote for Republicans, and acceptance of the New Deal among middle-class Republicans made them more willing to vote for Democrats. This set of changes in society and the parties also means that campaigns matter more, for there are now fewer voters with one-sided views of the two parties.

When General Eisenhower was elected president, many upper-income and upper-status southern Democrats began to reassess their antipathy to the Republicans, and the first cracks in the "Solid South" became apparent even before the civil rights explosions of the 1960s.[46] Throughout the country, when Eisenhower made no attempt to repeal New Deal programs, Democratic antipathy to the Republican party was moderated. Further, as moderate Republican governors, particularly in the Northeast, courted unions and Catholics, the distinction between parties became less clear. When Republicans accepted the New Deal politically and socially, Democrats were willing to vote for them.[47] The overwhelming vote against Goldwater in 1964 shows just how critical acceptance of the New Deal was to the Republican party.

Evaluating Candidates

The candidates themselves have more importance in the American system than in most other political systems. The American system vests power in a single individual with no formal ties to his party. The unity of the executive branch, the separation of the executive and legislative branches, and the weakness of the American party system combine to give the American president a degree of power and independence unknown in a parliamentary system.

Voters focus on the presidential candidate because American parties have never been teams unified behind a single centralized source of control, like parties in some other countries, and the president has a large effect on his party's programs. The American federal system is characterized by widely dispersed patronage centers, local primaries, local fund-raising, and local party organizations. Presidents, therefore, have wide latitude in deciding what course to follow in office.

There has been, throughout the century, an antiparty strain of reformism in America that argues for nonpartisan elections. Party labels, it is argued, give to voters the illusion of informed choice while allowing them to ignore important differences between the candidates on the newly emerging issues of the day. Take away party labels, the reformers argue, and voters will pay attention to the "real" differences between candidates on the issues. In reality, however, voters evaluate candidates and form their images of them by using the same types of information shortcuts they use to form their views of parties, and issue positions are by no means their only criteria in the evaluation.[48]

Voters care about the competence of the candidate, not just the candidate's issue positions, because they do not follow most government activity and because they care about what the candidate can deliver from government. They care about the policy preferences of the nominee, not just the party's platform, because parties are coalitions that exercise weak controls over presidents. And they worry about the character of the candidate, about his or her sincerity, because they cannot easily read "true" preferences and because they care about uncertain future situations.

Competence versus Issue Proximity

In an ideal, two-party, parliamentary democracy, it is assumed that voters practice "proximity voting"—voting for the candidate or party whose position is nearest to theirs. Under this assumption, however, voters consider all candidates and parties equally able to carry out their promises. In reality, voters sometimes care less about candidates' issue positions than they do about which candidate can deliver the most on these issues, and which candidate can do a better job of simply managing and running the government. In short, they care about competence.

Competence is a relevant dimension of candidate evaluation for three reasons: (1) The candidate's competence directly affects the probability of his or her being able to deliver benefits from the system once elected. (2) Much of what both the president and Congress do involves the general management of the country. Since the voter has only limited information, he or she may vote for a candidate who seems capable of managing the affairs of the country even if that candidate is not the "closest" to the voter's specific issue preferences. (3) Finally, if the candidate is elected, he or she will have to solve many problems that no one can anticipate on election day. Competence in unfamiliar areas may be inferred from the perceived competence of the candidate in other, more familiar, areas.

Competence, then, is a measure of ability to handle a job, an assessment of how effective the candidate will be in office, of whether he or she can "get things done." Many aspects of government are noticed only when something goes wrong, and in many other areas, maintaining minimal levels of performance is far more important than policy change. The voter as prudent investor is right to be concerned about the competence of the candidate.

When James "Boss" Curley of Boston was reelected mayor from his prison cell, Jerome Bruner surveyed Boston voters to discover the secret of Curley's success. The voters, he found, were aware of Curley's sins, but many—including proper Bostonians who disagreed with Curley's issue positions as well—were voting for Curley because none of the candidates with more desirable issue positions and better reputations appeared capable of controlling government and getting things done.[49]

General Dwight Eisenhower's victory in 1952 was largely a result of his perceived competence to deal with the issues of the moment. At the height of cold-war tension, with the nation apparently stalemated in a war in Korea against "Red China," a man regarded as one of the most successful military leaders of World War II (and known to be considerate toward enlisted men), a man who had been head of NATO and a university president, was "perceived as a person peculiarly able to cope with the nation's international problems."[50]

In a world of complete information about the past, even with uncertainty about the future state of the world, voters could assess the competence of the candidate by assessing how well he or she had dealt with past administrative and legislative problems, and then extrapolate from that performance to how the candidate would manage the affairs of office. But most voters take information shortcuts to avoid this long and arduous process. They do not seek out detailed information about how the candidate has managed government and delivered benefits. Instead they use shortcuts to assess competence, which is itself an information shortcut. They assess the candidate's competence on the basis of data that is new and easy to process, particularly information from the party conventions and the political campaign. The convention allows voters to hear what other, more familiar, political leaders have to say on behalf of the nominee; the campaign exposes the candidate to voters in complex and fast-breaking situations. As they watch the candidate handle crowds, speeches, press conferences, reporters, and squabbles, they can obtain information with which they imagine how he or she would be likely to behave in office.

There is a natural inclination to associate information shortcuts based on campaign behavior with the television era, during which there have been several well-publicized examples of campaign events that affected candidate ratings and votes. The most dramatic example from recent campaigns was in 1972, when Senator George McGovern, the Democratic nominee, lost considerable ground because he appeared weak and indecisive in handling the revelation that Senator Thomas Eagleton, the nominee for vice president, had received electroshock treatments. When McGovern wavered, many of his supporters concluded that he simply was not competent to be president.[51] More recently, Governor Michael Dukakis became the butt of jokes and received much ridicule for looking out-of-place and foolish in the helmet he wore when he went for a ride in one of the Army's new tanks, in an attempt to appear more familiar with defense issues.

Campaign behavior mattered to voters, however, well before television replaced radio and newspapers as the dominant medium in American national politics. During the 1948 campaign, Governor Thomas Dewey made uncomplimentary remarks about a workingman, a railroad engineer who had made a blunder with Dewey's campaign train. All knowledge of these campaign blunders came from radio and print media, and thus did not have the visual immediacy associated with television. Yet when a national survey asked respondents, "Do you think there was anything special about Dewey that made some people vote against him?" 26 percent of the respondents referred to Dewey's campaign behavior, and among respondents who actually voted, the proportion referring to Dewey's campaign behavior was 31 percent.[52]

What matters to voters when they assess competence can be expected to vary with the concerns of the moment and with how they view the office for which they are voting; thus honesty mattered more after Watergate, and military leadership experience mattered more during the Korean War. Nevertheless, voters also assess candidates' competence from past behavior and from political campaigns.

Policy Preferences and Sincerity

Voters use information shortcuts to assess candidates' policy preferences. Moreover, as we shall see in a moment, because of the problems of learning what the true preferences of candidates are in compromise situations, voters are also concerned with the integrity or "sincerity" of the candidates.

Demographic facts provide a low-information shortcut to estimating a candidate's policy preferences (though not to evaluating past public performance). Characteristics such as a candidate's race, ethnicity, religion, gender, and local ties (hereinafter, "localism") are important cues because the voter observes the relationship between these traits and real-life behavior as part of his daily experience. Where these characteristics are closely aligned with the interests of the voter, they provide a basis for reasonable, accessible, and economical estimates of candidate behavior.[53] It has often been noted that the use of demographic cues in voting probably plays a more important role in American campaigns than it does in those of more homogeneous countries.

There is a good deal of survey data to suggest that when voters believe government is closer to them, they are more likely to believe they get their money's worth from taxes. This belief finds its voting equivalent in the "friends and neighbors" vote that is so often disparaged as irrelevant.[54] Actually, it is an example of low-information rationality: using an easy-to-obtain cue to assess a candidate's positions. Particularly on distributive issues—which neighborhood to tear up for a highway, where to put the toxic-waste dump, where to build a prison, an airport, or a park, whether to allow offshore drilling, where to disburse patronage—localism may be an effective orientation for the voter to use in trying to predict a legislator's preferences. In addition, localism is of some value in determining the capabilities of the candidate. When a candidate is in some sense a neighbor, the voter at least has a better chance of knowing whether he or she is a blatant crook or an obvious fool. Given the problems of expensive, scarce, and unreliable information about the candidates, the voter is more likely to have confidence in a neighbor with a local reputation for competence.

Further, because voters are necessarily uncertain about what a candidate will do if elected, they take into account the demographic characteristics of the candidate's supporters. Endorsements from feminists, blacks, Christian fundamentalists, Jews, unions, military veterans, and many other demographic groups make a difference. This process of inferring the candidate's policy preferences from his or her demographic characteristics is the political equivalent of screening job applicants by reading their résumés instead of by evaluating their work, which would take more time and effort. Television appearances and televised convention proceedings offer quick visual clues to the candidate's support groups, and thus make it harder for candidates to pretend to be all things to all people. "If *they* are supporting him," a voter may ask, "how can he be good for *me?*" When candidates become aware of such an attitude, they try to change it by offering low-information cues that encourage support for demographic reasons. Thus the black mayor of Los Angeles, Tom Bradley, reminded voters of his experience as a policeman; the wealthy George Bush talked of his down-home love of pork rinds and horseshoe pitching; and Michael Dukakis, the governor of Massachusetts—a state thought to be liberal and therefore soft on defense—went for a ride in an Army tank.

When voters watch a candidate perform on television, making promises and taking hard-line rhetorical positions on issues, they question if there is congruence between avowal and actual feelings—whether the candidate's support for a cause represents a genuine personal commitment or only a campaign tactic.[55] We care more about sincerity and character when we are uncertain about what someone will do. As Aristotle noted, "We believe good men more readily and fully than others; this is true generally whatever the question is, and absolutely true where exact certainty is impossible and opinions are divided."[56] This is often the case in daily life, when we must make evaluations with limited information and no theory to guide us. How do we choose a new baby-sitter for our young children when we must make an emergency trip? How do we choose a nurse for a critically ailing parent who lives at the other end of the continent? We want to hire competent people, but without the time or resources to evaluate their past performance, we must make a judgment based largely on clues to personal character, from a conversation or from what our friends tell us; will this person do what we would like to have done? Delegation in such situations involves emotions and values and bonds between people. It involves evaluating empathy and understanding, deciding who shares one's own concerns. A voter wonders, therefore, about whether a candidate cares about people like himself or herself.

When voters estimate a candidate's preferences they take account of sincerity—whether the candidate really cares about their concerns. Because it is difficult, for example, to assess whether a compromise bill was the best that could be done, or whether a politician reneged on his commitments, they take shortcuts: they estimate public morality and character from private morality and character, assuming in the absence of better information that candidates treat their constituents like they treat their own spouses and children.

Incumbency

In 1940, the elaborate methods used to assess the effects of the media on the presidential vote produced no positive results. In that year, with Franklin D. Roosevelt running for a third term against Republican Wendell Willkie, only 8 percent of all voters changed their minds at any time during the six-month period from May through September.[57] This result is a striking demonstration of the fact that when the voter estimates competence, there is an asymmetry between candidates. For candidates who are incumbents or who have spent a long period of time in a prominent position, voters can make judgments about competence based on observation of "actual" behavior.[58] An incumbent has dealt with "real" events; the challenger can be judged only by talk and by those events he or she "manufactures." Thus public estimates of a challenger's competence must be based on how he or she talks, looks, and campaigns—criteria that are susceptible to more varied interpretation than the incumbent's actual job performance. Not for nothing were people who challenged a king called "pretenders."

In general, incumbents deal with acts of state, and challengers deal with media events. Presidents adopt Rose Garden campaign strategies so that evaluations of them rest on their records as presidents, not on their images as campaigners.[59] When President Richard Nixon elected not to campaign against George McGovern in 1972, his decision was based on just such reasoning. Nixon's aide H. R. Haldeman told him (as recorded on the White House tapes revealed during the Watergate investigation),

> So little is known about McGovern, you'll have a better chance of changing people's minds about him. To start with, you got 40 percent of the people who will vote for you no matter what happens . . . and you got 40 percent of the people who will vote against you no matter what happens, so you have got 20 percent of the people in the middle who may vote for you or who may not and that 20 percent is what you've gotta work on. Getting one of those 20 who is an undecided type to vote for you on the basis of your positive points is much less likely than getting them to vote against McGovern by scaring them to death about McGovern; and that, that's the area we ought to be playing.[60]

Because voters do not directly observe so much of what government does, an incumbent president—no matter what his rating in the polls—can claim credit for such things as keeping the nation out of nuclear war and preserving the basic structure of government.

Incumbents are increasingly attacking their opponents as risks because increases in education and the decline of party influence make incumbency the focal point of the campaign.[61] President Ford's 1976 campaign hammered away at how little was known about Jimmy Carter, and President Carter's 1980 campaign in turn did everything it could to raise doubts about what would happen with Ronald Reagan's finger on the nuclear button. In 1988 George Bush's strategists made essentially the same arguments: as *Newsweek* explained, the vice president "*had* to go bare-knuckle against Dukakis. . . . It was going to be a lot easier, a senior strategist said, to raise the other guy's negatives than to lower his own; if Bush could not pump himself up, he could at least tear Dukakis down."[62]

The victorious general, of which Eisenhower is the only twentieth-century example, is an exception to the rule that challengers are known mainly from campaigns. Having performed notable public service in an arena where his behavior is well publicized and closely watched, he may well be better known and more carefully evaluated, and feel more familiar to the electorate, than the incumbent.

The asymmetry of incumbents and challengers holds for elections to the Senate and House of Representatives as well. Because incumbents are generally better known, the competitiveness of campaigns is more affected by challenger spending than by incumbent spending. Incumbents may, and generally do, spend more money than their challengers, but the marginal return on money spent by challengers is much higher than that on money spent by incumbents. Elections are competitive when challengers have sufficient money to convey themselves and their messages to voters.[63]

Candidates, Parties, and Issues: Divided Government

It has become a near-permanent feature of American politics that the Republicans own the White House and the Democrats own the Senate and House of Representatives. Republicans have controlled the presidency for twenty-eight of the past forty years. Since Reagan was elected in 1980, furthermore, the Republican party has achieved virtual parity with the Democrats in party identification for the first time since 1946.[64] Despite Republican control of the presidency and parity in party identification, however, Democrats own the Congress. Democrats have controlled the House of Representatives for all but four years since 1932, and the Senate for all but ten years since 1940.

Republicans argue that the popular will is most accurately expressed in presidential elections. They charge that the Democrats own Congress because congressional seniority and gerrymandering have isolated Congress from the electorate and deprived the people of the fair chance to express their will that they have in presidential elections. The Republicans look for ways to eliminate the incumbency advantage in order to gain control of the House. Democrats counter that the will of the people is most accurately expressed in congressional elections, that they have been deprived of the presidency by primaries which resulted in unattractive candidates as their nominees, and that they were outspent by Republicans who could use their money to buy the White House. Democrats look for rules changes so their primary campaigns will produce candidates better able to capture the presidency, and for ways to nullify the Republicans' financial advantages. Partisans of each party are arguing that defeat of their pet agendas or candidates is proof of the corruption and incapacity of the system. They are arguing that elections do not work. They are wrong.

Gary Jacobson has refuted Republican arguments: incumbency is not responsible for Democratic advantages in congressional elections. In open-seat elections since 1968, the GOP has made no gains in Congress.[65] Democratic arguments are wrong as well. Democratic troubles begin with the changing nature of American society and the difficult problems of reconciling interests within the Democratic coalition. As noted above, the fact that white-collar voters are more sensitive to inflation while blue-collar voters are more sensitive to unemployment gives the Democrats a more difficult balancing act to achieve on national economic policy.

Ironically, while members of both political parties tend to explain divided government in candidate-centered terms—congressional incumbency on one hand, and poor campaigners on the other—the root cause of divided government is divided views about the political parties. People vote differently for Congress and president because they associate the two offices with different problems and issues, and they rate the GOP higher on issues with which the president deals. Recall that Republicans are seen as better in dealing with foreign policy, national defense, and inflation, and Democrats are seen as better in dealing with Social Security, domestic programs, unemployment, minority rights, and the environment. Party images are an important source of information which voters use to assess the candidates for whom they vote. Republicans win the White House because inflation, foreign policy, and national defense are all more important to voters when they vote for president than when they vote for legislators. Democrats win Senate and House races because people care more about domestic issues, Social Security, and unemployment when they elect legislators.[66]

Divided views of the party are based on voter reasoning about the differences between the job of the president and the job of the legislator, on one hand, and the images of the two parties, on the other. As John Petrocik notes, "Most voters recognize the policy strengths of the parties and respond to them."[67]

The Growing Importance of Campaigns

Divided government attests to both the limits and the importance of campaigns.

Divided government's roots in the different issue strengths of the two parties attest to the limits of voter manipulation—the limited ability of candidates in either party to use clever campaigns to obscure their historic performances with smoke and mirrors. Candidates' ability to stake out positions at variance with past party performance on long-standing issues is limited.

Information about past party performance is still important, however. The information shortcuts about party identification and party performance on different issues serve as reality tests against which campaign arguments are tested. The relative weights of party and candidate will vary both among issues and among offices. Candidates matter most where party matters least; the less well developed the party image, the more sensitive voters will be to the candidate.[68]

The roots of divided government, then, depend on reasoning about parties and candidates, which in turn depends on voters' use of information about party performance on issues and information about which issues are most relevant to different elections. Such information use and reasoning are connected to a campaign's ability to make connections between candidates, offices, and issues.

The early voting studies suggest that modern mass-media campaigns should have larger effects than the campaigns of the 1940s. At that time, a voter's strength of conviction was related to the political homogeneity of his or her associates. Most voters belonged to politically homogeneous social groups; the social gulf between the parties was so wide that a majority of voters had no close friends or associates voting differently from them.[69] A decline in the political homogeneity of primary groups should lead to weaker conviction among voters and therefore allow more latitude for the influence of the mass media. The political cleavages that exist today cut more across social groups, which means that voters are typically in less homogeneous family, church, and work settings.[70]

All voting studies have found that education is one of the prime indicators of voter ability to process information generated by campaigns and the mass media. In the 1940s, fewer than one in eight voters had been to college; today nearly half of all voters have been to college. In the 1940s, over 40 percent of the electorate had never reached high school; today this figure is 10 percent. This increase in educational level, then, gives greater potential import to political campaigns. The broadening of the electorate, discussed in chapter 2, means that voters are following more national and international issues. One striking example of this is the development of party images based on the party's ability to deal with the problems of women and senior citizens—two groups for whom it was not expected in the 1940s that distinctive voting patterns could emerge.

The more educated the electorate, the greater is its ability to follow news about national and international politics; the more issues the electorate follows, the more varied the images of the parties will be; the more varied the images of the parties, the more the choice of issue matters.

Democrats and Republicans today are generally much more willing to consider a vote for the other party's candidate than was true in the past. Further, a larger proportion of the electorate has no party loyalty at all, and even the "standing decision" of party members to vote the party line is not as firm as it used to be. In the 1940s, fewer than 25 percent of the voters in the entire country had ever voted for more than one party's candidate for president. Today, over 60 percent have voted for both Democratic and Republican candidates for president.[71] The extent of cross-party voting emphasizes just how much more politically fluid the country has become.

Whatever their level of education, voters use information shortcuts and cost-saving devices in thinking about parties, candidates, and issues. They use shortcuts to assess ideology, platforms, individual competence, and character. This leads to an asymmetry between the challengers and the incumbents, and to the explicit assumption that the election begins centered on the incumbent and his or her present performance.

Campaigns make a difference because voters have limited information about government and uncertainty about the consequences of policies. If voters had full information and no uncertainty, they would not be open to influence from others, and hence there would be no campaigns. In reality, voters do not know much about what government is doing or is capable of doing. Thus they are open to influence by campaigners who offer them more information or better explanations of the ways in which government activities affect them.

However, the shortcuts that voters use also limit the effects of campaigns. Before public opinion studies of voting, conventional wisdom held that "rational, independent voters" gathered and absorbed information, weighed alternatives, and made up their minds just before they voted. Because voters were assumed to gather and assess information, it was expected that voting would be affected primarily by the information to which they were exposed. Therefore, it was assumed that voting was a choice easily manipulated by "propaganda." But instead of direct media effects on rational voters without memory, there is a sophisticated pattern of transmission from past elections and interactions among and between people in the current election.

Voters also use information shortcuts when they assess candidates. They estimate a candidate's policy stands from demographic traits of both the candidate and his or her supporters. They estimate a candidate's sincerity and adherence to promises not by evaluating past behavior but by extrapolating from private morality to public morality. Voters care about the personal competence of the candidate—his or her ability to deliver benefits. They assess overall competence because they do not understand all the problems the president must deal with, and they do not make individual judgments in every case of what the president can do. When assessing competence, they also economize by judging campaign behavior, instead of researching the candidate's past governmental performance.

The focus on information shortcuts implies several assumptions about what kinds of information are easiest to obtain and process. These assumptions include: (1) It is easier to assess the real world than to make projections about the future. (2) It is easier to track a party by remembering its view of the good society than by trying to examine its past performance. (3) Current data are easier to use—and therefore are treated as more relevant—than past data. (4) Personal morality is easier to understand than institutional morality. (5) It is easier to assess an individual's competence than to assess his or her legislative performance. (6) Candidates can be understood if their demographic traits are known. And (7) candidates can be judged by who their friends and supporters are. In order to examine these assumptions and look more closely at how people process political information, chapter 4 explores the relevant findings of cognitive psychology.

FOUR

Going beyond the Data: Evidence and Inference in Voting

JEROME BRUNER once observed that the most characteristic thing about mental life is that "one constantly goes beyond the information given."[1] People go beyond the data they already have by using information short-cuts, cues that enable them to call on beliefs about people and institutions from which they can generate scenarios, or "scripts," as they are called in psychology. They absorb cues and then flesh out a scenario with their "default values," the information we assume to be associated with the cue in the absence of contradictory information about the specific situation.[2] While studying under Bruner, the sociologist Harold Garfinkel demonstrated how flexible and creative people can be in imagining a person and his probable behavior from a simple set of traits or demographic characteristics. Taking twelve traits from the standard psychological inventories—traits with positive and negative poles, such as energetic and lazy, honest and dishonest—Garfinkel selected combinations of positive and negative traits at random and then asked subjects to describe a person who had all of them. The result was dramatic: no matter how unlikely the combinations of traits, the subjects could *always* imagine people to fit them; not one subject complained of an impossible combination of traits. As Bruner noted of this work, "Perhaps there *can* be every kind of person. Or perhaps the better way to say it is that we can create hypotheses that will accommodate virtually anything we encounter."[3]

The cognitive psychology literature suggests that there are two modes of information processing, the statistical and the clinical, each with its own standards of evidence and truth. The statistical mode is concerned with logic and weighs evidence. The clinical mode is concerned with fitting information together and assembling a causal narrative. Anthony Downs's approach to decision making leads to neo-Bayesian statistics in which pieces of new and old evidence are combined in proportion to their information content. But this idea takes no account of how content is weighted.

The cognitive research suggests that a small amount of new information is usually given more weight than a large amount of old information whenever the new information is personal and the old information is abstract and hard to fit into a narrative. It also suggests that a small amount of old information may receive more weight than a large amount of new information in at least three situations: when the old information becomes more important in a new context, when the old information is easier to incorporate, or when the old information is easier to use in comparing candidates.[4]

Whereas the statistical mode asks whether an argument is persuasive, the clinical approach asks whether a story is lifelike, whether the pieces form a coherent narrative. Assembling, assessing, and incorporating information takes time and is a selective, hence creative, process. We assemble when we think, and the more we are stimulated, the more we think, computing on the fly, adjusting our categories and the data we use dynamically.[5] When we assemble our information, we don't use all we know at one time. The cognitive research which explains how narratives are assembled includes studies that focus on the representativeness, availability, and framing of information. We incorporate information that forms a narrative, which we assess by the clinical equivalent of "goodness of fit" testing, judgment by representativeness. We incorporate information which fits with our point of view, or frame, and we incorporate information which we have used recently—that is, information which is available.

From the research on cognition, we can draw several principles that help explain how voters make evaluations and choices. The findings about how people assemble information into narratives lead to a Gresham's law of information: just as the original Gresham's law was that bad money drives good money out of circulation, in campaigns, small amounts of new personal information can dominate large amounts of old impersonal information, permitting hitherto unknown candidates to surge ahead of better-known candidates.

The research on cognition has also uncovered calculation aids or shortcuts that people use when they estimate probabilities and compare different mixes of gains and losses. The effects of calculation aids, which I call pseudocertainty effects, help explain why virtually unknown candidates can be evaluated as highly as they sometimes are.

When people make choices between candidates, particularly in primaries, they "know" many things about the candidates from the information they obtain and the meaning they ascribe to it from their default values. They do not, however, have in mind the same characteristics for each candidate. This disparity means that the way voters evaluate candidates is affected by the ways in which they formulate comparisons of them. When people compare candidates on the differences that are most obvious, rather than those that are most important, they are conducting the equivalent of a Drunkard's Search, looking for their lost car keys under the streetlight only because it is easier to search there.[6] This search strategy reflects the ways in which voters formulate their choices. And the fact that people use this strategy explains much about the ways in which incumbents and front-runners frame the array of choices facing voters.

Representativeness

When millions of voters cast ballots for candidates of whom they knew nothing a few weeks prior to a primary, and when people judge a candidate's record on the basis of campaign appearances, they are assessing past or future political performance on the basis of assessments of how well a candidate fits their scenarios or scripts. Such goodness-of-fit assessments involve the use of the "representativeness" heuristic.[7] Representativeness is a heuristic, a "rule of thumb," for judging the likelihood that a person will be a particular kind of person by how similar he or she is to the stereotype of that kind of person. In other words, if we judge how likely it is that a candidate will "do the right thing" by how well he or she fits our ideas about what kind of person does the right thing, rather than by considering how likely it is that a person with a particular record would do the right thing, we are judging with the representativeness heuristic. In the case of voting behavior, the most critical use of this heuristic involves projecting from a personal assessment of a candidate to an assessment of what kind of leader he was in previous offices or to what kind of president he will be in the future.

When voters see a new candidate on television and assess what kind of president he would be from his media character and demographic characteristics, they are extrapolating from observed personal data to unobserved personal data, and from personal data to future presidential policies and performance. When voters judge how a candidate will run the government from how he manages his campaign, or whether he will have an honest administration from perceptions of his personal honesty, they are making large extrapolations with little or no discomfort, or even awareness that they are extrapolating. Thus: "In the absence of better evidence, people readily predict success in graduate school from an IQ test score, research productivity from performance in a colloquium, or the size of a mother's graduation gift to her daughter from the size of a tip that she gave to a waiter."[8]

When voters make these jumps—assessing character from interviews or from observing the candidate with his family, and then predicting future presidential performance from these personal traits—they are making intuitive predictions by representativeness.[9] When making political judgments by representativeness, people compare their evidence about a candidate with their mental model of a president. They judge the likelihood of a candidate's being a good president by how well the evidence about him fits the essential features of their model of a good president.[10] Representativeness, then, is a form of clinical goodness-of-fit testing.[11]

Demographics and résumés are important because of our talent for developing narratives about others. From fragments of information and random observations of behavior, we can develop full-blown causal narratives about kinds of people, and these narratives (or scenarios, or scripts) are so suggestive that we are not aware of the limited data from which we are generating them. Once a narrative about a person has been generated from fragmentary data, moreover, it may take a good deal of information to alter the narrative and change evaluations of the person. Thus, the representativeness research is also psychology's way of testing whether a picture is really worth a thousand words—or of learning just how many words it *is* worth.

When we generate narratives about people from specific traits, we are acting as clinicians, not as statisticians or scientists. As clinicians, we use different standards to test our ideas. As Bruner has noted, "With science, we ask finally for some verification (or some proof against falsification). In the domain of narrative and explication of human action, we ask instead that, upon reflection, the account correspond to some perspective we can imagine or 'feel' as right."[12]

In the statistical mode, we increase our confidence in a judgment by getting data about more trials or instances; in a clinical mode, we increase our confidence by getting a fuller picture. For example, when asked whether it was more likely that a student chosen at random was "depressed and quit college and attempted suicide" or simply "attempted suicide," a statistician would say that "attempted suicide" was *by definition* more likely, because you cannot be depressed *and* quit college *and* attempt suicide without at least attempting suicide; in other words, a conjunction of events is never more likely than any one of them. People judge likelihood by "fullness of picture" and thus commonly judge the other way; it is easier to think of someone being depressed, quitting college, and attempting suicide than just attempting suicide. The probability that someone is both an artist and a Republican is lower than the probability that a person is a Republican, but if the person resembles our *image* of a Republican artist more closely than our image of a Republican, we will estimate the probability of the conjunction higher than the probability of the single event.[13]

Character versus Incentives

The tendency to imagine whole people from specific traits and isolated observations of character is strengthened by our willingness to assume that we are learning about character whenever we observe behavior. We explain our own behavior in terms of situational constraints and incentives, but when we judge the behavior of others, we assume that it reveals character. Your behavior tells me what kind of person you are; mine reflects my environment.[14] Obviously, this critical difference increases the amount of information about character we acquire and subsequently use in assembling our views of others.

There is, then, an inferential asymmetry in representativeness: we do not make the same kinds of inferences about ourselves that we make about others. We take our own character for granted, explaining our behavior as a response to the situation we are in and the incentives we encounter. When thinking about others and describing their behavior, if we do not know them well, we cannot take their character for granted, and therefore we read their behavior for evidence about their character. This means that both racism and the use of demographic cues as shortcuts are intimately related to representativeness. One example may suffice. In the 1920s and 1930s, Jewish basketball players dominated the sport. Ed Sullivan, who later became famous as the host of a television variety show, was then a sports columnist for the *New York Daily News*. In a 1933 article entitled "Jews Are Star Players," he explained this Jewish athletic dominance as inherent in the Jewish mentality: "Jewish players seem to take naturally to the game. . . . Perhaps this is because the Jew is a natural gambler. Perhaps it is because he devotes himself more closely to a problem than others will."[15]

This inferential asymmetry between how we explain our actions and how we explain the actions of others is particularly sharp when we observe behavior we disagree with or judge negatively. Because we tend to overestimate the reasonableness of our own actions, we also overestimate the probability that others would do what we would do. For this reason, we tend to believe that people who make mistakes or blunders are revealing their true character.[16] This fact has an important effect on our voting behavior: we see politicians who vote against bills that we favor as showing their character and personal preferences, not as adapting to the unavoidable need to compromise or make trade-offs in order to achieve a result acceptable to a majority.

Background Information versus Personal Information

The original research by Kahneman and Tversky on representativeness suggested that no background information about a person would be integrated into the impression drawn from personal behavior. Subsequent research, however, has shown that historical information—what the psychological researchers call "base rate information"—will be integrated when it is comprehended as causally related to character formation and when it is not pallid, remote, or abstract.[17]

Past votes by a political candidate frequently are not easily assimilated into a picture, but there is a whole host of tags that do become integrated, such as environmentalist, union member, fundamentalist, right-to-lifer, militant, feminist, military veteran, draft dodger, Rhodes scholar, Eagle Scout, and astronaut. When candidates who were previously unknown to voters stump through the living rooms, supermarkets, and barbershops of Iowa and New Hampshire, voters use lists of background data. They learn that Jimmy Carter was an ex-governor of Georgia, Gary Hart a senator, and George Bush an ambassador, congressman, and CIA director. They also integrate this information into their images of the candidates. However— and this is the critical point—they will decide what kind of governor Carter was and what kind of president he will be *not* on the basis of knowledge about his performance as governor but on their assessment of how likely it is that Carter, as a person, was a good governor.

Personal versus Political Narratives

If people knew enough about politics, they could generate a picture of a politician in the same way they generate pictures of other people from knowing their demographics and personality traits.

Tell a "political junkie" how a politician has voted, and what kind of district or state he or she is from, and the junkie, after considering the interplay of personal preferences and political necessities, can tell you something about the politician's character and beliefs. But few people have enough knowledge about the organization of government and the dynamics of legislation to do this; most find it far easier to develop a personal narrative, and then assess political character from personal character. When they infer likely policy positions from a candidate's familiarity with tamales or biscuits or caviar, they are implicitly predicating their inferences on the "myth of tight linkage." Social scientists did this too when they searched for underlying dimensions like "need achievement" or an "authoritarian personality" or "attitudinal consistency." Social scientists have learned that the view of the brain as a large computer spreadsheet, where each piece of new data updates all relevant applications, is wrong; they have learned that people can tolerate much more inconsistency than they had once thought. But when people assess political character from personal character, they are assuming a high degree of consistency in interpersonal organization.

Gresham's Law of Political Information

Because we generate narratives about kinds of people, it is easier to take personal data and fill in the political facts and policies than to start with the political facts and fill in the personal data. This has an important political implication in decision making and evaluation: campaign behavior can dominate political history.

Judgment by representativeness means that people can quickly shift the data base from which they judge candidates. A voter may have information about the past accomplishments of a candidate, but when exposed to the candidate on television, may judge future performance solely by how "presidential" the candidate appears, ignoring evidence about past performance. Furthermore, personal evidence is so compelling that candidates known personally and recently come to appear more attractive than candidates with less recent images.[18]

Presidential appearance, particularly in the short run, can seem to voters to be an adequate basis for predicting presidential success in the future. This can occur because in comparing personal information with political behavior, one is comparing stories with facts. Personal data gathered from observing the candidate generates a story about the candidate—what he or she is like and is likely to do if elected. The information about votes, offices held, and policy positions taken in the past does not generate a full story and may not even be joined with the personal data. Narratives are more easily compiled and are retained longer than facts. Narratives, further, require more negative information before they change.[19] When judgments of likelihood are made by representativeness, people do not integrate personal data with background data easily, and often they do not do it at all.

Personal data can dominate or even obliterate background data; "when worthless specific evidence is given, prior probabilities are ignored."[20]

This is a point where the cognitive literature seems to me more optimistic than warranted about the use of information. Daniel Kahneman has written that "distant labels or incidents will be ignored when evidence that is closer to the target . . . is available."[21] But his own work shows that this does not always follow. Recent data of one form dominates distant data of the same form, but when some of the data are personal narrative and some are political facts, distant personal data can dominate more recent impersonal material.

In elections, Gresham's law of political information means that personal information can drive more relevant political information out of consideration. Thus there can be a perverse relationship between the amount of information voters are given about a candidate and the amount of information they actually use: a small amount of personal information can dominate a large amount of historical information about a past record. This dominance of personal campaign data over past political data is what I have called Gresham's law of political information. Just as bad money drives good money out of circulation, so does easily absorbed personal information drive more relevant but hard-to-assimilate political information out of consideration.

In one context—campaign information versus past voting records—Gresham's law is both strong and discouraging: personally uninspiring politicians with a career of solid accomplishments get bypassed in primaries for fresh new faces with lots of one-liners but no record of accomplishment. In the context of low-information rationality and information shortcuts, however, Gresham's law is somewhat less bleak; there are many low-information cues which are proxies for political records and which voters may pick up and incorporate into their assessments of future performance.

Gresham's Law and New Candidates

People's ability to judge by representativeness explains why it is possible for new candidates to do so well against established "heavies" in the early primaries. If people could not assemble full and coherent images from personal observations, well-established candidates with records would dominate primaries—except when voters were so unhappy with them that they were willing to gamble on new faces.

From a psychological point of view, voters do not necessarily gamble when they select new candidates over better-known candidates, because the comparisons they make are clinical. In comparing candidates, the process of projection—judging future likelihood by representativeness—does not automatically take account of different levels of information about the candidates. If voters were statisticians, they would integrate personal data with historical data and then adjust their predictions to account for the quantities of information upon which they were based. In statistical terms, they would regress for limited information, so that the extent to which they predicted performances that would deviate from the norm would depend on the quantity of data the prediction was based upon.

If a little data about one candidate suggests that he would be a good president, and a lot of data about another candidate suggests the same thing, statisticians would say that it is more likely that the second candidate will do well; they would discount the prediction based on less data. But voters are not statisticians, and they do not automatically discount, or regress, for limited data. They are, at best, clinicians, and they will be as confident in predictions made from flimsy and remote data as in those made from substantial and recent data.[22]

Jimmy Carter provides a clear example of how fast people can come to believe they know "something" about a candidate and feel able to rate him. Carter was an ex-governor of Georgia who had no television exposure at all prior to the 1976 primary. He won the Iowa primary in January, receiving some national publicity, and then received a lot of national publicity after winning in New Hampshire the next month, but few Americans outside Georgia and Florida could have heard of him a month before he won in New Hampshire. Gerald Ford had been president nearly nineteen months by February 1976 and had nearly as much media coverage for each month of his presidency as Carter had for his one month in the public eye. Yet despite the disparity in amounts of exposure and duration of time over which people had a chance to observe the two men, people who knew of Carter were able to place him on issues almost as readily as those who knew of Ford.[23]

Walter Mondale's famous campaign query about Gary Hart, "Where's the beef?" was an attempt to make voters aware of how little they knew about Hart. President Ford's campaign against Carter in 1976 was also focused in large measure on pointing out how little voters knew about Carter. The very fact that better-known candidates need to work so hard to remind voters how little they know about some of the new candidates emphasizes just how far a little personal data can go for new candidates, particularly when the data are consistent and clear.

Framing and Availability

While the representativeness literature emphasizes that information gets used when it can be incorporated into a coherent picture, the framing literature emphasizes formulation effects: what we incorporate into a picture or narrative depends on the point of view or frame we use. The decision frame has been defined as the "decision-maker's conception of the acts, outcomes, and contingencies associated with a particular choice. The frame that the decision-maker adopts is controlled partly by the formulation of the problem and partly by the norms, habits, and personal characteristics of the decision-maker."[24] The frame "determines how a task is conceived, what kind of evidence is considered, and the cognitive strategy employed."[25]

The frame, or point of view, determines how people think about gains or losses. It also matters because different reference points, or points of view, bring forth different information and attitudes.[26] As Aristotle noted, it adds to an orator's influence if "his hearers should be in just the right frame of mind."[27]

The seminal cognitive studies on choice and decision making are the experiments by Kahneman and Tversky, which demonstrate how the formulation of choices affects decision making.[28] Their experiments, and many subsequent studies as well, show that when people perceive themselves to be ahead, or in a good position, they are relatively cautious, preferring a bird in the hand to two in the bush; and that when they are behind, they are more likely to gamble, risking a bird in the hand to gain two from the bush. In psychological terms, they are generally risk-averse on gains and risk-seeking on losses. More important, however, these studies demonstrate that the way in which statistically identical alternatives are formulated can have a significant impact on the choices people make. A simple but classic example is the different ways that people perceive cash discounts and credit surcharges. Whether a store posts the credit-card price on its goods and gives a cash discount, or posts the cash price on its goods and charges a credit-card surcharge, is of no *cost* consequence to either cash customers or credit customers. However, people have a marked preference for cash discounts on posted credit-card prices over credit surcharges on posted cash prices, despite their exactly equivalent cost. Also, whether a choice is formulated in terms of the "good results" or the "bad results"—

whether, for example, people are offered a choice between medical policies in terms of lives saved or in terms of lives lost—affects the policy they choose.

The way a problem is formulated can even lead to a reversal of preferences. When it comes to choosing a lottery in which to buy a ticket, people prefer a lottery with high odds for a small prize over a lottery with low odds for a big prize. However, if they are given a chance to sell the tickets before the drawing, they place a higher value on the ticket with low odds for a big prize. This clear reversal of preferences is not a result of faulty mental arithmetic or inexperience with thinking about odds; the experiments have been replicated in Las Vegas![29]

Framing is to psychology as role theory is to sociology. Role theory tells us that we can present many different personas to others. At different times of the day, we can be a spouse, a parent, a child, a worker, a partisan, a customer, or a patient. By showing us this, role theory also says that we do not use all of ourselves at any one time. Framing tells us that since we cannot look at a person or situation from all perspectives at the same time, we cannot use all of ourselves when we view others. Both framing and role theory, then, are theories about the ways we divide ourselves and about which parts of ourselves we use in presenting ourselves or in viewing the presentations of others.

When Framing Matters

Framing effects occur whenever altering the formulation of a problem, or shifting the point of view of an observer, changes the information and ideas the observer will use when making decisions. Framing effects, in other words, occur only when there is differentiation in the ways that we can think about a subject. If the same information and metaphors always come to the fore no matter how questions about a subject are formulated, there is no differentiation and hence no possibility of framing effects. There is also no framing if there is a single dominant attitude about a subject. If people integrated all their attitudes about candidates and parties into a single measure, there would be no framing effects; the single measure would have the same explanatory power in all situations. Or if people had different attitudes about a candidate or a party but had one attitude that dominated all others, again, framing wouldn't matter.

Framing effects are not an artifact of casual, "top of the head" responses to low-salience subjects. People who care about a subject, who think about their responses, and who are certain of their beliefs are just as susceptible to framing effects.[30] Whenever there is more than one way to think about a subject there can be framing effects.

There are limits to framing. Certainly there is some information that is always brought to the fore regardless of perspective. People who wear rose-colored glasses see the same objects that we see; no matter what the perspective from which a subject is viewed, their view will be rosier than the view of people without rose-colored glasses. Similarly, some subjects, no matter how they are viewed, and no matter how choices or problems are formulated, evoke the same dominant attitudes and ideas. In general, you can frame all of the people some of the time and some of the people all of the time, but you cannot frame all of the people all of the time.[31]

It is, of course, always an empirical issue whether framing matters: that is, whether there is so little information that differentiation is impossible, or whether there are such strong dominant evocations or such specific lenses that perspectives don't matter.

A particularly valuable example of framing comes from Shanto Iyengar's work on the types of causal reasoning people use in narratives. The difference between how people think about a person when they are told he or she is poor, and how they think about the same person when they are told he or she is unemployed, is a clear example of framing effects. Iyengar has examined the types of causal reasoning people do when they think about poverty and unemployment. He coded the stories into two general types: stories which focus on *dispositional* explanations for the subject's predicament, such as motivation, cultural background, or skill; and stories which focus on *systemic* explanations for the subject's predicament, such as government policy or economic conditions.[32] Poverty evokes more dispositional and less systemic narratives than does unemployment. In other words, poverty is thought to be caused by individual actions, while unemployment is seen as due to systemic causes.

Furthermore, Iyengar has shown that differences in the type of causality have political consequences. People who attribute the causes of a problem to systemic forces are more likely to link the problem to their political judgments than people who attribute the story to dispositional causes.[33] Just as people are more likely to see the causes of inflation in political terms than the causes of unemployment, unemployment is seen as more systemic than poverty.

Framing the President

The evidence is strong that framing matters in presidential politics, and it matters in ways that follow directly from our discussions up to this point. When the Columbia studies found that the 1948 campaign changed the relative salience of domestic and international issues and that this change affected votes, they were finding, in psychological parlance, framing effects. People formulated their voting choices in terms of what they thought a president would be doing or what they wanted him to be doing. When voters in 1948 thought more about a president dealing with domestic affairs and less about how he would deal with international affairs, this change of viewpoints on the presidency affected evaluations of the parties and candidates.

The Columbia studies suggested, and Shanto Iyengar and Donald Kinder have experimentally confirmed, three points: there is enough differentiation in people's images of presidents for formulation effects to matter; changing people's ideas about problems facing the president changes the way people think about presidents; and changing the ways people think about presidents affects their assessments of presidents as well as their votes.[34]

Iyengar and Kinder do not discuss framing explicitly in their book *News That Matters*. They focus on how television news affects the public political agenda, and how the political agenda affects the way presidents are evaluated. Nevertheless, their experiments and their parallel statistical analyses of public opinion polls and network news offer strong evidence of formulation effects—i.e., framing—in politics.

Iyengar and Kinder devised a complex series of experiments for testing the extent of agenda setting, and these experiments controlled for, or took account of, prior knowledge and awareness by viewers.[35] They recruited groups of residents of New Haven and Ann Arbor to watch television newscasts and to answer questions before and after their viewing. Some of the network newscasts that the viewers watched, however, had been subtly altered; stories from previous news shows about energy, inflation, unemployment, or arms control were put into some of the programs but not others, so that some viewers saw no stories about these subjects.

Iyengar and Kinder also did time-series analyses of public opinion polls and network news coverage. They analyzed relations between the changes from month to month in four series of data: the proportion of respondents in national polls who named a particular problem, such as energy, as the most important problem facing the nation; the number of network news stories about the subject; the actual price of gasoline, or the actual rate of inflation or unemployment; and the number of presidential speeches about the subject.

Both the experiments and their time-series analyses demonstrated that both television news programs and presidential speeches change voters' agendas. During the energy crisis of 1974–80, voters' concerns with energy reflected not just shortages and prices, but also stories on the evening network news and presidential speeches.[36] Even when there is extensive information about a problem, such as energy during the late 1970s, news and speeches focus more attention on the problem as a problem of national policy.

Not surprisingly, when the news media change the agenda, they change the president's performance rating for the policy area being featured in the news stories. When a story is highlighted on the television news, the president's ratings for the area of the story are affected. Energy stories change the president's energy ratings, defense stories change the president's defense ratings, and economic stories change the president's economic ratings.

Changing the news focus also changes the relation between a specific problem rating and the overall rating of the president. A voter's overall rating of the president ("Overall, would you say the president is doing an excellent, good, fair, or only poor job?") can be seen as a weighted combination of the ratings that he or she gives the president on specific problems. When television news includes stories about defense or energy or the economy, for example, the relative importance or weight of the specific rating of the president in that area to the president's overall rating can double.[37] That is, energy stories can make a voter's rating of the president on energy twice as important in his or her overall assessment of the president.

This research is significant not only because it confirms the extent of the gatekeeping function of television news, but also because it shows how different varieties of stories on the same subject can have different effects on presidential ratings and votes. For problems that voters assume are intimately connected to the presidency, like foreign policy and defense, news stories affected the president's ratings for those areas whether or not the president was mentioned in the story. For problems that less-informed voters did not automatically associate with the president, the ratings did not change unless the story mentioned the president. For example, many people did not automatically assume that presidents were responsible for energy policy; for such people the effect of stories on presidential ratings depended on whether the story provided the link.

Television news stories frame the president, affecting people's conception of the acts and outcomes associated with him. Even in the middle of an energy crisis, or a bout of high inflation or unemployment, when people see news stories about these problems, their overall assessments of the president, and their assessments of how he is dealing with the specific problem, are both affected. Voters who have seen stories about energy place more weight on energy relative to other issues when they rate the president's overall performance.

Television, in other words, can bring problems from the mental back burner to the front burner of presidential images, making voters more aware of particular subjects when they think about the president and evaluate him. This goes well beyond the by-product and daily-life information theories from the last chapter. Some of the effect, some of the time, can occur because people who are concerned about certain problems in their own lives did not know that other people were also concerned about them, or that they were presidential problems. That is, news stories can tell you that crack cocaine is everywhere and that many people are worried, not just you and your friends. However, some of the effect is formulation effect; the news story makes the problem more prominent among all problems when you create your mental image of the president.

As there are limits on framing, so are there limits on availability. Availability tells us that data we have dealt with recently are more likely to be used than older data; this raises the troublesome possibility that a barrage of exposure to a minor issue will push important issues out of consideration. However, importance restrains the effects of availability because important attitudes are more accessible than unimportant attitudes.[38] Therefore, if a voter is exposed to a number of messages about a secondary issue, older, more important attitudes will still be available alongside the newly obtained information.

It is often difficult to sort out framing effects from availability effects. Either way, what you can picture and incorporate into scenarios is what you can use, and the same political effects hold. I believe, however, that the examples discussed above fit far more easily into the category of framing effects than into that of "mere" availability effects.

Framing and availability also have implications for causal thinking and assessment in politics. Iyengar's work on dispositional and systemic causality, discussed above, demonstrates that the type of causal reasoning voters do about a problem is also affected by the causal reasoning of the story. The problems we think about and the way we explain the problems we think about are affected by television. Similarly, sins of commission will hurt more than sins of omission, because it is easier for people to generate scenarios based on what they have seen than scenarios based on what they have not seen.[39] This is one more way in which incumbents and challengers differ; incumbents will have more sins of commission.

Frames That Matter

If the differences in how voters rate presidents on different issues were minimal, the change in focus prompted by television stories or presidential speeches would be insignificant. However, the variations between problem areas in presidential ratings are large enough to determine the outcome of an election. When the issue that voters focus on is changed, ratings of presidents and challengers vary enough to change the vote.

There are five changes of frame that occur repeatedly in presidential politics, and each can have substantial effects on the vote. Each one affects the way voters formulate their evaluations and their choices by changing their information and point of view.

First, an incumbent running for another term can be thought of as a candidate or as a president; the Rose Garden strategy assumes that a president who chooses not to stray beyond the White House Rose Garden will be seen as rightfully confident of victory, unlike the campaigner, who must crisscross the nation in an effort to win votes. I discuss this at length below.

Second, a candidate can be thought about in terms of the kind of person he is or in terms of the kind of record he has; this was discussed at length in the earlier section on representativeness.

Third, a candidate can be thought of either as a candidate battling to win a nomination or as the chosen representative and nominee of a party; as noted in the discussion of the two-step media flow in chapter 3, political conventions have a major effect on the way candidates are viewed. This effect is particularly strong for vice presidents, like Ford in 1976 and Bush in 1988; the party convention transformed them from candidates to nominees and from subordinates to commanders.[40]

The fourth change of frame which is important in presidential elections is the change from domestic to international issues. Since 1948 we have known that voters think about domestic and international presidential issues differently enough to matter. As I noted in chapter 3, there are differences between an incumbent who is known from performance in office and a challenger who is known only from a campaign. International issues are accessible when people think about the president because they assume he is responsible in some manner for foreign affairs. There is no equivalent activity for challengers, with the rare exception of a victorious general like Dwight Eisenhower.[41] The importance of hostages to Jimmy Carter is but one such example of the importance of foreign affairs, but John Aldrich, John Sullivan, and Eugene Borgida have shown that foreign and defense attitudes have played some role in every election since at least 1952.[42] The asymmetry, however, does not always benefit the president, as the hostage example discussed in the prologue emphasizes. Candidates can say, as did Ronald Reagan during the 1980 campaign, that they hope the president has a secret plan, because it would be terrible "if the president isn't doing more than he has told us he is doing."

The fifth is that voters think about inflation, unemployment, and poverty very differently, and which economic problem is uppermost in their minds has important consequences for how they think about and evaluate presidents. The extent to which they link economics to the presidency varies between the three issues first of all, as I have shown above and in chapter 2. Further, as noted in chapter 3, there are substantial differences in how the parties are viewed on the issues; the three economic problems vary in how political they are and how much of a bonus or onus they give the parties as well. When people think about inflation there is more of an edge for Republicans than when people think about unemployment or poverty, where Democrats have an edge in party heats.

Framing and the Rose Garden Strategy

Rose Garden strategies are a prime example of campaigning predicated on framing effects. Incumbents try to increase their psychological and political distance from their challengers by planting their incumbency firmly in voters' minds. Incumbents want to be invested with authority, to be seen as more solid, certain, and credible. As Downs had intuited, incumbency is a cognitive reference point.[43] Politicians believe that incumbency per se is generally a good thing, and they are right.

It is easier to picture someone in a position who has already been there, and when we think about an office or about a real officeholder and a challenger, we will generally be able to develop a fuller picture of the incumbent. Theoretically, then, there should also be enough differentiation for framing to affect ratings and choices at critical junctures of a political campaign. If Rose Gardens favor incumbents, then there might also be changes in the ratings of political figures when they first are framed in a campaign context. If the assumption behind the Rose Garden strategy—that an incumbent is seen as stronger than a campaigner—is correct, there should be a drop in support for unpopular presidents when they are seen in campaign contexts. There is extensive polling data from 1980 that demonstrates a move away from President Carter in his primary battle with Senator Edward Kennedy.

Primaries are two-stage elections. In the first stage, for weeks or even months, voters hear about the campaign on national news, where the reports of distant battles and the reports of national government are commingled. In the second, the last few weeks before their state primary, they are also exposed to campaign commercials, rallies, and campaign contacts. We might call these the Rose Garden phase and the bread-and-circuses phase. President Carter did not campaign in 1980 until the end of the primary season, until the last primaries in California, Ohio, and New Jersey, so that his presidential image would dominate over his campaign image. Senator Kennedy campaigned extensively. In every single primary, voters who decided their vote in the last week, when the campaign in their states was in full bloom, gave Kennedy a larger share of their votes than did voters who made up their minds earlier.

Further, there is even stronger evidence from New Hampshire that placing voters in a campaign frame was detrimental to President Carter. Campaigns concentrate their door-to-door visits and their phone calls on their most likely supporters. Thus, it is about as universal a finding as one can get in politics that voters contacted by a campaign are more likely to support that candidate than voters who have not been contacted. Despite this, in the 1980 New Hampshire primary, a CBS News/*New York Times* survey showed that people contacted by Carter's campaign had more negative evaluations of him than Democrats who had not been contacted by his campaign. Among registered Democrats who were contacted by Carter's campaign, 53 percent had favorable opinions, 38 percent had unfavorable opinions, and 9 percent were undecided. Among registered Democrats who had not been contacted by his campaign, 65 percent rated him favorably, 25 percent rated him negatively, and 10 percent were uncertain.[44]

Placing a president either in the Rose Garden or on the campaign trail, then, can change the way he is viewed, although it is not likely that popular presidents would be hurt as much as Carter was by the change of frame.

Television, Candidates, and Campaigns

Our discussion of the narrative mode and the ways in which people assemble pictures of politicians leads naturally to a focus on television, for the growth of TV news broadcasting, at the expense of newspaper coverage, is a prime explanation for the historic shift toward a candidate-centered politics. There is now ample theoretical reason to support beliefs that the differences between television and newspapers are important.

Richard Rubin compared television news with the front pages of major newspapers; television news was both more national and more political, and also focused more narrowly on individual politicians rather than institutions. Not only was there more politics on television newscasts than on the front page, more of it was about national, as opposed to state or local, politics. Rubin also found that the national political stories on television were more often centered on the president rather than Congress. This was true even of stories about economic matters, 80 percent of which were presented with explicit links to the presidency.[45] Since Rubin has shown that television news covers the president more intensively, and that it more often links national political problems such as those relating to the economy directly to the president, it can be expected that voters will link more problems to the president. Further, the increased linkage of politics to the federal level, and of federal politics to the presidency, generally ignores institutions and emphasizes the personal calculations of the president. Television coverage puts more emphasis on the president as a politician who must think of election at all times; as Paul Weaver has noted, considerations of policy are only a backdrop against which personal ambitions are played out.[46] Television news, basically, is national news linked to the president as an individual.

The Rubin research, coupled with Iyengar and Kinder's work on the effects of television, lead to a different conclusion about the role of television than the original expectations at the beginning of the television age. In 1952, when there were enough television sets and news shows to begin to study the effects of television on presidential politics, a major research concern was how television would change the kinds of personality attributes that voters looked for and found in candidates. In that year Stevenson and Eisenhower both were perceived somewhat differently on television than in newspapers or on radio, but the differences were small and the effects were limited to those two candidates. That is, there was no general tendency for television to enhance particular features for all candidates, or for people who watched television instead of listening to radio broadcasts to be aware of different personality characteristics for all candidates.[47]

This early research, however, missed the major effect of television. Television's major impact came not from emphasizing certain personality traits and deemphasizing others, but from a general focusing on the individual politician at the expense of parties and institutions. Talks between leaders of the United States and Russia became global prize fights, and TV debates became like the World Series, as Samuel Lubell found in 1960.[48] As Paul Weaver argued in 1972, television news systematically portrays politics as conflicts between individuals, not between institutions or principles.[49] Television, in Scott Keeter's felicitous phrase, provides the "illusion of intimacy."[50]

Furthermore, the increased educational level of the country heightens the potential effects of framing and hence the effects of television news and campaigning. Educated people are more able to develop complex narratives, and as complexity increases, judgments about people become less extreme and hence more ambiguous and open to framing effects.[51]

Calculation Shortcuts

In addition to the research on how people assemble information about people, the cognitive literature has also considered how people use calculation aids as they search among candidates in their decision making. Making complex calculations in order to "maximize expected value" is difficult for all of us, and we are frequently unsure of our choices or projections. We are more confident in some of our choices than in others. An examination of the situations in which people are most confident in their calculations shows that when we are able to use calculation shortcuts, we are more confident and more comfortable in our estimations and choices.

One problem in making choices is resolving contradictions and inconsistencies. When all the evidence points the same way because all the data are consistent, we do not have to resolve contradictions or decide how to weigh the evidence for one conclusion against the evidence for another. Internal consistency raises confidence also. People's confidence in predictions increases when all the evidence points in the same direction.[52] At the beginning of a primary campaign, the data offered to voters are often all positive or all negative; therefore people are often most confident in the predictions most likely to be inaccurate and subject to later revision.

Another problem is assessing probabilities. People are confused, even repelled, by vague probabilities.[53] When people find themselves in situations where they must implicitly compare the likelihood of different outcomes, they become less confident. When they are dealing with easy calculations of likelihood, however, they are more confident in their choices. When they can think of "always" or "never," the probabilities of one or zero, they overrate the accuracy of their predictions.[54] People also find it difficult to calculate when choices require separate assessments of gains and losses. Lotteries with only gains are more attractive than bets with gains and losses, even if the mixed bet has a higher expected return.[55] Finally, people are more confident in making predictions from the more reliable to the less reliable measure, even though actual accuracy is the same in either direction.[56]

Some types of data and probabilities make it easier for people to calculate and choose. People overvalue consistent information and find it easier to use than inconsistent information; they find information that is all good or all bad more valuable than mixed information; and they prefer positive bets to mixed bets. When people use these shortcuts, they are more confident in their decisions. The most confident projections are made when there are what can be termed *pseudocertainty effects,* the types of data and probabilities which give people strong assurance in their predictions by offering them easy and clear calculations.

When people can use "always" or "never," for example, they are making predictions near the tail of the distribution; when they are more confident in a little consistent data than in a large amount of inconsistent data they are not correcting for the amount of data but for the ease of assessing the data. Because of pseudocertainty effects, overvaluing "the always and the never," finding information that is all good or all bad more valuable than mixed information, and preferring positive to mixed bets, people are most confident about their least accurate projections.[57]

The Drunkard's Search

The calculation shortcuts which people use in making choices of all kinds, and the pseudocertainty principles underlying their calculations, demonstrate that people have difficulty making choices when they must integrate data about several factors.[58] When there are several factors, or when some indicators point to one choice and other indicators to a different choice, people are, in effect, being pushed to weigh the pluses and minuses, to assign weights to the different features they care about. People have a general aversion to making trade-offs and instead search for a way to make their choices one-dimensional. As Robyn Dawes has noted, "People are good at picking out the right predictor variables and coding them . . . People are bad at integrating information from diverse and incomparable sources."[59]

People particularly need search aids in situations like primaries when they possess different kinds and quantities of information about each candidate. The way they make use of shortcuts in searching among complex choices results in a Drunkard's Search, a search among obvious differences.

Technically, of course, the Drunkard's Search, as the very name implies, is a shortcut to easier information *acquisition.* Here I am referring to a decision about how to compare candidates, about the criterion on which to compare candidates and make a choice, because a decision about where to look, or a decision about which information to retrieve, becomes a decision about how to decide. People are particularly likely to use one-dimensional searches, focusing on a single issue or attribute, when there is no dominant alternative. Such a procedure "avoids mental strain and provides a compelling argument."[60]

When complicated choices involving many different issues are simplified to a single dimension, which dimension is chosen is important. Designation of an attribute as focal tends to increase the mutability of that attribute, and increased mutability increases the weight of an attribute. Since increased awareness of alternatives tends to increase the perceived importance of a feature, the search process, by focusing on a particular feature among many, gives disproportionate weight to the focal, comparative feature, even if this feature originally was of lesser importance.[61]

Front-runners can be a reference point for voters and for other candidates. At the beginning of a primary season, voters will not know anything about many of the candidates, and will consider information about only a few from the whole field. If there is a front-runner, the voter is likely to consider that candidate when evaluating other candidates, both because the front-runner is likely to be known and because the front-runner is likely to be considered viable.

A Drunkard's Search among candidates is dependent upon the characteristics of the front-runner and can lead to peculiar dynamics. Do front-runners affect the agenda in primaries? Candidates and their strategists believe that they do.[62] Research about decision making, in fact, does support the idea that it matters whether there is a front-runner, and that it matters who the front-runner is. The way in which front-runners set the stage does affect the dynamics and affects the relative fortunes of the other candidates. Whether it is always bad to be the front-runner, however, is a more complicated question without a simple answer.[63]

When there is a front-runner, the other candidates frequently describe themselves with reference to how they differ from this candidate; the features of the front-runner which other candidates discuss become focal points of candidate comparison. The increased attention placed on the focal features leads to increased awareness of alternatives, which in turn increases the importance voters place on the focal features in their evaluation of candidates. This places relatively less importance on the features of the front-runner which are ignored, which are taken for granted. For example, as I discuss in chapter 9, in 1984 as the other candidates made numerous references to Walter Mondale's endorsement by the AFL-CIO, the salience of attitudes toward union political endorsements increased.

When the front-runner is well enough known so that voters know his warts and blemishes, these faults can be magnified in the primaries. Just as people are more comfortable assessing blame for sins of commission than for sins of omission, and more confident making predictions from the more reliable to the less reliable measure, they will be more comfortable with searches made comparing the better-known with the lesser-known candidates, or the incumbent with the challenger. Therefore, it can be a disadvantage to be the front-runner. If voters had the same types of information about each candidate, these voters could compare the candidates on the feature they considered most important, or even on many criteria, not just those advantageous to the challengers.

The relationship between awareness of alternatives and the importance of a trait means that changing the front-runner can change the choice. New search orders over the array of candidates, or comparisons with a different candidate, will be made on different criteria and will affect the weight of all criteria.

Candidates will also try to create obvious differences between themselves and the other candidates to give voters easy ways to separate themselves from the other candidates. A classic example of this was the Republican primary campaign of Congressman John Anderson in 1980, who campaigned on a "new politics" theme. Asked why, if his campaign represented a new politics, he hadn't come up with any new ideas during nineteen years in Congress, Anderson replied, "Well, I have to make an abject confession at this point. I hadn't really sat down and wrestled with myself to the point where I felt it was imperative to come up with new approaches, new ideas. I guess it was the stimulus of a presidential campaign, particularly when you're trying to separate yourself from a field of . . . candidates."[64]

The cognitive literature shows ways that voters process and absorb information and infer meaning. This gives back to voters some of the reasoning they lose when scrutinized with a textbook civics approach to knowledge. Taken together, the Drunkard's Search, Gresham's law of information, and pseudocertainty effects provide a theoretical explanation consistent with the patterns of the rises and falls of new candidates in presidential primaries, a topic explored at length in chapter 6. When we understand these quirks, we can predict how and when the overconfident projections of voters will collapse.

At the same time, the cognitive literature, by showing us ways that personal information and campaign behavior can dominate past political history, also raises new questions about the content of political decisions. A full assessment of the implications of the cognitive contribution, however, depends upon just how well voters are able to make connections between the cues about candidates they absorb and the future political programs of these same candidates. In the next chapter I examine the ways that campaigns matter to voters from the perspective of low-information rationality. I then turn to an examination of primaries and the new candidates that emerge to show just how much political content there is to the support for these candidates.

F I V E
Attributable Benefits and Political Symbols

WOODY ALLEN once wrote that the Russian revolution, after simmering for years, erupted "when the serfs finally realized that the Czar and the Tsar were the same person."[1] This wry joke actually illustrates a truth we shall explore in this chapter: a new understanding of the links between hitherto unconnected people and events can have large political consequences. In any political system with multiple principals and agents, the members, be they serfs or voters, have incomplete information about the relation between the world they see and the actions of officials. Thus, information that changes their beliefs about the connections between officials and outcomes can affect their political preferences. This insight can lead us to an expanded appreciation of campaigns that differs substantially from the original Columbia analysis.

A campaign, from the voters' perspective, is a search for connections. Voters will equate some present actions with future results and some present results with past actions. They will not always make these equations in an objectively correct manner, but they will always have a rationale for which actions they equate with which results and vice versa. Therefore, candidates' campaign strategies are designed to offer voters the appropriate rationales for connecting candidates to policies, offices, and voters. When voters learn to connect benefits to specific offices and policies, the benefits become attributable benefits, which thus depend upon both the knowledge and the beliefs of the voters. Candidates strive to provide the links between their actions and the voters by finding symbols that can make these connections efficiently.

Attributable Benefits

If voters had a full understanding of the organization of government, and no uncertainty about what policy choices candidates would make, and no uncertainty about the result of government policies, they would be able to weigh all issues and assess the impact of each on future benefits. As we have seen, however, these conditions are never present. Voters consider only the few issues they can connect with particular offices and with results they care about.

Voters vote on actions that they equate with results, and on results that they equate with actions. An example of an action equated with results would be a vote to restore or eliminate the death penalty; its consequences are so clear and direct in the minds of voters that they feel little need to see actual results. An example of a result equated with actions would be inflation; it is easily noticed and readily assumed to be the consequence of actions by politicians, even though the voter doesn't know which actions. A result equated with actions is an information shortcut because when the voter sees the result, he or she "knows" that it follows from past actions and does not have to make any further evaluations.

This focus raises two questions that are central to our inquiry at this point: (1) When will voters consider a candidate's performance in terms of benefits received ("What have you done for me lately?"), as opposed to considering his personal image and character ("How have you looked to me lately?")? And (2) when will voters evaluate performance by considering the means politicians use for accomplishing goals, as opposed to reasoning backwards from results?

I have suggested that the single question that best captures the voter's frame of mind when thinking about a candidate in the voting booth is, "What have you done for me lately?" Richard Fenno, studying the ways congressmen developed "home styles"—ways of presenting themselves to constituents—found that the question voters generally asked themselves when thinking about their congressman was "How has he looked to me lately?"[2] Fenno's finding may seem to imply a different concern, but the difference disappears with a moment's reflection. Voters are always concerned with performance (not just "looks" in the cosmetic sense), but when they are short of both information and understanding of government, as they often are, they may ask instead, as a second-best question, How has he looked to me lately? It is harder to unravel the work of a legislature and determine an individual representative's contribution than to understand the actions of an executive, and since congressmen get less media coverage than presidents, voters usually have less information and understanding about congressmen. Thus on many occasions a voter falls back on a general assessment of a congressman's cultural style and personal character as a second-best alternative to figuring out what the congressman has actually done for him lately. In other words, congressmen generally act as if constituents judge the likelihood that they are good congressmen by using the representatives heuristic, as described in chapter 4.

Generally, voters judge presidents for what they have done and congressmen for how they have looked, but the two positions are sometimes reversed. When a president is dealing with a complex problem like arms control or preventing nuclear war, voters who are unable to judge easily what the president has done will resort to assessments of general style, of how the president has looked. On the other hand, when an issue like gun control or offshore drilling appears clear to them and leads to a specific vote, they will judge congressmen by what they have done lately and not by how they have looked.

What portion of their benefits voters attribute to any candidate or office depends first upon the structure of the political system and the ease with which benefits and individual actions are connected. In the American system of government, which is both federal and presidential, the benefits that can be connected to the actions of an incumbent or challenger will depend on the office, the voter's information, and the voter's beliefs about government. The difficulty of sorting out individual contributions means that candidates and incumbents seek to associate themselves with the largest possible attributable benefits; this means finding policies and programs which the voter associates with the office. If the voters search under streetlights, then that is where candidates will campaign.

A simple program of small local benefits may win more votes for a congressman than a complex budget compromise that revives the national economy, because 435 congressmen can claim partial credit for approving it. For the same reason, presidents try to emphasize their contributions in areas where voters readily see the president in control, namely foreign policy.

Any candidate who assumes that total benefits and attributable benefits are the same is vulnerable to a candidate who knows how and why the two are different. The knowledge voters have of the links between issues and offices, as discussed in chapter 4, is malleable—even for as prominent and visible an office as the presidency of the United States. It is not just news stories explicitly linking certain problems to presidents that change how voters connect issues with offices. The incumbent president's performance also affects views of the scope of the presidency, and thus affects voters' consideration of issues when they vote for a particular office. In the wake of the Watergate investigations and President Nixon's resignation, Jimmy Carter emphasized the need to reduce secrecy in government and to reorganize the bureaucracy. Only a minority of voters rated secrecy and reorganization as the most important problems facing the country, but many more voters thought these issues were among those the president could do most about.[3]

Benefits become attributable only when the voter credits, or attributes, them to a particular politician. Different voters connect different aspects of the economy with the president, for example. Some may assume that the president has enough authority over the economy to control inflation and unemployment; they will judge him directly by the performance of the economy (an example of a result equated with actions). Other voters, with a more complex causal understanding of the economy, may allocate responsibility for inflation and unemployment among the president, Congress, and foreign governments; they may rate the president according to how well he responds to OPEC or Japan. Of course, in judging his response, they may use information shortcuts that are no more sophisticated than those used by other voters to judge the president directly from the rate of unemployment or inflation.

As these examples of economic evaluations indicate, the connections voters make between offices and issues presume political reasoning.[4] Most Americans believe, for example, that the best way to cut inflation is by cutting government spending. In April 1980, when inflation was in double digits and interest rates were near 20 percent, a CBS News/*New York Times* poll asked whether the best way to cut inflation was by wage and price controls, tax cuts, or spending cuts. Half of the respondents said the best way to cut inflation was by cutting government spending, while only 29 percent said wage and price controls, and 13 percent said tax cuts.[5] It is not surprising, then, that when inflation rises, there is far less support for government spending on social programs. At the beginning of American involvement in Vietnam, Lyndon Johnson ordered bombing campaigns that he did not believe would be effective because so many Americans believed otherwise; he sensed that he would not be able to get support for sending in troops until bombing had failed.[6]

Voters generally care about ends, not means; they judge government by results and are generally ignorant of or indifferent about the methods by which the results are achieved.[7] They are likely to know if there is a sharp rise in interest rates or energy prices, but not what specific actions caused the increases. However, this general rule has important exceptions. When voters have clear beliefs about the effects of specific government actions or laws, they will care about means, because they will equate specific results with government actions. The search by politicians for attributable benefits leads them to select means that voters associate directly with ends. Thus, while voters may care far more about the economy or the end of communism than they do about death penalties, sex education, abortion, or gun control, candidates devote a disproportionate amount of time to these areas that seem to promise quick, direct results to voters. In addition, ends are sometimes diffuse and hard to evaluate, but means are clearly visible. It is hard, for example, to assess whether the death penalty and gun-control laws actually deter crime, but if voters take it as an article of faith that they do, then politicians will support the death penalty and gun-control laws to associate themselves with attributable benefits. Many voters take it as an article of faith that an Equal Rights Amendment has clear and direct effects, and many voters believe that sex education and school prayer have similarly obvious and clear results.

When voters equate actions with results, they need no evidence to confirm their belief. In direct contrast, when they equate results with actions, they know specific results and assume that a particular official is responsible for them, even if they do not know exactly how, or under what policies. Many voters assume that a president is partly responsible for inflation and unemployment, although they may know nothing about prime rates, deficits, and trade flows. Hostages are a clear international example of a result that voters equate with actions. President Carter was held responsible for not getting the hostages back, although many voters had no ideas at all about how they could be released or why they had been taken.

When voters know and understand specific actions by a politician they are less concerned about looks and will focus on deeds. In contrast, when voters estimate the performance of a politician by inferring backward from results, because they are uncertain about the specific connections between a politician and the results they are observing, looks will be more important than deeds. They will be judging by likelihood, or representativeness. If George McGovern had established a long record of support for Israel, asking for a glass of milk with his kosher hot dog wouldn't have worried anyone. If Gerald Ford had been intimately involved with the American Hispanic community, the unshucked tamale would not have hurt him.

Effective Campaign Issues

Issues can be effective in a campaign only if the voters see three connections: (1) between the issue and the office; (2) between the issue and the candidate; and (3) between the issue and the benefits they care about. On some issues, voters have information, and on others the candidate must provide it. And on some issues the connections between the political office and candidate, on one hand, and the voters' benefits, on the other, are clear, whereas on other issues the connections must be spelled out by the candidates.

It is easier to campaign on an issue that involves information obtained as a part of daily life than on one involving information that must be supplied to the voters. Data about inflation and interest rates are more widely known by voters than data about Social Security solvency, deficits, and exchange rates. It is also easier to campaign on an issue that is clearly connected both to the president and to the voter's concerns, like hostages, than on an issue which is not directly connected, like the budget deficit. For most voters and in most elections, budget deficits are not obviously related to inflation and unemployment or to other immediate concerns, even though for a decade fiscal conservatives have been using analogies between national deficits and family deficits. Nor has the balance of payments been clearly linked in the minds of most voters with their standard of living or the country's well-being.

In some cases, though, voters perceive clear connections if they are provided the data. A $600 ashtray and $700 coffeepot purchased by the Pentagon will receive more attention from politicians and the media during campaigns than weapons systems costing billions of dollars. Voters, and politicians, find it easier to judge the value of ashtrays and coffeepots than to decide whether a multi-billion-dollar electronics project, like a cruise missile or a weather satellite, is fairly priced, well managed, or necessary.

In some cases the data about a potential issue are obtained in daily life and the connections to the concerns of the voter are clear, but the political links are not established. The quality and cost of residential phone service, the price of electricity, and the price of a pound of sugar are related directly to federal policies on antitrust and communications, on one hand, and to tariffs and import quotas, on the other. Yet how many voters know how phone service and sugar prices relate to politics?

The hardest issues to use in a campaign are those in which both the connections and the data are unclear to many voters. These issues may have great potential when understood, but sometimes the connections are difficult to make. It is hard to connect budget deficits, for example, to the president and to the state of the economy, because many people do not understand how presidents can cause or alter deficits, and many never see links between national deficits and their own standard of living. On such issues, also, the symbols may be so unclear as to suggest the opposite of what they are intended to mean. A strong dollar sounds good, not bad, and the links between strong dollars, exports, jobs, and deficits are not easily

clarified in a short period of time. President Nixon expressed his understanding of this problem during a campaign discussion with his chief
of staff, H. R. Haldeman. When Haldeman said that Arthur F. Burns,
chairman of the Federal Reserve Board, was concerned about speculation
in the Italian lira, Nixon replied, "Well I don't give a [expletive deleted]
against the lira. . . . There ain't a vote in it. Only George Schultz and
people like that think it's great [unintelligible]. There's no votes in it,
Bob."[8]

Contemplating the three conditions necessary for an issue to be salient in
a campaign can tell us a great deal. When there is either no information or
no linkage, supplying the missing element can stimulate a rapid change
in preferences and attitudes. This is particularly true in primaries. Thus
whether voters are assessing political competence by campaign behavior
or estimating political character from personal character, new information
from campaign flubs or personal revelations can have striking effects. New
linkages are the other source of rapid changes. In 1989, when the Supreme
Court decided in *Webster v. Reproductive Health Services* that states could en-
act stringent regulations on abortion, abortion suddenly became more
firmly linked to state and local elections. In that year Democrats scored major victories in New Jersey and Virginia, and, in both states, far more
people said abortion was a critical issue in their vote for governor than had
been the case in previous gubernatorial elections. And, after the Supreme
Court decision, when President Bush announced that he would veto a bill
funding abortions for rape and incest victims, attitudes about abortion became more closely linked to evaluations of the president, exactly as in the
Iyengar and Kinder experiments discussed in chapter 4.

Why Campaigns Create Symbols

Candidates seeking to make an issue part of their campaign must connect
the issue to the candidate, the office, and important consequences for the
voter. To communicate their opinions rapidly, candidates and their strategists search for concrete symbols that serve as information shortcuts, as
cognitive placeholders and focal points, to their position on larger abstract
problems. These symbols must also appeal to many different types of
voters. For some the symbol will be but the tip of an intellectual iceberg,
while for others it may be all they know. The Panama Canal symbolized a
host of issues involving America's relations with the "third world" for
some voters, while for others it was a beloved part of the American
heritage, like the Statue of Liberty, the Empire State Building, or Rockefeller Center.

The connections between data and office and policy are far easier to grasp when they are evoked by a specific concrete symbol. In 1976, New York City's brush with bankruptcy was easier to grasp than discussions of fiscal responsibility, bond ratings, and future solvency. In 1957, the flight of Sputnik raised more alarm about Soviet military power than reports on Russian military spending. The Soviet invasion of Afghanistan, a direct use of Russian troops, raised more concern about the Soviets than their proxy interventions in Angola and Mozambique and Ethiopia, because the proxy interventions were easy for many to shrug off as exaggerated cries of "wolf" at a time when many people had decided that the costs of involvement in third-world brush fires were higher than the benefits. Clear, direct events like Sputnik and Afghanistan are more likely to become part of campaigns because they are more clearly and simply connected with national defense and security than other, more serious, foreign actions. Sputnik made candidate John Kennedy's baseless charges of a missile gap credible. The Russian invasion of Afghanistan created more support for President Reagan's greatly increased defense budget than all the stories about SS-20s, throw weight, and hardened silos.

Campaigns communicate, when they are successful, by linking symbols which are already clear and well known. Fiscal conservatives warned for years about the disasters that would befall American cities if they did not change their profligate ways of welfare spending, union pampering, and patronage. New York City's fiscal crisis was a watershed event that became a referent for every presidential candidate in 1976. Many other cities were in deep financial trouble, but it was the plight of New York that became the focal point of the tightfisted fiscal mood that prevailed throughout the country after the first oil shocks of the 1970s. When Gerald Ford refused federal aid to the city, in large part to cover his conservative flanks in the Republican primaries, the headline put out by the *New York Daily News*, FORD TO NEW YORK: DROP DEAD, was reproduced throughout the country and displayed prominently on television. Ronald Reagan told his supporters, "I have included in my morning and evening prayers every day, the prayer that the federal government not bail out New York."[9] George Wallace observed, "The City of New York has taken the advice of the *New York Times* all these years and has finally gone completely broke. The least thing we can say about Alabama is that we're not about to close down."[10] In 1982, when unemployment was the highest it had been for fifty years, the symbol of President Reagan's alleged indifference to the working person was the new White House china service that his wife purchased for state occasions at a cost of $250,000.[11]

Much opposing campaign rhetoric in any election focuses on the same symbols. Both candidates talk at length about peace, prosperity, or arms control. From all this talk about symbols over which there is no disagreement, some scholars conclude that voters are not concerned with policies or the benefits they derive from government actions.[12] Even when the two candidates discuss the same symbol, they are debating whose definition, whose performance, and whose approach is better.

Ironically, the slogan "Mother, God, and Country," which arose in the 1950s to denigrate politics as entirely symbolic and devoid of policy concern, lists symbols for three of the most divisive issues of the 1970s and 1980s. The nature of motherhood was the core issue in acrimonious debates about abortion, the Equal Rights Amendment, and the proper role of women in the labor force and in the family.[13] The proper role of God and religion in society sparked battles about the Moral Majority, homosexuality, fundamentalist and mainstream churches, sex education, and private schools. The nature of patriotism and how it was defined became a battle over the role of force, whether Vietnam was a "noble cause," and whether the UN should be allowed to practice "anti-Americanism." Even the debate over the appropriate Vietnam memorial reflected these undercurrents; to say that it was lacking in depth or politics simply because no one opposed "honoring war dead" is a serious misreading of politics. Does anyone believe that when George McGovern and Ronald Reagan both say "No more Vietnams," they are saying the same thing to voters? And finally, whether the Constitution should be altered to forbid desecration of the flag was one of the most difficult issues for politicians who supported free speech to deal with in 1990.

Rather than using factual arguments against one symbol, campaign strategists often attempt to counter it with another symbol. An example of fighting one symbol with another is Carter's use of the Camp David talks against Reagan's references to U.S. hostages taken by Iran. Carter argued that Camp David stood for prestige and progress toward peace, whereas the hostages were a minor issue that would be solved. The welfare cheat versus the hungry child and the $600 ashtray versus Star Wars are also examples of symbols being used against each other. When Republicans argued in 1982 that the social "safety net" was intact and that only waste and fraud had been eliminated from the welfare budget, Democrats illustrated the callousness of the cut by holding up the symbol of a Chicano (read "not black") Congressional Medal of Honor winner who had lost his disability benefits but could not work. Similarly, when right-to-life advocates use the helpless fetus as a symbol of the victims of abortion, pro-choice advocates counter not with arguments about fetal viability but with the image of the rape or incest victim or the teenage mother.

All principles have exceptions and voters are therefore inconsistent, but this does not mean that principles are of no consequence to them. Their reliance upon principles and symbols is another form of information cost-saving, and the contradictions mean only that the world is complex. Just as our party identification can remind us what to do when we have no other information, our symbols and principles orient us when we have no other information. The inconsistencies that exist between the general and the particular are what make campaigns and the choice of issues and symbols so important.

Some of the premises on which Americans base their political reasoning are so universal, and so deeply felt, that they are noticed only by an outsider from a society that operates on different assumptions. In the 1840s, when a friend wrote Alexis de Tocqueville to ask what he had learned about American beliefs, Tocqueville noted particularly how the American attitude toward education was linked to the belief in democracy:

> You ask me in your last letter if there are *beliefs* here. . . . What strikes me is that the immense majority of people are united in regard to certain *common opinions*. . . . That the majority can be fooled once, no one denies, but people think that necessarily in the long run the majority is right, that it is not only the sole legal judge of its interests but also the surest and most infallible judge. The result of this idea is that enlightenment must be diffused widely among the people, that one cannot enlighten the people too much. You know how many times we have been anxious (we and a thousand others) to know if it is desirable or fearful for education to penetrate through all ranks of society. This question, which is so difficult for France to resolve, does not even seem to present itself here. I have already posed this question a hundred times to the most reflective men; . . . to them even stating the question had something shocking and absurd about it.[14]

Our symbols and premises, such as a belief in the absolute value of education, are the assumptions we make when there is no further information. Reactions are most visceral and violent when deeply felt assumptions are challenged. Such challenges threaten moral and intellectual chaos from the loss of sustaining and orienting principles.[15] Two examples will suffice. After World War II it was assumed by many that America was secure because our superior technology assured us a monopoly on nuclear weapons.[16] Thus, when Russia did explode a nuclear device, it was taken for granted that the Russian breakthrough had been made possible only by espionage. The question was not whether there was a spy, but who the spy was. Similarly, millions of Americans were deeply committed through their church missionary activities to a future Christian China. When Communists won the civil war in China, the feeling of broken bonds for many Americans was so deep that the question was not a self-examining "How could we ever have believed in a Christian China?" but an angry "Who lost China?"[17]

Voters may not have specific or even accurate knowledge about the details of legislation or public policy, but they have deeply held views that influence their reactions to public policy. During the energy crisis, general attitudes about corporations and the fairness of corporate profit levels were strongly related to opinions about whether the profit on a gallon of gas was too high and whether the large oil companies should be broken up.[18] There was no relation, however, between whether respondents had accurate knowledge of corporate profits, or of oil-company profits, and their opinions about government policy toward the oil companies. Similarly, when there is a toxic-waste spill today, many Americans assume the corporation guilty until proven innocent, and others assume the corporation innocent until proven guilty.

When there is a protest in the United States against an autocratic foreign leader, such as Diem, Rhee, Somoza, the Shah of Iran, or Ferdinand Marcos, some Americans assume, without any information, that the protesters are idealists with legitimate grievances and are worthy of support. Others, without any more information, assume that the protesters are Communists, or at least their dupes, and that the grievances are therefore phony or exaggerated. When Bernhard Goetz shot four black youths on a New York subway and became an instant celebrity, attitudes about his presumed innocence or guilt depended on deeper attitudes about race, crime, and guns.

Depending on the distribution of opinion about the underlying assumptions, one side in a campaign debate will have the wind at its back, and the other will have to work doubly hard to make its case an exception to the general rule. And these general rules or prevailing sentiments are themselves changed by clear and dramatic events. The Vietnamese boat people and the Ayatollah Khomeini each changed the center of gravity on U.S. demonstrations in favor of third-world movements, and the Three Mile Island, Bhopal, and Exxon *Valdez* calamities hardened attitudes on corporate responsibility for health and safety. It is harder today than in 1970 to argue for support for a third-world movement (except for the African National Congress) or for a relaxation of toxic-waste controls.

Corporations, unions, computers, welfare cheats, and $600 ashtrays become important symbols in politics because they are so easily grasped that candidates can use them as focal points to organize debate. These symbols, and well-placed phrases like "There you go again," also have an important sustaining effect, keeping memories of a speech or a position alive long after remembrance of specifics has faded.

Changing Constituencies

In both primary and general elections, a presidential candidate faces new opponents and new constituencies. The constituency of his or her home state differs from the constituency of the party primary, which in turn differs from the constituency of the presidency. The candidate's opponents also differ from home state to primary to general election. Since changing the constituency or changing the opponent changes the way a candidate will be viewed by voters, candidates are constantly making decisions about how to position themselves as they adapt to new contexts. Adapting includes choosing which issues to emphasize, which symbols to use, and when to change position on an issue.

Traditional academic theories of elections have emphasized that a candidate's main strategy option is deciding which position to take on an issue. However, as they change constituencies and try to appeal to new groups, candidates can change their own positions, minimize their distance from new groups, multiply issues and symbols, or try to push the other candidate away from the majority opinion.

Moving to new positions creates new problems. A candidate whose positions and emphases were developed to win a Democratic or Republican primary will want to change some positions, or at least some emphases, for the general election; but doing so will confuse supporters, divide the party base, and make a candidate look like an unprincipled opportunist—and politicians who flip-flop on issues are among the most popular targets of attack in American politics.

Instead of changing long-held positions, a candidate can stand fast and argue that he or she is not as far from voters as they had thought. Ronald Reagan showed in 1980 that it was not necessary to move to the center, wherever that was, to become president. He simply argued that he was not as far from the mainstream as he had been portrayed. He also argued that Jimmy Carter was farther from voters than they had realized. As Roger

Ailes defined his role as strategist for George Bush in 1988 against Michael Dukakis, "Every single thing I did from debates to rhetoric to speeches to media was designed to define the two of them and push them farther apart."[19]

Campaigns and Issue Salience

The Columbia studies of the 1940 and 1948 campaigns looked only at the last stages of the presidential campaign and ignored variables we now know to be critical to the importance of an issue. We now know of three ways in which campaigns can increase the importance of an issue: (1) by increasing the perceived importance of an issue; (2) by strengthening the connections between an issue and an office; and (3) by increasing the perceived differences between the candidates on an issue. The second and third, though not considered in the original Columbia studies, naturally complement the original work and follow from information shortcuts and framing.

The original studies by the Columbia sociologists showed that campaigns can increase the importance of an issue in an election by raising its perceived importance among voters. Campaigns activated old attitudes and changed the salience of different issues—by moving voters from a primary concern with international affairs to a primary concern with domestic programs, for example. Campaigns, they found, did not change attitudes as often as they changed priorities.

When *Voting* said that not all voters were voting *on* the same election, that meant that many members of the same party did not share the same issue priorities. Since people identified with a party because of its stance in different past elections, there were differences within the party on what were the most important issues. There were also disagreements within the party on issues; what unified members of a party before the election was that they were all opposed to the other party on some issue that mattered to them. As the campaign brought forth issues from both sides, the parties had to remind voters of the positive side of their own party.

Giving voters a positive view of their own party meant, in particular, selling voters on issues where they did not initially agree with their own party. When the campaign was effective in converting voters—in getting them to vote against their party loyalty or against the party for whom they had voted in the prior election—it was effective because it succeeded in reinforcing the importance of secondary issues.

Defection was related to the salience of core party issues, compared to secondary issues or new issues. In 1948 there were many Democrats who supported their party on New Deal issues and disagreed with their party's positions on civil rights or emerging cold war issues. There were also many Republicans who supported their party's positions on cold war issues but supported the Democrats on domestic, New Deal issues.[20] Whether these voters voted for their own or for the opposition party depended on the priorities they assigned to each set of issues. *Voting* tracked the changes over the course of the campaign and found that the aggregate changes followed initial policy priorities. "In other words, voters with an attitudinal foot in each camp, so to speak, tend to choose the party that corresponds to their own positions on those issues to which they assign particular weight."[21]

Thus *Voting* found that the most important effects of the campaign were related to the salience of issues. Voters whose issue saliences before the campaign were not supportive of their standing decision about party preference were moved by the campaign to vote their priorities. Further, there were voters whose priorities were changed by the campaign, and who voted their priorities. The important effects of the campaign, then, were not in changing attitudes, but in changing priorities.[22]

Second, the campaign can increase the importance of an issue by connecting it with a particular office. The Columbia researchers presumed that in 1948 voters connected the issues of the day, namely the cold war and the New Deal, with the office of the president. They did not bother to study ways in which the campaign may have affected the perceived importance of issues by making a connection for voters between the issue and the office. Thus they ignored the possibility that the reason domestic issues were more influential after the campaign was that the campaign connected issues the voters already cared about with the actions and office of the president. Harry Truman's campaign speeches reminded black audiences, for example, that it was an executive order that began the desegregation of the armed forces.

Even for an office as prominent and well publicized as the presidency, voters do not automatically connect relatively important parts of the national political agenda with the president. Thus, even during the energy crisis of the late 1970s, many voters who cared about energy policies connected them with the presidency only when news stories explicitly reminded them of the connections. The research of Shanto Iyengar and Donald Kinder, discussed in chapter 4, confirms this; the connections between problems and offices are a variable that is affected by communications, and therefore by campaigns.

Third, the campaign can increase the importance of an issue by increasing the perceived differences between the candidates on an issue. The

Columbia researchers simply assumed that the long-standing, traditional positions of the parties and the perceived positions of the parties' presidential nominees were synonymous. And they did not study ways in which campaigns may provide information that alters voters' perceptions of the differences between the candidates on an issue. But we now know that the salience of an issue may change when voters acquire new information about the candidates during the campaign.

In 1952, for example, many voters who perceived a large difference between Democrats and Republicans on support for New Deal programs like Social Security may have grown less concerned about a rollback of the New Deal as they learned more about General Eisenhower, who had never been associated with the more virulent Republican attacks on Social Security and unions. In other words, new information may have moved Eisenhower away from the "default value," or preexisting image held in the absence of other information, that voters assumed for the Republican position on the New Deal programs in the absence of new information about the candidate. Although candidates today are generally given more exposure before nominations, campaign information is just as likely to move voters' perceptions of where a candidate stands on an issue closer to their perceptions of long-standing party positions. Jimmy Carter was a southern governor, assumed to be different from recent Democratic nominees like George McGovern and Hubert Humphrey. After the Democratic convention of 1976 showed Carter and Humphrey praising each other and Carter choosing the northerner Walter Mondale as his vice president, perceptions of Carter changed, moving him closer to the "default value" voters had for the party.

When little information about candidates is available, the policy perceptions of voters are based on relevant party images. However, if there is substantial information about the candidates, then perceptions based on party images will be modified during the campaign as perceptions based on candidates replace them. This conclusion suggests that nominating conventions are still important in an age when the nominees have already been determined earlier, by primaries. From conventions, voters get information that helps them locate candidates within the party (by showing them in relation to party figures they already know something about) and form an opinion about what their future programs are likely to be.

Tamales and Helicopters Reconsidered

The tamales and helicopters introduced in the Prologue were important symbols that require cognitive and economic principles for their explanation. They connected presidential candidates to important concerns of voters. They were information shortcuts with symbolic meaning, and they were both predicated upon views of how government works and what the president can do.

In 1976, when President Ford tried to eat an unshucked tamale, he committed a faux pas far more serious than spilling mustard on his tie or ice cream on his shirt. To Hispanic voters in Texas, he betrayed an unfamiliarity with their food which suggested a lack of familiarity with their whole culture. Further, tamales were a way of projecting from the personal to the political, of assuming that personal familiarity with a culture and the acceptability of a candidate's policies to a group were linked.

In 1980, the helicopters that crashed in the abortive desert rescue mission symbolized President Carter's failure to bring the hostages home from Iran. The hostages were a powerful symbol of American weakness and humiliation, a personalization of foreign policy, because they were individuals with whom Americans could directly identify, enduring a situation in which most Americans could picture themselves. Further, rightly or wrongly, the hostage question was assumed to be a clear and detachable aspect of foreign policy—unclouded by treaties, bureaucracies, and the layers of government—directly within the purview of the president, so that an inability to bring the hostages home reflected directly on his competence.

In similar fashion, many Americans picture state governors as directly responsible for all pardons and furloughs handed out to prisoners, as in the old Jimmy Cagney gangster movies where suspense builds while the governor decides whether to stay an execution. The release of Willie Horton on furlough was effective against Michael Dukakis in 1988 because furloughs, pardons, and death penalties are to governors what hostages are to presidents.[23]

Symbols like tamales and helicopters, and memorable rejoinders like "There you go again," lay down traces that are activated when subsequent events provide reminders.[24] Sometimes these symbols can even re-create our memories, literally "inventing" our history. By way of illustration, I note how Robert Darnton, the distinguished French historian who has contributed so much to our understanding of popular culture, has inadvertently demonstrated the power of Edmund Blair Bolles's insight that "memory is an act of imagination."[25] Commenting upon the unraveling of Communist rule in East Germany, Darnton wrote, "The hunting lodges have doomed the Communists in the GDR just as Imelda Marcos' shoe collection delegitimized the dictatorship in the Philippines and Marie

Antoinette's diamond necklace brought down the monarchy in France."[26] The luxurious hunting lodges of the Communist leadership were publicized when the Communist party was already reeling from mass protests, and this publicity may have helped doom the Communists. But Imelda Marcos's three thousand pairs of shoes—now taken as the single most powerful image of the Marcos dictatorship—were not discovered until *after* the Marcos family had fled the country and the presidential palace was occupied by forces loyal to the new government. This illustrates how, in remembering, we often revise chronology to let a single symbolic event carry the meaning of a complex process. Memory is an act of imagination, and so the shoes can dominate earlier individual memories of the Marcos dictatorship, and the temporal sequence of events becomes reversed in our minds—as in Darnton's analysis, when the shoes that were discovered after the overthrow come to symbolize the reason why the Marcoses were overthrown. The overthrow was a collective action, and collective actions call common symbols to mind; "our last straw" supplanted "my last straw" after the fact. People think in terms of causal schemas, but we generally store schemas with a single cause. If different people had different causes it would be harder to store and use the memories.

If Imelda's shoes can symbolize the reasons for the fall of the Marcos dictatorship, it is understandable that journalists and scholars would attribute Senator Edward Kennedy's fall, when the 1980 primaries began in 1979, to a poor performance in an interview with Roger Mudd. Kennedy led Jimmy Carter in the primary preference polls throughout 1978 and 1979 before he actually declared his candidacy on November 7, 1979. Three days before that, on a Sunday evening, an interview with the senator by Roger Mudd of CBS News was shown nationally. Kennedy provided no new information about Chappaquiddick (a muted scandal from his past); when asked why he wanted to be president, he was silent for nine seconds before beginning his answer—and on television, nine seconds is a lot of "dead air." That interview has been credited by academics, campaign strategists, and journalists alike with a critical role in Kennedy's poor showing in the primaries and in the drop in his personal popularity.[27] Millions of people, when they began to think about Kennedy, Chappaquiddick, and the presidency, began to have doubts. What better common event with which to express doubts felt by millions than an interview in which the senator himself seemed to reveal doubts? The fallacy here was to make the implicit assumption that a single new event was *necessary* to explain millions of individual changes of attitude. That the Kennedy-Mudd interview was given so much importance by so many scholars and campaign operatives attests to the power of television, or at least to the power it is assumed to have. If the Kennedy-Mudd interview had never occurred, some other media event would have provided a television-oriented explanation for Kennedy's fall. The interview was singled out as the simplest, most economical explanation for a complicated process of change in voter attitudes.

Just as the Kennedy-Mudd interview and Imelda's shoes became focal points, Jimmy Carter's "lust in my heart" interview became the focal point in his 1976 campaign against President Ford. Carter gave an interview to *Playboy* magazine in which he confessed that despite his deep commitment to Christianity, he too sometimes had "lust in his heart." He gave the interview in a conscious attempt to allay fears of intolerance. His deep commitment as a "born-again Christian" was well known, and there was concern about whether his policies as president would reflect his religious commitment so strongly that he would launch divisive moral crusades. The juxtaposition of *Playboy* and Jimmy Carter was so startling that the interview confession quickly disseminated throughout the electorate.

However, like Imelda's shoes, Carter's lust became much more important in retrospect than it was at the time. For a month after the Republican convention of August 16–19 Carter had been falling in the polls; Ford was developing a more positive image and raising doubts about Carter's experience and his connections to traditional Democratic groups and programs. The interview, which was scheduled to appear in the November *Playboy,* made the national news on the evening of September 20, and appeared in newspapers for the first time on September 21.[28] Thus the interview became news after nearly all of Carter's fall in the polls had already taken place. In fact, three days later, on September 23, the first presidential debate was held, and attention shifted from the interview to the debate.

Campaign mythology necessarily overstates how much some of the memorable events matter, because the memorable event provides a credible and easily grasped symbol, a focal point to represent and explain a diffuse process. We use the essence of a process, a "critical event," to provide a common collective explanation or representation for earlier decisions by countless individuals. After the fact, these symbols serve to encapsulate the process better than anything we knew at the time. We can use such explanations credibly only because we believe in the power of images and the power of television.

Imelda's shoes, Kennedy's interview, and Carter's lust demonstrate two points. First, incidents become important only when they draw upon many other related incidents and concerns. Second, it is frequently the case that the many less dramatic incidents were the effective agents of change, and the single dramatic incident becomes the archetypical incident only in our historical re-creation of the moment. Images matter, but they are based upon far more reasonable and defensible considerations than their specific content. As we develop a richer and fuller picture of the political reasoning that goes on within the mass electorate, I believe that we will see increasingly that there is less reason to attribute so much significance to trivial incidents.

SIX

Expectations and Reassessments: Surges and Declines in Presidential Primaries

PRESIDENTIAL PRIMARIES are among the more intriguing and distinctive features of American elections, fascinating and bedeviling participants and bystanders with their volatility. Virtually unknown presidential candidates, like Jimmy Carter in 1976, can in a matter of weeks become the preference of a plurality of their party; other candidates, like Senator Edward Kennedy in 1980, can lose commanding three-to-one leads to become decided underdogs even before the first vote. Candidates strapped for cash can scrape together money for a few commercials and rise immediately in the polls, as Gary Hart did in Iowa in 1980; others, like John Connally in 1980, can spend $14 million and win only one delegate to the party's convention.

Given such surges and declines, it needs to be asked whether a primary election is a giant crapshoot in which a person lucky enough to do well in an early primary simply gets on a roll that takes him or her to a nomination. In fact, voters in primaries have little or no information about many of the candidates when the primaries start, pay little attention to primaries being held in other states, and make up their minds at the last minute when the primary campaign finally reaches their state. Furthermore, even if voters paid a lot of attention to media coverage of primaries, most of the coverage is horse-race news about strategy and results elsewhere.

The volatility and unpredictability of primaries have led some observers to conclude that the outcomes have no relation to any policy preferences of the electorate. Indeed, if candidates who are virtually unknown can quickly gain the support of a plurality of their party, and if most media coverage concentrates on the horse race, it is plausible that people know nothing about the candidates they are supporting beyond the fact that they are winners; these candidates earn their votes on little more than name recognition. The center of an old-fashioned political victory parade, of course, was the wagon carrying the band, and to climb on the bandwagon has

115

come to mean rushing to join victorious campaigns for the excitement and attraction of victory, being *persuaded* to support a candidate simply because others are doing so. Such a persuasion theory is troubling because it explains volatility as a product of a lack of knowledge about candidates.

In fact, primaries are volatile precisely because they are political, and because they generally present voters with more than two candidates. Surges and declines of support for candidates are related to the ways voters think about the kind of person they want to be president, and about the policies they want their party to pursue. They reflect the ways in which people use and acquire information, the way elections are framed, the ways people read the array of candidates, and the fact that people vote strategically.

Part of the volatility comes from the decline of candidates who had large followings before the primaries began. These declines reflect political reasoning about what kind of person a president should be. They also reflect how the reasoning that voters do in primaries is affected by the new information they receive as they go, in effect, from a politician's preprimary résumé to an electronic "interview" with him or her via the campaign.

Part of the volatility also comes from the fact that voters engage in strategic voting, which means voting for a so-so candidate with a good chance of beating an undesirable candidate, instead of voting for a great candidate with a poor chance of beating the same undesirable candidate. These strategic-voting considerations involve reasoning about public policy.

Further, surges of support for new candidates reflect voters' ability to read candidates and the media. These surges are politically meaningful because they are based on information about issues that voters pick up from observing the array of candidates, as well as on the low-information signals they obtain about the new candidate. These surges show the power of low-information signaling. The way people absorb information and read the array of candidates also explains why surges for new candidates are followed by falls, and why a surge for one candidate often is followed by a surge for another candidate.

The idea that bandwagons based on *nothing* but victories can persuade people is simply wrong. Voters do not always follow the loudest band or join the biggest parade. People learn to read the political and personal strengths and weaknesses of individual candidates. This should not surprise us. Most people may not be able to read sheet music, but they know something about the tunes the new bands are playing, and they most certainly know what tunes the older, more established bands have been playing.

Primary victories generate two kinds of low-information signals. One is the victory signal, the televised victory celebration from campaign headquarters on election night and the blitz of media coverage of the winner in the following days. Bandwagon theories concentrate on victory signals that tell voters which candidates are doing better than expected and are gaining momentum. The second low-information signal tells voters about the personal characteristics and policies of a candidate. Both kinds of information structure the changes in preferences that occur after primary victories. These signals change alternatives and focus the voters on reduced sets of alternatives. In judging these alternatives, voters take account of whom they want to win and whom they want to lose, as well as who is actually winning.

Momentum and Expectations

In primaries, particularly in the early states, candidates are concerned with how their performances affect later primaries. Candidates want publicity that gives impetus or momentum to their campaign. As Elizabeth Drew reported from Iowa in 1976, "For the candidates, a win in Iowa, or even a strong showing, will provide the strong press coverage that those now dwelling in crowded obscurity need. It will provide what is commonly referred to as momentum. The candidate who looks like a 'winner' will get more money and other forms of help."[1]

This phenomenon has bedeviled academics as much as it has fascinated journalists. Studies of primary voting and campaign strategy have typically concentrated on analyzing this slippery concept known as momentum.[2] Larry Bartels has offered the single best definition of momentum; he defines it as the "demonstration effects of important primary victories."[3]

Momentum is troubling because it suggests that a mindless following of the mob, not reasoned policy preferences, determines who wins the nomination. This concern took firm hold after 1976, when unknown outsider Jimmy Carter won the Democratic nomination over candidates whose cultural and political credentials were more deeply revered by academics and journalists alike. The most frequently quoted complaint that Carter's win was a result of momentum comes from a one-time candidate, Congressman Morris Udall: "It's like a football game, in which you say to the first team that makes a first down with ten yards, 'Hereafter your team has a special rule. Your first downs are five yards. And if you make three of those you get a two-yard first down. And we're going to let your first touchdown count twenty-one points. Now the rest of you bastards play catch-up under the regular rules.' "[4]

There are few things in American politics that match the outpourings of enthusiasm for a candidate with momentum. Those moments when candidates suddenly surge forward from the pack are comparable to "moments of madness," when suddenly there are no constraints and "everything is possible"—like Tiananmen Square in May and June of 1989, or the day Paris was liberated from the Nazis in 1945.[5] Candidates who have had to work years to become known to voters, desperately seeking them out at factories and bowling alleys, suddenly find that the voters are looking for *them,* full of unbridled hopes for their candidacies.

When candidates and campaign strategists talk about gaining momentum, they talk about getting more votes or finishing in a higher position than they were expected to do by voters and the media. For exceeding expectations, they make the news and receive positive publicity. Candidates and strategists are assuming that changes in expectations cause changes in preferences—that when primary voters have increased expectations that a candidate will win, then their preference for that candidate also increases. Indeed, they often believe that the effect of expectations is so strong that the early winner cannot be stopped. As Ann Lewis, Senator Birch Bayh's political director, wrote in late 1975, "Momentum is more important than position in the delegate selection process. If the domino theory holds anywhere in the world, it is in the Democratic nominating process."[6]

If expectations determine preferences, then early primary victories will create bandwagons. Voters will rush to become associated with the winner as rising expectations keep increasing preferences for that candidate. If voters are susceptible to bandwagons, whoever wins the first primaries should win the nomination. Indeed, the Republican strategist Lance Tarrance stated before the first 1980 primary, "The early primaries are no longer early signals but have basically become the determinants."[7] In a similar fashion, Nelson W. Polsby has argued that voters know little about the candidates and that primary voting reduces to media expectations and candidate name recognition.[8]

Attentiveness to Primaries

Concerns that primaries are crapshoots determined by little more than the momentum generated by early victories are plausible because primaries differ from general elections in three ways: voters pay less attention to primaries than to general elections; the candidates are less well known (and the information value of party labels is nullified); and voters decide on their candidates much later in the campaign. Low levels of attentiveness and knowledge, and the emphasis of media coverage on the horse-race aspects of the primaries, make expectation theories plausible.

Primaries are really two campaigns. There is the long national campaign that begins early in the year in Iowa and New Hampshire and ends on the first Tuesday in June. Then there is the actual primary campaign in any state, the period when candidates are actually campaigning for votes with personal appearances, paid media ads, mailings, and phone banks. After the Iowa and New Hampshire primary campaigns, which begin the year before the election, these other state campaigns are essentially one or two weeks long. Low levels of attention within the electorate and the concomitant lack of knowledge about candidates until the primary occurs in a particular state means that voters are deciding upon their candidates in the full heat of the local battle, after the most recent battles in other states have been decided. This means that information about recent results is available when voters choose.

Voters definitely pay less attention to primaries than to the general election. In 1980, 1984, and 1988, the monthly CBS News/*New York Times* polls asked, "How much attention have you been able to pay to the presidential campaign so far—a lot, some, or not much?" Only after months of campaign news and primary results are more than two-thirds of the party electorate paying at least some attention to the ongoing campaign; and in no survey of registered Republicans in 1980, or registered Democrats in 1980 or 1984 or 1988, were more than 75 percent paying at least some attention to primaries.[9]

Until the week of the election in their state, when the pace of local media coverage increases dramatically, many primary voters are not even familiar enough with the candidates to give them a general favorability rating. Robert Dole had been the Republican nominee for vice president in 1976, but at the start of his 1980 campaign only 32 percent of Republicans were familiar enough with him to rate him positively or negatively. Howard Baker asked, "What did the President know and when did he know it?" on national television day after day during the Watergate hearings, and still he was evaluated by only half of the Republicans at the time he ran. Governor Jerry Brown won four primaries in 1976, but was ratable by only 40 percent of registered Democrats at the beginning of his 1980 quest.[10]

Because primary campaigns are short, and not decisive in the way the general election is, voters are much more likely to decide on a candidate at the last minute. There are usually at least ten weeks between the last nominating convention and the general election—ten weeks for voters to focus intensively on a single choice between two candidates. This difference is reflected in the frequency of last-minute decisions in primaries compared to general elections. In every presidential election since 1952, the University of Michigan SRC/CPS election surveys have asked voters when they made up their minds about their votes. The highest proportion ever to say that they decided on the day of the November election was 9 percent in 1980, when election day coincided with the first anniversary of the taking of fifty-five American hostages in Iran. In 1984, ABC/*Washington Post* exit polls in twelve states asked voters when they made up their minds in the Democratic primary. In no primary exit poll did less than 9 percent of the voters say they made their choices that day, and the average was 13 percent. In presidential elections, the largest proportion making their final decision in the last two weeks, including election day, was 26 percent, in 1980. In 1984 exit polls, the proportion deciding in the last week ranged from a high of 49 percent in the New Hampshire primary to a low of 27 percent in the late primaries in Ohio, New Jersey, and California. In 1988, the proportion arriving at a decision in the last week showed a similar range for both parties; in New Hampshire, 55 percent of the Democrats and 47 percent of the Republicans came to a final choice in the last week, and the percentage declined as the race progressed.

Horse-Race Knowledge

Most people pay little attention to primaries, know little about many of the candidates, and make their decisions in the last week of the campaign, when the results of other primaries are available. Thus it is plausible that voters are affected by results from earlier states, and that they consider expectations when they vote, whether the expectations are a catalyst or a causal element in their choice.

Despite low levels of attentiveness, the public most definitely does learn the results of earlier primaries. In March of 1984 a CBS poll asked respondents whether they watched news reports of the results of primaries and caucuses; 75 percent of registered voters and 90 percent of those with interest in the primaries said they watched the news reports.[11] Voters clearly pay attention to news about primary winners. In addition, they also absorb information about the "horse race" for party nominations very quickly. The first delegates of the 1984 Democratic primary season were selected in caucuses held in Iowa on February 20, a week before the New Hampshire primary. In the next five days a national CBS News/*New York Times* poll asked "Who won the Iowa caucuses?" In response, 68 percent of all regis-

TABLE 6.1

Primary Voters Who Made Their Decision in the Last Week, by State

	NH (%)	MA (%)	AL (%)	FL (%)	GA (%)	NC (%)	IL (%)	NY (%)	WI (%)	PA (%)	OH (%)	NJ (%)	CA (%)
Democrats													
1988	55	21	27	33	31	32	35	16	27	35	11	9	9
1984	49	41	35	27	36		44	34		30	27	24	27
1980		16		12			22	22	33	24	20	19	18
1976		33											
Republicans													
1988	47	21	18	10	25	18	33		40				
1980		34		20			38		40	32	9	14	10
1976		14		21		18				19			

Source: All 1988 data are from CBS News/*New York Times* exit polls. All 1984 data are from ABC News/*Washington Post* exit polls; 1980 and 1976 Massachusetts data are from CBS News/*New York Times* exit polls; other 1976 GOP data are from NBC News exit polls.

Note: Since so many polls use different categories, a finer breakdown is impractical for any comparative purpose. There are many polls where this question is not asked because space is at a premium on exit polls, and because the place on the exit poll where decision time is asked is also a good place to ask voters about gubernatorial and senatorial primaries. On the 1988 polls, only for New Hampshire, Massachusetts, and Pennsylvania do the exit-poll categories break at one week; on all the other 1988 exit polls, the number given is the number who made up their minds since Saturday.

tered Democrats answered correctly that Walter Mondale had won in Iowa, and only 1 percent gave incorrect answers.[12] In 1988 a CBS News/*New York Times* tracking poll in New Hampshire began the day after the Iowa caucuses. Within the first 24 hours after the Iowa results were announced, more than 70 percent of registered Democrats knew that Richard Gephardt had won, and 84 percent of registered Republicans knew that Robert Dole had won.[13]

That voters are influenced by these results is not disputed. Every month during presidential election years since 1936, the Gallup Poll has asked Democrats and Republicans which candidate they prefer among those seeking their party's nomination. Comparing the polls taken before and after the New Hampshire primary—until 1976 the first in the nation—James Beniger found that from 1936 to 1972 the winner of the New Hampshire primary gained an average of 8.4 points in the next national poll.[14] Since Beniger's research, there have been seven more presidential primaries, and the effect of early results on national preferences has almost doubled. Moreover, Iowa has joined New Hampshire as a second early primary with a major effect upon later primaries.

Between 1976 and 1988, the effect of a win in New Hampshire on national preferences rose to 14 points.[15] In 1976 Jimmy Carter began his rise in the polls after the Iowa caucuses, which preceded New Hampshire's. Since then, so much attention has been placed on these once insignificant caucuses that they have become, in Howard Baker's phrase, "the functional equivalent of a primary" for candidates and the media.[16] Candidates seeking an early boost, and reporters and commentators seeking early clues about the electorate, give as much attention to Iowa as to New Hampshire. Since 1976, a victory in Iowa has been worth an average of 14 points in the national polls.[17]

How Results Matter: Information and Expectations

Voters know who wins the early primaries, and the winners of early primaries do rise in the polls. There are three possible reasons why candidates who do well in early contests *could* rise in the polls: (1) because they receive publicity that provides voters with *information;* (2) because changes in expectations can have a *persuasion* effect, changing our evaluations of the candidate; and (3) because changes in expectations can make a candidate look like a better or worse *strategic* alternative to another candidate. The first and third reasons, information and strategic voting, are in fact why winners *do* rise; the second possibility, persuasion, has a minor role.

Two of the three ways that early results can affect voters, persuasion and strategic voting, involve expectations. The difference between them is critical to evaluating primaries. If changed expectations change evaluations of a candidate, then people are liking candidates just because they are winners; this is persuasion and is without political content. It is akin to following a band merely because it is playing loudly, without regard for what music it is playing or what other bands there are to follow.

However, if people use expectations to consider which of two candidates is the stronger alternative to a third candidate, then they are using expectations for strategic voting, to help them make the best use of their choice. That, in fact, is where expectations matter most in primaries.

Information Effects of Primary Results

Victories, particularly in early primaries, mean more media coverage, which can also increase vote shares without any change in expectations.[18] Research in 1984 suggests that the information effects of early victories are more important than the persuasion effects of changes in expectations.[19] As Henry Brady and Richard Johnston have demonstrated, expecting a candidate to do well does not increase liking for the candidate.[20] In Brady

and Johnston's untangling of the interactions of expectations and evaluations, then, there are no persuasion effects.

Brady and Johnston's research on the effects of horse-race information is
consistent with Steven Chaffee's findings in 1980 that although horse-race
information helped voters structure the field of candidates, it did not persuade them simply to go with winners. Chaffee followed voters in Wisconsin over the first months of the 1980 primary season. As the primaries
progressed, voters received information about primaries in other states;
how much information they received depended, of course, on how attentive they were to the media and how interested they were in politics.
Chaffee found that exposure to news about primary results did not persuade voters to follow winners: "The impact of media reports was not mass
persuasion on behalf of these few candidates but simply uncertainty-
resolving information that permitted the high-exposure sub-audience to
focus in on a reduced list of plausible candidates."[21]

When Expectations Change

Candidate information and horse-race information both affect voters' expectations about candidates. This demonstrates that people think of expectations as "estimates of electoral potential." Expectations are affected by
(1) thinking more about a candidate; (2) the results of earlier primaries
and news about the horse-race aspects of the campaign; and (3) learning
more about a candidate. They do matter politically whenever there are
more than two candidates in a primary, so that voters will consider strategic voting.

First, as estimates of electoral potential, expectations reflect what people
think of candidates. Thinking more about a candidate, or thinking about a
candidate in a different frame, affects expectations for that candidate. This
explains why some candidates can lose support before there are any primary results, without any changes of information. (I discuss the effects of
thinking about old information in new contexts in a later section.)

Learning the results of primaries does affect expectations for a candidate.
Henry Brady has demonstrated that voters' expectations for a candidate are
exceedingly sensitive to news about how the candidate has actually done.
He compared survey data and media coverage of the 1984 campaign and
showed that stories about the horse-race aspects of the campaign had
effects on how well or how poorly people thought each candidate was
doing.[22]

However, learning more about a candidate also affects expectations. Expectations reflect how well people think candidates will do based on their

assessments of the candidates' positions. There is some wish-fulfillment here; liking a candidate has a powerful effect on expecting him to do well.[23]

Expectations also reflect people's assessments of how well they think other people will like a candidate's positions. In an ingenious set of experiments, Brady has shown that newspaper articles that discuss issues also affect expectations. These experiments demonstrate that when voters learn about a candidate's positions they judge not just how they like the positions but how they think others will like the positions as well.[24] Brady's experiments emphasize one of the themes of this book, that voting is collective action that involves social reasoning about the preferences and actions of others, as well as reasoning about candidates and government. When people estimate expectations for a candidate, they do not simply project from past primary results; their reasoning about expectations takes account of their own judgments about candidates as well.

Information and Reassessment

Reassessment—thinking anew about a candidate and acquiring new information—will occur when there is information that changes expectations. Information that others like oneself have changed their opinions, or information that is surprising, will prompt people to reexamine what they know about a candidate and look for more information about him or her. One of the critical considerations will then be whether to vote for the preferred candidate or for a candidate with a better chance of winning.

A signal that people like oneself have changed their opinions will prompt reassessment. Catherine Marsh's research on the effects of public opinion polls on voters supports this proposition. In her study, some voters were shown poll reports of the opinions of other voters, and some voters were shown reports indicating that the opinions of voters were changing. Reports of opinions did not affect voters; nor did voters who were shown polls which indicated that they were in the minority switch to the majority. However, reports of changing opinions within the electorate did affect voters; some who were shown reports of change from their side to the majority side did change opinions themselves.[25] A signal that others like themselves had changed provoked reexamination and change; a signal that people like themselves were in the minority did not lead to change. An indication of change is a signal that new information is emerging and should be taken into account.

Surprise also leads to reassessment. When people evaluate current outcomes they go through backward processing; they try to explain these

outcomes with their prior knowledge. We are surprised when our conceptual organization is inadequate to account for reality, when our presuppositions are violated.[26]

Thus it is failure of imagination that provokes reassessment and reorganization.[27] The reorganization of expectations and perceptions is most
likely to occur when presuppositions and outcomes cannot be reconciled.
Thus, Jerome Bruner: "[Expectations], whether realistic or wishful, continue to operate so long as they are reinforced by the outcome of events. In
short, [expectations] continue to mold perceptual organization in a self-
sustaining fashion so long as they are confirmed. It is when well-
established [expectations] fail of confirmation that the [individual] may
face a task of perceptual reorganization."[28]

When we are surprised, we reorganize our thoughts. When people do
not have the information to imagine how and why a candidate performed
as he did, they are stimulated to rethink what they already know and to
look for more information. A good deal of research supports the finding
that surprising information has the most impact; that is, the less expected
the information is, the greater its impact on judgments.[29] Certainly, candidates themselves believe that victories which come as a surprise have more
impact.[30] Unexpected victories tell people that there are real outcomes
they had never imagined, and therefore that they ought to reassess their
estimates of electoral potential.

Further, when people reassess they will be interested in getting new information, making the candidate's job much easier. When people come to
the candidate for information, rather than the candidate struggling for an
audience, exposure to his message increases and the rate of conversion, for
a successful candidate, rises. In 1984, it took three weeks of intensive campaigning in Iowa for Gary Hart to go from 5 percent in surveys to 17
percent of the actual primary vote. In New Hampshire, it took him five
weeks to move from 5 percent to 13 percent in surveys, but after news of
his second-place finish in Iowa, it took him only five days to go from 13
percent to 37 percent.

Strategic Voting and Expectations

Expectations, of course, do matter. While increases in expectations may
not cause voters to like a candidate more, voters do take expectations into
account. They vote strategically, which is one reason why candidates
can rise so fast in primaries. The rises occur because voters consider expectations that a candidate has the best chance of defeating another candidate.

A voter votes strategically if he or she votes against his or her preferences in order to gain a more preferred final outcome. To give a primary example, in 1984 a New Hampshire voter who preferred John Glenn to both Mondale and Hart, but preferred Hart to Mondale as well, would be voting strategically if he or she voted for Hart as the candidate with a better chance of beating Mondale.

In fact, several kinds of strategic voting are critical in primaries. In November, in a two-person election for president, voters vote for the candidate they most want as president. In contrast, primaries choose nominees, not presidents, so that there are strategic factors as well as different uses of the vote to consider. Voters can, and do, take account not only of their preferences but also of a candidate's chances of getting nominated, or of stopping another candidate, or of winning the presidency, or of sending a message.

The expected value of a candidacy to a voter may depend only on whether the candidate is able to maintain a campaign and get his message across to party members. When George Wallace shocked Democratic party leaders with his strong showing in the 1968 primaries, his theme was "Send them a message." In the 1984 Democratic primaries, 77 percent of black voters voted for Jesse Jackson. Nearly half of them voted for Jackson "to show their support for a black candidate," not because they thought he could win.[31]

When Jimmy Carter beat George Wallace in the 1976 Florida primary, a "startling victory" in Morris Udall's words, his campaign theme was "Send them a president, not a message." Carter's victories in Iowa and New Hampshire made more credible his claims that a southerner could win his party's nomination. Because he had won primaries in the Midwest and East, he argued, it made sense to vote for him and get a good president, rather than vote for Wallace and send a message. (For many southerners, the distinction between New England and the East was a line too fine to consider.) When Carter said, "Send them a president, not a message," he was arguing for strategic voting, for voting that took account not only of the voter's most preferred candidate, but also of likely outcomes.

Do voters actually vote strategically? Certainly it would be rational to consider probabilities of success as well as preferences when there are more than two candidates, but it does not follow automatically that voters do consider strategic factors in their voting. There is data, however, to support the argument that enough voters consider strategic factors in their voting to affect the outcomes of primaries. When Hart came in second in Iowa and immediately began to rise in the New Hampshire polls, his first gains came from voters who opposed Mondale and moved to Hart because his candidacy was clearly more viable than that of the candidate they had earlier supported against Mondale—particularly that of John Glenn, who finished sixth in Iowa and immediately lost most of his New Hampshire voters to Hart.

In 1984, when 77 percent of black voters voted for Jesse Jackson in the Democratic primaries, most blacks preferred Mondale over Hart as their second choice for the party nomination. Mondale got 19 percent of the black vote and Hart 3 percent, and whenever national surveys or exit polls asked voters for their second choice, blacks overwhelmingly chose Mondale. Thus if black votes for Jackson could help give the nomination to Hart, their least favored candidate, strategic considerations could urge a vote for Mondale. Also, when Mondale's campaign appeared to be in trouble, he should have gotten more black votes than when he was doing well. This was indeed the pattern. After Hart won the New Hampshire and Vermont primaries, he surged ahead of Mondale in the national polls. The media were filled with reports that Mondale was in trouble, and Mondale himself stated that he would need help from his old friends if he were to get the nomination. The raised expectations for Hart led not to a black bandwagon but to black support for the new underdog, Mondale, and fewer votes for Jackson.[32] In the Alabama, Georgia, and Florida primaries on Super Tuesday, Jackson averaged 59 percent of the black vote. After Mondale regained the lead, Jackson averaged 80 percent of the black vote in the rest of the primaries.[33]

Primary voting can also be based logically on considerations of a candidate's relative chances of either winning the nomination or winning the presidential election in November. In the 1976 Republican primary between Ronald Reagan and President Gerald Ford, many Republicans who preferred Reagan both on the issues and on personal qualities nevertheless voted for Ford on the grounds that he had a better chance of beating the Democrats. If every primary voter had voted for his personal favorite, without considering strategic factors, Reagan would have won the nomination. In the Ohio primary, for example, 10 percent of Ford's votes were cast by people who said they preferred Reagan on the issues but rated Ford's chances of winning higher than Reagan's. Without these Ohio votes, Ford would not have won the nomination.[34]

Because primaries lead to a convention, voters can vote against a likely winner in the hope of keeping the nomination open. In 1976, after Carter's victories against Wallace, Udall, and Henry Jackson placed him far ahead in the race for the nomination, Governor Jerry Brown of California entered the race and won primaries in Maryland, Rhode Island, Nevada, and California. In the California exit poll, 30 percent of Brown's voters said they voted for him to "stop Carter."[35]

Coordinating Expectations

I have argued above that the rise of new candidates reflects strategic voting, not the bandwagon effect. The best-documented primary surge is that of Gary Hart. It is clearly the case, as I will elaborate in chapter 9, that Hart's second-place finish in Iowa in 1984 made him the most obvious and viable alternative to Walter Mondale; it also brought him the votes of many "anybody but Mondale" voters and many "Mondale because there isn't anybody else" voters. This means that at the very moment of Hart's sudden rise, within days of his New Hampshire victory, expectations that he would win the nomination did not account for his support. Voters were taking account not just of who would eventually win the nomination, but of who had the best chance of defeating Mondale in the primaries.

Usually media surveys do not ask questions about expectations, either about the chances of the individual candidates or about which candidate the respondent thinks is most likely to win the nomination.[36] However, extensive CBS News/*New York Times* polling data casts doubt on an expectations-centered explanation for preferences for Hart. In 1984, two CBS News/*New York Times* polls asked, "Who do you think will win the nomination?" One poll, taken just after Hart had won primaries in Vermont, Massachusetts, and Florida, and Mondale had won primaries in Alabama and Georgia, contained 411 registered Democrats and independents who said they were likely primary or caucus voters.[37] The other survey was a panel survey, which reinterviewed 376 of the 467 likely registered Democratic primary voters who had been interviewed just after Mondale's Iowa caucus victory.[38]

Hart voters in general, and those who switched to Hart from Mondale in particular, expected Mondale to win the nomination. In the survey conducted just after Super Tuesday, 44 percent of Hart's voters expected Mondale to win the nomination, 41 percent expected Hart to win, and the rest did not know. On the panel survey, the voters who moved from Mondale in late February to Hart in March expected Mondale to win the nomination 57 percent to 35 percent. Among all other voters who moved to Hart, 55 percent thought Mondale would win the nomination and 25 percent thought Hart would win the nomination.[39] It is hard to make expectations the chief explanation of support for Hart when half of his supporters had higher expectations of victory for a different candidate.

Of course, increased expectations were critical for Hart, but there are various kinds of expectations—including the important expectation that one candidate has the best chance of defeating another. After he came in second in Iowa, Hart took off in the New Hampshire polls, his victory there giving him a boost nationally. Hart may not have had the highest expectation of victory, but he did appear to have the best chance of defeating Mondale. Hart picked up voters who wanted someone besides Mondale, and he picked up Mondale voters who had been for Mondale because there wasn't anybody else. Thus both information effects and strategic voting contributed to Hart's rise.

Cognition and Coordination: The Rise of New Candidates

The rush to new candidates like Carter in 1976, Bush in 1980, and Hart in 1984 is a form of "coordination game" that depends on the way people process information and frame candidates. Taken together, the Drunkard's Search, Gresham's law of information, and pseudocertainty effects provide a theoretical explanation consistent with the pattern of rises and falls among new candidates in presidential primaries. Further, the same cognitive principles suggest explanations for the falls of older, established candidates before the first results are known.

In game theory, a coordination game occurs when people want to meet at a common point; they may value some points more than others, but they value meeting together at most places over going to any one place alone. Thus a coordination game would occur when two people try to meet for lunch, both knowing the agreed-upon time but neither remembering the name of the restaurant. Another example would be two people who get separated in a subway when one gets on the car and the other doesn't, so that each must decide where to wait for the other person.[40]

When Bush won the Iowa primary over Reagan in 1980 and when Hart came in second to Mondale in 1984, they became rallying points for people who wanted an alternative to Reagan or Mondale. Their standing in national polls rose overnight when people saw them as the most obvious and best alternative to the dominant figures. Each of these men became the focal point for voters in an implicit coordination game, a situation in which a group of voters all win if they can coordinate support for a single candidate to oppose another candidate.[41]

The way people compare candidates creates the potential for a coordination game. In primaries, voters have vastly different kinds and amounts of information about the candidates. When that happens, they will use the

Drunkard's Search to compare the candidates, sorting them out by a few prominent criteria.

The Drunkard's Search makes it easier for the new candidates to define themselves. When there is a well-known trait by which the other candidates distinguish themselves from the front-runner, the communications of the lesser-known candidates become easier. They can communicate via negatives, telling voters what they are not, and letting voters fill in the rest with default values and representativeness. It was easy for voters to decide that Bush was not a voodoo economist or a bomb thrower, that Carter was not a politician, that Jerry Brown was not a southern fundamentalist, and that Hart was not a tool of unions or blacks.

But why jump to a new candidate in the first place? If people are generally risk-averse, preferring a bird in the hand to two in the bush, how can so many be willing to support a candidate for president whom they have known about for only a few weeks? First, the criteria upon which they seize will become more important to them. If the criteria are faults of the front-runner, then the frame of the Drunkard's Search will make them less risk-averse; this is because people are cautious (risk-averse) about moves away from a positive status quo, but gamblers in moving away from a negative status quo. Jumps to a new focal candidate are most likely, then, when there is dissatisfaction with the front-runner. Second, people pick up more information about the new candidates than is generally recognized, and they can also use representativeness to fill in much that they do not know.

Negative Framing and Surges

The creation of constituencies, however, is a dialectical process. The creation of one constituency alerts potential counterconstituencies. A political party can divide into many different political interests, because there are many aspects of political identity that people can focus upon. Primaries mobilize these identities by making people realize that they belong to a constituency. This is done by showing them that their interests are shared by others, that those interests belong on the political agenda, and that there are enough other people like them to make their constituency viable.

Because poorly known candidates can communicate through negatives, framing themselves as "not" whatever people don't like about the front-runner, it is not always an advantage to be the better-known candidate. Since people fill in missing information with "default values," they can "know enough" about the new candidate to support him for president because they have combined what they know about his attributes with what they know about the front-runner. Thus Hart and Bush embody not only their own attributes but their contrasts with the front-runner as well. No candidate has ever acknowledged this more trenchantly than Hart did. In 1984, after he won two primaries in the middle of the campaign, Senator Hart told an interviewer, "Mondale's had to face cruelly twice, *twice*, the fact that a majority of this party wants somebody else. . . . He thinks *I'm* his problem. I'm not his problem. *He's* his problem."[42]

In 1987, exactly a year before the first ballots were to be cast in the 1988 Democratic primaries, and before Hart's well-publicized tryst with Donna Rice aboard the yacht *Monkey Business*, one hundred prominent political reporters for television and the print media gathered socially to toast the impending primaries. Although the occasion was social, the reporters were, naturally, asked whom they expected to get the nominations the next year. By a wide margin they predicted that Hart would win the Democratic nomination. Hart had nearly won in 1984 and had spent the next three years preparing for the 1988 campaign.

Hart promptly wrote the hosts a note saying, "I demand a recount."[43] He was aware of the ways front-runners set the context for primaries and of the ways in which being a front-runner can be a disadvantage. He was also, perhaps, uniquely aware of how much easier it is for new candidates to define themselves by what they are not, in order to mobilize constituencies against the status quo.

The first stage in the creation of constituencies is likely to be the "not" stage, where disparate constituent elements rally around a candidate on the basis of the ways in which he differs from a well-known candidate—on the basis of what he is not. A new candidate is most likely to emerge, therefore, in situations where this type of communication is easiest; and a surge of support for that candidate is most likely when he or she appears to be the obvious solution to a coordination game. The situation most favorable to this phenomenon is when the field of candidates is, like "Snow White and the Seven Dwarfs," a prominent and well-known candidate and a host of poorly known challengers.[44]

Patterns of support for the front-runner determine where support for fresh faces comes from, and the image of the front-runner determines which issues and personal characteristics other candidates emphasize. Further, the issues that other candidates use to distinguish themselves from the front-runner become more salient as the campaign progresses. Gary Hart (1984) and George Bush (1980) are clear examples of the new candidate who rises to sudden prominence by contrast with a well-known front-runner to whom he becomes the most viable alternative. (I illustrate this dynamic for the Republicans in 1979 and 1980 in chapter 8, and for the Democrats in 1983 and 1984 in chapter 9.) I see a difference between these two cases and the rise of Jimmy Carter in 1976. Carter also emerged from the pack by distinction from the other candidates, but there was no "Snow White" in 1976. There was, however, a particularly clear and powerful backdrop framing the 1976 election: Richard Nixon and Watergate. Carter was able to distinguish himself clearly from the other candidates by his personal qualities, his approaches to government, and his "outsiderness." He was the "non-Washington" un-politician.

The sudden emergence of new candidates in the context of a coordination game occurs only when there is dynamic framing—when the categories people use to examine the candidates are constructed out of the array of candidates. People do not assess the candidates separately and vote for the one with the highest expected value; they use a Drunkard's Search over the whole field. The coordination game also presupposes a critical inferential rule: "My enemy's enemy is my friend." People can switch to a new candidate when their initial favorite fares poorly because their negative framing of the candidate—as "not-Reagan" or "not-Mondale," for example—precludes the possibility that the voter is closer to Reagan or Mondale than to this new candidate.[45]

New candidates excite interest because they tap hopes created by thinking about the better-known candidates. When there is an explicit or implicit discontent with our existing choices, victories by newcomers trigger surges of hope. As different as politics and love may be, the initial euphoria of new love and the utopian enthusiasm for a newly emergent candidate are both examples of low-information infatuation. The bubbles that lift new candidates recall Stendhal's observation in *De l'Amour* that "realities model themselves enthusiastically on one's desires." The way we see little-known objects of desire, in other words, depends upon what we are looking for. Our hopes frame our realities. Elizabeth Drew noted this element in the Gary Hart bubble of 1984: "Charisma involves an interchange between the candidate and the public, in which the public begins to sense something exciting about the candidate, and the candidate, buoyed by that, gets better at projecting himself. Charisma is a chemical reaction between a candidate and the people. Charisma also probably involves an ingredient of hope; the charismatic candidate is one who is raising hopes."[46]

Additional constituencies can be created, however, only if there is a leader who can give them a clear focus. John Connally, John Glenn, Howard Baker, and a number of other candidates with early followings could not fill this role once voters started to think about them more seriously. To assemble a coalition, to hold diverse interests together, to create a "we," requires more than the correct issue positions. As Jerome Bruner has noted, others are required for the realization of self; a great leader, one who can inspire others, is a person who appears limitless, whose extravagance appears to need no return on investment in others. Such leaders never seem to hedge, as if they would be "the richer for giving": "When this human extravagance is combined with great talent, it becomes a form of community renewal—if the time and climate are right. The extravagant great create self in others in a manner that, finally, makes others more easily able to share self. It is not that the world becomes like them. Rather, they create a medium of exchange."[47] This is the psychological side of the political-economy notion that the primary task of a political entrepreneur is to coordinate expectations so that people begin to feel that their contributions will be effective.

There was a great deal of unease among Republicans about George Bush in 1987, about his policies and Reaganomics as well as about his leadership, but Robert Dole could not use this unease to build a constituency for change within the party. There was a great deal of uneasiness about Walter Mondale in 1984, and Democrats initially looked to John Glenn, who quickly lost his potential constituency. There was also widespread discomfort with Reagan among Republicans in 1980, but Senator Robert Dole could not hold the constituency that turned to him after his victory in Iowa; he could not convince people who were ambivalent about the presidential legacy of Ronald Reagan that he represented the modifications they wanted. Neither Dole nor Glenn nor Bush could inspire the hopefulness that Elizabeth Drew noted among Hart followers in 1984, or that Stendhal found in new lovers; in Bruner's felicitous phrase, they did not appear "the richer for giving."

Low-Information Signaling

The criticism that primary campaigns test little more than name recognition and ill-founded expectations ignores the amount of information with political substance that voters get from low-information signals. Voters learn about the traits and characteristics of the new candidates, and they also see their behavior in contrast to that of the other candidates in the field. They learn directly from observing the candidate, and indirectly from seeing how the candidate fits into the array of candidates. Indeed, the history of voting research is a history of scholars learning how to discover what voters know. As Larry Bartels notes, "Part of the perception that issues are unimportant reflects the overly narrow conception of 'issues' prevalent in mainstream voting research. If we focus more broadly on prospective voters' political predispositions—predispositions based on a wide variety of social characteristics, policy stands, and group attachments—the role of politics in the campaign looks more significant and more comprehensible."[48]

If people are shown pictures of pennies or of nickels and are asked which ones are real and which ones lack features of actual coins, Donald Norman points out, their answers will display a lack of knowledge of money. If, on the other hand, you give them pictures of both coins and ask them which are nickels, their answers will show that they do know something about money.[49] The point is that when making decisions, people use many cues for some dimensions and few cues for others. When they choose between candidates, choices that appear uninformed may in fact be choices on a dimension that scholars have not yet found. If voters have been listening for a long time to the tune one band plays, it will not take them very long to recognize the difference between that tune and the tunes other bands are playing.

There is much more behind the surges of support for new candidates than vague personal information and generalized expectations. Voters relate candidates to the past performance of their parties and to their desires for the future. In deciding how to place candidates in the field, they consider media reports of exchanges between candidates, the perceived relation of candidates to specific interest groups, and endorsements by prominent politicians. In 1980, for example, when the mayor of Chicago, Jane Byrne, endorsed Jimmy Carter over Senator Edward Kennedy, 78 percent of the Illinois primary voters knew of her endorsement.[50] Immediately after Gary Hart's New Hampshire victory, when he surged ahead of Walter Mondale in the national polls, voters had picked up enough information about the candidates so that their attitudes about unions, which had endorsed Mondale, corresponded very closely to their preferences between Hart and Mondale. Voters favorable to the AFL-CIO preferred Mondale over Hart by 41 percent to 29 percent, and voters unfavorable to the AFL-CIO supported Hart over Mondale by a whopping 48 percent to 17 percent.[51]

Crystallization

The implicit coordination game I have described above depends on the particular framing of the candidate against the front-runner; the game can break down when the framing changes because voters use more information about the challenger and make more complete comparisons of the two candidates.

New candidates are likely to be known mainly from campaign behavior and personal attributes, and the publicity given to the early winners is often all personal data and all positive. These candidates can get large lifts from the negative framing of better-known candidates. As Elizabeth Drew described the surge in support for Gary Hart after his unexpected win in New Hampshire, "The very fact that numerous people now tell reporters that they favor Hart even though they don't know much, or anything, about him is part of the phenomenon . . . people can impute to him what they want. Hart is, as of now, the inkblot candidate. The fact that voters have seen little of him until now and know little of him is an advantage."[52]

As noted in chapter 4, the use of the representative heuristic makes it easy for people to assess future political performance by projecting from personal data about the candidate. Further, when the data are consistent and all positive, the ease of using these data leads to pseudocertainty effects—overoptimistic projections from limited data. The collapse of the bubble for the fresh new candidate is most likely when pseudocertainty effects no longer operate in projections of future performance. Regardless of how much new information about a candidate becomes known, pseudocertainty effects do not operate when data are inconsistent, and when the "always" and "never" in a voter's projections are replaced by "sometimes."

This explains why negative campaign behavior—such as Carter's "ethnic purity" remark, Bush's inept handling of the debate flap with Reagan in New Hampshire in 1980 (discussed in chapter 8), and Hart's inability to pull a commercial off the air in Illinois or to decide whether the U.S. embassy in Israel should relocate (discussed in chapter 9)—can have so much impact at a particular point in a campaign. Each of the new candidates I examine in chapters 7–9 who has had a surge in support has later fallen back after a campaign incident that has caused voters to reassess their information.

Henry Brady and Richard Johnston, in an important analysis of voter evaluations of candidates, show that as candidates become known, their images become more differentiated, or "crystallized"; that is, people evaluate and rate candidates differently in different situations.[53] As they develop a more differentiated picture, they become less dependent on personal attributes for projecting future behavior and more concerned with the candidates' political positions.

When pseudocertainty effects are eliminated, projections of future performance become less extreme, and the choice becomes one between two candidates who both have positive and negative traits and positions. Thus the sudden collapses that occur in primaries and general elections depend on quirks in the ways people process data and frame their information about candidates. When we understand these quirks, we can predict how and when the overconfident projections of voters will collapse.

Ignoring for the moment the cognitive principles involved in these choices and evaluations, the fall of Hart in 1988, for example, or that of Bush in 1980, could theoretically be attributed to changing expectations. The importance of differentiation, or "crystallization," as Brady calls it, is illustrated by the changing evaluations of Hart in the period after New Hampshire and Super Tuesday. At a time when there were no changes in Hart's overall familiarity or favorability ratings, there were large drops in assessments of his experience, particularly with respect to foreign affairs. My analysis of Hart's campaign, in chapter 9, shows that the big drop in support for him came *without* any change in expectations, and also without any change in his overall favorability ratings. It occurred, instead, because of a major drop in voter assessments of his experience and competence as voters developed a more differentiated picture of Hart and his strengths and weaknesses.

In all three classic instances of new faces surging into prominence in the early polls—Carter in 1976, Bush in 1980, and Hart in 1984—there were easily absorbed cues that allowed voters to place the candidates in perspective. As voters learn more about a candidate, or as they discover that they know less than they thought, they sometimes learn that they prefer a different candidate. The rapid decline of early "surge" candidates occurs because of new information about their stands or competence, not because of changes in voter expectations about the candidates' chances of electoral success.

Any analysis of candidates based only on name recognition and expectations will understate the importance of learning during the campaign. But as all our discussions of framing have indicated, no single, overall measure can incorporate or reflect all the information —let alone all the meaning imputed to the information—that a voter has about a candidate. Further, no single measure of familiarity can incorporate all the changes in information and all the learning about a candidate that take place during a campaign. When voters see a candidate in new situations, they learn to differentiate and view him or her differently in disparate situations. The critical question, as Henry Brady has noted, is not whether voters learn about new candidates, but whether they learn before they vote.[54]

Old Information in New Contexts: The Cases of Edward Kennedy, John Glenn, John Connally, and Gary Hart

Fascination with the Carters and Harts has diverted attention away from the failures like John Glenn, John Connally, Henry Jackson, Howard Baker, and Edward Kennedy, men with substantial preprimary support who flopped once the local campaigning started. On theoretical grounds, the falls of these men are important for two reasons.

First, their falls demonstrate the importance of thinking and framing. Evaluations of candidates change as candidates enter primaries and are seen in a presidential frame and in comparison with other candidates. The falls of these "turkeys"—large birds that couldn't get off the ground—occurred because new information and new frames get brought to bear only once the primaries start. Further, if these men didn't falter, the Harts and Carters could never soar.

Second, they show that voters do not accept just *any* prominent candidate as the alternative to a front-runner. Bush in 1980, and Hart in 1984, became the focal point for opposition to front-runners only *after* other candidates who started with that position flopped. In this light, the surges of Carter, Hart, and Bush hardly look driven by name recognition and expectations; even in the negative-framing context, enough material is considered for candidates to fail, and for expectations to change before there are any votes taken.

The research on representativeness, framing, and availability shows that people do not incorporate all their information about political figures into one specific overall assessment. If we had ready-made categories in which *all* our information were stored, changing the perspective would not affect what information is used. But that is not the case, and since we are not using and integrating all our information all the time, any change of frame or any stimulation that increases the amount of time we spend thinking about a person or a choice can affect our evaluations and preferences.

When the presidential primaries begin, there can be rapid changes in evaluations and preferences. In particular, there are always relatively well-known political figures who are unable to convert preferences based on their records into votes at the polls. Henry Jackson, John Connally, John Glenn, and Howard Baker, to name four prominent examples, were preferred by 10 percent to 30 percent of their party before the primaries began, but had little or no success in converting these early preferences into actual votes. In 1983, for example, Senator Glenn was within three points of Walter Mondale for months; he had as much support in 1983, in fact, as Ronald Reagan had in 1979 or 1975, yet his ratings and support faded rapidly. The most famous case, of course, was that of Senator Edward Kennedy. In 1980, he fell in the national polls almost as soon as he announced his candidacy for president—a bandwagon effect in reverse. These declines illustrate how changing the context can change the evaluation of the candidate.

Edward Kennedy's Campaign

How could so many people accept the Roger Mudd interview, discussed in chapter 5, as the explanation for Senator Kennedy's fall? In this view, millions of people with favorable opinions of Kennedy, who already were saying that they wanted him to be their nominee for president, are supposed to have changed their opinion of him in part because he was generally inarticulate and failed to give a prompt answer when asked why he wanted to be president. No writer attributes the change in primary preferences between Carter and Kennedy solely to the interview, since the hostages were taken at the American Embassy in Teheran at this time, and there was a great rallying of support for President Carter. But all writers have given the interview great weight in explaining the fall in Kennedy's popularity ratings.

I suggest that the event made such powerful sense to journalists and political insiders only because of what they were already thinking about Kennedy, and what they were already thinking about was far more serious than a nine-second hesitation on television. In other words, as I suggested in chapter 5, the interview has come to represent a more complex process because the press had no better theory with which to explain how Kennedy actually fell.

I argue that the drop in Kennedy's ratings does not demonstrate the effect of new information but rather the effect of a new perspective in which old information becomes more troubling or difficult to deal with, a context in which people are thinking more about facts they already know.[55] This can be seen from a brief review of the facts surrounding Kennedy's fall.

Kennedy was seen on television countless times in 1978 and 1979, and he consistently led President Carter in preference polls among Democrats by nearly two to one. Just to consider one national network: between January 1, 1978, and October 31, 1979, he was either mentioned by a correspondent or shown on the CBS evening news 316 times; he was mentioned by a correspondent 226 times; he spoke in person on the show 90 times; and he was shown in film footage 139 times.[56]

Furthermore, before Kennedy ever announced his candidacy, the Chappaquiddick incident was about as well known as any nonpresidential political scandal or tragedy or event; in a national poll taken in July 1979, nearly all Democrats said they remembered it.[57] Clearly, then, the drop in Kennedy's favorable ratings after he became a candidate cannot plausibly be attributed to new information, to facts that voters did not have before he declared for office.

Yet from the summer of 1979 to the winter of 1980, the proportion of Democrats saying that the Chappaquiddick incident would affect their vote doubled, from 14 percent in July 1979 to 30 percent in March 1980, while at the same time Kennedy dropped in the polls. The proportion saying that they believed he was lying about Chappaquiddick also doubled.[58] In November of 1980, the day before he announced his formal challenge to Carter, Kennedy led the president by 54 percent to 20 percent. But by January he trailed by 32 percent to 46 percent, and he fell to 23 percent to 58 percent by the time the primaries started in February. I suggest that this is a powerful example of how changing the context and stimulating more thinking about a candidate changes the way in which the candidate is evaluated. After Kennedy's announcement of his candidacy, concern among voters about his ability to handle a crisis increased. Despite years of discussion, his 1968 automobile accident at Chappaquiddick on Martha's Vineyard, which resulted in the death of Mary Jo Kopechne, once again became an issue: was there immoral behavior, had Kennedy panicked, was there a cover-up? When asked "Because of what happened at Chappaquiddick, are you more likely or less likely to vote for Senator Kennedy for President, or doesn't it matter?" the proportion who said it made them less likely to vote for him rose from 14 percent in November to 31 percent by January.[59]

Also in November, at about the time that Kennedy formally entered the race, Iranian students took fifty-five Americans hostage at the U.S. embassy in Teheran, and in late December, Russia invaded Afghanistan. These events led to a great increase in public concern with foreign policy and a rise in the proportion of Americans favoring expanded defense spending and a more militant international posture. This certainly must have contributed to the senator's fall; the more that people were concerned about international crises, the more that questions about his judgment under pressure would matter.[60]

Even without Iran and Afghanistan, though, questions about Kennedy's character would have arisen simply because he was placed in a presidential context and judged as a possible president in his own right, rather than simply as a means to dump an unpopular president. For many voters considering a future Kennedy administration, opinions about the candidate's personal behavior at Chappaquiddick outweighed years of public service in the Senate. Many who believed at the time that Kennedy would be a better leader than Carter simply could not vote for a man whose judgment they did not trust or whose personal morality they doubted. Kennedy's advisers told Elizabeth Drew in January 1980 that they had not anticipated the extent of renewed concern with the issue. This lack of anticipation was a conceptual failure on their part, not a limitation of survey methodology or voting theory.[61]

John Glenn's Campaign

Since Senator John Glenn was one of the major flops of the 1984 Democratic primary campaign, it is generally forgotten—particularly by reporters who prefer to repress faulty predictions—that he was in a near tie with former vice president Walter Mondale in the 1983 national polls. He had a high recognition rate among Democratic voters because of the publicity he had received as an astronaut and national hero during the JFK years. In June and September of 1983 slightly over half of all Democrats nationwide had a favorable impression of him; after he declared his candidacy, but before his campaign had received much national publicity, his favorable rating fell to 31 percent. He had given no famous interview, and there was no new information about him. Nevertheless, a large fraction of people who had thought favorably of him before he entered the race for president became uncertain about how to rate him.[62] The increase in undecided voters in the race for the nomination, then, was also made up in large measure of former Glenn supporters.

I believe that the best explanation for this change is that when people began to see Glenn in a presidential frame, they did not have enough information to complete the picture. Clearly, being asked to rate an announced contender in the context of an actual campaign, and being asked to rate a potential candidate a year in advance, are two different things. There were too many differences between an astronaut and a president for many people to make the extrapolation easily. The hero-astronaut data was not enough to complete a presidential narrative. In terms of his presidency, Glenn was considered generally competent but was otherwise a blank slate, as his strategists realized from their polls.[63]

Although Glenn was considered a hero, he was never able to fill in the blank slate and move beyond being a hero for most voters. A CBS News/

New York Times poll taken in Iowa a month before the Iowa caucuses found that Democrats still had no idea what he would actually do as president, and that only half of those who had a favorable view of him even thought that he cared about people like themselves.[64]

Glenn fell, despite the initial high expectations for him, because people could not fill in the picture. This is an important reminder about the limits of expectations, for if high expectations and a positive personal image were sufficient to gather votes, Glenn would not have fallen. Clearly, as voters begin to think about the candidates and project to the future, they need more than expectations and a blank slate to complete the picture. Voters cannot project from past feats to a future presidency unless they feel they can grasp the person about whom they are constructing future scenarios. And a favorable rating is clearly not an indication that voters have enough information to make these projections.

John Connally's Campaign

The failure of John Connally in the Republican primaries of 1980 supports these arguments that personal characteristics begin to matter more as voters think about the election, and that voters do not integrate all their information about candidates into a single overall assessment.

In the public opinion polls for most of 1979, Connally was one of the leading challengers to Ronald Reagan. He had been a very popular governor of Texas, secretary of the Navy, and secretary of the Treasury under Richard Nixon. In 1979 he impressed Republican activists in several Midwest states and even won a straw poll taken after one Republican gathering in Indiana.[65] He had also been indicted during Watergate, but was acquitted. Having received campaign contributions from 25 percent of the chief executive officers of Fortune 500 corporations, he refused federal matching funds in 1980 in order to avoid incurring campaign spending limits and take advantage of his ability to raise more money than the other candidates could.

Emphasizing his corporate connections, Connally presented himself as the most effective power broker in the circles of the governing elite. When his campaign staff told him that this was not working, and that he ought to identify more with the average voter, he began to argue that his involvement with Watergate really demonstrated his concern for average citizens. Speaking to a group of dairy farmers in Iowa, he said, "Let me tell y'all something. None of you have made the sacrifices for the dairy industry that I have. I got indicted because of it, if you want to know something. You think I don't know about milk producers and milk prices, you're crazy."[66] But this sort of appeal failed.[67]

Gary Hart's 1988 Campaign

In 1986 and 1987, Gary Hart was the leading contender for the Democratic nomination for president, until he was involved in a personal scandal aboard the yacht *Monkey Business* with Donna Rice. When the scandal occurred, Senator Hart's ratings dropped, but he still led a field of candidates who were, except for Jesse Jackson, unknown nationally. However, his support after the scandal did not reflect a lack of perceived alternatives among voters who knew Hart and no other candidates; much of his support came from knowledgeable and interested voters. Polls in 1988 in Iowa, for example, showed that he still had support from a quarter of the potential Democratic caucus electorate, and he was even supported by 20 percent of the people who had gone to caucuses in 1984. He also had strong early support in New Hampshire. Nevertheless, he received less than 1 percent of the votes in Iowa and less than 4 percent in New Hampshire. As voters were contacted by the campaigns and were stimulated to watch debates and think about the candidates, Hart's support began to sink.[68]

As Hart's support began to erode, he addressed the relationship between personal and political rectitude: "As a public official, I would never lie to the Congress or the American people on their business. I would never shred documents. I would never sell arms to terrorists. And I would never condone anyone in my administration who breached the highest standard of the sacred trust of the public duty."[69] Hart was arguing that the best way to assess his future political behavior was from his past political behavior, not from his personal behavior. He had no success at all.

The falls in support for Kennedy, Glenn, Connally, and Hart are consistent with the argument that when voters evaluate candidates as potential presidents, they try to imagine what they will do in office. This increases the weight they give to personal factors, which means that personal information matters more as voters begin to think about their choices. Thinking about the future involves evaluating scenarios. If people find it easier to project from personal data than from political data, then representativeness, coupled with a limited knowledge of politics, increases the importance of personal data as thinking goes on during the primaries. Thus drops in ratings are consistent with the notion that most voters have vague and ill-defined notions of all the jobs that presidents do, and that they therefore evaluate presidential aspirants on personal grounds, projecting from personal characteristics and competence to future performance. It is possible that these changes in support are due to more thinking, and not to framing, but it is the new context that prompts more thinking. Either way, these falls are consistent with Gresham's law of information, which says that small amounts of personal information can dominate large amounts of impersonal information.

The decline of candidates like Senator Kennedy becomes more intelligible when explained in terms of the decision processes of voters. In those terms, it also becomes clear that well-known candidates do not fall because horse-race news in the media changes voters' expectations, for these falls often take place before the first primary results are known.

Favorite Sons

The persistence of favorite-son candidates is further evidence against the possible role of expectations as persuasion. Before the reforms that both parties enacted in the late 1960s and early 1970s opened up the presidential nominating system to the wide-open fifty-state brawl of today, many delegates to the national conventions were accorded their positions automatically by virtue of their local party positions. In addition, many primaries were not heavily contested by national candidates; there were fewer public appearances and much less paid advertising about the actual candidates. Primary voters, with little knowledge of the candidates, often voted for a prominent state politician—usually a governor, mayor, or senator. This local politician, known as a "favorite son," would then vote for one of the actual candidates at the national convention.

After the reforms, it was generally assumed that favorite sons would disappear from primaries. With so much more national publicity and so much more active campaigning by candidates in every state, it was assumed that voters would vote only for a candidate with a real chance to win the nomination. Further, momentum theories, and consideration of the ways in which expectations could determine votes, seemed to preclude the possibility of favorite sons. As Henry Brady has acknowledged, "Two things I thought I would never see again were favorite sons and open conventions."[70]

The Case of Senator Paul Simon

Peter Hart Associates did two polls in Illinois for the *Chicago Tribune* in the days before the Illinois primary of 1988. As a result, it is possible to show how strategic factors operate even in votes for favorite sons, and to make some informed speculations about voting for local candidates or message candidates.[71] After Super Tuesday, the week before the Illinois primary, there were three candidates with earlier wins who were actively campaigning: Dukakis, Jackson, and Senator Albert Gore. Dukakis, who had pulled ahead of Gephardt and Gore on Super Tuesday, had a poll rating in Illinois of 47 percent positive, 10 percent neutral, 28 percent negative, and 18 percent "don't know."

Jackson, a well-known figure in Illinois, was supported by nearly all the blacks in the state, but he was not popular among white voters. White voters who did not support Jackson could vote for Dukakis, Simon, Gore, or Gephardt (whose name was on the ballot although he did little active campaigning). Little was known about Dukakis beyond the fact that he had won the most delegates so far. His campaign managers, in an effort to show that he had at least a modicum of familiarity with these midwestern "outsiders" from Chicago and Peoria, ran TV spots showing blue-collar white males in taverns talking about his record as governor of Massachusetts.

The first poll, on the Wednesday and Thursday before the campaign, had Simon at 35 percent, Jackson at 30 percent, Dukakis at 18 percent, Gephardt at 6 percent, and Gore at 4 percent. The second poll, on the next two days, was very heavily publicized throughout the state, for it showed that Jackson had taken the lead at 32 percent, with 29 percent for Simon and 20 percent for Dukakis. After the results of the second poll came out, Simon's share of the non-Jackson vote began to rise. The actual primary result was Simon 43 percent, Jackson 31 percent, Dukakis 17 percent, Gore 5 percent, and Gephardt 2 percent.

It is plausible that many voters went with Simon because they did not know enough about Dukakis, even though he was a front-runner with a high personal rating. Further, the moment it appeared that Jackson could actually win and that Simon was the best alternative because he was ahead of Dukakis, many more voters turned to Simon strategically.[72] Thus it appears that voters had strategic purposes in mind when deciding whether to vote for Dukakis or Simon in order to stop Jackson.

The Case of Senator Albert Gore

Albert Gore's vote on Super Tuesday across the South was similar to Simon's favorite-son vote, but on a regional scale. Gore campaigned hard as a southerner, presenting himself as an alternative to candidates who didn't understand the South. Among whites who voted in the thirteen southern states on Super Tuesday, Dukakis got 26 percent of the vote and

Gore received 25 percent. Half of all the white voters in the thirteen states were migrants to the South; they voted for Dukakis over Gore 41 percent to 22 percent. Among the half who were native southerners, Gore beat Dukakis 45 percent to 25 percent.[73]

Gore's favorite-son vote is a prime example of low-information signals and the ways in which advertisements communicate them. Among people who knew Gore well enough to rate him, those who hadn't seen his commercials were much less likely than those who had seen them to know that he was a southerner. Two weeks before Super Tuesday, there was a CBS News/*New York Times* poll in the southern states holding primaries on Super Tuesday. At that time Gore's favorability rating among likely Democratic primary voters was 20 percent favorable, 17 percent unfavorable, and 26 percent undecided; 37 percent did not know his name. Looking only at likely primary voters who were able to rate Gore either favorably or unfavorably, 38 percent knew he was from Tennessee. Still looking only at voters who could rate Gore, 68 percent of those who had seen his commercials knew he was from Tennessee, while only 28 percent of those who had not seen his commercials knew where he was from.[74] The Gore commercials increased the number of people who could rate him, but they also communicated information about him which other people who already knew him either did not know or did not readily recall.

Both George Wallace and Jesse Jackson, as different as they may be, have had some of the characteristics of favorite sons. Wallace argued that voters should "Send them a message." Many blacks voted for Jackson because he was black. In both cases, many voters were sending an agent to the convention to vote for a nominee rather than voting directly for a potential winner themselves.[75]

The Gore and Simon votes, as well as votes for candidates like Jesse Jackson, emphasize that it is still possible for favorite-son candidates to receive votes when the front-runners are not clearly understood or established among segments of the electorate, and they confirm that a favorable personal evaluation is not an adequate measure of information about a candidate. Dukakis was known well enough to be rated positively by most voters on Super Tuesday and by most voters in Illinois, but that emphasizes again that it takes more than a favorable rating to be known well enough to get presidential votes. Many native southerners were more comfortable with Gore and many voters in Illinois were more comfortable with Simon, despite the very low expectations for these men after their earlier defeats. However, the persistence of favorite-son candidates shows that more theorctical work is needed to explain when voters will vote for favorite sons as opposed to front-runners or national alternatives.

Favorite sons and "message" candidates simply don't fit easily into persuasion theories of momentum. If expectations are a direct determinant of votes, and are shaped by what voters know about previous primary results, it is unclear how a candidate with no track record, or a poor showing in earlier primaries, can get votes.

Candidacies like Jesse Jackson's also show the possibilities that are present for national favorite-son candidacies as more media coverage establishes nationwide constituencies of such diverse groups as senior citizens, environmentalists, religious fundamentalists, and women. If there were a one-day national primary, there would be many new opportunities for candidates to become electronic favorite sons and daughters. This would be particularly true if the parties made it easy for candidates with small proportions of the vote to receive convention delegates, so that there would be little to lose by voting for a person to represent a specific interest group, such as pro-choice or pro-life advocates, minorities, senior citizens, or environmentalists.

The volatility of primaries, particularly evident in the rise and fall of new candidates, results from the ways in which voters acquire and use information, from the ways in which they frame their decisions and view the office of president, and from the decision rules they use to compare candidates. Primary voters rely on low-information cues, such as demographics and endorsements, to predict the policy positions of candidates. They rely on TV presentation and "home style" to judge personal competence and to extrapolate from personal to political competence. In addition to projecting from personal characteristics to issue positions, and from personal morality to public morality, voters also obtain information about individual candidates by observing them in relation to the full array of primary contenders.

Despite their low levels of information about many aspects of politics, and despite the fact that they do not know very much about many of the candidates, voters do manage to make more sense out of the array of candidates than they are usually given credit for. They know about past divisions within the party, and they pick up information in the campaign about endorsements and a candidate's relations to groups within the party. They also learn about the demographics of the candidates and where the candidates are looking for voters. Finally, they learn with amazing rapidity about the results of early primaries.

My analyses in chapters 7, 8, and 9 show the low-information issue effects in the rise of new candidates. They also show that the falling-off of support for these candidates occurs not because of changes in expectations but because of changes in the evaluations voters make of them—a phenomenon that bears witness to the learning about candidates which takes place during primaries.

The primaries I investigate in the following chapters illuminate the cognitive and strategic principles I have used to explain the dynamics of primary campaigns. Further, they demonstrate the critical importance of issues in intraparty battles, the place where they might be expected to matter least. Given the many overlapping constituencies and interests within the parties, looking for the cleavages that emerge is a bit like cutting a diamond: there are many but not an infinite number of ways in which it can be cut. Nevertheless, certain preoccupations arise repeatedly in each of the parties. In Democratic primaries, we see relations between the party and unions, attitudes toward the use of American power overseas, and the problems of race; in Republican primaries, we see attitudes toward the use of force in international conflicts, the role of women, and the proper role of the government in helping the less advantaged.

Presidential primaries are intraparty struggles that express more than cleavages among races, religions, geographic regions, and ethnic groups; they expand to create conflicts over the past performance and the future direction of the party—as illustrated by the Mondale-Hart and Reagan-Bush battles and the emergence of Jimmy Carter in 1976. My analysis of fights within parties and the concurrent emergence of new candidates for president reinforces the argument in chapter 3 that party identification is a political identification and that parties are best viewed as coalitions. Ironically, the political view of party identification is best shown by examining the fights within parties.

Expectations play a role in primaries because voters in most states have knowledge of the results of earlier primary elections in other states, and because there are typically more than two candidates running. But expectations are a catalyst, not a causal agent, in primaries. The role of momentum—the "demonstration effects of important primary victories"—is overstated by popular theories that ignore low-information issue cues, strategic voting, and framing. As estimates of electoral potential, expectations are, of course, sensitive to primary results. And as estimates of the stature or plausibility of the candidate, they can change when voters simply think about the candidates in a presidential frame.

Primaries are so volatile because they are the first presidential auditions for the candidates, because the change of frame from thinking about a candidate to thinking about a future president is so big, and because voters care about some of the policies of their party and their country.

There are, however, still troubling questions about primaries to keep in mind as we examine the cases presented in the next three chapters.

First, do primaries resolve policy conflicts or create them? While primaries mobilize discontent, do they also create it? Do the issues that get raised as candidates attempt to differentiate themselves within parties bear on important questions of public policy? Are the low-information signals that voters receive about candidates and their policies about real issues and concerns or about contrived and trivial differences?

Second, how meaningful are the "screen tests" that candidates like John Glenn fail to pass during primaries? Would voters be better off voting on the résumé alone? Candidates need a screen test, it can be argued, because if they cannot communicate successfully on television they will fail even if they get nominated in a smoke-filled room without primaries. But is the primary screen test too exacting and quirky? Does it throw out candidates who do poorly in New Hampshire but would be great in a general campaign? On one hand, Senator Robert Dole of Kansas was ineffective as Gerald Ford's vice-presidential candidate in 1976, and was hardly any better as a presidential candidate in 1980 and again in 1988. On the other hand, Senator Lloyd Bentsen of Texas was a total flop in 1976 as a presidential candidate, but was an extremely popular and effective national candidate as Michael Dukakis's nominee for vice president.

Finally, when a new candidate emerges in the primaries, a critical moment for his or her campaign is the period just after a surprising showing has provoked reassessment and curiosity. When people suddenly want to know more about the candidate, how good a job do they and the media do in evaluating his or her political history? When people judge what kind of senator Gary Hart was, or what kind of congressman George Bush was, are they judging only by watching the candidates talk about their past political service, or are they also getting information from the media about their actual accomplishments and character?

SEVEN

The Democratic Primaries of 1976: Watergate and the Rise of Jimmy Carter

JIMMY CARTER's victory in 1976 remains the most surprising in the history of primary elections. In February of 1975, for example, a Gallup poll asked Democrats whom they favored for their party's nomination the next year among thirteen Democrats who had been mentioned as possible candidates. Carter, a former one-term governor of Georgia, came in last with 1 percent of the vote.[1]

Carter began receiving national coverage in January 1976, after winning the first event of the 1976 Democratic primary season, the Iowa caucuses. In the February CBS News/*New York Times* poll soon after, Carter was the choice for president of 12 percent of Democrats nationally. He then won the New Hampshire primary, received extensive national television exposure, made the covers of *Time* and *Newsweek*, and won important primaries in Florida and Illinois. By mid-March, after winning these primaries, the CBS News/*New York Times* poll showed him to be the clear leader for the nomination, as the first choice of 46 percent of all Democrats. This early publicity and the boost he got in the polls led to a number of arguments, exemplified by Morris Udall's complaint (discussed in chapter 6) that Carter's early victories gave him a special advantage over the other candidates, who were reduced to playing catch-up under disadvantageous rules.

Udall's charges were certainly plausible, for if ever there was a candidate about whom people may have known nothing except that he was a winner, it was Jimmy Carter. Because he was virtually unknown outside the South before the primaries began, nearly all voters in nonsouthern states, and most southern voters as well, voted for him on the basis of new information gained after the campaign had begun. Some voters *may* indeed have voted for him simply because he was shown in a positive light as a winner. But many more people felt they had acquired enough information about him in barely a month to want him to be their president. Carter's victory provides an unusually dramatic example of negative framing, by which a candidate comes into clear focus for voters when seen against a certain backdrop—which in Carter's case was the Watergate scandal and the collapse of the Democratic party's national leadership. Jimmy Carter was *not* a Democratic insider and he was *not* part of Watergate. My analysis of this phenomenon offers a clear illustration of how information about a candidate is used by voters to create a picture of what kind of president he will be.

The 1976 primary exposed the glaring inability of the Democratic party's traditional leadership to defend its programs before its faithful. An outsider could win the party's nomination not because he was lucky, had a better strategy, or used momentum, but because the party insiders could not put together a credible program. They could not do so because of policy splits over race, Vietnam, and the role of unions within the party, and also because unions could not deliver the vote for their preferred candidates in the party. As this chapter will show, Carter won the Democratic nomination in 1976 because the party leadership was discredited, because he made sense out of Watergate, and because he was a southern governor who could assemble a coalition of blue-collar whites and blacks, something none of the other candidates could do.

Carter was often ridiculed by reporters for his emphasis on personal honesty and his talk about how government reorganization could help solve the problems of mismanagement. Few of them acknowledged that he was communicating themes with which a broad array of Americans, particularly the less well educated, were in general agreement. His triumph in the 1976 New Hampshire primary and his subsequent rise in the national polls thus demonstrates the importance of easily absorbed messages and simple voting cues. The criticisms that Carter had no program, or that he won because of momentum, fail to account for his personal appeal, his response to Watergate, and his appeal as a moderate southerner who could affects blacks as well as whites.

Finally, in discussing the late primary battles between Carter and Jerry Brown, I will illustrate how the campaign front-runner creates his own antithesis. As Carter became better known, the campaign tactics of the other contenders increasingly became reactions to Carter. And as Carter rose against the backdrop of Watergate and a discredited party elite, Brown rose in contrast to Carter.

The Democratic Party in Disarray

In the same 1975 poll in which Jimmy Carter was the choice of 1 percent of Democrats, the leading choice for the nomination was George Wallace, with 22 percent. He was followed by former vice president Hubert Humphrey, with 16 percent; Senator Henry Jackson of Washington, a favorite of the AFL-CIO and a highly visible and extreme supporter of Israel, with 13 percent; Senator George McGovern of South Dakota, the party's nominee in the 1972 debacle, with 10 percent; and Senator Edmund Muskie of Maine, with 9 percent, to name the leading vote-getters. Senators McGovern and Muskie never entered the race, and Humphrey chose to wait on the sidelines and see if there was sentiment for a draft later in the primary season.

Jackson, Wallace, and Carter were joined as official candidates by Senator Birch Bayh of Indiana; Congressman Morris Udall of Arizona, who had been at 3 percent in the Gallup poll mentioned above; Senator Lloyd Bentsen of Texas, also at 3 percent in the Gallup poll; former senator Fred Harris of Oklahoma, at 1 percent in the poll; former North Carolina governor Terry Sanford; Pennsylvania governor Milton Shapp; and the former Peace Corps director and Kennedy family in-law, Sargent Shriver. The campaigns of Bentsen, Shapp, and Sanford never got off the ground, and Bayh and Harris never made it past the first primaries; Shriver lasted until his home state of Illinois and quit the race after a poor showing there. Wallace left the race after he was beaten by Carter in both Florida and Illinois, and Jackson left after he was beaten by Carter in Pennsylvania. Of the starting field this left only Carter and Udall. At that point, Senator Frank Church of Idaho and Governor Jerry Brown of California entered the race to make runs at stopping Carter.

That there was no declared candidate ahead of Wallace in the 1975 preference poll speaks to the disarray within the party after the events of the previous decade. The two most prominent Democrats in the country besides Wallace were Humphrey and Senator Edward Kennedy, and neither was willing to bring his policies and character before the party in 1976. Democratic prospects should have been excellent: President Nixon had resigned in 1974 in the aftermath of the Watergate investigation, and citizen identification with the Republican party was at its lowest point in decades; Cambodia and South Vietnam had fallen to the Communists in 1975; there had been a major energy crisis and a bout of inflation; and the Republican party was not united behind President Ford. Yet in this highly favorable political climate, the leading contender as of 1975 was a onetime third-party candidate for president who had been one of the most ardent champions of segregation and who had been left crippled by an assassination attempt in 1972.

Senator Kennedy could not run in 1976 because it was only eight years since he had apparently panicked and lied about, or at least seriously

mishandled, the Chappaquiddick incident. Questions about his character and morality had not been resolved sufficiently for him to risk running. Further, he faced the same domestic policy liabilities in 1976 as
Humphrey.

Humphrey was the most eloquent and ardent defender of the New Deal
tradition within the party, a tradition of support for Social Security, unemployment insurance, unions, Medicare, and a host of other federal
programs that were the foundation of the modern American welfare state.
He was also an ardent proponent of civil rights for minorities, particularly
blacks, and an unabashed anti-Communist who, as Lyndon Johnson's vice
president, had been a defender of American involvement in Vietnam.
Within the party, Humphrey's favorability ratings reflected the sources of
disgruntlement with recent Democratic policies. His rating among Democrats was 51 percent favorable and 34 percent unfavorable at the beginning
of 1976. He had particularly strong negatives among whites opposed to
busing and among young and educated Democrats who disagreed with his
stance on Vietnam.

Wallace was in the lead in 1975, and Humphrey couldn't face his party's
rank and file because racial issues were so salient in 1976. As the primary
season began, only one in five white Democrats still supported busing for
racial integration, and half of all white Democrats believed that the federal
government was paying too much attention to blacks and other minorities.[2] Furthermore, in the wake of the inflation set in motion after OPEC
had managed to increase oil prices in 1973, white-collar Democrats were
expressing increased concern with fighting inflation, and a corresponding
suspicion about (possibly inflationary) programs for full employment.

Congressman Udall's plan for the early primaries was to clear out his
competitors on the left, to be the last surviving member of the party's progressive wing. He called himself a progressive instead of a liberal because
liberal had taken on such a negative connotation with so many voters in
the furor over racial issues and government spending, among other
issues.[3]

Udall's main competitors among the "progressives" were Birch Bayh
and Henry Jackson. Birch Bayh's ads stressed that "it takes a good politician to be a good President." Bayh claimed that he had "written more of
the Constitution than any President since Madison," and that he was able
to accomplish passage of the Twenty-fifth and Twenty-sixth Amendments
to the Constitution because he was a good politician.[4] Even if people knew
what these amendments were, certain links between such claims and a
Bayh presidency were unclear. First, Bayh was claiming individual credit

for a collective project, the passing of amendments; and second, in asserting a link between such activities and the possibilities and benefits of a Bayh presidency, he was making a claim that was hard to assess.

Senator Jackson had been an ardent proponent of the war in Vietnam and an outspoken champion of unions and Israel. He was also an outspoken opponent of busing. He did well in Florida and New York among Jews, and he won the primary in Massachusetts, where court-ordered busing was a volatile issue, with a strong campaign featuring his total opposition to busing.

Senator Jackson's main hope was that the unions could deliver votes for him in Pennsylvania and other union states, and that these delegates would give him enough of a bloc to win at the convention. By 1976, however, the unions were also the object of more than a little opposition within the Democratic party. While Democrats by three to one believed that unions were important to protect workers from management, a plurality of Democrats believed that unions were too often opposed to changes that would increase productivity. Most important, 46 percent of all Democrats believed that unions were too involved in politics, while only 30 percent disagreed. Furthermore, even union members were hostile to union political involvement.[5]

Jimmy Carter's win in 1976 makes sense only in terms of the unpopularity of unions and the illegitimacy of the party establishment in the eyes of so many Democrats. The party elites were discredited and did not know how to communicate with their own voters. Governor Carter was an outsider, a man with no Washington experience or connections, but in the wake of Watergate that was an advantage. Further, Carter approached the problem of rejuvenating the government and the party in moral rather than programmatic terms, and that also was not entirely a disadvantage. In 1976 a significant portion of the electorate looked away from Washington and away from specific programs toward moral values as a solution to the malaise symbolized by Watergate. Without comparable data from other years, of course, we can only guess how much of this concern arose in direct response to the moral decay suggested by Watergate and how much came from disaffection with the party itself. However, it is clear that in 1976, Democrats, particularly less-educated blue-collar Democrats, looked to outsiders rather than insiders, and to restoration of moral values rather than programmatic responses, as the cure for their disaffection. And it is also clear that in 1976, college-educated and non-college-educated voters differed markedly in the way they responded to specific programs as opposed to general themes, such as restoring morality in government.

Many people, particularly those without college education, felt that a non-Washington president was now preferable. A CBS News/*New York Times* poll of April 1976 asked respondents the following question: "Do you agree or disagree: We should elect someone who has spent most of his political career outside Washington"?[6] Among respondents with a high school education or less, 45 percent agreed and 39 percent disagreed; among those with some college education, 34 percent agreed and 49 percent disagreed. According to the poll, the totals of all the respondents who agreed and disagreed "were thus the same—42 percent." This national response was similar to the mood expressed in New Hampshire. When Democrats there were asked in January 1976, "Do you think it would be better for the next president to have Washington experience or to be from outside Washington?" 40 percent said Washington experience and 35 percent said outside experience.[7]

A CBS News/*New York Times* poll in May 1976 asked, "If you had to choose between two candidates, which of the following would appeal more to you . . . one who proposes specific programs to deal with major national problems, or one who wants to restore moral values to our government?" Among respondents with a high school education or less, moral values were favored by a margin of 52 percent to 32 percent; among those with some college education, specific programs were favored by 50 percent to 41 percent. The total response thus favored moral values, 49 percent to 37 percent.[8]

Watergate

When Carter spoke about mismanagement and reorganization, he was speaking about activities generally believed to be within the purview of the president, and he was speaking directly to the common belief that Watergate was a mess that affected everyone in Washington, not just the president.

What was Watergate? Why did it occur? The answers given by voters depended on how well they understood the intricacies of government and how much faith they had in the underlying system of government. Watergate stood for more than a president who lied about a campaign "dirty trick" and was forced to resign. It stood for a long series of contentious confrontations between the president and legislators of both parties. This series of struggles left many Americans believing that government itself did not work, and that the connections between the president and government had been weakened. Thus an explanation for Watergate contains within it an implicit program for preventing future Watergates.

In the 1976 primary season, voters mindful of Watergate and President Nixon's resignation were particularly concerned with a president's personal honesty and whether a candidate had been part of the "Watergate mess." Furthermore, Watergate affected beliefs about what presidents could do about various issues, and the long struggle between President Nixon and Congress affected views of the presidency itself.

Honesty and Trust as Campaign Issues

All the candidates in 1976 believed, or said they believed, that honesty was the one issue underlying all others. Senator Birch Bayh, for example, promised voters that he would restore confidence and trust, and Morris Udall said, "Give the people some leaders they can trust—that's the unspoken issue of the year."[9]

In 1976, the first presidential election year after Watergate, voters in every primary, both Republicans and Democrats, indicated that they were more concerned with honesty than with leadership or positions on issues. In every CBS News/*New York Times* exit poll during the 1976 primary season, Republican and Democratic voters were asked, "Which of these qualities best describes why you voted for your candidate today?" The list of qualities included honesty, competence, leadership, and "his position on the issues." In every primary, for both parties, "he is honest and has integrity" was chosen as the most important quality more often than any other. Indeed, over all the exit polls in all the primaries throughout 1976, honesty was the most common reason given for voting for every candidate in every state except one: in Wisconsin, Udall voters, who were a highly educated group, placed honesty second to issue positions in their voting priorities.

Honesty was clearly a more salient concern in 1976 than in other presidential elections, and this was clearly a response to Watergate. In the 1976 New Hampshire exit polls, for example, 55 percent of all voters for the two parties selected honesty as *the* most important quality in their candidate. But in 1980, asked for the *two* most important qualities, only 34 percent named honesty as one of the two most important personal characteristics influencing their choice. In other words, voters were much more likely to mention honesty in 1976 than in 1980, although exact comparisons are difficult because some surveys asked for two choices and others for only one.[10]

Mismanagement, the Presidency, and Watergate

Carter emphasized the success of his administrative reorganization of government in Georgia and his desire to have less government secrecy.

While this was disparaged by many reporters, management of the federal government was a major concern in the wake of Watergate. Further, Carter was speaking about issues that a majority of voters assumed to be directly under the president's control.

As noted in chapter 4, the research of Shanto Iyengar and Donald Kinder has shown that news stories which explicitly connect the president with a government policy provide information that many voters use in evaluating presidents. Many people, for example, do not know that the president is involved with energy policy unless a television story explicitly mentions that fact. In other words, the range of presidential authority is affected by the news.

In this context, Watergate can be viewed as negative linkage, one that diminished beliefs about how much either the president or government itself can do. To use the analogy of government as an automobile and the president as a driver, Watergate suggested not only that Nixon was a reckless driver, but that the automobile had a failing transmission, which made it uncertain whether shifting gears would actually change its speed.

In 1975 and 1976, government mismanagement, a perennial theme in national politics, became a dominant concern. In November 1975, a Florida survey asked citizens how much blame for the country's economic problems (from "none" to "a lot") they would place on various domestic and international factors: excess spending by Congress, oil companies, mismanagement by the federal government, excess federal regulation of big business, big-business practices, or the Arab oil-producing countries (see table 7.1).

The two factors most often assigned "a lot" of the blame were federal mismanagement (66 percent) and excess spending by Congress (60 percent). These particular factors were further linked because so many people throughout the country believed that mismanagement was the real *source* of excess spending, and that better management could cut spending without reducing programs. Voters in this same Florida poll were asked, "Some people say that we should cut back on federal programs in order to reduce the size of the federal budget. Others say we could cut the budget if we just managed things better. Do you think we *really* could cut the budget much simply by better management?" In response, 79 percent said yes, 14 percent were not sure, and only 7 percent disagreed. This was not a transitory opinion; when the same question was repeated in February 1976 in Florida, the responses were the same. And when the question was asked in

TABLE 7.1

Response to: "How much blame—a lot, some, only a little, or none at all—do you feel each of the following deserves for our current economic problems?"

	A Lot (%)
The president	33
Excess spending by Congress	60
Oil companies	53
Mismanagement by federal government	66
Excess regulation of big business by federal government	40
Big business	49
Arab oil-producing countries	44

Source: Cambridge Survey Research poll #457, November 1975.

Note: This was a field survey in Florida of 800 registered Democrats who said they voted regularly in primaries.

Wisconsin in April 1976, 87 percent said that the federal budget could really be cut by better management.[11]

As these responses make clear, voters associated federal mismanagement with economic problems as well as with the size of the federal budget. Furthermore, and most important of all, voters in the 1975 Florida poll believed that mismanagement was a problem that presidents could do a lot about. When given a list of the problems that were most frequently mentioned on other surveys, and asked to rank them in the order in which they would like to see them solved, they did not rank federal mismanagement ahead of inflation, unemployment, or crime in the streets. But when asked how much the president could actually do about these problems, they ranked federal mismanagement as high as inflation (both at 26 percent) and ahead of unemployment (at 23 percent) (see table 7.2). Furthermore, voters do discriminate between problems they care about personally and problems they think a president can do the most about. As the same 1975 poll done for Carter showed, many more people cared about crime in the streets than about mismanagement, but many more believed that the president could do something about mismanagement and much less about crime in the streets.[12]

New Hampshire and Beyond: The Carter Coalition

While the candidates with Washington experience criticized Carter for having no program, he had something else: a response to Watergate and an

TABLE 7.2
Perceptions of Presidential Ability to Solve National Problems

	Problems Want Solved (First + Second Choice) (%)	President Has Most Control over (First + Second Choice) (%)
Mismanagement by federal government	14	26
Inflation	38	26
Unemployment	42	23
U.S. foreign policy	3	20
Maintaining strong national defense	7	18
High taxes	10	16
Energy crisis	18	15
Crime in the streets	23	10
Reducing government secrecy	2	9
Improving Social Security	10	8
Race relations	5	8
Controlling growth and development	2	6
Health care	9	5
Air and water pollution	7	3
The Mideast conflict	2	3
Drug abuse	6	2
Abortion	2	0
Pornography	0	0

Source: Cambridge Survey Research Poll #457, Florida, November 1975.

Note: The total number of respondents was 800, all of whom were likely Democratic primary voters. Survey members were given a card reading:

"Please look at this card. On it are a list of problems. Which problem would you most like to see solved? That is, if you could pick one problem what would it be? Which problem would be second?

"When you think about the president of the United States, which problem on the list do you think he can do most about? In other words which problem does he have the most control over? Which problem would be second?"

alternate image of public policy that was more acceptable to blue-collar and black Democrats.

There is a striking and unexpected pattern to the voting in the 1976 Democratic primaries. In New Hampshire, Carter defeated a field of union-supporting, program-oriented, Senate-insider "liberals" because he overwhelmed them among blue-collar and less-educated voters. The liberals—

who were supposedly fighting over the working-class vote left up for grabs by the absence of Hubert Humphrey and Edward Kennedy—divided the educated and white-collar voters. Among blue-collar voters, Carter received 44 percent of the vote; among white-collar voters he received 22 percent. Among voters who had at least some college education, Birch Bayh, Morris Udall, Fred Harris, and Sargent Shriver received together 72 percent of the vote and Jimmy Carter 18 percent. Among voters without any college education, Carter received 44 percent—exactly the same percentage as the four "liberals" combined![13] In the North, Carter was the candidate of less-educated and blue-collar voters; in the Florida primary, he was much more an upscale "New South" candidate. Only in the South did Carter run as well or better among educated and white-collar voters as among less-educated and blue-collar voters.

In New Hampshire, Carter did not have to battle Wallace for the working-class vote, for Wallace had chosen to make the Florida primary his first major contest. Of the Washington insiders, only Henry Jackson was willing to enter the Florida primary against Wallace and Carter. Jackson had taken a strongly anti-busing position, but the other Washington candidates, particularly Udall, were willing to let Carter try to beat Wallace, particularly since it would allow them to avoid clarifying their positions on race and busing.[14] In November 1975, a Carter poll showed Wallace at 38 percent among likely primary voters, Jackson at 18 percent, and Carter at 15 percent. After his win in Iowa and his initial campaigning in Florida, a second Carter poll showed Wallace with 30 percent, Carter with 26 percent, and Jackson with 14 percent.[15]

Carter's gains in Florida had come not from among Wallace supporters, but from among people to whom his record as a "New South" governor made him an alternative to Wallace, on one hand, or someone like Jackson, on the other. From November 1975 until just before the New Hampshire primary, Carter's biggest gains in Florida came among people who said that mismanagement was one of the problems a president could do most about. Before he started campaigning in Florida he had one-sixth of the vote among people who thought mismanagement and waste were something a president could do a lot about. After he began campaigning, his vote among this group doubled.

In Florida, Carter could not beat out Wallace among blue-collar whites, although he got 32 percent of their vote to Wallace's 38 percent in the CBS News/*New York Times* exit poll. He was able to beat Wallace because he won so much of the "New South" white-collar vote from Wallace and because he was able to win almost all of the black vote.

Carter and the Black Vote

Much of the bitterness toward Carter and resentment at his victories arose during the primaries because Carter did so well among both less-educated whites *and* blacks. The candidates who as legislators had supported busing had taken a lot of heat from white constituents for their policies to help blacks; how could they now lose the black vote to Carter as well? From Udall's point of view, this was a logical inconsistency that could arise only if Carter was misperceived by one of the two groups.[16] Udall's problem, however, was not that Carter was misperceived, but that whites who distrusted Washington required litmus tests of insiders that need not be required of a southern governor.

Carter was able to win the black vote because he had an effective network of black supporters like Andrew Young and Martin Luther King, Sr., whom he had come to know well as governor of Georgia. Blacks of this stature told black Democrats that one of Carter's first acts as governor of Georgia was to hang a picture of Martin Luther King, Jr., in the state capitol. This two-step media flow of information mediated by reliable elites provided effective cues to black communities throughout the country. Further, Carter was experienced at talking with blacks and could demonstrate that he was comfortable in their homes and churches; he could speak eloquently about his unsuccessful efforts to integrate his local Baptist church. Udall, in contrast, had no black leaders spreading the word about him and could not show any comfort among blacks. Indeed, of the original candidates, only one ever received as much as one-third of the black vote in any primary; in Sargent Shriver's home state, Illinois, where he was well known as a Kennedy in-law, Shriver won 38 percent of the black vote from Carter.

Carter could also attract blue-collar and less-educated voters because he had been a southern governor. As a southern governor, he did not draw a strong antiblack vote from whites (which always went to Wallace), but he was assumed to be moderate, so that voters did not need to be convinced that he had not gone too far, as they assumed people like Udall had. The perception of southern governors as moderates who had not "gone too far" on busing and other racial issues explains why Carter was able to reassure both whites and blacks and reassemble the coalition. This was something the insiders could not do and the most prominent Democrats did not even dare attempt. As scholars studying the general election between Carter and Ford also intuited, perceptions of Carter were strongly influenced by his being a southerner.[17]

The failure of the insider candidates to mobilize blue-collar voters continued throughout the primary campaigns. For that reason, the only times an insider won were when Henry Jackson mobilized a large Jewish vote and capitalized on anti-busing sentiment in Massachusetts and New York, and when Senator Frank Church won in Nebraska, a state he had worked long and hard. In the Ohio primary, Church and Udall both made well-financed, all-out attempts to derail Carter before the Democratic convention. But as the exit polls again made clear, voters were not attracted by their traditional approaches to government programs. More strikingly, Church and Udall between them managed to draw barely one-quarter of the vote among voters who had not been to college. As in New Hampshire, not one of the traditional Washington-based candidates was able to gather substantial support among less-educated Democrats.

After Carter had beaten Wallace in both Florida and Illinois, forcing Wallace out of the race, the major industrial unions mounted an all-out campaign against Carter. The critical test was in Pennsylvania, where the labor unions made a major effort among their members to win support for Henry Jackson. Their effort failed miserably. Among union households, Carter beat Jackson 36 percent to 24 percent—only slightly less than his margin among nonunion households, where he beat Jackson 39 percent to 23 percent.[18] Significantly, the only person who could make an effective challenge to Carter was another outsider, Governor Jerry Brown of California. Brown's success, however, can be explained only with reference to Carter's religion as well as his "southernness."

Religion and Primary Voting

When Carter began receiving national publicity, he was perceived as an outsider, a former governor, and a southerner. As he began to get more coverage, a good deal of attention was also given to his personal religious beliefs, to his description of himself as a born-again Christian for whom religion was an important part of daily life. Carter had done missionary work, and his sister, Ruth Carter Stapleton, was a well-known evangelist. As this information became part of Carter's image, voting patterns changed to reflect attitudes about Carter's religion and its influence on his approach to government. When Carter won early primaries in New Hampshire, Florida, and Illinois, he received an average of 40 percent of the Protestant vote and 38 percent of the Catholic vote. After his religious beliefs became better known, however, his support began to divide along religious lines. In the

New York, Pennsylvania, Michigan, Ohio, and California primaries, he averaged 47 percent of the Protestant vote and 35 percent of the Catholic vote.[19]

The results in the New York primary are particularly interesting because the size of the exit poll and the proportion of Jews in the population make it possible to look at the vote for Protestants, Catholics, and Jews. Carter received 51 percent of the Protestant vote, 36 percent of the Catholic vote, and 4 percent of the Jewish vote. Dividing each religious group into educational categories, the results are even more striking. Among Protestants, Carter received 57 percent of the less-educated vote and 40 percent of the college-educated vote; among Catholics, he received 40 percent of the less-educated vote and 30 percent of the college-educated vote; and among Jews, he received 6 percent of the less-educated vote and 2 percent of the college-educated vote.[20]

The success of the union attempt to stop Carter in favor of a more pro-union candidate depended on Carter's religious appeal. The union efforts were more successful with Catholic union members than they were with Protestant union members. When the unions began to mobilize in an all-out effort against Carter in Pennsylvania, the difference in vote between Protestants and Catholics was twice as large among union households as it was among nonunion households. Where there was less attraction to Carter on personal grounds, the counterappeals were more successful (see table 7.3).

TABLE 7.3
Religion, Union Membership, and Democratic Primary Vote
in Pennsylvania, 1976

	Union Households			Nonunion Households			
	Protestant (%)	Catholic (%)	All (%)	Protestant (%)	Catholic (%)	All (%)	All (%)
Jackson	17	27	24	14	20	23	25
Carter	42	32	36	48	44	39	37
Udall	15	18	17	22	13	21	19
Wallace	19	13	15	11	12	10	11
Other	7	10	8	5	11	7	8
Total	(227)	(374)	(698)	(194)	(285)	(642)	(1,507)

Source: CBS News/*New York Times* exit poll for Pennsylvania Democratic primary.
Note: The last column includes respondents who did not indicate whether they were from a union household.

In Michigan the United Auto Workers, the state's largest union, endorsed Carter, and the combined pull of religious attraction and union endorsement made the religious divide far bigger among union members than it had been in Pennsylvania. Among Michigan UAW members, Protestants voted 66 percent for Carter and 20 percent for Udall, while Catholics voted 48 percent for Carter and 45 percent for Udall.[21]

As more and more information about Carter came into use, concerns about secular and religious approaches to politics became more salient. At the end of the primary campaign, in the California and Ohio elections, religious cues were more important in evaluating Carter than they had been in the early contests. In both states, Protestants who attended church at least once a week gave Carter twice as high a proportion of their votes as Protestants who did not attend church weekly.

Among Protestants in Ohio and California, Carter was more highly regarded among the more religious, those who attended church services frequently. In contrast, among Catholics, Carter was more highly regarded among the less religious, those who did not attend services at least once a week. Carter wasn't simply a religious man; he was a religious *Protestant.* Therefore religious Protestants liked him *more* than less-religious Protestants, and religious Catholics liked him *less* than less-religious Catholics (see table 7.4).

The single most effective challenge to Carter came late in the campaign from Governor Jerry Brown of California. Brown could do what none of the insiders like Udall or Jackson could do because he was an outsider, a Californian, and a Catholic. Brown entered after it was clear that Udall, the only survivor from the original field, could not catch up with Carter. He immediately won in Maryland, Rhode Island, and Nevada, and had a highly successful write-in effort in Oregon. Then he won overwhelmingly in California, one of the least religious states.

In 1976, both parties were operating for the first time under new post-Watergate reform rules. Candidates were uncertain how to allocate their resources, which were limited by new federal election laws, and how to decide where to campaign actively. Further, Carter chose to contest every state. As the campaign progressed, this turned out to be a critical decision; by the time opposition to him began to coalesce, he had so many delegates that last-minute stop-Carter movements could not succeed. Had Brown entered sooner, however, he would have had a far better chance against Carter than any of the insider candidates.

TABLE 7.4

Church Attendance and the Democratic Vote in Ohio
and California, 1976

| | Church Attendance | | | | |
| | Weekly or More | | Monthly or Less | | |
	Protestant (%)	Catholic (%)	Protestant (%)	Catholic (%)	All (%)
	OHIO				
Carter	77	44	48	50	52
Udall	7	16	30	32	21
Church	13	21	9	13	14
Wallace	3	7	11	1	7
Other	1	10	2	4	6
Total *N*	(155)	(202)	(226)	(91)	(983)
	CALIFORNIA				
Carter	46	13	20	18	20
Brown	40	68	57	65	58
Other	14	19	23	17	22
Total *N*	(160)	(147)	(390)	(150)	(1,492)

Source: CBS News/*New York Times* exit polls for Ohio and California Democratic primaries, 1976.

Note: Numbers in parentheses are *N*s. The last column includes other religious affiliations.

Morality and Political Reasoning

Reactions to Carter depended on whether voters preferred programmatic or moral responses to government in addition to their religion and their level of church attendance. This demonstrates that attitudes toward him reflected implicit moral reasoning, not simply attitudes about religion. Religious Protestants liked Carter because he was a religious Protestant, and religious Catholics disliked him for the same reason. In each of the four groups—religious and less-religious Protestants, and religious and less-religious Catholics—those who wanted candidates to propose specific programs were less positive about Carter than those who wanted candidates to concentrate on restoring morality to government. Thus people's views of themselves and their religion, and their beliefs about how the world works, combined to affect their responses to Carter.[22] Attitudes toward him reflected not only responses to his religion but responses to his moral approach to government as well (see table 7.5).

When a party's nominee for the most important office in the country turns out to be a political outsider, it will be asked whether the selection process has contributed to the demise of the party. The answer is no. Jimmy Carter's victory over candidates who had been more involved with the party's

TABLE 7.5

Religion, Church Attendance, Programs versus Morality as Preferred Approach to Government, and Ratings of Jimmy Carter among White Democrats

	Church Attendance						
	Weekly or More			Monthly or Less			
Ratings of Carter	Programs (%)	Morality (%)	All (%)	Programs (%)	Morality (%)	All (%)	All (%)
	PROTESTANTS						
Favorable	29	58	49	41	37	40	45
Unfavorable	32	26	26	32	20	26	26
Undecided	22	4	10	13	10	10	10
Don't know	16	12	14	14	33	24	18
Total N	(32)	(81)	(139)	(42)	(48)	(108)	(247)
	CATHOLICS						
Favorable	39	38	41	45	59	51	46
Unfavorable	49	31	35	28	27	27	31
Undecided	10	13	12	5	7	6	9
Don't know	2	18	12	22	7	16	15
Total N	(26)	(54)	(98)	(43)	(49)	(98)	(196)

Source: CBS News/*New York Times* poll, May 1976.
Note: I have included only white Catholics and Protestants so that the Catholic/Protestant comparisons are not tilted by the strong positive support for Carter among blacks. Respondents were asked the following questions:
"If you had to choose between two candidates, which of the following would appeal more to you . . . one who proposes specific programs to deal with major national problems, or one who wants to restore moral values to our government?"
"Do you have a favorable or unfavorable opinion about Jimmy Carter or don't you know enough about him to have an opinion?"
"How often do you attend religious services? More than once a week, once a week, once a month, a few times a year, almost never, or never?"
The "All" columns include people who answered "don't know."

legislative program did not send the Democratic party into decline. Rather, it was an out-of-touch, comatose national leadership that made the election of a total outsider possible. The 1976 primary was played out against the backdrop of both Watergate and a discredited national elite which could not defend its programs to members of its own party. It foreshadowed the fights of 1984 between Walter Mondale, Gary Hart, and Jesse Jackson about how to reassemble a traditional Democratic coalition of blacks, workers, and white-collar voters.

Carter did not beat Udall in 1976 because "the momentum" from a few early wins rigged the game in his favor; Jerry Brown managed to win four primaries against Carter at the end of the campaign. Nor did he beat Udall and his other challengers because the "liberal" votes were divided between Udall and several other candidates, including at various times during the campaign Sargent Shriver, Senator Fred Harris of Oklahoma, Senator Birch Bayh of Indiana, Senator Frank Church of Idaho, and Governor Milton Shapp of Pennsylvania.

Nor did Carter win the nomination in 1976 because he was the only candidate to talk about honesty. He won because he fashioned a campaign and a message that connected voters' concerns to a credible program for the presidency. He did not convince people that he was more honest than the other candidates; he convinced them that he could do more about dishonesty. And he could convince people who knew next to nothing about his record as governor of Georgia because his personal qualities made his policies and programs credible. Carter is a textbook example of the ways in which voters can use personal information about a candidate to assess his past performance and then extrapolate to his future performance.

Arguments that Carter won because of momentum fail to account for Carter's appeal as an outsider, as a southern governor, and as a man with a moral approach to restoring confidence after Watergate. Further, the momentum theory cannot explain how Jerry Brown could win four primaries after a string of Carter victories. Brown could do so well because the better Carter became known, the clearer his religiousness became.

During the 1976 Democratic primary season, an initial concern with honesty was transformed into a contest between moral and pragmatic responses to government, and about the relation of personal morality to political performance. The better-known Carter became, the more easily a nonsouthern outsider could appeal to Catholics and less-religious Protestants. Indeed, one of Brown's campaign strategists later said that Brown's method for deciding where to challenge Carter was elegantly simple: "pick the states with the most Catholics."[23]

E I G H T

The Republican Primaries of 1980: George Bush, Ronald Reagan, and the Legacy of '76

THE REPUBLICAN PRIMARIES of 1980 were a battle about whether the party needed to change its approach to domestic programs and adapt to changing constituencies inside and outside the party. The results of these primaries demonstrate how the front-runner's relation to past political splits within the party can open fault lines between constituencies. Besides illustrating how sensitive people are to changes in the direction of their party, the 1980 primaries show how the activation of one constituency activates another one that opposes it. A "we" requires a "they."

After his near victory over President Gerald Ford in the 1976 Republican primaries, Ronald Reagan was the acknowledged front-runner for the nomination in 1980. Reagan had a strong political identity going back to 1964, when he made his national transition from actor to politician with an ardent, well-received speech championing Senator Barry Goldwater, the 1964 Republican presidential candidate. During that campaign, when many moderate Republicans—like the governors of Pennsylvania and New York, William Scranton and Nelson Rockefeller—attacked Goldwater for his aggressive defense posture and his attacks on government programs to advance civil rights and regulate business, Reagan ardently promoted Goldwater and his views. In the ensuing years, Reagan had built a following throughout the country, particularly among Republicans disgruntled with their party's accommodations to the New Deal and its less confrontational approaches to the Soviet Union and China.

In 1980 Reagan was the focal point; Republicans divided into pro- and anti-Reagan camps, and the other candidates compared themselves to him. The mobilization of anti-Reagan party members was a two-stage process. In the first stage, when the Republican rank and file knew little about any of the candidates except Reagan, George Bush was able to mobilize the national anti-Reagan constituency behind himself; his victory in Iowa made him the preferred alternative to Reagan among voters who began the

primary season opposed to Reagan or ambivalent about him, and also
made him the candidate with the best chance of beating Reagan. In the
second stage, beginning during the New Hampshire primary, which Bush
lost to Reagan, new campaign information—concerning both issues and
personal characteristics—led many initially anti-Reagan Republicans to
decide that they were now closer to Reagan than to Bush.

Ronald Reagan's Meager Surge

In 1980, from an initial field of seven declared candidates, only two—
Reagan and Bush—won any Republican primaries. (The others were John
Anderson, Howard Baker, Robert Dole, John Connally, and Philip Crane.)
After winning in Iowa, Bush jumped ahead of Baker, Dole, Connally, and
Crane, and was within striking distance of Reagan in the New Hampshire
polls. After Reagan pulled away from Bush, winning New Hampshire with
50 percent of the vote compared to Bush's 23 percent, no declared candi-
date ever came close to him in the national preference polls (see table 8.1).
But despite his showing in New Hampshire, and despite his subsequent
victories, Reagan gained only 8 points in the March CBS News/*New York
Times* preference poll. This put him exactly where he had been before the
Iowa primary. Indeed, this was only 6 percentage points ahead of where he
had stood in 1979 before the primaries began.

TABLE 8.1
National Preferences for Candidates by Month,
1980 Republican Primary

	Nov. '79 (%)	Jan. (%)	Feb. (%)	March (%)	April (%)
Anderson	1	2	2	7	10
Baker	13	11	13		
Bush	3	6	24	11	12
Connally	15	11	6		
Crane	3	1	2		
Dole	3	4	2		
Reagan	37	43	35	43	58
Ford[a]	2	1	2	26	6
Other/ don't know	23	21	14	13	14

Source: CBS News/*New York Times* polls.
[a]These are volunteered responses; Gerald Ford was not a declared candidate and his
name was not given to respondents.

On the face of it, Reagan's gains from New Hampshire and his subsequent victories look minimal indeed. By the time of the March poll, Reagan had dispatched every serious rival. He had gone on from his New Hampshire victory, where he was one of the few candidates *ever* to receive 50 percent of the vote, to overwhelming victories in Florida, Alabama, and Georgia. Baker, Dole, Connally, and Crane had withdrawn, and Bush's popularity had plummeted. Nevertheless, Reagan had no more support among Republicans at the midpoint of the primary season—with all his rivals vanquished—than he had at the beginning, when there was a whole field of plausible rivals.

Clearly there was more at work here than voter expectations about who would win the nomination horse race. Why did a candidate who greatly increased his prospects of winning the nomination get very few new votes in the process? The answer is that Reagan's string of victories not only consolidated a party constituency that supported him but also mobilized other constituencies that opposed him.

After Bush's loss in New Hampshire and Reagan's victories in Florida, Alabama, and Georgia made Reagan a near-certainty for the nomination, the big gains in the March CBS News/*New York Times* poll were registered by an undeclared candidate: 26 percent of Republicans, when asked whether they preferred Reagan, Bush, or John Anderson for their party's 1980 nomination, *volunteered* the name of Gerald Ford! (see table 8.1).

There is no way in which this result can be explained away as an artifact of the questionnaire—a result prompted by the wording of the preference question or the content of previous questions. Before the preference question, respondents were asked to rate the declared candidates in both primaries: "I'm going to name some possible Presidential candidates and ask what you think of them. If you haven't heard much about someone I name, just tell me. Do you have a favorable or not favorable opinion about . . . , or don't you know enough about him to have an opinion?" The list of candidates that respondents were then asked to rate did not even include Ford; the six names on the list were Ronald Reagan, Jerry Brown, Edward Kennedy, George Bush, John Anderson, and Jimmy Carter.

While the above-mentioned poll did not include Ford's name, his name had been in the news. In the week after the New Hampshire primary, Ford said that he would respond should there be a "broad-based" draft asking him to run, because he did not think Reagan could beat President Carter. Clearly, Republicans were aware of this statement.[1] In the wake of Bush's collapse, Ford became the coordination point for Republicans seeking an alternative to Reagan. This groundswell of support for an undeclared candidate emphasizes the depth of splits within the Republican party. Indeed, later in the same CBS News/*New York Times* poll, when Republicans were asked how they would vote if former president Ford was also a candidate, he led Reagan 45 percent to 21 percent!

Reagan was a near certainty for his party's nomination, yet this did not translate into any surge in the polls. Reagan's failure to gain from the collapse of expectations for Bush, the withdrawal of Baker, Connally, and Dole, and the meager improvement in Reagan's ratings that followed from the much-increased prospects for his nomination—all these emphasize again that when it comes to voting, expectations are a catalyst, not a causal agent. The Reagan "juggernaut" and the Bush collapse did not lead—either because of increased expectations or because of the decline in alternatives—to a surge or bandwagon for Reagan.

When voters began thinking about Reagan, it created a surge by one group to Reagan, a surge by another group to Bush. Indeed, when Bush edged Reagan in Iowa, he jumped from 6 percent to 24 percent in the CBS News/*New York Times* national poll. This was the largest gain that any candidate in any party has yet received from a victory in Iowa. After the Bush "bubble" popped and he dropped from 24 percent to 11 percent in the national polls, thinking about Reagan triggered a surge for Ford. This emphasizes, as I noted in chapter 6, that the mobilization of one constituency prompts the awareness of those opposed to the constituency, which in turn facilitates the formation of counterconstituencies.

In 1980, Reagan was the focal point of the campaign, and Bush's rapid ascent after he won in Iowa was the result of strategic voting among anti-Reagan Republicans. Antipathy to Reagan was antipathy not to his personal characteristics but to his policies and the direction in which he would steer the Republican party. Furthermore, a vote for Bush was not merely a "blind" vote for "anybody but Reagan." First, other viable candidates were assessed and rejected before Bush came to the fore. Second, as the campaign progressed and people learned more about Bush, some of them moved to Reagan.

The Ford-Reagan Split

Why did Reagan gain so little from his overwhelming victory in New Hampshire? Why did 26 percent of Republicans look to Ford when asked to choose between Bush, Anderson, and Reagan? The answer to both questions is that deep party splits created by the 1976 primary had not yet healed, despite four years of Jimmy Carter. The 1976 split, furthermore, was a policy split, not merely a disagreement over the personal leadership abilities of the two men. Republicans understood that a move to Reagan was a move with important consequences for the party and the country.

In the 1979 polls, the best predictor of 1980 primary preference among Republicans was which candidate they had preferred in the 1976 primary season, Reagan or Ford. In November 1979, before the primaries, two-thirds of the Republicans who had supported Reagan in 1976 supported him again; and no other candidate received as much as 10 percent of their support. In contrast, Republicans who had supported Ford gave only one-quarter of their support to Reagan, putting him just ahead of Connally and Baker, who had the support of 20 percent and 19 percent, respectively, of former Ford supporters.

In March, after Bush had been beaten two to one in New Hampshire, and Dole, Connally, and Crane had withdrawn, still only one-third of Ford's 1976 supporters were willing to support Reagan, despite the fact that his nomination was a virtual certainty. Instead, they turned to the un-declared Ford. When there were no challengers in the race with a chance to beat Reagan, they voluntarily named Ford as their preferred candidate (see table 8.2).

In the 1979 poll, 61 percent of Republicans said they had supported Ford, and 30 percent said Reagan; in the March 1980 poll, 69 percent said Ford and 24 percent said Reagan. The actual figures at the end of the primary campaign in the June 1976 CBS News/*New York Times* poll were 52 percent for Ford and 33 percent for Reagan. That more Republicans re-member supporting Ford in that primary than actually did so is not surprising, since there was an ensuing campaign against Carter in which many Republicans who had not supported Ford against Reagan committed to Ford. What is surprising is that Reagan's near certain nomination in 1980 did not prompt revised memories of 1976. People had strong reac-tions to Reagan which were not easily changed.

Strong reactions to Reagan were also apparent in his favorability ratings. Ford Republicans did not begin to think of Reagan more positively as his nomination became inevitable. The publicity that Reagan got from his pri-mary victories in New Hampshire increased the proportion of 1976 Ford voters who rated him favorably by only 4 percentage points, from 46 per-cent to 50 percent (see table 8.3).

The Ford-Reagan primary fight in 1976 left many Ford Republicans be-lieving that they were closer to Carter than to the Reagan wing of the Republican party. At the end of the primaries in June 1976, Ford and Rea-gan voters were asked how they would vote between Ford and Carter and between Reagan and Carter. Fewer than half of the Republicans who sup-

TABLE 8.2

1980 Republican Primary Preferences by 1976 Primary Preference

	November 1979			March 1980		
	1976 Primary Choice			1976 Primary Choice		
	Ford (%)	Reagan (%)	All (%)	Ford (%)	Reagan (%)	All (%)
Anderson	2	0	1	9	2	7
Baker	17	6	13			
Bush	4	3	3	10	9	11
Connally	20	9	15			
Crane	1	6	3			
Dole	3	2	3			
Reagan	26	65	37	33	78	43
Ford[a]	2	2	2	35	4	26
Other	9	3	8			
Don't know/ no answer	17	4	16	13	7	13
Total N	(280)	(138)	(459)	(253)	(88)	(367)

Source: CBS News/*New York Times* polls for November 1979 and March 1980.

Note: No other polls during this campaign asked Republicans who they supported in 1976. The 1979 poll did not include registration, whereas the 1980 poll is reported for registered Republicans only.

The "All" columns also include Republicans with a preference other than Ford or Reagan.

[a]Volunteered responses.

TABLE 8.3

1976 Republican Choice and 1980 Rating of Ronald Reagan among Republicans

	November 1979			March 1980		
	1976 Primary Choice			1976 Primary Choice		
	Ford (%)	Reagan (%)	All (%)	Ford (%)	Reagan (%)	All (%)
Favorable	46	77	54	50	90	59
Unfavorable	35	13	28	26	7	21
Undecided/ don't know	19	10	18	24	3	20

Source: CBS News/*New York Times* polls, November 1979 and March 1980.

ported Ford or Reagan were willing to support the other candidate in an election against Carter. When Ford's Republican supporters were asked to choose between Carter and Reagan for president, 33 percent chose Carter, 41 percent chose Reagan, and 26 percent were undecided; when Reagan's Republican supporters were asked to choose between Carter and Ford, 31 percent chose Carter, 49 percent chose Ford, and 20 percent were undecided.[2] In November, a majority of Reagan's supporters finally did vote for Ford, but the reluctance among the supporters of each to support the other candidate against Carter emphasizes just how divisive the primary battles were.

Ford vs. Reagan: Issue Differences

The Reagan-Ford split reflected issue divisions within the party. Republicans, whether for or against him, believed that Reagan would change party policies. In particular, Reagan was considered willing to reverse the moderating trends of the party under Richard Nixon and return to earlier, more orthodox Republican positions, such as less concern with protecting the environment or regulating business, more interest in the aggressive use of military force, and desire for a federal government less supportive of the rights of women and minorities. On standard Republican issues like the size of government, balanced budgets, military spending, Social Security, or whether to place the highest priority on fighting inflation or fighting unemployment, the differences between Ford and Reagan Republicans were smaller than on the new issues of the 1960s and 1970s. The biggest disagreements over government policies concerned the use of military force in foreign policy and the use of federal government programs and laws to improve the status of minorities and women in society.

The simplest way to assess the relative importance of a particular issue to Republican voters choosing between Ford and Reagan is to look at the difference in net support for the two candidates between those who agree and those who disagree with a particular policy. For example, in June 1976, Republicans who wanted a smaller, less costly government offering fewer services preferred Ford over Reagan by 54 percent to 36 percent, a difference of 18 percent. Republicans who preferred a bigger, more costly government offering more services preferred Ford by 51 percent to 33 percent—again, a difference of 18 percent. Thus between the two sides on this issue, there was a net difference of 0 percent in support for Ford. In the same survey, Republicans who thought most welfare programs should be eliminated preferred Ford by 44 percent to 41 percent, and Republicans who did *not* think most welfare programs should be eliminated preferred

Ford by 62 percent to 23 percent—a net difference of 36 percent in presidential preferences between pro-welfare and anti-welfare Republicans.

Throughout 1976, the biggest differences between Ford and Reagan Republicans were whether or not to eliminate welfare; to do less for minorities; to relax federal antipollution controls; to strengthen Social Security; and to keep the Panama Canal. Reagan Republicans were less supportive of welfare, aid to minorities and women, environmental controls, and strengthening Social Security. The only area in which they were in favor of more government action was in foreign policy; they were more likely to want to keep the Panama Canal, and more likely, as shown on later surveys discussed below, to be willing to use force to protect or enhance American interests around the world. There were other smaller differences in support for Reagan and Ford on questions about military spending, balancing the budget, whether to attack unemployment or inflation, and whether to seek a smaller or a larger government. Ford and Reagan Republicans agreed on emphasizing inflation over unemployment, increasing the size of the military budget, and having a smaller government providing fewer services overall. The disagreements were about the use of force in foreign policy, advancing the status of women and minorities, protecting the environment, and strengthening Social Security (see table 8.4).

With Ford out of the race for the 1980 nomination, the divisions between Reagan Republicans and the rest of the party persisted. On standard, long-standing Republican issues, such as the size of government, defense spending, and balancing the budget, there were small differences in support for Reagan between people on opposite sides of the issues. The larger differences in support for Reagan in 1980 were on approximately the same issues as in 1976: the use of military force to protect oil fields, government treatment of minorities, and the social role of women. Reagan Republicans, in fact, might be described as Republicans who opposed the policy adaptations of the Nixon years. They were supportive of strong defense, the use of force abroad, a balanced budget, and small government. They were far less likely than other Republicans to support the policy changes of the Nixon era, which included arms control, the Environmental Protection Agency, and moderate programs to advance women and minorities (see table 8.5).

Despite the depth of their reservations about Reagan and his positions, the Republicans who sought an alternative to him did not simply follow the challenger who gained a lead in the early polls. Connally and Baker were both well funded and had early strong support, yet their support evaporated as people spent more time getting to know them in the Iowa

TABLE 8.4
Policy Choice and Reagan versus Ford in 1976

		Agree (%)	Disagree (%)
Most welfare programs should be eliminated.	Reagan	36	22
	Ford	59	72
	Neither/don't know	5	6
	Total %	43	42
In general, the government has paid too much attention to the problems of blacks and other minorities.	Reagan	36	21
	Ford	62	70
	Neither/don't know	2	9
	Total %	48	48
Laws against polluting the environment should be relaxed to help solve the energy crisis.	Reagan	33	22
	Ford	62	72
	Neither/don't know	5	6
	Total %	53	37
The Social Security system should be strengthened even if it means raising taxes.	Reagan	24	36
	Ford	67	61
	Neither/don't know	9	3
	Total %	52	37
Government spending for military defense should be reduced.	Reagan	30	28
	Ford	64	68
	Neither/don't know	6	4
	Total %	27	50
Our government should return control of the Panama Canal to the government of Panama.	Reagan	31	36
	Ford	59	50
	Neither/don't know	10	14
	Total %	18	59
The government should pay more attention to unemployment rather than inflation.	Reagan	31	38
	Ford	52	51
	Neither/don't know	18	11
	Total %	31	56
A smaller government providing less services is preferable to a larger government providing more services.	Reagan	36	33
	Ford	54	51
	Neither/don't know	10	16
	Total %	58	29

Source: The first five issues are from a CBS News/*New York Times* poll for March 1976 which included 659 Republicans. The other three issues are from a CBS News/*New York Times* poll for June 1976, including 505 Republicans.

TABLE 8.5

Attitudes about Government and Presidential Preference
among Republicans, March 1980

	GOVERNMENT ATTENTION TO MINORITIES		
	Too Much (%)	Right Amount (%)	Not Enough (%)
Reagan	54	42	32
Bush	13	8	19
Ford[a]	19	33	27
Others	14	17	22

	GOVERNMENT SERVICES	
	More Services (%)	Less Services (%)
Reagan	44	46
Bush	11	12
Ford[a]	26	26
Others/ don't know	19	16

Source: CBS News/*New York Times* poll, March 1980.
Note: The specific questions asked were:
"Do you think the government in Washington is paying too much,
not enough, or about the right amount of attention to blacks and other
minorities?"
"In general, government grows bigger as it provides more services. If
you had to choose, would you rather have a smaller government
providing fewer services, or a bigger government providing more
services?"
[a]This is respondents who volunteered Ford. Divisions for the question
listing Ford as a candidate are larger.

and New Hampshire campaigns. This result is what opened the way for
Bush to challenge Reagan head-to-head in New Hampshire.

The New Hampshire Primary

Bush's Iowa win at the beginning of the 1980 primary season put him on
the covers of most news magazines and established him as the most prominent alternative to Reagan. Although Reagan had a large following in New
Hampshire, where he had almost beaten President Ford in the 1976 primaries, it was possible that Bush could win in New Hampshire, or at least
finish a close second and force Reagan into a long-drawn-out campaign.

Bush's support came from Republicans who had opposed Reagan in 1976, and, in New Hampshire, Ford Republicans were even more negative about Reagan than Ford Republicans nationally.[3]

Bush's strategy in New Hampshire was to mobilize anti-Reagan Republicans, both those who opposed him on the issues and those who opposed him because they didn't think Reagan could win the presidency. Just after Bush won Iowa, one of his strategists described their search for issues to emphasize in the battle against Reagan: "You look for issues that overlap different wings of the Party, or issues that make conservatives happy but don't bother moderates, such as some civil-liberties issues—but no social ones—or Taiwan; and you try to find some moderate issues that don't alienate conservatives, such as conservation."[4] In other words, in assembling a coalition within the party, candidates try to take advantage of the differential salience of issues to different groups by finding issues that are important to one group but relatively unimportant, or unknown, to the others. The policy issue with which Bush chose to differentiate himself from Reagan and attract former Ford supporters was the Equal Rights Amendment to the Constitution; whereas Reagan had opposed it, Bush supported it unequivocally.

The Notorious Microphone Incident

During the New Hampshire primary, however, an incident completely unrelated to any policy issue turned the tide against Bush. The way in which this incident changed the coalition supporting Bush demonstrates that the use of new information is not automatic, and that much information comes into use by voters only when they are prompted to reassess the candidates and reconsider their choices.

After the Iowa primary, the *Nashua Telegraph* scheduled a two-way debate between Bush and Reagan for the weekend before the New Hampshire primary. However, the Federal Election Commission ruled that if the newspaper financed the debate it would constitute a campaign contribution. Because Reagan was far behind Bush in the polls, the Reagan campaign directors agreed to pay the entire cost of the debate. Reagan's strategists reasoned that he was most effective one-on-one and needed the opportunity to cut into Bush's strength.

After agreeing to a two-person debate, the Reagan campaign later decided it would get more benefit from a debate with all the candidates. In the period after agreeing to the two-person debate, Reagan's aggressive campaign began to activate his New Hampshire supporters and regain their support. Further, all the other candidates began attacking Bush; they believed they would be out of the race if they did not displace Bush as the alternative to Reagan. With Reagan doing well in the polls and the other candidates all attacking Bush, the Reagan campaign decided to ambush Bush. They *secretly* invited the other candidates to take part in the debate, to dilute Bush's exposure and reduce any chance that Bush could decisively outshine Reagan.

What occurred next was television at its best—or its worst. The night of the scheduled debate, when Bush realized that he was about to be denied his chance to go head-to-head with Reagan, he refused to debate with all the other candidates. Instead he sat on the stage, silently, while the *Nashua Telegraph* editor and moderator tried to get the originally uninvited candidates—Baker, Dole, Anderson, Connally, and Crane—to leave.[5] When Reagan began to defend the right of the others to be present, the moderator instructed technicians to turn off his microphone. Before they could do so, Reagan grabbed his microphone and said, "I paid for this microphone, Mr. Green," at which the audience burst into applause. The next day the *Manchester Union Leader,* the largest paper in the state, wrote that Bush had looked like "a small boy who had been dropped off at the wrong birthday party."[6]

When Reagan delivered his famous line, he got the moderator's name wrong (it was Breen, not Green), and when he presented himself as a defender of fair play, he was really acting selfishly to dilute any impact of the debate on his own candidacy. He wanted to involve the other candidates because their main target was Bush, not because leaving them out was unfair. In addition, he was double-crossing Bush, breaking a gentleman's agreement and trapping him in a setup. Nevertheless, the negative effect on Bush was dramatic. And finally, when Reagan said "I paid for this microphone," he was using a line from an old Spencer Tracy movie, *State of the Union.* In that movie, when the "bosses" attempted to shut up Tracy and keep his messages from getting to the people, Tracy grabbed the mike and said, defiantly, "I paid for this microphone."[7]

The microphone incident occurred on the Saturday night before the Tuesday primary; the day after the election, 85 percent of the Republican electorate had heard of the event. Furthermore, Reagan had clearly struck a chord. When the same CBS News/*New York Times* survey after the election asked New Hampshire Republicans who was to blame for the incident, only 20 percent of Republican voters said that Bush was at fault. What mattered to them, for better or worse, was not who was to blame but how Bush handled the situation.

News of this confrontation had a sudden negative impact on Bush's campaign. Before the incident, the CBS News/*New York Times* New

Hampshire survey had completed 82 percent of its 456 interviews with registered Republicans or likely Republican primary voters, and in these interviews Reagan led Bush by 37 percent to 27 percent. In the interviews taken the day after the incident, Reagan led Bush by 50 percent to 16 percent. On Tuesday, Reagan won the election with 50 percent of the vote; Bush received 23 percent. In interviews taken before the incident, Bush's favorable-unfavorable rating was 51 percent to 22 percent; the day after the incident it was 47 percent to 35 percent; and the day after the election, it was 32 percent positive and 48 percent negative. Among voters who had supported Ford in 1976, Bush led Reagan 35 percent to 21 percent before the incident; by Tuesday that had changed to 32 percent for Bush and 37 percent for Reagan.

In short, Bush appears to have lost more votes and more popularity in two days of media barrage than in the preceding three weeks, when all the other candidates had tried to knock him off to keep their own campaigns alive. Many people, apparently, did not reassess him until after the nondebate. Were they responding only to their prejudices about personal character—notions about how to stand tall at the O.K. Corral or face down a challenge in the old saloon—or were they also thinking about *political* character?

We can begin to answer this question most effectively by looking at the polls. Because the CBS News/*New York Times* New Hampshire preelection poll respondents were called back after the election to see whether they had voted, we can compare the turnout rates of people who had supported either Bush or Reagan before the microphone incident. Of those intending to vote for Bush before that event, only 54 percent actually voted; of those intending to vote for Reagan at that time, 68 percent actually went to the polls. Among all respondents who had supported Ford in 1976, the actual turnout rate was 59 percent; among those who had supported Reagan in 1976, the turnout rate was 74 percent.

The interaction of issues and candidate personality in this case becomes clear when we divide former Ford voters by issue position. Before the microphone incident, the 1976 Ford supporters who favored the ERA, which both contenders had discussed in 1980, preferred Bush to Reagan by 39 percent to 10 percent; their voting figures at the exit poll were 39 percent to 23 percent. The 1976 Ford supporters who opposed the ERA preferred Bush over Reagan by 40 percent to 38 percent before the microphone incident. Afterward, according to the exit poll, their preference changed dramatically: they voted 23 percent for Bush and 56 percent for Reagan (see Table 8.6).

TABLE 8.6
The Microphone Incident, the ERA, and the 1980 Vote
in New Hampshire among 1976 Supporters
of Gerald Ford

	Before Incident		Actual Vote	
	Pro-ERA (%)	Anti-ERA (%)	Pro-ERA (%)	Anti-ERA (%)
Bush	39	38	39	23
Reagan	10	38	23	56
Other/ don't know	51	22	38	21
Total N	(131)	(57)	(222)	(182)

Source: CBS News/*New York Times* 1980 New Hampshire telephone survey for "Before Incident" and CBS News/*New York Times* New Hampshire exit poll for "Actual Vote."
    Note: I am including only the respondents in the telephone poll who were interviewed before the incident. I am using the exit poll instead of the sample called back for reliability, although the findings hold for the voters located in the callback.

As Bush's personal ratings dropped, turnout among former Ford supporters dropped, and there was a move away from Bush and toward Reagan and the other candidates. The extent of movement away from Bush, however, depended on issues as well as on assessments of Bush personally. From just before the microphone incident until the election, the net movement to Reagan among 1976 Ford supporters was twice as big among those who opposed the ERA as it was among those who supported it. In the same period, Bush lost no (net) votes among pro-ERA Ford voters, and Reagan gained 13 percent from other candidates; among anti-ERA Ford voters, however, Bush dropped from 40 percent to 23 percent, and Reagan went from 38 percent to 56 percent. Ford voters were also more likely to move to Reagan if they supported the use of force to protect oil fields. In contrast, on balancing the budget by law there were minimal differences between Ford Republicans who stayed with Bush and Ford Republicans who moved to Reagan (see table 8.7).

We must conclude, then, that the long New Hampshire campaign did bring more issue information about Bush into play after people began to make fuller comparisons of Reagan and Bush. Bush's bubble burst, furthermore, when negative information about his campaign behavior— information inconsistent with his positive image after Iowa—caused

TABLE 8.7

Policy Differences between Bush and Reagan Voters in
the 1980 New Hampshire Republican Primary Exit Poll

	Ford Voters in the 1976 Primary		All 1980 Republican Primary Voters	
	Favor (%)	Oppose (%)	Favor (%)	Oppose (%)
Use U.S. troops to protect Middle East oil supplies if they are threatened				
Reagan	43	32	59	37
Bush	28	34	20	26
Others	29	34	21	37
Total %	50	34	49	32
Balanced budget should be required by law				
Reagan	39	36	50	51
Bush	31	33	24	23
Others	30	31	26	26
Total %	48	35	47	34
Equal Rights Amendment				
Reagan	23	56	31	69
Bush	39	23	31	15
Others	38	21	38	16
Total %	49	40	43	42
Party should modify principles to attract more voters				
Reagan	49	20	62	30
Bush	28	37	20	31
Others	23	43	18	39
Total %	57	37	57	31

Source: CBS News/*New York Times* 1980 New Hampshire Republican primary exit poll.

voters to reassess whether they were, in fact, closer to Bush than to Reagan on the issues that mattered to them.

The 1980 Republican primaries demonstrate the roles of both substantive issues and personal assessments in primary voting. The issues that were salient in the 1976 split between Reagan and Ford were just as central in 1980 in producing support for Reagan. The division over issues was not merely a reflection of regional differences in public opinion, or of the greater popularity of Reagan in the South and West and of Ford in the Midwest and East. The same debates that divided Ford and Reagan Republicans nationally—over the use of force, the ERA, and the general direction of the party—divided them in New Hampshire as well. These conflicts also demonstrate that party identification has real political content, and that political partisans are sensitive to changes in the overall direction of their parties. The fights between Bush and Reagan, and between Reagan and Ford, concerned issues, not just personalities. Support for Bush reflected a reasoned search for a "Ford-like" Republican alternative to Reagan, not an undiscriminating willingness to accept "anybody but Reagan." Voters who chose Bush over Reagan were not blindly assuming that their enemy's enemy was their friend, without any information about Bush. They knew that Bush's positions in 1980 were closer to Ford's than were Reagan's.

The fights between Ford and Reagan in 1976, the concerns about how to react to the programmatic changes of the party under Nixon, and the debates of 1979 and 1980 were implicitly and explicitly concerned with whether the party should be a Republican party as defined by Reagan, or a party more attuned to newer issues like protecting the environment and the rights of women and minorities. For example, the Republican party had actively supported the ERA for years, but Reagan explicitly opposed it. John Anderson raised these questions explicitly throughout the 1980 campaign, and they were clearly salient to voters in New Hampshire, as table 8.7 shows. Voters who wanted a party that did not modify its approaches in order to seek more members supported Reagan over Bush by three to one; those who wanted a more moderate party and a broader base split evenly between the two.

Anderson received very favorable network coverage during the campaign as the Republican with the most ardent and innovative calls to his party. Early in the Iowa primary, in fact, he had been the candidate who most impressed voters during a widely covered debate.[8] Yet Anderson never benefited from Bush's failure or Ford's decision not to enter the campaign when Bush faltered. This emphasizes, I believe, that voters could discriminate between Bush and Anderson as well as they could discriminate among Ford, Bush, and Reagan. On traditional Republican issues, Bush was seen as more acceptable than Anderson, and thus as a credible Republican alternative to Reagan. Bush, unlike Anderson, was careful to join Reagan in stressing a strong military and a balanced budget, issues on which there was little disagreement among Republicans in 1980. Anderson stood near Bush on issues like the ERA and the environment, but he did not demonstrate any commitment to the core issues, like defense. (Anderson, in fact, appealed to the same kinds of intellectuals who had supported Morris Udall in the Democratic primaries in 1976.)

Ironically, after the 1964 Republican primary in which Senator Barry Goldwater's insurgency captured control of the party, and after the fall debacle when so many Republicans voted against Goldwater and for Lyndon Johnson, Angus Campbell argued that voters were unconcerned about policy differences within parties. "The public," he wrote, "is typically unconcerned about the intra-party debates over specific issue positions which agitate the party leadership and command copious space in the newspaper."[9] But sixteen years later, Republicans were still fighting over the same issues that Goldwater raised in 1964. Republican voters in the 1980 primaries were sensitive to the implications of a shift from a party led by Gerald Ford to a party led by Ronald Reagan. Instead of jumping on the bandwagon for Reagan when all the other candidates withdrew or performed poorly, many Republicans looked back to Ford as the candidate who best represented the direction they wanted their party to follow.

N I N E

The Fight to Redirect the Democratic Coalition in 1984

THE DEMOCRATIC PRIMARIES of 1984, like the Republican primaries of 1980, were in part a battle about whether the party needed to change its approach to economic management, foreign policy, and domestic programs. The primary campaign of 1984 illustrates how the images of the parties and beliefs about their ability to deal with specific problems are affected by the failures and successes of recent presidents. Jimmy Carter's unpopular performance as president, in contrast with Ronald Reagan's first term, generated a widespread perception among Democrats that something was wrong with the approach of the Democratic party.

In February of 1984, Senator Gary Hart won the New Hampshire primary and surged ahead of former vice president Walter Mondale in the national preference polls. As a result, a great deal of media attention was suddenly given to Hart's theme of "new ideas" and his call for a "new generation" to take over the Democratic party. He associated himself with John Kennedy and talked about the promise of high technology and the need to move away from the ideas and policies of the past. But Hart himself did not create the demand for his ideas. Well before the primaries began, when he was still a blip in the polls and no one had heard his call, there was already support for new ideas within the Democratic party. He simply used the phrase in an attempt to mobilize the widespread demand for change after Senator John Glenn failed to fulfill the initial expectations for his candidacy.

The 1984 primary battle between Hart, Mondale, and Jesse Jackson was a battle between different social bases. Younger voters' support for Hart reflected the experiences of postwar-generation Democrats under Reagan, their increased education, and their increasingly white-collar, middle-class outlook on life. Indeed, throughout the primary season, Mondale, even in his darkest hour, was never behind Hart among voters over forty-five years old; Hart's lead in early March reflected his appeal to voters who came of age during and after the 1960s.

As we saw with the candidacies of Bush and Carter, the fault lines that open in primaries are related both to the personal characteristics of the front-runner and to the front-runner's position in relation to past political splits within the party. Mondale was the focal point of the 1984 campaign, and so the campaign centered on his relations with unions, his ties to the New Deal traditions of the party, and public perceptions about whether he was too subservient to interest groups within the party.

More surveys were taken at critical points in the 1984 primary campaign than in either 1976 or 1980, and they clearly show that Hart's sudden rise was related to discontent with Mondale and the failure of Glenn to sustain his early support. It is also clear that Hart did not lose his lead over Mondale because of changes in expectations about his chances of winning, but rather because of changed perceptions of his ability to handle the job of president. These surveys also make it possible to examine more carefully than in any other case the roles of expectations, personal evaluations, and issues in the rise of new candidates.

The Search for "New Ideas"

As candidates and would-be candidates prepared for the 1984 Democratic primaries, candidates and strategists took for granted that the "old ways" of the Democratic party were a problem, that many Democrats were concerned about whether their party was capable of addressing important issues.[1] For four years, Republicans had been crowing that the country's problems had been caused by the old "tax, tax—spend, spend" mentality of the Democrats, and the Republicans fervently believed they would solve these problems by rejecting the Democrats' reliance on bureaucracy in favor of reliance on the market and private enterprise.

The most recent Democratic president—indeed, the only Democrat to gain the White House since 1964—had received some of the lowest popularity ratings ever given to any president. Jimmy Carter had presided over double-digit inflation, high unemployment, gasoline lines, a hostage crisis, and the Soviet invasion of Afghanistan. Under the succeeding Republican president, inflation had been controlled, OPEC had lost control of petroleum prices, and unemployment, which soared in 1981–82, was coming down. There was a major budget deficit, to be sure, but there was a marked contrast between the economic conditions of 1984 and those of 1980. Furthermore, there had been a major military buildup and a markedly changed rhetoric about the role of force in international affairs. The combination of Reagan successes and Carter failures, and a perceived change in the climate of support for government programs, fired a widespread belief among party leaders that the Democratic party needed to modify its approaches to government.

There is public opinion data which confirms the beliefs of the candidates and their pollsters that the 1984 Democratic primary would be framed as a contest between new and old ideas. As table 9.1 indicates, there was a great deal of support among all Democrats for the proposition that the president should be someone who would "try new and unusual ways of solving the country's problems," not someone who would "follow generally familiar approaches and do them better."

In 1984 young Democrats had no adult experience of a popular Democratic president. The last popular Democratic president was John Kennedy; in the two decades since his assassination in 1963, no Democrat had left office with the party united behind him. Not surprisingly, Democrats under forty-five years of age in 1983, who had less direct experience with past Democratic success, were the Democrats most supportive of new approaches to the country's problems.[2]

There were differences in attitudes between Democrats above and below forty-five years of age in evaluations of the first four years of the Reagan administration. These differences, moreover, related to changing beliefs about the relative abilities of the Republican and Democratic parties to deal with the nation's problems (see table 9.1).

As the attitudes about unions, protectionism, Reagan, and Reaganomics shown in table 9.1 suggest, younger voters in 1984 were part of a different political culture than older Democrats. Younger Democrats were more inclined than older ones to credit Reagan and the Republican party for their record since 1980.

For those Democrats under forty-five, Reagan was simply more central to their thinking about government than for older Democrats. Whether they thought the economy better or worse in 1983 than it was in 1980, in open-ended questions, younger Democrats were more likely to cite Reagan as the cause of the change. Younger Democrats were less familiar with the AFL-CIO and Hubert Humphrey than older voters, and, if they did know them, were less favorable toward them. Younger Democrats were also far less supportive of protectionist trade policies.

TABLE 9.1
Attitudes of Democrats by Age, 1983–1984

		Under 45 (%)	Over 45 (%)	All (%)
Do you think that a president should be someone who will try new and unusual ways of solving the country's problems or would you be more comfortable with someone who will follow generally familiar approaches and do them better?	New, unusual	52	34	43
	Familiar	42	45	44
	Don't know/ no answer	6	21	13
Do you approve or disapprove of the way President Reagan is handling his job?	Approve	52	34	43
	Disapprove	39	56	47
	Other/ don't know	9	10	10
Are you better off today [1983] than you were three years ago?	Yes	60	34	47
	No	33	57	44
	Don't know	7	10	9
Do you think (Ronald Reagan's) economic program eventually will help or hurt the country?	Help country	54	43	48
	Hurt country	36	33	34
	Don't know	10	24	18
Which party is better able to keep the economy strong?	Republican	33	21	30
	Democratic	55	63	58
	Other/ don't know	12	16	12
Which party do you think can best handle [the most important problem facing the country]?	Republican	22	10	15
	Democratic	53	50	51
	Other/ don't know	25	40	34
If the United States put additional restrictions on foreign imports, would that do more to protect American jobs or would that do more to raise the prices of things people buy?	Protect jobs	32	45	38
	Raise prices	49	17	33
	Other/ don't know	19	38	29

(continued)

TABLE 9.1 (*Continued*)

		Under 45 (%)	Over 45 (%)	All (%)
Do you have a favorable	Favorable	37	67	52
or not favorable attitude	Not favorable	16	16	16
toward Hubert	Don't know	47	17	32
Humphrey?				
Do you have a favorable	Favorable	32	44	38
or not favorable attitude	Not favorable	29	27	28
toward the AFL-CIO?	Don't know	39	29	34

Source: In order, with the number of respondents for each poll in parentheses, the questions are from the CBS News/*New York Times* polls for June 1983 (423); January 1984 (470); January 1984 (470); June 1983 (423); September 1983 (523); June 1983 (423); October 1984 (478); March 1984 (567); March 1984 (567)).

Note: While the 1984 poll reports for the primaries include independents who vote in Democratic primaries, the 1983 polls do not include the same screening questions for independents and are based only on registered Democrats. I have checked every 1983/1984 comparison and the inclusion of independents has no effect on the intra-year comparisons.

Walter Mondale, John Glenn, and "New Ideas"

In 1984 President Carter's former vice president, Walter Mondale, was the front-runner for the nomination. He was linked not only to the Carter administration but to the New Deal and Great Society traditions of the party. His mentor, Senator Hubert Humphrey, had been a lifelong champion of civil rights and governmental activism, and, as Lyndon Johnson's vice president, had been one of the major architects of the Great Society programs.

Yet even Mondale—a champion of unions, the welfare state, and civil rights—believed, even before 1983, that the 1984 primaries would be a campaign of "old ideas" against "new ideas." He even acknowledged that in order to succeed, he would have to "disavow a return to the old ways."[3] Mondale was popular among all Democrats, but there was a marked difference in his ratings according to the age of the respondents. Among Democrats over forty-five, his favorable to unfavorable rating was 67 percent to 13 percent; with Democrats under forty-five, it was only 49 percent to 25 percent. Further, it was already clear by the start of the campaign that large numbers of Democrats acknowledged that President Reagan had managed to stop inflation and turn the economy around. Half of all Democrats thought that the eventual impact of Reagan's economic program would be positive, and Glenn led Mondale among those Democrats by 34 percent to 30 percent, while Mondale led Glenn among Democrats who thought the eventual impact of Reaganomics would be negative.[4]

Because of resistance from younger white-collar Democrats in particular, Mondale was barely ahead of Senator John Glenn of Ohio in the polls during 1983. At that time Glenn was as popular as Mondale among Democrats, and he was within 3 points of Mondale on the preference questions in the June and September CBS News/*New York Times* polls.

Glenn was the high-tech candidate, the first American space hero, the man who rode in ticker-tape parades with President Kennedy, the man who ran for the Senate at Kennedy's urging. And as a much-decorated Marine who had fought in World War II and Korea, Glenn could counter President Reagan's patriotic bravura by saying, "I went through two wars . . . I wasn't doing *Hellcats of the Navy.*"[5] He was also considered a good media candidate.[6] In the September 1983 CBS News/*New York Times* poll, 46 percent of Democrats said they considered him a national hero, and his campaign research showed that voters associated him with honesty, bravery, and strength.[7] Glenn's campaign strategy was to portray himself as a leader looking to the future, painting Mondale as a politician of the past.

From the time they announced their candidacy, each of the other Democratic contenders—former senator and presidential nominee George McGovern, Jesse Jackson, former Florida governor Reuben Askew, and Senators Allan Cranston, Ernest Hollings, John Glenn, and Gary Hart—described themselves in both implicit and explicit contrast to Mondale. They made their reference points Mondale's endorsements and his connections with the party's past. Implicit in their messages was the need for the party to change, or at least to update its traditions. Hart, for example, used futuristic computer typefaces in his posters, and said when declaring his candidacy, "A president who owes his election to special interests risks an administration that is owned by them." Glenn associated himself with John F. Kennedy, the space program, and high technology, and said in his announcement that the Democrats would lose if they were seen as "a party that can't say no to any group with a letterhead and a mailing list . . . [or] wants to replace the Reagan program of the twenties with programs of the sixties." Glenn's advertising stressed that he "doesn't play to special interests, doesn't play the old political game."[8]

The Emergence of Gary Hart

As is rarely the case, the time at which Gary Hart began to rise can be fixed precisely. It was the afternoon of Sunday, January 15, 1984, when all the candidates for the Democratic nomination gathered at Dartmouth College in Hanover, New Hampshire, for a three-hour nationally broadcast debate.

One-quarter of the Iowa caucus electorate and 42 percent of the New Hampshire primary electorate watched this debate.[9] They saw Glenn engage Mondale in an argument about the difference between "gobbledygook" and "baloney." They also saw Hart call for new ideas and a new generation of leaders not wedded to the past. And voters could see that the only candidates without gray hair were Hart and Jackson.

By comparing evaluations of the candidates made by watchers and nonwatchers, we can obtain a reasonable assessment of the debate's effect on the race. The only way to obtain a completely satisfactory evaluation of its impact, of course, would be by doing surveys before and after the debate and comparing the responses; or even better, by interviewing the same people before and after the debate and comparing the opinion changes among viewers with the opinion changes among nonviewers. These data unfortunately do not exist. However, a reasonable first approximation of the impact of the debate can be obtained by comparing responses of viewers and nonviewers to a CBS News/*New York Times* poll conducted in Iowa just after the debate (see table 9.2).

Iowa

Candidate ratings by viewers of the debate show just how well Hart projected himself. At the time, his favorable to unfavorable rating among all respondents in Iowa was only 16 percent to 9 percent, but his rating among all respondents who had seen the debate was 27 percent to 11 percent. The difference in overall ratings for Glenn before and after the debate was insignificant, and Mondale's negative ratings after his performance were actually higher among viewers than among nonviewers. The differences between the attitudes of viewers and nonviewers was particularly striking for respondents younger than forty-five. Mondale was perceived far more negatively by viewers than by nonviewers. Glenn, overall, was more popular with younger respondents than with older respondents, but younger respondents who had seen the debate were less favorable to him than were nonviewers of the same age.

Hart, by contrast, was substantially more popular with younger viewers than with older viewers or nonviewers. His favorable rating among young-

TABLE 9.2

Candidate Ratings and Presidential Preference by Debate Viewing
and Age, Iowa, 1984

	Under 45			Over 45			All Respondents		
	Watched Debate?			Watched Debate?			Watched Debate?		
	Yes (%)	No (%)	All (%)	Yes (%)	No (%)	All (%)	Yes (%)	No (%)	All (%)
	CANDIDATE RATINGS								
Gary Hart									
Favorable	36	12	16	21	10	16	27	12	16
Unfavorable	3	5	5	16	16	16	11	10	10
Don't know/ can't rate	61	83	79	63	74	68	62	78	74
John Glenn									
Favorable	40	44	44	41	28	32	40	36	38
Unfavorable	19	10	11	16	16	16	11	10	10
Don't know/ can't rate	41	46	45	43	56	52	49	54	52
Walter Mondale									
Favorable	59	63	63	73	73	73	67	68	68
Unfavorable	25	14	16	15	8	12	19	11	14
Don't know/ can't rate	16	23	21	12	19	15	14	21	18
	PRESIDENTIAL PREFERENCE								
Walter Mondale	39	44	43	56	67	61	49	55	53
John Glenn	15	24	22	11	10	11	13	17	16
Gary Hart	10	2	4	6	2	3	7	2	3
Others/ don't know	36	30	31	27	21	25	31	26	28

Source: CBS News/*New York Times* poll, Iowa, January 1984.

Note: This poll was based on 480 Iowa Democrats and Democratic primary voters interviewed in the week after the debate, 232 of whom were less that 45 years old; 23 percent of the younger voters and 32 percent of the older voters said they saw the debate.

er viewers was 36 percent to 3 percent and his rating among nonviewers was only 12 percent to 5 percent! Hart simply projected better than Glenn to people who didn't yet know him, and he projected particularly well to younger voters.[10] Thus we have another piece in the explanation of Glenn's fall: he could not articulate or focus his differences with Mondale as well as Hart could.

Hart's ability during the debate to project his "new approach" and to focus the differences between himself and Mondale began to change preferences as well as candidate ratings. Prior to the debate, his Iowa poll standing was nearly zero, but among viewers of the debate there was a clear gain, particularly among younger voters. At the same time, there was a clear drop in support for Glenn. In fact, among younger viewers Hart was closing in on Glenn (see table 9.2). At the same time, Mondale's lead was being eroded among the activated in Iowa; debate viewers, particularly younger voters, were less likely to support him than others. Hart, on the other hand, was able to substantially cut into Glenn's votes and eventually win the position of main challenger to Mondale. Hart's gains continued and he eventually came in second, although a very distant second, to Mondale in the caucuses (see table 9.2).

New Hampshire

At the same time that the CBS News/*New York Times* poll was being conducted in Iowa, William Hamilton & Staff, the pollsters for Senator Glenn, were conducting a poll in New Hampshire; the results were similar to the results of the Iowa poll. In New Hampshire, as in Iowa, Glenn received far *fewer* votes from viewers than from nonviewers, and Hart far *more* votes from viewers than from nonviewers[11] (see table 9.3).

When the Iowa caucuses were held a month after the debate, Glenn received 3 percent of the actual vote, a fall from the 17 percent he received in the January CBS News/*New York Times* Iowa survey. Hart received 17 percent of the actual vote, a rise from 3 percent in the survey. Iowa was a strong victory for Mondale, but the results showed that he still was much less appealing to voters who had come of political age after 1960. Among voters under forty-five, his edge over Hart was 32 percent to 18 percent, while among older voters it was 57 percent to 17 percent.[12]

In the seven days after the Iowa primary, Mondale went from a 37 percent lead (over Glenn's 20 percent and Hart's 13 percent) to a stunning defeat, with 27 percent of the vote to Hart's 37 percent. His vote share dropped one-fourth while Hart's tripled—in exactly one week!

Before his Iowa second-place finish was known in New Hampshire, Hart's share of the New Hampshire vote was approximately the same as his share in Iowa; once the Iowa result was known, his New Hampshire share surpassed his Iowa results. Without a strong signal of viability, and a signal that Glenn was not viable, Hart would have earned from 13 percent to 17 percent of the vote. Once his viability was demonstrated by his showing

TABLE 9.3

Presidential Preference and Debate
Viewing, New Hampshire 1984

	Watched Debate?		
	Yes (%)	No (%)	All (%)
Mondale	43	36	39
Glenn	13	25	20
Hart	9	2	5
Jackson	3	2	3
Others/ don't know	32	35	33

Source: This table is derived from table 2 in
Harrison Hickman, "Presidential Election Debates: Do
They Matter?" p. 11.

Note: Viewers were 42 percent of his sample of
425. Hickman shows the viewers were more likely to
be male, white-collar, and retired than the nonviewers, but the demographic differences were not
large, certainly not large enough to account for the
differences in preference. The differences between
those who watched more than half the three hours of
debate and others, however, were pronounced.

TABLE 9.4

New Hampshire Preferences by Day

	Jan. 18 (%)	Pre- Iowa (%)	Wed.– Fri. (%)	Sat. (%)	Sun. (%)	Mon. (%)	Actual Vote (%)
Mondale	39	37	38	36	26	27	28
Hart	5	13	24	23	33	35	37
Glenn	20	20	14	14	14	14	13
Others/ don't know	36	30	24	27	27	24	22

Source: The January numbers come from Hickman and the other numbers come from
ABC News/*Washington Post* polls reported in *The 1984 Vote* and the *Washington Post*, Feb.
26. Before the Iowa results were known, the ABC News/*Washington Post* polls reported
that Hart was at 10 percent, whereas Hickman had him at 13 percent much earlier.

in Iowa, he became the focal point for voters who didn't like Mondale, and for voters who had gone along with Mondale when they thought they had no choice (see table 9.4).

Wholesale and Retail Campaigning

Looking at Hart's rapid rise in New Hampshire after his second-place finish in Iowa, David Moore has argued that New Hampshire is now a state where political outcomes are determined by "wholesale," or television, campaigning; that it is now a state dominated by media blitzes and expectations, as opposed to its traditional image as a state where votes are determined by "retail," face-to-face campaigning.[13] The research presented in this chapter, however, indicates the powerful influence of the local campaign as well as that of the national media, and the presence of strategic voting based on the results in Iowa.

The fall of John Glenn and the impact of the debates in Iowa and New Hampshire demonstrate the importance of the local primary campaigns in these two states. Glenn's fall began before the campaign, but it accelerated as people in these two states saw him during the race. Hart's rise as the alternative to Mondale, first in Iowa and then in New Hampshire, occurred only because of his long months of canvassing and the small-group interactions he undertook in the month before the campaign began.

Hart did not get a "blind" vote in New Hampshire—a vote from people who knew only that he was "not Mondale." Glenn was the early, obvious, and well-known alternative to Mondale, but he failed his interview despite an interesting résumé. Hart built up his favorability ratings in both Iowa and New Hampshire because people who were stimulated by local campaign activity watched television and paid attention to events like the debates, where they could see and compare the candidates. As they made their comparisons, Hart emerged as the clearest and most attractive alternative to Mondale.[14]

Mondale vs. Hart: The National Battle

On the day Hart won the New Hampshire primary, only one out of six Democrats and independents intending to vote in Democratic primaries reported a favorable image of him in the national CBS News/*New York Times* poll; seven days later, in the next national poll, one-half rated him favorably. National favorability ratings of the candidates and national preferences changed in February and March faster than in any previous primary. Three days before the New Hampshire primary, Mondale led his nearest opponent by 50 points, 57 percent to 7 percent; one week later, he trailed Hart by 7 points, 31 percent to 38 percent. In two more weeks he was again ahead, 42 percent to 35 percent. In no other primary year have there been such rapid changes in preferences for the candidates.

If ever there was a plausible case for the proposition that primary support depends on little more than expectations and good looks, Gary Hart provided it. When people flocked to him in the week after New Hampshire, how much did they know about where he stood on "the issues"? The national polls suggest that the people who moved to Hart picked up a good deal of information about him in that week. This demonstrates just how much information people can access when comparing candidates, and how much they can learn from "reading" them as they campaign.

In the week after his win in New Hampshire, Democrats across the country were more confident of Hart's ability to deal with the Russians than they were of Mondale's.[15] It is important to note that there was no discussion whatsoever of foreign policy in this period; voters assessing Hart's ability to deal with the Soviet Union were projecting solely from observations of campaign behavior and domestic policy evaluations. This is low-information reasoning. Clearly, people projected on the basis of newly acquired impressions of the candidate, assuming the best where little was known. This emphasizes how strongly campaign behavior influences the images that voters build of candidates and the assessment they make of the candidates' abilities to govern. It also suggests that the credibility of the candidates, and the extent of projections from campaign behavior to White House behavior, is increased when candidates are perceived as winners. Charisma, as Hart told Elizabeth Drew, comes from winning.[16]

The reasoning about Hart from his campaign behavior raises directly all the questions about the kinds of information people pick up in primaries, as well as the possibility that people were merely voting for him as a winner, without any sense of what he stood for or how he differed from Mondale. As I reported in chapter 6, however, the extensive CBS News/ *New York Times* polling data casts doubt on any expectations-centered explanation for Hart preferences. Voters who switched to Hart from Mondale actually gave Mondale a better chance at winning the nomination; voters who switched to Hart from Glenn did the same. Voters didn't move to Hart because they thought he had a better chance of winning the nomination. They did so because he was an attractive and viable alternative to Mondale.

Even during the first week after New Hampshire, people acquired information about the ways in which Hart differed from Mondale; this fact was reflected in the social and issue-oriented bases of their support. Indeed, this case suggests that people pick up information about a candidate's position

on issues faster than they absorb information about character and competence.[17] It is easier for people to understand candidates in relation to one
another than to assess their personal qualities individually. Comparisons,
that is, come easier than evaluations.

Low-Information Reasoning: Policy Content

In the week after the New Hampshire primary, 82 percent of the Hart voters
in the CBS News/*New York Times* poll thought that Hart did indeed have
new ideas for dealing with the country's problems, though only one in five
could suggest what even one of them was. Knowledge of specific proposals, however, is an inadequate measure of issue information about a
candidate. Even in the period immediately after the New Hampshire primary, when media emphasis was on the horse race and the Vermont
primary, voters learned about the positions of the candidates and related
the issue information to their preferences. Voters did acquire usable data
from candidates' presentations of themselves. They did see the kinds of
supporters the candidates had, and who endorsed them. They read character and competence from campaign behavior, and they inferred policy
preferences from demographic information. And they learned about the
priorities of the candidates from the ways in which they defined themselves in opposition to each other, and from the ways in which they
elaborated their priorities.[18]

The rhetoric used by Mondale and Hart during this period did convey
some sense of the differences in the priorities, and the social bases, of the two
men. Hart emphasized the private sector: "I think we can meet the basic
human needs and commitments of the people of this country by restoring
entrepreneurship." His call for new leadership was an implicit move away
from the traditional Democratic agenda; he called for "new leadership that
will move this nation beyond the irrelevant debate between the two parties
and beyond outworn agendas . . . new leadership that will ask everyone to
share the burdens of putting our country back on the track."[19]

Mondale, in contrast, emphasized generosity and caring when he talked
about the traditional Democratic agenda. He made this his focal point for
comparing himself and Hart:

> Listen to [Hart's] speeches. . . . You don't hear him talking
> about restoring the sense of social justice, reaching out and
> helping the vulnerable, [or emphasizing] Social Security and
> Medicare. . . . He wrote a book about his vision of America.
> You need an FBI investigator to find one word in there ex-
> pressing concern about people in trouble.[20]

We're about to decide whether we'll be a generous party and a caring nation or whether we won't. . . . There's a new argument in this land—a new idea about the Democratic Party and where it should go. This new idea is the essence of the battle we're in. The idea is this: If you fight for the values the Democratic Party has always believed in you're supposed to go on a guilt trip. But if you fight against them you're supposed to be applauded. If you fight for better schools, you're old. But if you fight for big oil you're new. . . . If a worker wants a raise that's greedy. But if a plant closes down that's trendy. If you want corporations to pay their share of taxes you're old hat. But if you want working families to pay more taxes you're high tech.[21]

This campaign rhetoric successfully pointed out the different policy or issue biases of the two candidates; voters definitely made use of this information. Voters who left Mondale for Hart were more negative about unions, more negative about Jimmy Carter, more concerned about inflation than about unemployment, and more concerned about the deficit than about the poor. These issue effects are apparent in two instances: (1) when we compare early Mondale supporters who switched to Hart with Mondale supporters who stayed with him, and (2) when we examine policy differences between Hart and Mondale supporters.

Two CBS News/*New York Times* national polls taken in the three weeks after the New Hampshire primary can be used to assess the bases of support for Mondale and Hart. The first poll was taken the week after New Hampshire; it shows the support for Hart at its highest point of the campaign, at the peak of his surge, when he led Mondale by 38 percent to 31 percent. In the second poll, respondents from the Democratic primary electorate who were interviewed in the February CBS News/*New York Times* poll, just after Mondale won in Iowa, were interviewed again after the Illinois primary, which was the week after Super Tuesday.

The first of these polls, taken the week after New Hampshire, asked voters not only about their current preferences but also whether they had changed preferences.[22] With the information about previous support, it is possible to compare Mondale supporters who stayed with Mondale after Hart's victory in New Hampshire, with Mondale supporters who switched to Hart. The second poll, the reinterview of respondents from the survey conducted between Iowa and New Hampshire, also makes available a panel that follows the electorate from the height of the Mondale wave to the steady state that ensued after Hart peaked and Mondale regained the lead.

Attitudes about unions and union endorsements were important to early Mondale supporters in deciding whether to stay with Mondale or switch to Hart.[23] Respondents with negative attitudes toward the AFL-CIO or union endorsements in general were twice as likely as those with positive attitudes to leave Mondale for Hart. Half of the voters who had earlier supported Mondale and who had a negative attitude about the AFL-CIO switched from Mondale to Hart the week after New Hampshire; only one-quarter of the early Mondale supporters with pro–AFL-CIO attitudes switched to Hart. On the panel survey taken after Super Tuesday, only one-quarter of the February Mondale voters who approved of union endorsements changed to Hart, whereas 41 percent of those who disapproved of them moved to Hart.

In the panel, Mondale was far more likely to lose supporters who cared about deficits than supporters who cared about the poor. Panel respondents were asked, "What do you think is more important in a president, being concerned about people who are poor or really cutting down the federal budget deficit?" Responses indicated that half of the early Mondale supporters who cared more about the deficit had moved to Hart, but only one-fifth who cared more about the poor had made that move.[24] Further, when voters were asked about the most important problems facing the country, Mondale proved to have lost 40 percent of the voters whose priority was deficits or inflation, but only one-quarter of those who were most concerned about unemployment.

By the week after New Hampshire 40 percent of the national primary electorate knew that the AFL-CIO had endorsed Mondale. As noted earlier in the discussion of fault lines within parties, the campaign provided information about the AFL-CIO's endorsement of Mondale and tightened the connection between attitudes about the union and the vote. Voters favorable to the AFL-CIO (38 percent) favored Mondale over Hart by 41 percent to 29 percent, while voters not favorable preferred Hart over Mondale by 48 percent to 17 percent. Among voters who had a favorable attitude toward the AFL-CIO, those who knew about its endorsement supported Mondale 49 percent to 33 percent, whereas those who did not know of the endorsement favored Hart 36 percent to 33 percent. Obviously, when there was a favorable attitude already, awareness of the endorsement had a powerful effect upon preference.[25]

In addition to feelings about unions, attitudes about Jimmy Carter also affected decisions about whether to stay with Mondale after Hart won in

New Hampshire. Among participants in the survey taken immediately after New Hampshire, Mondale lost 40 percent of his early supporters who gave negative ratings to Carter's performance, and 25 percent of those who had positive evaluations of Carter. Carter may not have been mentioned by either candidate during this period, but explicit connections were hardly necessary. Mondale had been Carter's vice-president and could not escape ties to his record.

In all of these polls, the differing preferences for Hart and Mondale reflected the different approaches and priorities of the two candidates. In the wake of the political and economic debates of the first Reagan administration, voters had a sense of what "new ideas" in America were about, and they weren't about caring for the elderly, the poor, or blacks. Thus despite Hart's highly publicized similarities to John F. Kennedy, all the exit polls in all the state primaries throughout the entire election showed that Hart received a grand total of 3 percent of the black vote for the year.[26]

It seems clear enough that even while the media were emphasizing horse-race tactics over substance, voters who paid attention to the campaign statements of the two men gained information about how their positions on various issues differed. It is also clear that support for "new ideas" was not just a follow-the-leader, bandwagon effect. When Hart's band began to play, people already had ideas about what music they wanted to hear. The campaign sharpened the salience of concerns that people had expressed well before they had even heard of Gary Hart.

Campaigns and Issue Salience

Forty years ago, *Voting* concluded that campaigns do much more to change the relative importance of issues than they do to change opinions on issues. As table 9.5 demonstrates, this was true in 1984 as well. During the Democratic campaign, the discussion of interest-group endorsements and "new ideas" versus "old ideas" did very little to change the distribution of attitudes about either subject. What the campaign did, however, was increase the salience of these issues.[27] It did not affect net support for new ideas or net support for unions, but it did widen the vote division between the two sides on these questions. Further, the changes in the relationship between these questions and the primary vote occurred *after* the primaries began.[28] The constant campaign references to unions and old ideas did in fact raise the importance of these issues for voters; it made them more aware of alternatives, and it led them to base their preferences for various candidates more and more on these issues as the campaign progressed (see table 9.5).

TABLE 9.5
Democratic Attitudes and Candidate Preference, 1983–1984

	Union Endorsements					
	Appropriate			Inappropriate		
	Sept. 1983 (%)	Feb. 1984 (%)	March 1984ᵃ (%)	Sept. 1983 (%)	Feb. 1984 (%)	March 1984ᵃ (%)
Mondale	33	59	53	30	53	41
Glenn	25	6		30	8	
Hart	2	7	33	1	8	45
Jackson	5	11	9	10	7	6
Total %	42	43	43	50	48	48

	Governmental Style			
	New Ways		Familiar Approaches	
	June 1983 (%)	March 1984ᵇ (%)	June 1983 (%)	March 1984ᵇ (%)
Mondale	32	31	35	53
Glenn	37		31	
Hart	1	44	1	28
Jackson	7	11	8	6
Total %	43	47	44	37

Source: CBS News/*New York Times* polls, June 1983, September 1983, February 1984, and March 1984.

Note: The complete questions asked were:

"Do you think it is appropriate for labor unions to endorse candidates for president or is this something they shouldn't get involved in?"

"Do you think that a president should be someone who will try new and unusual ways of solving the country's problems or would you be more comfortable with someone who will follow generally familiar approaches and do them better?"

ᵃThis is a panel from February 21–24, 1984, with reinterviews March 21–24, but the union question was not repeated, so that these columns record attitudes about endorsements in February and candidate preference a month later, March 21–24.

ᵇThis is the second of the two March surveys, taken March 21–24, not the panelback to the February sample.

Social Bases of Support for Hart and Mondale

The contest between Mondale and Hart reflected the different priorities of blue-collar and white-collar (college-educated) voters within the Democratic party. This fight extended even to the union ranks. There are almost as many white-collar as blue-collar union members in the United States today, and white-collar union members are more critical of AFL-CIO political activity.[29] Not surprisingly, even within unions, there is a difference in the vote of white-collar and blue-collar members. The exit poll taken at the November general election asked Democrats who they had supported for their party's nomination. The size of the poll, over 9,000 voters, makes possible a separation of union members by occupation. Mondale did substantially better among blue-collar than among white-collar and professional union members (see table 9.6). Thus, an increasingly white-collar union movement is simply unable to deliver the same percentage of its vote as once was possible.

The different outlooks of Hart and Mondale voters went far beyond attitudes about union political involvement. The September CBS News/*New York Times* poll asked, "Where do you think there is more waste, in the defense budget or the welfare budget?" Democrats who thought there was more waste in defense preferred Mondale 31 percent to 27 percent, and Democrats who thought there was more waste in welfare preferred Hart 33 percent to 22 percent. Mondale voters thought about import barriers and tariffs predominantly in terms of jobs and unemployment; Hart voters thought more about the effect on prices. White Democrats who thought the government should do more for blacks preferred Mondale 48 percent to 32 percent.

TABLE 9.6
Primary Preference among
Democratic Union Members
According to Occupation

	White Collar (%)	Blue Collar (%)
Mondale	36	42
Hart	31	25
Jackson	10	11

Source: CBS News/*New York Times* poll, November 1984.
Note: If independents were also included, or if retired union members were included, the divide would be much stronger. This table is based on 672 employed union members divided nearly equally into the two categories.

Hart's talk of the future and the importance of high-technology industries was noticed by Democrats and affected their perceptions of the
candidates. In the exit polls, voters who drove Japanese cars or worked
with computers voted more for Hart than other voters. For example, in the
California Democratic primary, where Hart beat Mondale 40 percent to
38 percent, his victory margin came from his two-to-one margin (50 percent to 26 percent) among voters who used computers or drove foreign
cars (who accounted for one-third of the vote); the other voters preferred
Mondale 43 percent to 37 percent.

That computer users and drivers of foreign cars voted more for Hart than
for Mondale reflects the cultural differences between the two groups, even
beyond the relatively higher education, youth, and income of Hart voters.
The November CBS News/*New York Times* exit poll asked voters whether
they used computers at home or at work. Because the sample is large
enough to control for age, political party, and profession, it can definitively
test whether computer users did indeed identify more with Hart. Hart was
portrayed in campaign coverage as both the high-technology advocate and
the "yuppie" (young urban professional) candidate. In fact, he even fared
far better among high-tech young urban professionals than among other
yuppies. Table 9.7 demonstrates just how much difference there was in
support for the candidates between the more technologically oriented sectors of young urban professionals and the less technologically oriented
sectors.

TABLE 9.7

Computer Usage and Primary
Preference among Urban Professional
Democrats under Age Forty-five

	Computer Usage		
	Yes (%)	No (%)	All (%)
Mondale	22	37	32
Hart	40	33	35
Others	38	30	33
Total *N*	(338)	(642)	(980)

Source: CBS News/*New York Times* national
exit poll, November 1984.

The contrasting social bases of support for Hart and Mondale emphasize how changes in the American economy have made it more difficult for Democrats to hold their coalition together than in the past. As noted in chapters 2 and 3, blue-collar workers are more sensitive to unemployment than to inflation in their political evaluations and policy preferences, while white-collar workers are more sensitive to inflation. White-collar and professional workers are also more resentful of union political involvement. Democrats who want to rely on unions to mobilize working-class and poor Democrats, and who embrace union support, run into opposition if they emphasize unemployment and jobs over control of inflation. This exacerbates the age splits within the party between a younger, more white-collar cohort (who remember unions for their support for Vietnam and their opposition to George McGovern more than for their support for the New Deal and their opposition to George Wallace, and who resent union political involvement) and an older, more blue-collar cohort. Union demands for protectionist support for dying industries were not well received by a cohort driving Japanese cars or working in high-technology growth areas. In every 1984 primary, voters who believed that unions had too much political power were more likely to vote for Hart, and this question was as good a predictor of voting among union members as it was among the primary electorate as a whole.

Reasoning about Leadership and Competence

The primary process can work to the advantage of newcomers like Gary Hart. Successful politicians get things done, but in order to do so they bargain and compromise, and in that process they do not always do exactly what they said they would do when they were campaigning. To bargain and compromise is by definition to abandon ideal solutions in favor of coalitions that can produce workable solutions. In examining, or framing, a well-known candidate, the voter can emphasize either the results or the compromise. When one candidate is all promise for the future and the other has a known record, the known candidate will often look insincere.

Mondale's problems with union endorsements and sincerity were partly self-inflicted. They were due not just to resentment of the political role of unions, but to the way he appeared to deal with unions and other groups that supported him. More than once Mondale was challenged, "Name a single time you have ever differed with the AFL-CIO," but he never answered.[30] There were no union issues on the agenda in 1984, and unions had been less active and less successful than in recent years. Mondale, however, lost many votes because voters did not like the way he dealt with interest groups within the party, especially unions.

It was not just the endorsements themselves but how Mondale handled them that mattered. He appeared to many like a man following the agenda of others, not a man inviting others to join the fight for his own agenda. Compared to Hart, he did not come across like a man who stood up for his own beliefs. Over half of the primary electorate thought he told the public what it wanted to hear, not what he believed; only one-third thought Hart did so (see table 9.8).

Mondale did not appear willing to say what he believed if it was at variance with what the public wanted to hear. Even among respondents favorable to him, half still said he "says what the public wants to hear." Among those favorable to Hart, by contrast, only one-quarter said Hart "says what the public wants to hear." Even pro-union Mondale supporters felt he did not stand up for his own beliefs. One-third of the respondents who were both favorable to Mondale and favorable to the AFL-CIO thought he said mainly what the public wanted to hear.[31] In another CBS News/*New York Times* poll, also in March 1984, respondents were asked

TABLE 9.8
Voter Perceptions of Candidate Candor

		Hart	Mondale
Do you think that most of the time (Gary Hart/Walter Mondale) says what he really believes or do you think he says what people want to hear?	Says what he believes	48	31
	Says what public wants to hear	34	56
	Don't know	18	13

		Hart Supporters	Mondale Supporters	All Democratic Primary Voters
Which candidate would say what he believed even if he thought you wouldn't like it?	Hart	59	26	37
	Mondale	13	39	32
	Both	10	12	12
	Neither/ don't know	18	23	20

Source: CBS News/*New York Times* polls, March 5–8 and 21–24, 1984.
Note: The complete preamble to the second question is "Here are some things people say about the candidates they see on television. I'd like you to tell me whether you think each comment applies more to Gary Hart, or more to Walter Mondale. If you think a comment applies to both of them or neither of them, just tell me."

which candidate was better described by different phrases; one of the phrases was "He would say what he believed even if he thought you wouldn't like it." Again, Hart was believed to be more willing to affirm his beliefs than Mondale (see table 9.8).

Thus how Mondale dealt with his friends, not just who his friends were, affected his support in the primaries. People read his relations with unions and other traditional Democratic constituencies as relations in which he did not display the ability to rise above his supporters' demands, display candor, and exert leadership. Many simply did not believe that a man who was unwilling to criticize labor, a man who promised to maintain all the traditional Democratic commitments at a time when many were saying that Social Security was not viable and that the budget had to be cut, could be telling people what he really believed (see table 9.8).

The Fall of Gary Hart

As Gary Hart's ascent began with a debate, so did his decline. In a debate the Sunday before Super Tuesday, Mondale, along with Jesse Jackson, John Glenn, and George McGovern, criticized Hart for lacking substance and implied that he had neither the ideas nor the experience to be an effective president. This was where Mondale first asked Hart the most famous question of the campaign, "Where's the beef?"

Exit polls in Alabama and Georgia asked voters whether they had seen the debate, and in both states Mondale did substantially better among voters who had. Without the extra margin the debate gave him, Mondale probably would have lost the Georgia primary, albeit by a small margin, for Hart beat him by 1 percent among voters who did not see the confrontation (see table 9.9).

In the two weeks between the New Hampshire primary and Super Tuesday, there were stories on all the networks about inconsistencies in Hart's personal biography: he had changed his date of birth, his name, and his signature, and there were irregularities in the way he had received his Naval Reserve commission before he ran for reelection to the Senate. Mondale's use of the famous ad slogan "Where's the beef?" sought to summarize and focus attention on both how little was known about Hart and the difference between Hart's talk of new ideas and his actual record as a senator. Along with "Where's the beef?" came the predictable commercials with a red phone, to remind voters that the president faces onerous duties and is the one with his finger on the button.

TABLE 9.9

Debate Viewing and Voting on Super Tuesday

	Alabama			Georgia		
	Debate Viewers (%)	Nonviewers (%)	All (%)	Debate Viewers (%)	Nonviewers (%)	All (%)
Mondale	42	34	37	30	31	32
Hart	18	25	22	25	32	28
Glenn	16	20	18	19	17	18
Jackson	24	20	22	23	15	19
Others	1	1	1	3	4	4
Total N	(455)	(779)	(1,349)	(501)	(706)	(1,293)

Source: CBS News/*New York Times* exit polls.

Note: The "All" columns include voters who did not answer the debate question on the exit polls.

Clearly the debate before Super Tuesday cut Hart's share of the vote in the primaries held the following Tuesday. Yet the public opinion data for the next two weeks show conclusively that Hart's standing in national surveys was not dramatically changed until much later.[32] Mondale did not overtake Hart nationally until more than a week after Super Tuesday, when stories about campaign mismanagement and about confusion within the campaign over some of Hart's statements were widely covered.

On Super Tuesday Hart won in Florida, Massachusetts, and Rhode Island, while Mondale won in Georgia and Alabama. The network theme was that Mondale had "hung on," that he had managed—albeit barely—to survive. CBS News, for example, even asked on the regular evening news and the special primary show whether Mondale was considering dropping out of the race in the face of Hart's continuing successes.[33]

The week after Super Tuesday, in the Illinois primary campaign, Hart attacked Mondale for airing commercials which discussed his name change and the confusion over his age; Mondale had never aired the alleged commercials. Hart then showed some anti-Mondale commercials. When they raised controversy, he publicly announced he had ordered the commercials off the air. However, although Hart announced he had recalled the commercials on a Friday, they continued to play for two more days. Mondale then criticized Hart, asking how a man who took forty-eight hours to get commercials off the air could ever run the government.

In the days after the Illinois primary, Hart became embroiled in another campaign controversy about remarks he made at the end of the Illinois campaign. The new controversy centered on whether Hart was inconsistent in his positions on moving the American embassy in Israel to Jerusalem, and whether his campaign literature was a truthful reflection of his record. Hart and some members of his campaign organization insisted that his current position had been his position for a long time; some of his staff (and the record) said it was new.[34]

The available evidence suggests that these campaign incidents did more to damage Hart than the stories which established irregularities in his past behavior or which questioned whether his Senate record was consistent with either his descriptions of his past policies or his platform. The evidence also supports the arguments made in chapter 4 that past data and data about current behavior are not easily integrated and that current personal evidence will dominate past historical evidence. The evidence also emphasizes that as people are exposed to the combat between candidates during the primary, they do learn to differentiate their views of the candidate and to see variations in his or her competence and experience by policy area.

The CBS News/*New York Times* poll of March 21–25 covers the four days after the Illinois primary, the days during which news was disseminated about Hart's campaign controversies. There are enough interviews in this survey to divide it in half and treat each half of the survey independently. During the first half of this poll, the two days after the Illinois primary, when the commercials fracas was getting some publicity, Hart still led Mondale nationally, 41 percent to 38 percent. In the second half of the survey, when the campaign news centered on Hart's embassy position(s) and his campaign management, Mondale jumped ahead 49 percent to 27 percent! This extraordinary turnaround is one more demonstration of how fragile the image and votes can be for candidates like Hart, or Bush in 1980, or Carter in 1976, when voters are projecting future performance from campaign behavior.[35] It reemphasizes the discussion in chapter 3 of the logic of incumbents' attacking their challenger(s) instead of trying to change opinions about themselves.

At some point, for some reason, Gary Hart had changed his name from Hartpence to Hart. He had also on different occasions listed two different ages—one year different—and he had changed his signature when young. These stories had been on the air between New Hampshire and Super Tuesday. The major changes in attitude toward Hart, however, and the drops in his experience ratings, occurred not when those stories ran but when the campaign controversies were aired. In these four days, Mondale's "Where's the beef?" apparently hit home, for there were large changes in attitudes about Hart which appear linked to these campaign controversies.

Between the poll taken before Super Tuesday and the poll taken after Illinois there was a drop in Hart's favorable rating and a drop in the percentage who believed he had enough experience to be an effective president. Between the first and second halves of the post-Illinois poll, his favorable rating did not change, but there was another large drop in his experience rating and a large drop in the proportion of respondents who believed that he had the ability to deal with an international crisis (see table 9.10).

It was not the questions about his past personal behavior, then, as much as it was negative news about his campaign management which damaged Gary Hart. Voters projecting from current images of Hart were not as much disturbed by past historical data about name changes as they were by current campaign behavior which did not square with the initial image of the competent, and confident, "upset" winner facing the future. I suggest that it was hard for voters to integrate the name-change data into their projections; as noted in chapter 4, voters do not easily integrate background data about a candidate into the images they project from their observations of campaign behavior. When the stories about Hart's name, age, and signature appeared they were not automatically integrated with current observations of Hart.

When the controversies about the Illinois commercials and stories about Hart's position, or positions, on the location of the American embassy in Israel were aired, concerns about Hart increased and his vote dropped. I suggest these stories were more damaging because they were easier to incorporate into further thinking about a Hart presidency; a name change is a less usable piece of information than an inability to decide where an embassy should be or the failure to manage a campaign properly.

My argument that campaign behavior was responsible for the national decline in support for Hart, not the inconsistencies in his personal record, is open to dispute. It is also possible that the cumulative effect of the many small "media hits"—the nicks and cuts over name and age—did the damage, not the controversies over the Illinois ads and the U.S. embassy. We do not yet have adequate theory or data to eliminate this possibility. However, my argument is supported by the fact that changes in Hart's image were related particularly to international behavior and crises. Further, I am convinced that most current behavior is easier to relate to future policies than most past behavior, whether the past behavior be personal or

TABLE 9.10

Changing Attitudes about Gary Hart and Walter Mondale

		Pre–Super Tuesday	Post–Super Tuesday and Illinois		
		March 5–8 (%)	March 21–22 (%)	March 23–24 (%)	Total Sample (%)
Preference for Democratic nomination	Mondale	31	38	49	42
	Hart	38	41	27	35
	Jackson	7	7	11	9
	Other/ don't know	24	14	13	14
Who do you think will win the nomination?	Mondale		64	68	66
	Hart		22	17	20
	Jackson		0	1	0
	Other/ don't know		14	14	14
Is your opinion of Gary Hart:	Favorable	49	40	41	41
	Not Favorable	4	12	11	12
	Uncertain/ don't know	47	48	47	47
Do you think Gary Hart has enough experience to be a good president?	Yes	45	36	31	34
	No	28	34	44	39
	Don't know	27	30	25	27
Do you have confidence in Gary Hart's ability to deal wisely with a difficult international crisis or are you uneasy about his approach?	Confident		33	28	31
	Uneasy		37	51	43
	Don't know		30	21	26
Is your opinion of Walter Mondale:	Favorable	48	47	57	51
	Not Favorable	24	27	18	23
	Uncertain/ don't know	28	26	25	26
Do you think Walter Mondale has enough experience to be a good president?	Yes	79	75	82	78
	No	13	19	11	16
	Uncertain/ don't know	8	6	7	6
Do you have confidence in Walter Mondale's ability to deal wisely with a difficult international crisis or are you uneasy about his approach?	Confident		44	53	48
	Uneasy		42	36	39
	Don't know		14	11	13
	Total *N*	(573)	(235)	(176)	(411)

Source: CBS News/*New York Times* polls, March 5–8 and 21–24, 1984.

political. Hart's experience with Donna Rice in 1987, however, reminds us that some personal behavior can be used.

The plunge in Hart's support came with no changes in his favorability rating, and no changes in expectations about the eventual winner of the nomination. This emphasizes the limitations of current theories about the role of expectations in primaries and emphasizes the importance of framing. A strong case can be made that the changes in support for Hart were due not to changes in expectations, but to changes in views of his experience and competence.

Hart's overall favorability rating did not change between the two halves of the CBS News/*New York Times* national survey taken after the Illinois primary. With no change in overall positive and negative assessments of Hart, evaluations of his experience and evaluations of his ability to deal with an international crisis did change. This emphasizes the importance of Henry Brady's findings about the third stage of learning about a candidate. When images become differentiated, people no longer project from the same information about a candidate to all situations, but use different information depending on the frame or point of view. This analysis also shows that there was a change in information about Hart, and that "ability to rate" a candidate does not capture changes in information about that candidate. I have also shown that there were no changes in expectations during the period when Hart's vote changed. Underestimating changes in kinds and levels of information overstates the importance of expectations.[36]

The effects upon the 1984 Democratic primary of recent political experience with Carter and Reagan emphasize two of Anthony Downs's key insights: uncertainty is necessary for ideological differences between parties to persist, and different party ideologies can remain distinct from each other only insofar as no one of them is clearly more effective. Gary Hart, and John Glenn before him, was an alternative to Mondale in the wake of Reagan's repudiation, in word and deed, of Carter.

In February of 1984, Hart won the New Hampshire primary and surged ahead of Mondale in the national preference polls. As a result, a great deal of media attention was suddenly given to Hart's theme of "new ideas" and his call for a "new generation" to take over the Democratic party. But Hart did not create the demand for these ideas; instead, he mobilized existing sentiment. There was already support for new ideas within the Democratic party well before the primaries.

Although Hart did not win the nomination, he remained a contender and won several large primaries, notably in Ohio and California, at the end of the season. Why could he remain viable when George Bush, for example, fell so much farther and faster? My analyses show three reasons for Hart's continued viability and strength in the polls.

First, Mondale had a serious problem with perceived credibility and sincerity. Even his own supporters did not believe that he always said what he believed instead of what people wanted to hear. In a battle of appearances, his relationships with groups that had endorsed him became a source of doubt and suspicion about his sincerity. Reagan did not have a similar problem.

Second, in the Democratic race in 1984, three candidates—Mondale, Hart, and Jesse Jackson—remained after the other early contenders dropped out. The willingness of blacks (and a small segment of whites) to support Jackson as a candidate who could bargain on their behalf for more influence over the platform—and the nominee—made it possible for Hart to do much better than he would have done in a two-way race. At least 85 percent of Jackson's vote came from voters who preferred Mondale over Hart. Without Jackson's presence, Hart would have lost Florida, California, and Ohio—his only victories in the larger states—as well as most of his victories in smaller states.

Third, divisions within the Democratic party are wider than within the Republican party. The Democratic nominee must appeal to white voters as well as black voters, and to poor and blue-collar voters as well as white-collar voters. This means that the nominee must straddle the divisions on minority rights between equality of access and equality of results, on inflation versus unemployment and protectionism versus free trade. These splits, as we have noted, occurred even within the ranks of labor unions, a traditional source of party strength.

T E N
Conclusion

IN RECENT DECADES, journalists and reformers have complained with increasing force about the lack of content in voting and the consequent opportunities for manipulating the electorate. And yet over the same period academic studies of voting have begun to expose more and more about the substance of voting decisions and the limits to manipulation of voters. The more we learn about what voters know, the more we see how campaigns matter in a democracy. And the more we see, the clearer it becomes that we must change both our critiques of campaigns and our suggestions for reforming them.

In this chapter I summarize my findings about how voters reason and show how some modest changes which follow from my theory could ameliorate some defects of the campaign process.

I have argued throughout this book that the term *low-information rationality,* or "gut" rationality, best describes the kind of practical reasoning about government and politics in which people actually engage. I have emphasized that low-information reasoning is by no means devoid of substantive content, and is instead a process that economically incorporates learning and information from past experiences, daily life, the media, and political campaigns. As Tony LaRussa, the manager of the Oakland Athletics, put it: "When you trust your gut you are trusting a lot of stuff that is there from the past."[1]

Gut rationality draws on the information shortcuts and rules of thumb that voters use to obtain and evaluate information and to choose among candidates. These information shortcuts and rules of thumb must be considered when evaluating an electorate and considering changes in the electoral system.

How Voters Reason

It is easy to demonstrate that Americans have limited knowledge of basic textbook facts about their government and the political debates of the day. But evaluating citizens only in terms of such factual knowledge is a misleading way to assess their competence as voters.

Because voters use shortcuts to obtain and evaluate information, they are able to store far more data about politics than measurements of their textbook knowledge would suggest. Shortcuts for obtaining information at low cost are numerous. People learn about specific government programs as a by-product of ordinary activities, such as planning for retirement, managing a business, or choosing a college. They obtain economic information from their activities as consumers, from their workplace, and from their friends. They also obtain all sorts of information from the media. Thus they do not need to know which party controls Congress, or the names of their senators, in order to know something about the state of the economy or proposed cuts in Social Security or the controversies over abortion. And they do not need to know where Nicaragua is, or how to describe the Politburo, in order to get information about changes in international tensions which they can relate to proposals for cutting the defense budget.

When direct information is hard to obtain, people will find a proxy for it. They will use a candidate's past political positions to estimate his or her future positions. When they are uncertain about those past positions, they will accept as a proxy information about the candidate's personal demographic characteristics and the groups with which he or she has associated. And since voters find it difficult to gather information about the past competence of politicians who have performed outside their district or state, they will accept campaign competence as a proxy for competence in elected office—as an indication of the political skills needed to handle the issues and problems confronting the government.

Voters use evaluations of personal character as a substitute for information about past demonstrations of political character. They are concerned about personal character and integrity because they generally cannot infer the candidate's true commitments from his past votes, most of which are based on a hard-to-decipher mixture of compromises between ideal positions and practical realities. Evaluating any sort of information for its relevance to politics is a reasoning process, not a reflex projection directly from pocketbook or personal problems to votes. But in making such evaluations, voters use the shortcut of relying on the opinions of others whom they trust and with whom they discuss the news. These opinions can serve as fire alarms that alert them to news deserving more than their minimal attention. As media communities have developed, voters have the additional shortcut of validating their opinions by comparing them with the opinions of political leaders whose positions and reputations people grow to know over time.[2]

People will use simplifying assumptions to evaluate complex information. A common simplifying assumption is that a politician had significant control over an observable result, such as a loss of jobs in the auto industry. This saves people the trouble of finding out which specific actions really caused the result. Another example of a simplifying assumption is the notion that "My enemy's enemy is my friend."

People use party identification as running tallies of past information and shortcuts to storing and encoding their past experiences with political parties. They are able to encode information about social groups prominent in the party, the priorities of the party, and the performance of the party and its president in various policy areas. This generalized information about parties provides "default values" from which voters can assess candidates about whom they have no other information. In keeping generalized tallies by issue area, they avoid the need to know the specifics of every legislative bill.

As a shortcut in assessing a candidate's future performance, without collecting more data, people assemble what data they have about the candidate into a causal narrative or story. Because a story needs a main character, they can create one from their knowledge of people who have traits or characteristics like those of the candidate. This allows them to go beyond the incomplete information they have about a candidate, and to hold together and remember more information than they otherwise could. Because these stories are causal narratives, they allow voters to think about government in causal terms and to evaluate what it will do. Narratives thus help people incorporate their reasoning about government into their projections about candidates; their assumptions "confer political significance on some facts and withhold it from others."[3] They offer people a way to connect personal and political information, to project that information into the future, and to make a complete picture from limited information.

Finally, people use shortcuts when choosing between candidates. When faced with an array of candidates in which some are known well and some are known poorly, and all are known in different and incomparable ways, voters will seek a clear and accessible criterion for comparing them. This usually means looking for the sharpest differences between the candidates which can be related to government performance. Incorporating these differences into narratives allows them to compare the candidates without spending the calculation time and the energy needed to make independent evaluations of each candidate.

Working Attitudes

People do not and cannot use all the information they have at one time. What they use will depend in part on the point of view or frame with which they view the world; attitudes and information are brought to bear if they fit the frame. Of the attitudes and bits of information available, people tend to use those they consider important or those they have used recently. As the changes in voter attitudes entailed by the emergence of new candidates in primaries suggests, attitudes and information will also be brought to the foreground when they fit with what is *expected* in a situation. Our realizations, the thoughts that come clearly to mind, depend in part on what others say about their own thoughts and perceptions.

Thus, as options change, expectations change. If a Democrat were asked in early 1984 what he or she thought of Walter Mondale as a presidential candidate, and the reply was "He'll be all right," that response could be interpreted as coming from a nonthinking voter who was passively following a media report about the thinking of others. But the same response could also be interpreted as an indication of a complex ability to come to grips with the available choices, with issue concerns that cannot be satisfied simultaneously, and with the compromises considered necessary to reach consensus with other people. Similarly, if the same voter were asked a few weeks later what he or she thought about Gary Hart and the reply was "He's just what we need," the response could be interpreted to mean that this voter was simply following the media-reported bandwagon. On the other hand, it could be interpreted to mean that reported changes in public expectations had brought other attitudes and concerns forward in the voter's mind. As this example suggests, the information voters use depends on the reasoning they do, and the reasoning they do depends in part on their expectations. It also indicates that the way in which the content of a voter's response is interpreted depends on a theory about how voters use information and make choices. And I am convinced that any such theory must account for the "working attitudes" of voters—the combinations of feeling, thought, and information they bring to bear when they make their choices at the polls.

Why Campaigns Matter

Changes in government, in society, and in the role of the mass media in politics have made campaigns more important today than they were fifty years ago, when modern studies of them began. Campaign communications make connections between policies and benefits that are of concern to the voter; they offer cognitive focal points, symbolic "smoking guns," and thus make voters more aware of the costs of misperception. Campaigns attempt to achieve a common focus, to make one question and one cleavage paramount in voters' minds. They try to develop a message for a general audience, a call that will reach beyond the "disinterested interest" of the highly attentive, on one hand, and the narrow interests of issue publics, on the other.[4] Each campaign attempts to organize the many cleavages within the electorate by setting the political agenda in the way most favorable to its own candidates. The description of this process given in *Voting* (1948) is still accurate today:

> At the start of any political campaign the individual voter agrees with some issues, disagrees with others and is indifferent to some. As a result there are potential or actual conflicts over issues within individuals, within social groups and strata and within parties. Then the campaign goes on, and somehow the combination of internal predispositions and external influences brought to bear on the content of the campaign (the issues) leads to a decision on election day that one or the other party shall control the presidency for the following four years.
>
> Thus, what starts as a relatively unstructured mass of diverse opinions with countless cleavages within the electorate is transformed into, or at least represented by, a single basic cleavage between the two sets of partisans . . . disagreements are reduced, simplified and generalized into one big residual difference of opinion.[5]

The spread of education has both broadened and segmented the electorate. Educated voters pay more attention to national and international issues and they are now connected in many more electronic communities—groups of people who have important identifications maintained through media rather than direct, personal contact. There are also today more government programs—Medicare, Social Security, welfare, and farm supports are obvious examples—that have a direct impact on certain groups, which become issue publics. Other issue publics include coalitions organized around policies toward specific countries, such as Israel or Cuba;

various conservation and environmental groups; and groups concerned with social issues, such as abortion and gun control. Furthermore, there are now a great many more communications channels with which these people can keep in touch with those outside their immediate neighborhoods or communities. Such extended groups are not new, and modern communications technology is not necessary to mobilize them, as the abolitionist and temperance movements remind us; but the channels to mobilize such groups are more available today, and I believe that the groups they have nurtured are more numerous.[6] When the national political conventions were first telecast in 1952, all three networks showed the same picture at the same time because there was only one national microwave relay; today, with the proliferation of cable systems and satellite relays, television and VCRs can now show over a hundred channels. Furthermore, as channels and options have proliferated, and as commuting time has increased and two-career families become more common, the proportion of people watching mainstream networks and network news is also dropping.

Over the past fifty years, as surveys have become increasingly available to study public opinion, there have been many gains in knowledge about voting and elections. There have also been losses, as national surveys have replaced the detailed community orientation of the original Columbia studies. We know much more about individuals and much less about extended networks, and we have not adequately examined the implications for society and campaigning of the transitions from face-to-face to electronic communities.

Both primaries and the growth of media communication have increased the amount of exposure people get to individual candidates, particularly the quantity of personal information they get about the candidates. This increases the importance of campaigns because it gives voters more opportunities to abandon views based on party default values in favor of views based on candidate information, and also more opportunities to shift from views based on a candidate's record to views based on his or her campaign image. Moreover, as primaries have expanded, parties have had to deal with the additional task of closing ranks after the campaign has pitted factions within the party against each other. Primaries have also changed the meaning of political party conventions. Conventions no longer deliberate and choose candidates; instead, they present the electorate with important cues about the social composition of the candidate's coalition and about the candidate's political history and relations with the rest of the party. The more primaries divide parties, the more cues are needed to reunite parties and remind supporters of losing candidates about their differences with the other party.

The Implications of Shortcuts

Recognizing the role of low-information rationality in voting behavior has important implications for how we measure and study attitudes, how we evaluate the effects of education, and how we evaluate electoral reforms. To begin with, we must acknowledge that the ambivalence, inconsistency, and changes in preference that can be observed among voters are not the result of limited information. They exist because as human beings we can never use all of what we know at any one time. We can be as ambivalent when we have a lot of information and concern as when we have little information and limited concern.[7] Nor do inconsistency, ambivalence, and change result from a lack of education (especially civic education) or a lack of political interest. Ambivalence is simply an immutable fact of life. Economists and psychologists have had to deal with the inconsistencies people demonstrate in cognitive experiments on framing and choice: preference reversals and attitude changes can no longer be attributed to a lack of information, a lack of concern, a lack of attention, low stakes, or the existence of "non-attitudes."

The use of information shortcuts is likewise an inescapable fact of life, and will occur no matter how educated we are, how much information we have, and how much thinking we do. Professionals weighing résumés and past accomplishments against personal interviews, or choosing from an array of diverse objects, have the same problems and use the same shortcuts as voters choosing presidents. What we have called Gresham's law of information—that new and personal information, being easier to use, tends to drive old and impersonal political information out of circulation—applies not only to the inattentive and the uneducated but to all of us. We must therefore stop considering shortcuts pejoratively, as the last refuge of citizens who are uneducated, lacking in the political experience and expertise of their "betters," or cynically content to be freeloaders in our democracy.

Drunkard's Searches and information shortcuts provide an invaluable part of our knowledge and must therefore be considered along with textbook knowledge in evaluating any decision-making process. As Abraham Kaplan has noted, the Drunkard's Search—metaphorically, looking for the lost keys under the nearest streetlight—seems bothersome because of the assumption that we should begin any search rationally, in the most likely places rather than in those that are the best lit and nearest to hand. He adds, "But the joke may be on us. It may be sensible to look first in an unlikely place just *because* 'it's lighter there.' . . . The optimal pattern of search does not simply mirror the pattern of probability density of what we seek. We accept the hypothesis that a thing sought is in a certain place because we remember having seen it there, or because it is usually in places of that kind, or for like reasons. But . . . we look in a certain place for additional reasons: we happen to be in the place already, others are looking elsewhere."[8] At least when people look under the streetlight, they will almost certainly find their keys if they are there; if they look by the car, in the dark, they are far less likely to find them even if they are there.

Before considering the most serious criticisms of our present primary election process, and my suggestions for improving it, we should keep in mind the main features about how voters obtain information and reason about their political choices. The Drunkard's Search is an aid to calculation as well as an information shortcut. By telling us where to look, it also tells us how to choose, how to use easily obtained information in making comparisons and choices. As long as this is how we search and choose, people will neither have nor desire all the information about their government that theorists and reformers want them to have.

The faith that increased education would lead to higher levels of textbook knowledge about government, and that this knowledge in turn would enable the electorate to measure up to its role in democratic theory, was misplaced. Education doesn't change *how* we think. Education broadens the voter, because educated voters pay attention to more problems and are more sensitive to connections between their lives and national and international events. However, educated voters still *sample* the news, and they still rely on shortcuts and calculation aids in assessing information, assembling scenarios, and making their choices. Further, an educated, broadened electorate is a more diffuse electorate, an electorate segmented by the very abundance of its concerns. Such an electorate will be harder to form into coalitions. The more divided an electorate, the more time and communication it takes to assemble people around a single cleavage.

Since all citizens sample the news and use shortcuts, they must be judged in part by the quality of the "fire alarms" to which they respond. They must be judged in part by *who* they know and respond to, not simply by *what* they know. Furthermore, this use of fire alarms has an important implication. Since people can only respond to the fire alarms they hear, it matters how the fire alarms to which they are exposed are chosen. If it matters whether the responses to a policy or crisis are mediated electronically by Jesse Jackson and Jesse Helms, or by Bill Bradley and Robert Dole, then attention must be given to how the mediators are chosen by the networks.

Since attitudes depend on which information we use and how we view a problem, framing is an inevitable part of life. So long as framing is inevitable, campaigns will be important in a democracy. Therefore, campaign reform should focus on improving the shortcuts available from campaigns and campaign coverage, not on getting citizens to stop using them. Taking the high road and trying to eliminate shortcuts will work no better than promoting more civic education.

Criticisms of the Primary Process

Three serious charges have been leveled at primary elections: (1) they are insubstantial and lacking in issue content and are decided on favorability ratings and momentum; (2) they elect candidates who lack the insider political skills needed to pass legislation; and (3) by weakening party identification, they further decrease the already low American voter turnout. The first charge is simply wrong. The other two charges, however, have merit and deserve serious consideration here.

Chapter 6 and the case studies have shown that even with the newest and greenest candidates, primaries are heavily laden with issues; and that they are fought over the general direction people want their party to take, and over what groups they want to see dominant within it. Two incidents in particular demonstrate that the role of expectations is significantly less, and significantly different, than many popular views of primaries assume. First, when Ronald Reagan's nomination was a virtual certainty in 1980, after George Bush self-destructed in New Hampshire, there was a surge in support for Gerald Ford because thinking about Reagan prompted consideration of an alternative to Reagan, not votes for Reagan. Second, when Gary Hart fell behind Walter Mondale after the Illinois primary, his fall came without any change in expectations or in his favorability ratings; the fall came when Hart's problems with managing his campaign and stating his positions on Israel prompted increased awareness of his inexperience in foreign policy and general concerns about his competence.

Political Character and Personal Character

The second major criticism of primaries is that they emphasize campaigning skills over legislative skills. Primaries certainly favor candidates who can rally voters in the bowling alleys and restaurants of New Hampshire, and who are good at selling themselves in thirty-second "sound bites." Candidates who excel in this area—Carter and Reagan come to mind—need not have skill at actually working with legislators or with bureaucrats; and as Nelson Polsby has noted, presidents who cannot work effectively with their own party's representatives allow the national government to remain divided and thereby thwart the legislature.[9] I am not sure that the smoke-filled rooms of yore produced better presidents than primaries produce today. Otherwise, I agree with Polsby. Primary campaigns seldom offer voters information about a candidate's ability to make effective personal bargains and compromises with others in order to produce legislation. As the case studies of new candidates show, it is easier for voters to pick up low-information cues about issues than it is for them to pick up cues about the *political* character of the candidates.

Indeed, I believe that the single greatest danger of the primary system is that it promotes the assessment of political character by *personal character as displayed on television*. Given only a short period of time, voters inevitably use what they know about a candidate's personal character to judge the competence and integrity with which he or she is likely to work with other politicians. That might be tolerable if voters had access to full and reliable information about personal character. But when they make their judgments about personal character from the media caricatures presented on TV and radio, we have judgments of political character made on the basis of unreliable and misleading estimations of personal character.

It was suggested in chapter 6 that when shown pictures of pennies and nickels, people may not be good at separating real coins from coins that lack critical identifying features, but they are very adept at sorting nickels from pennies, just as they are at sorting candidates in Drunkard's Searches. In primaries, however, voters are called on not only to sort but also to evaluate candidates. Is it possible for voters to separate the Carters from the Bayhs and Udalls, the Bushes from the Reagans, and the Harts from the Mondales, and simultaneously decide whether the Carters, Bushes, and Harts are counterfeit or not? It is easier to tell chicken from beef than it is to grade the beef.

Every form of electoral competition has a bias. Because most primary contests are so short, and because most voters pay much less attention to them than to general elections, there is a bias in primaries in favor of candidates who are easy to grasp quickly, easy to judge from their media character. Ronald Reagan, for example, was portrayed and perceived on television as a particularly warm and friendly person. From the memoirs written by his senior associates as well as by his children, however, it is clear that he was a cold, distant, unengaged man with no friends other than his wife.[10] When Gary Hart's adultery was sinking his candidacy in 1988, he countered that he had not lied to Congress, shredded documents, or sold arms to terrorists—in effect, that his political rather than his personal character ought to be the issue. His retort should have been taken seriously, but it was not. The media—and television in particular—chose to discuss Hart's suitability for the presidency chiefly by publicizing his adultery.

While I have been unable to find a completely satisfying analogy, I suggest media character is to personal character as manners are to integrity. Judging a candidate's political character from his or her personal character, having first judged personal character from media character, is far more inaccurate than judging a book by its cover. Both politicians and authors have incentives to present a misleading character, in order to get elected or to increase sales, respectively. An author may want a sensational cover for his book, but his publisher has a clear incentive to resist this idea. The sales success of even a few books with misleading covers could lead to a long-term loss of sales; book-browsers might decide to reject all of his further titles because the covers of a few misrepresented them. Political parties have no such control over the media character of primary candidates.

Voter Turnout, Party Identification, and Primaries

The other chief criticism of primaries relates to the general decline in voter turnout in American national elections. Walter Dean Burnham has cogently argued that low turnout reflects the weakness of party identification and party organizations.[11] To the extent that primaries do indeed weaken party identification and reliance on party cues in general elections, they can be held responsible for some demobilization of the electorate. The extent, however, is debatable.

Turnout in America has always been low for an industrial democracy, and for presidential elections it has decreased from about 60 percent of the voting-age population to about 50 percent in the last forty years. Further, whereas in every country the better-educated are more likely to vote than the less well educated, differences are much larger in the United States than anywhere else.[12] One reason for our low turnout and for the large difference in turnout between the educated and the uneducated is the diffusion of authority in America and the confusion which results. Federalism combined with a separation of powers results in a system in which it is particularly hard to connect problems and votes, and a plethora of different campaigns and election dates.

It might be argued that low turnout and some of the education differential came about because Americans must register to vote long before the general election, and early registration dates are more likely to exclude people with less precampaign information about politics.[13] However, while it has become easier to register in recent decades, turnout has continued to decline. This supports the contention that low turnout and the education differential are due to the weakness of long-standing electoral cues and the concomitant need, in an already confusing and diffuse political system, to go through a political reorientation for every election.

In primaries, people must learn about candidates in a short period of time. This places a premium on quickly absorbed personal and issue cues. Because these cues are only imperfectly related to the cues people use in the general election, primaries have the effect of increasing the demands on individuals to absorb new information during the general-election campaign, while at the same time weakening the sources of political stimulation and solidarity. But I see no reason to believe that eliminating primaries would increase turnout by making it easier to use long-standing electoral cues about the parties instead of new information about the candidates. As noted in chapter 4, it is the rise of television that has made candidate-centered politics possible. Eliminating primaries would not change television or campaign advertising, or reverse the changes occurring in the nature and kinds of social stimulation available.

American media coverage of politics, and of American culture in general, is becoming increasingly personalistic. If primaries were eliminated, general elections would still be candidate-centered and people would know even less about the candidates than they do after primaries. It is true that Robert Dole, Howard Baker, and Morris Udall did not do well in primaries; it does not follow that they would have done better had they been nominated by conventions. After the nominating convention they would be prone to the kinds of falls that John Glenn and Edward Kennedy suffered at the beginning of the primaries. Dole, after all, did no better as a vice-presidential candidate than as a candidate for president, and Senators Thomas Eagleton and Dan Quayle were savaged by the media, and the public, after party conventions introduced them to the American electorate. As long as résumés are followed by interviews, parties need a "screening test" for whether their candidates can master modern communication. This is one more reason why a single national primary would be the worst reform of all.

It is true, as Martin Wattenberg notes, that divisive primaries are followed by losses in the ensuing presidential election, but divisions within the parties were exploitable and exploited long before the present primary system developed.[14] Some Democrats have pointed to the popularity of Jesse Jackson as a problem created by primaries, with the implied suggestion that if a black didn't run or make demands on the party, conservative whites wouldn't notice that the Democratic party is more sensitive to the interests of blacks than the Republican party. But eliminating primaries would not eliminate the powerful media appeal of national political figures like Jackson. The fact is that America is becoming a country of electronic as well as geographical communities, and an increasing number of people in and out of our electoral institutions have national followings. The power of individual media politicians and advocates does not depend on primaries.

Furthermore, primaries are not the source of the present-day public's unquenchable thirst for personal information about national figures, and abolishing them would not restore the boundaries between public and private life. The growing accent on news and information about the personal lives of presidents can be clearly illustrated by comparing the coverage of President Franklin D. Roosevelt's polio with that of President Reagan's cancers of the colon and nose. By gentleman's agreement with the press, FDR's polio was never discussed, and he was never pictured being lifted from his wheelchair to the lectern for a speech or press conference. Forty years later, the minutest details of President Reagan's colon cancer were discussed on television with illustrations and diagrams; there was more open discussion of Reagan's colon in one week in 1985 than there was of FDR's disability in all his years in the White House. Indeed, one can wonder whether FDR could have been elected today. Would it have been possible for him to separate questions about the soundness of his policies from questions about the strength of his legs?[15] This open scrutiny of the lives of presidents and presidential candidates is relatively new.

All the barriers between elites and their publics are lower today. As recently as 1948, for example, Governor Harold Stassen of Minnesota, a prominent Republican with a good chance for his party's presidential nomination, was criticized in the press for "amateurish" campaign tactics that one might expect in a race for sheriff but not in a contest for the presidency. What he had done was hold question-and-answer sessions with members of his audiences to establish rapport, and then stand by the door to shake hands with them as they left[16]—an approach too folksy then, but de rigueur today.

On the evidence, then, primaries are not the reason turnout in the November presidential elections is down. Primaries are not the reason our politics is becoming increasingly candidate-centered, nor are they the reason for the increased focus on personal information about the candidates.

More Campaigning

If it is impractical to eliminate primaries, and implausible to believe that going back to smoke-filled rooms would strengthen party voting in a television age, what can be done? How can we get primaries that will increase concern with political character, and how can we halt the decline in voter turnout in general elections? My suggestions, though modest enough, will differ from those of most reformers, because I believe that a cure for both problems may be found mainly in increasing the amount of political stimulation that campaigns provide.

There is no electoral problem in America that would be solved by restricting television news to the MacNeil-Lehrer format and requiring all the candidates to model their speeches on the Lincoln-Douglas debates.

Successful reform is possible only if we begin by looking at the ways in which voters actually reason, and then alter the system to give them more of the information and stimulation they need to reduce the chance of unacceptable outcomes. If voters engage in a Drunkard's Search for the keys to political choice, then campaigns should give them more, not fewer, streetlights to look under. The place where the candidates are shining their lights may not be the best place to find the information about the issue a voter cares most about. But at least when people look there, they are likely to see whatever electoral keys are there to be seen.

The one change in primaries I would urge would be a spacing of three weeks between primaries so that the local campaigns in primary states would run for twenty-one days instead of a single week. I believe that this combination of national news and intensive local campaigning would give people enough exposure and stimulation for complex pictures of new candidates to develop. This is enough time for crystallization to develop, in Brady's formulation, or for expectations to become less important, in Bartels's approach.[17] If the New Hampshire primary were held the third week in January and regional primaries were held every third Tuesday, the entire season could end in early May.

More campaign competition among the candidates, and more voter exposure to this competition, would give the candidates more time to move from personal character to general political competence and to introduce into the campaign questions about the candidates' records. Walter Mondale had to ask "Where the beef?" and force Gary Hart to come to grips with specific policy proposals. The more time and stimulation in such campaigns, the better.

I would like to see more time provided between the end of the convention and the election for the parties and the candidates to prepare themselves. The challenging party's candidate can always use additional time to get to know the people that he or she will have to work with in campaigning and, if elected, in governing. I would also like to see the networks recognize the role that conventions play in an age when the nominee is already known. It is commonly assumed that because conventions no longer pick presidential candidates, they have little substantive importance. In fact, conventions gain new importance in an age of primaries. They are the key source of cues for the party followers about whether the party elites have reunited, and about what ammunition the party platform provides for the battles ahead.

Turnout and Social Interaction

I believe that voter turnout has declined because campaign stimulation, from the media and from personal interaction, is also low and declining, and there is less interaction between the media and the grass-roots, person-to-person aspects of voter mobilization. The lack of campaign stimulation, I suggest, is also responsible for the large turnout gap in this country between educated and uneducated voters.

The social science research shows clear relations between the turnout and social stimulation. Married people of all ages vote more than people of the same age who live alone.[18] And much of the increase in turnout seen over one's life cycle is due to increases in church attendance and community involvement.[19] I believe that in this age of electronic communities, when more people are living alone and fewer people are involved in churches, PTAs, and other local groups, interpersonal social stimulation must be increased if turnout is to increase. The research discussed in chapter 3 on interpersonal influence and focus groups showed the role that social stimulation played in helping people form opinions and bring them into use. More research will be needed before we can say whether there has been a decline in overall stimulation, or whether the stimulation people are getting is more diverse and less reinforcing. In either case, though, I believe that only an increase in overall social stimulation will increase turnout.

Political parties used to spend a large portion of their resources bringing people to rallies. By promoting the use of political ideas to bridge the gap between the individual "I" and the party "we," they encouraged people to believe that they were "links in a chain" and that the election outcome would depend on what people like themselves chose to do.[20] Today, less money and fewer resources are available for rallies as a part of national campaigns. And parties cannot compensate for this loss with more door-to-door canvassing; in the neighborhoods where it would be safe to walk door-to-door, no one would be home!

Some of the social stimulation that campaigns used to provide in rallies and door-to-door canvassing can still be provided by extensive canvassing. This is still done in Iowa and New Hampshire. These are the first primary states, and candidates have the time and resources to do extensive personal campaigning, and to use campaign organizations to telephone people and discuss the campaigns. In research reported elsewhere, I have analyzed the effect of the social stimulation that occurs in these states. People contacted by one political candidate pay more attention to all the candidates and to the campaign events reported on television and in the papers. As they watch the campaign they become more aware of differences between the candidates. And as they become more aware of the differences, they become more likely to vote.[21]

This suggests a surprising conclusion: The best single way to compensate for the declining use of the party as a cue to voting, and for the declining social stimulation to vote at all, might be to increase our spending on campaign activities that stimulate voter involvement. There are daily complaints about the cost of American elections, and certainly the corrosive effects of corporate fund-raising cannot be denied; but it is not true that American elections are costly by comparison with those in other countries.[22] Comparisons are difficult, especially since most countries have parliamentary systems, but it is worth noting that reelection campaigns to the Japanese Diet—the equivalent of our House of Representatives—cost over $1.5 million per seat.[23] That would be equivalent to $3.5 million per congressional reelection campaign, instead of the current U.S. average of about $400,000 (given the fact that Japan has one-half the U.S. population and 512 legislators instead of 435). Although the differences in election systems and rules limit the value of such comparisons, it is food for thought that a country with a self-image so different from America's spends so much more on campaigning.[24]

I believe that voters should be given more to "read" from campaigns and television, and that they need more interpersonal reinforcement of what they "read." Considering the good evidence that campaigns work, I believe that the main trouble lies not with American politicians but in the fact that American campaigns are not effective enough to overcome the increasing lack of social stimulation we find in a country of electronic as well as residential communities. This confronts us with some troubling questions.

What kinds of electronic and/or social stimulation are possible today? To what extent can newspaper and television coverage provide the kinds of information citizens need to connect their own concerns with the basic party differences that campaigns try to make paramount? Is there a limit to what electronic and print stimulation can accomplish, so that parties must find a way to restore canvassing and rallies, or can electronic rallies suffice? Does watching a rally on television have the same effect as attending a rally? Could a return to bumper stickers and buttons, which have become far less prominent since campaigns began pouring their limited resources into the media, make a difference by reinforcing commitments and encouraging political discussions?

The problem may also be not simply a *lack* of social stimulation, but the growing *diversity* of social stimulation, and a resulting decline in reinforcement. In 1948, Columbia sociologists collected data about the social milieu of each voter and related the effects of the mass media on the voter to the political influences of family, friends, church, etc. They found that a voter's strength of conviction was related to the political homogeneity of the voter's associates. At that time, most voters belonged to politically homogeneous social groups; the social gulf between the parties was so wide that most voters had no close friends or associates voting differently from them.[25] A decline in the political homogeneity of primary groups would lead to less social reinforcement; since the political cleavage patterns which exist today cut more across social groups, voters are in less homogeneous family, church, and work settings and are getting less uniform reinforcement.[26] Whether there is less overall social stimulation today, or whether there is simply less uniformity of social stimulation, the demands on campaigns to pull segments together and create coalitions are vastly greater today than in the past.

What Television Gives Us

Television is giving us less and less direct communication from our leaders and their political campaigns. Daniel Hallin, examining changes in network news coverage of presidents from 1968 to 1988, has found that the average length of the actual quote from a president on the news has gone from forty-five seconds in 1968 to nine seconds today. Instead of a short introduction from a reporter and a long look at the president, we are given a short introduction from the president and a long look at the reporter.[27]

In the opinion of Peggy Noonan, one of the most distinguished speechwriters of recent years, who wrote many of President Reagan's and President Bush's best speeches, the change from long quotes to sound bites has taken much of the content out of campaigning: "It's a media problem. The young people who do speeches for major politicians, they've heard the whole buzz about sound bites. And now instead of writing . . . a serious text with serious arguments, they just write sound bite after sound bite."[28] With less serious argument in the news, there is less material for secondary elites and analysts to digest, and less need for candidates to think through their policies.

We also receive less background information about the campaign and less coverage of the day-to-day pageantry—the stump speeches, rallies, and crowds. Moreover, as Paul Weaver has shown, the reporters' analysis concentrates on the horse-race aspect of the campaign and thus downplays the policy stakes involved. To a network reporter, "politics is essentially a game played by individual politicians for personal advancement . . . the game takes place against a backdrop of governmental institutions, public problems, policy debates, and the like, but these are noteworthy only insofar as they affect, or are used by, players in pursuit of the game's rewards."[29]

As a result of this supposedly critical stance, people are losing the kinds of signals they have always used to read politicians. We see fewer of the kinds of personalized political interactions, including the fun and the pageantry, that help people decide whose side they are on and that help potential leaders assemble coalitions for governing.

Gerald Ford went to a fiesta in San Antonio because he wanted Hispanic voters to see his willingness to visit them on their own ground, and to demonstrate that some of their leaders supported him. He also wanted to remind them of his willingness to deal respectfully with the sovereignty issues raised by the Panama Canal question. But when he bit into an unshucked tamale, these concerns were buried in an avalanche of trivial commentary. Reporters joked that the president was going after the "klutz" vote and talked about "Bozo the Clown."[30] From that moment on, Ford was pictured in the media as laughably uncoordinated. Reporters brought up Lyndon Johnson's contemptuous jibe that Ford "was so dumb he couldn't walk and chew gum at the same time." Jokes circulated that he had played too much football without his helmet. For the rest of the campaign, his every slip was noted on the evening news. Yet the news photos supposedly documenting the president's clumsiness reveal a man of remarkably good balance and body control, given the physical circumstances—not surprising for a man who had been an all-American football player in college and was still, in his sixties, an active downhill skier.

Similarly, during the 1980 campaign, Ronald Reagan visited Dallas and said, in response to a question, that there were "great flaws" in the theory of evolution and that it might be a good idea if the schools taught "creationism" as well. This statement was characterized in the media as the sort of verbal pratfall to be expected from Reagan, and much of the coverage related such gaffes *entirely* to questions about his intellectual capacity, not to the meaning of his appearance or the implications of the appearance for the coalition he was building.[31]

What difference would it have made if press and television reporters had considered these actions by Ford and Reagan as clear and open avowals of sympathy for political causes dear to their hearts? What if Ford's political record on issues dear to Hispanics had been discussed, or if the guest list for the fiesta had been discussed to see which prominent Hispanics were, in fact, endorsing him? The nature of the gathering Reagan attended was noted at the time, but it was never referred to again. It was not until 1984 that Americans uninvolved in religious fundamentalism understood enough about what the Moral Majority stood for to read anything from a politician's embrace of Jerry Falwell, its president, or a religious roundtable such as the one Reagan attended in 1980. By 1988, as more people on the other side of the fundamentalism debates learned what the Moral Majority stood for, the group was disbanded as a political liability.[32]

Television, in other words, is not giving people enough to read about the substance of political coalition building because it ignores many important campaign signals. That rallies and other campaign events are "staged" does not diminish their importance and the legitimate information they can convey to voters. When Richard Nixon met Mao Tse Tung in 1972, the meeting was no less important because it was staged. And when Jesse Jackson praised Lloyd Bentsen by noting the speed with which he could go from biscuits to tacos to caviar, he was acknowledging the importance of coalition building and trust. He was also acknowledging another fact of great importance: in building coalitions, a candidate must consider the trade-off between offering symbols and making promises.

If politicians cannot show familiarity with people's concerns by properly husking tamales or eating knishes in the right place with the right people, they will have to promise them something. As Jackson noted, the tamales may be better than promises, because promises made to one segment of voters, or one issue public, will offend other groups and therefore tie the politician's hands in the future policy-making process.

Is it more meaningful when a governor of Georgia hangs a picture of Martin Luther King, Jr., in the statehouse, or when a senator or congressman votes for a bill promising full employment? Is it better for a politician to eat a kosher hot dog or to promise never to compromise Israel's borders? When voters are deprived of one shortcut—obvious symbols, for example—they turn to another shortcut—obvious promises, for example—instead of turning to more subtle and complicated forms of information.

How good a substitute are electronic tamales for the real thing? Does watching a fiesta provide any of the stimulation to identification and turnout that attendance at a fiesta provides? How long does it take to bring us together, at least in recognizable coalitions? We need not have answers to these questions to see that they speak to the central issue of stimulating turnout and participation in elections in an age of electronic communities. The media *could* provide more of the kinds of information people use to assess candidates and parties. However, I do not know if electronic tamales provide the social stimulation of interacting with others, or the reinforcement of acting with others who agree, and I do not know how much more potent are ideas brought clearly to mind through using them with others. The demands placed on television are greater than the demands ever placed on radio or newspapers because the world is more diverse today and there are more segments which need to be reunited in campaigns.

Objections and Answers

Two notable objections can be made to my suggestions for increasing campaigning and campaign spending. The first is the "spinmaster" objection: contemporary political campaigns are beyond redemption because campaign strategists have become so adept at manipulation that voters can no longer learn what the candidates really stand for or really intend to do. Significantly, this conclusion is supported by two opposing arguments about voter behavior. One objection is that voters are staying home because they have been turned off by fatuous claims and irrelevant advertising. A variant of this is that voters are being manipulated with great success by unscrupulous campaign advertising, so that their votes reflect more concern with Willie Horton or school prayer or flag burning than with widespread poverty, the banking crisis, or global warming. The second objection is that popular concern with candidates and with government in general has been trivialized, so that candidates fiddle while America burns. In the various versions of this hypothesis, voter turnout is down because today's political contests are waged over small differences on trivial issues. While Eastern Europe plans a future of freedom under eloquent spokesmen like Vaclav Havel, and while Mikhail Gorbachev declares an end to the cold war, releases Eastern Europe from Soviet control, and tries to free his countrymen from the yoke of doctrinaire communism, in America Tweedledum and Tweedledee argue about who loves the flag more while Japan buys Rockefeller Center, banks collapse, and the deficit grows.

Both of these critiques of the contemporary system argue that campaigns themselves are trivial and irrelevant, that campaign advertising and even the candidates' speeches are nothing but self-serving puffery and distortion. This general argument has an aesthetic appeal, especially to better-educated voters and the power elite; campaign commercials remind no one of the Lincoln-Douglas debates, and today's bumper stickers and posters have none of the resonance of the Goddess of Democracy in Tiananmen Square. But elite aesthetics is not the test of this argument; the test is what voters learn from campaigns.

There is ample evidence that voters *do* learn from campaigns. Of course, each campaign tries hard to make its side look better and the other side worse. Despite that, voter perceptions about the candidates and their positions are more accurate at the end of campaigns than at the beginning, and exposure to campaigns is still the best predictor of whether perceptions of the candidates are accurate. Furthermore, as noted in chapter 2, there is no evidence that people learn less from campaigns today than they did in past years. This is a finding to keep in mind at all times, for many of the criticisms of campaigns simplistically assume that because politicians and campaign strategists have manipulative intentions, campaigns necessarily mislead the voter. This assumption is not borne out by the evidence; voters know how to read the media and the politicians better than most media critics acknowledge.

George Orwell overestimated the ease with which controlled media could manage minds, as even the Rumanian and Albanian Communists have discovered. Voters remember past campaigns and presidents, and past failures of performance to match promises. They have a sense of who is with them and who is against them; they make judgments about unfavorable news and editorials and advertisements from hostile sources, ignoring some of what is favorable to those they oppose and some of what is unfavorable to those they support. In managing their personal affairs and making decisions about their work, they collect information that they can use as a reality test for campaign claims and media stories. They notice the difference between behavior that has real consequences, on one hand, and mere talk, on the other.

Among those who read Orwell several decades ago, and among the disillusioned or alienated of more recent vintage, the ability of television news to manipulate voters has been vastly overstated, as one extended example will suggest. In television reporting—but not in the academic literature—it was always assumed before 1984 that winning debates and gaining votes are virtually one and the same. But on Sunday, October 7, 1984, in the first debate between Walter Mondale and Ronald Reagan, this assumption was shown to be flawed. Mondale, generally a dry speaker, was unexpectedly relaxed and articulate, and Reagan, known for his genial and relaxed style, was unexpectedly tense and hesitant. Mondale even threw Reagan off guard by using "There you go again," the jibe Reagan had made famous in his 1980 debate with Jimmy Carter. Immediately after the debate, the CBS News/*New York Times* pollsters phoned a sample of registered voters they had interviewed before the debate, to ask which candidate they were going to vote for and which they thought had done a better job in the debate. Mondale was considered to have "done the best job" by 42 percent to 36 percent, and had gained 3 points in the polls. As a result of similar polls in the next twenty-four hours by other networks and news organizations, the media's main story the rest of the week was of Mondale's upset victory over the president in the debate. Two days later, when another CBS News/*New York Times* poll asked voters about the debate and about their intended vote, Mondale was considered to have "done the best job" not by the 42 percent to 36 percent margin of Sunday, but by 65 percent to 17 percent. Media reports, then, claimed that millions of voters had changed their minds about what they themselves had seen just days earlier. Yet in the three days during which millions changed their minds about who had won the debate, the same poll reported, few, if any, changed their minds about how they would vote.[33]

This example emphasizes just how complex the effects of television can be. Voters now have opinions about opinions. When asked who won the debate, they may say not what they think personally, but what they have heard that the majority of Americans think. It is easier to change their opinions about what their neighbors think than to change their own opinions. And most important of all, it is clear that they understand the difference between a debater and a president, and that they don't easily change their political views about who they want to run the country simply on the basis of debating skills.

Critics of campaign spinmasters and of television in general are fond of noting that campaigners and politicians intend to manipulate and deceive, but they wrongly credit them with more success than they deserve. As Michael Schudson has noted, in the television age, whenever a president's popularity has been high, it has been attributed to unusual talents for using television to sell his image. He notes, for example, that in 1977 the television critic of the *New York Times* called President Carter "a master of controlled images," and that during the 1976 primaries David Halberstam wrote that Carter "more than any other candidate this year has sensed and adapted to modern communications and national mood. . . . Watching him again and again on television I was impressed by his sense of pacing, his sense of control, very low key, soft."[34] A few years later this master of images still had the same soft, low-key voice, but now it was interpreted as indicating not quiet strength but weakness and indecision. Gerald Rafshoon, the media man for this "master of television," concluded after the 1980 campaign that all the television time bought for Carter wasn't as useful as three more helicopters (and a successful desert rescue) would have been.

As these examples suggest, media critics are generally guilty of using one of the laziest and easiest information shortcuts of all. Assuming that a popular politician is a good manipulator of the media or that a winner won because of his media style is no different from what voters do when they evaluate presidents by reasoning backward from known results. The media need reform, but so do the media critics. One cannot infer, without astonishing hubris, that the American people have been successfully deceived simply because a politician wanted them to believe his or her version of events. But the media critics who analyze political texts without any reference to the actual impact of the messages do just that.[35]

Negativism and Triviality

Campaigns are often condemned as trivial—as sideshows in which voters amuse themselves by learning about the irrelevant differences between candidates who fiddle over minor issues while the country stagnates and inner cities burn—and many assume that the negativism and pettiness of the attacks that candidates make on each other encourage an "a pox on all your houses" attitude. This suggests a plausible hypothesis, which can be given a clean test in a simple experiment. This experiment can be thought of as a "stop and think" experiment because it is a test of what happens if people stop and think about what they know of the candidates and issues in an election and tell someone what they know.[36] First, take a random sample of people across the country and interview them. Ask the people selected what they consider to be the most important issues facing the country, and then ask them where the various candidates stand on these issues. Then ask them to state their likes and dislikes about the candidates' personal qualities and issue stands, and about the state of the country. Second, after the election, find out whether these interviewees were more or less likely to vote than people who were not asked to talk about the campaign. If the people interviewed voted less often than people not interviewed, then there is clear support for the charge that triviality, negativism, and irrelevancy are turning off the American people and suppressing turnout.

In fact, the National Election Studies done by the University of Michigan's Survey Research Center, now the Center for Political Studies, are exactly such an experiment. In every election since 1952, people have been asked what they care about, what the candidates care about, and what they know about the campaign. After the election people have been reinterviewed and asked whether they voted; then the actual voting records have been checked to see whether the respondents did indeed vote.

The results convincingly demolish the triviality and negativism hypothesis. In every election, people who have been interviewed are more likely to vote than other Americans.[37] Indeed, the reason the expensive and difficult procedure of verifying turnout against the voting records was begun in the first place was that the scholars were suspicious because the turnout reported by respondents was so much higher than either the actual turnout of all Americans or the turnout reported in surveys conducted after the election. So respondents in the national election studies, after seventy minutes of thinking about the candidates, the issues, and the campaign, were both more likely than other people to vote and more likely to try to hide the fact that they did not vote! Further, if people are reinterviewed in later elections, their turnout continues to rise. Still further, while an interview cuts nonvoting in a presidential election by up to 20 percent, an interview in a local primary may cut nonvoting by as much as half.[38]

The rise in no-shows on voting day and the rise of negative campaigning both follow from the rise of candidate-centered elections. When voters do not have information about future policies they extrapolate, or project, from the information they do have. As campaigns become more centered on candidates, there is more projection, and hence more negative campaigning. Negative campaigning is designed to provide information that causes voters to stop projecting and to change their beliefs about a candidate's stand on the issues. As Peggy Noonan commented on the 1988 Willie Horton ads, "Willie Horton . . . was a legitimate issue because it speaks to styles and ways of governance. In that case Dukakis's."[39]

As Noonan has also noted of the 1988 campaign, "There should have been more name-calling, mud-slinging and fun. It should have been rock-'em-sock-'em the way great campaigns have been in the past. It was tedious."[40] Campaigns cannot deal with anything substantive if they cannot get the electorate's attention and interest people in listening to their music. Campaigns need to make noise. The tradition of genteel populism in America, and the predictable use of sanitary metaphors to condemn politicians and their modes of communication, says more about the distaste of the people who use the sanitary metaphors for American society than it does about the failings of the politicians.[41]

The challenge to the future of American campaigns, and hence to American democracy, is how to bring back the excitement and the music in an age of electronic campaigning. Today's campaigns have more to do because an educated, media-centered society is a broadened and segmented electorate which is harder to rally, while today's campaigns have less money and troops with which to fight their battles.

When I first began to work in presidential campaigns I had very different ideas about how to change campaigns and their coverage than I have today. Coverage of rallies and fiestas, I used to think, belonged in the back of the paper along with stories about parties, celebrity fund-raisers, and fad diets. Let the society editor cover the banquets and rubber chickens, I thought; the reporters in Washington could analyze the speeches and discuss the policy implications of competing proposals.

I still wish that candidates' proposals and speeches were actually analyzed for their content and implications for our future. I still wish that television told us more about how elites evaluate presidential initiatives than what my neighbors said about them in the next day's polls. However, I now appreciate the intimate relationships between the rallies and governance which escaped me in the past. I now appreciate how hard it is to bring a country together, to gather all the many concerns and interests into a single coalition and hold it together in order to govern.

Campaigns are essential in any society, particularly in a society that is culturally, economically, and socially diverse. If voters look for information about candidates under streetlights, then that is where candidates must campaign, and the only way to improve elections is to add streetlights. Reforms can only make sense if they are consistent with the gut rationality of voters. Ask not for more sobriety and piety from citizens, for they are voters, not judges; offer them instead cues and signals which connect their world with the world of politics.

E L E V E N
The Election of 1992

IN THE PRESIDENTIAL ELECTION of 1992, a president once acclaimed as unbeatable was defeated by a candidate initially declared unelectable.

In March 1991, after the international coalition George Bush had assembled liberated Kuwait from Iraq in Operation Desert Storm, Bush had the highest approval rating of any modern president. According to the Gallup Poll, 89 percent—the highest in the nearly sixty-year history of that poll—approved of the way he was handling his job.[1] Many columnists and commentators declared him "unbeatable" in 1992: columnists Roland Evans and Robert Novak wrote, "There is something more intangible and mystical in the new relationship that now appears to bind the president and his country, affording him precious new strength," and *Newsweek*'s preview of the Democrats' prospects in 1992, headlined DREAM ON, DEMOCRATS, described the scenarios that the Democrats offered for their coming victory in 1992 as "fantasies."[2] Since many Democrats in both the Senate and the House of Representatives had voted to give sanctions against Iraq additional time before using ground forces against Sadaam Hussein, some strategists and commentators thought the division between the parties on when to start the war might become a realigning issue. Republican Senator Phil Gramm of Texas called the Democrats a party of "appease and run liberals" without the ability to lead the world:

> As you know, the Baath Party in Iraq and the Democratic Party in the United States are both working on their domestic agendas to make us forget the war. . . . Why is this [anti-force authorization] vote to undercut the president and to deny him the ability to lead the world so damaging to Democrats? Because it fits a pattern that is 20 years old . . . the pattern of Jimmy Carter and Walter Mondale and Michael Dukakis.[3]

By contrast with President Bush, the Democratic governor of Arkansas, Bill Clinton, had the lowest personal poll ratings of any recent major party

237

candidate for the presidency. Most voters first heard of him before the New Hampshire primary when he and his wife, Hillary, appeared together on the CBS program *60 Minutes* to refute tabloid stories of his alleged affair with a would-be nightclub entertainer named Gennifer Flowers. Throughout the primary campaign he was plagued by damaging stories concerning his alleged adultery, draft evasion, and marijuana use. Further, he was constantly accused of giving evasive, "slick" responses to questions about these charges. When he finally admitted that he had smoked marijuana during his days as a Rhodes Scholar, his follow-up line, "I didn't inhale," became as well known as the classic phrase of George Bush in 1988, "Read my lips." As a result, in the CBS/*New York Times* polls, Clinton was rated negatively by more than twice as many voters as had rated him positively, and most Americans thought he was telling them only what he thought they wanted to hear rather than what he actually believed.[4]

If momentum generated by the media was sufficient to sway voters, George Bush would have been reelected president of the United States. However, less than a year after he was declared unbeatable, President Bush was unable to win even 60 percent of the Republican vote in the New Hampshire primary against Pat Buchanan, a challenger who had never held elective office. And in November he received only 38 percent of the vote, one of the lowest totals ever received by an incumbent president. Moreover, this was the first time a Democratic challenger had beaten an elected incumbent Republican since 1932, when Franklin Roosevelt had defeated Herbert Hoover. In 1932, the country was in the midst of an historic economic crisis; unemployment was at 24 percent and no relief was in sight. In 1992, however, the economy was improving. Indeed, the election forecasts that had been based solely on the state of the economy predicted that Bush would win.

If voters had been unable to separate military leadership from domestic leadership, George Bush would have been reelected. A man who had been one of the youngest heroes of World War II, and the leader of a successful international effort in the Middle East, was defeated by a man who had avoided the draft and was thought by many Americans to have been dishonest about how and why he did so. Indeed, if voters had been unable to separate personal and political evaluations of candidates, Bill Clinton would never have received his party's nomination, let alone been elected president.

If voters had been unable to distinguish between current and future economic prospects, George Bush would have been reelected. Neither inflation nor unemployment was high in 1992, and a standard economic model of presidential elections, based on changes in inflation and economic growth, predicted that President Bush would win comfortably with 57 percent of the vote.[5] The economy *did* matter in 1992; in fact, a slogan on the wall in the Clinton campaign's "war room"—"The economy, stupid"—became so well known that it was used in campaigns throughout the world. That while the economy mattered traditional economic models could not predict the election emphasizes what an unusual year 1992 was. George Bush was not defeated because knee-jerk pocketbook voters voted against him, but because voters who were concerned about their long-term economic future no longer believed that the Republican party had a program for prosperity and for governing the country.

Finally, if voters had not remembered past campaigns, George Bush would have won reelection. In other words, if the "visceral power of ad pollution"—typified by the Willie Horton and "Read my lips" gambits in Bush's 1988 campaign—had been as effective as critics maintained, Bush would have been reelected. But in fact it proved harder to recycle an incumbent—even a heroic war leader—who had broken well-known promises than to promote a vice-president. The road to Washington is littered with the geniuses of campaigns past.

The dramatic turnaround in the ratings of President Bush is powerful confirmation that when people's beliefs about the main problems facing the president change the way they think about presidents and parties also changes. In 1992, voters reasoned that the collapse of the Soviet Union meant that diplomatic and military skills were less important. They believed that the economy was the main problem facing the country and that trade was the most important international issue. Candidates in both parties had to try to demonstrate to voters that their policies were relevant to the new domestic and international contexts.

With the collapse of communism, the Republican record on defense was no longer as relevant as it had been and their domestic economic record was mixed at best. After twelve years, Reaganomics had not brought lower taxes, less government spending, or sustained growth. President Bush had to use his campaign to try to convince voters that his military and diplomatic skills could open markets in Japan, and that he would focus on domestic issues in his second term.

Bill Clinton successfully used his campaign to persuade voters that he would change the policies of his party, and that he was a different kind of Democrat, who would emphasize jobs and personal responsibility instead of the social programs of a traditional, "tax and spend" Democrat. Clinton's campaign had to provide such assurance to voters; the party's past record and the acrimonious battles between the Democratic-controlled Congress and President Bush had also left voters unsure whether the party's policies were adequate, or even relevant, to the economic crisis they perceived.

In fact, the 1992 Democratic primaries became battles over *how* to change the party, not battles over whether or not the party needed to change. In 1984 the success of President Reagan in strengthening national defense and controlling inflation led to a primary battle over whether the Democratic party needed to change its ways. In 1992, the failures of Reaganomics and the collapse of the Soviet Union led some primary candidates to argue that the party should now return to its previous liberal path. However, instead of a rerun of 1984, the Democratic primary electorate responded mainly to the two Democrats, Bill Clinton and Paul Tsongas, who used their campaigns to tell voters about detailed economic plans and debated over which plan's variant of a new direction made most sense for the party.

Before Bill Clinton could persuade voters that he was a new kind of Democrat he had to provide voters enough additional details of his personal life so that the initial allegations of adultery and draft evasion were not the central features of his personal biography. He circumvented the nine-second sound-bite barrier of conventional network news to communicate about himself with voters by utilizing the alternate media channels and new formats. Once he had established his character, he defended his claim that he was a different kind of Democrat by using the campaign to detail the welfare reform and job creation policies he had implemented as governor. Finally, he reinforced his claim to being a new kind of Democrat by selecting a running mate, Senator Albert Gore, Jr., who was also perceived as a nontraditional Democrat.

Desert Storm

Polls conducted immediately after Operation Desert Storm that gave President Bush a record high job approval rating showed no increase in the salience of military issues, no increase in the public's confidence in the country's ability to win economic competitions with other countries, and no increase in public confidence in the president's leadership in economic matters either at home or abroad. Despite the intense focus by the media on the dangers of aggression by Iraq's Sadaam Hussein and the prospect of another oil crisis, the public did not place concerns about national security above concerns about a stagnant economy. In the CBS/*New York Times* poll taken immediately after the 100-hour ground war to liberate Kuwait, more than half of all the respondents listed an economic concern as the major problem facing the country, while only 7 percent cited any international or military concern.

At the time that President Bush's military ratings and overall ratings were at a record high, only 42 percent of all respondents had a favorable impression of the job he was doing on the economy. Moreover, four out of five said they believed the economy was in recession, and 75 percent blamed the state of the economy on the policies of either George Bush or Ronald Reagan.[6] The majority of respondents placed the lion's share of the blame on the policies of President Reagan; but Bush had made correcting the perceived excesses of the Reagan policies a cornerstone of his 1988 campaign with his talk of a "kinder, gentler nation" and his pledge, "I am the change."

The collective displays of buoyant patriotism following Operation Desert Storm did not put an end to pessimism about the future. In the afterglow of international acclaim for American leadership, when President Bush was receiving record ratings, only slightly more than one out of three Americans were optimistic about their collective future. Since 1984, CBS News/ *New York Times* polls have asked the question, "Do you think the future for the next generation of Americans will be better, worse, or about the same as life today?" During the postwar elation, in the first week of March 1991, only 36 percent were optimistic, while 35 percent expected no change and 26 percent expected things to be worse for the next generation.[7] Although these figures showed slightly greater optimism than in the previous year, they reflected, as well, a pessimism about the future that had been increasing throughout the four years of Ronald Reagan's second term.[8]

Expectations about the economic future were far lower than would have been expected on the basis of actual measures of the economy. For decades the Conference Board, a business think tank, and the University of Michigan's Institute for Social Research had been calculating indices of consumer confidence based on surveys which asked people their evaluations of local employment opportunities and economic activity, and their expectations about employment opportunities, family income, and economic activity in the future. For decades, both of these measures of consumer confidence had closely mirrored actual changes in employment opportunities and economic activity. When Iraq invaded Kuwait, however, consumer confidence dropped far below where it would have been based on the historic relationship with the aggregate predictors of consumer confidence. After the victorious 100-hour air war, moreover, there was only a momentary upsurge in consumer confidence before it once again dropped far below the predicted level of consumer confidence, and stayed there for the rest of the Bush presidency.[9]

Potential voters had a pervasive sense of stagnation and of a slow economic decline. The long-term economic future looked uncertain compared to their own past, and they doubted whether their country would remain a world economic leader. Even in the immediate afterglow of victory, a plurality of Americans believed that the world's leading economic power in the next century would be Japan.[10]

In short, the media's prolonged and intensive focus on Operation Desert Storm did not distract citizens from concerns about their long-term economic future, and the prominent display of the president's military and diplomatic competence did not improve their evaluations of his economic performance. Despite his apparently solid position, President Bush's future troubles were evident at the moment of his greatest triumph, because the polls already indicated that voters did not see success in international affairs as proof of competence in managing the domestic economy. Operation Desert Storm failed to have a long-term effect on what voters were looking for in a president, nor did it have a long-term effect on what they saw when they looked at George Bush. By the next year, he had suffered the most precipitous drop in favor of any president in the history of the Gallup Poll.

Japan

If Operation Desert Storm was the high point of George Bush's career, the low point was his trip to Japan in January of 1992. The sluggish American economy was not producing jobs, the trade deficit with Japan was increasing, and there were challenges to the President's laissez-faire approach to international trade within his own party as well as from the Democrats. As the election year began, President Bush flew to Japan with a group of American business executives, including the leaders of the three major automobile manufacturing companies. The trip was intended to bring home trade agreements and to demonstrate that the president's international military and diplomatic skills were indeed relevant to producing domestic economic benefits.

The most disastrous moment of the trip occurred at a state dinner, when the tired, flu-stricken president suddenly became nauseous and vomited directly onto the Japanese prime minister before collapsing with his head in the lap of his appalled host. The president's illness launched a wave of jokes, editorials, and metaphors. On *The Tonight Show,* for example, Johnny Carson joked:

> President Bush is doing just fine. . . . If you had to look at Lee Iacocca while eating raw fish, you'd barf too. [Afterwards] the president got some more bad news: Japan also bars the import of Kaopectate. . . . At first they thought everyone at the dinner had the stomach flu because all the American auto executives were on their knees too. Turns out they were just begging.[11]

The Bush trip had turned into a political nightmare, and the Carson monologue touched on all of the major problems the president encountered. The trip touched on public insecurity about whether America would be able to compete economically with Japan in the post–Cold War world. The perception that Americans were going hat in hand to Japan, with a president seeking economic help to stay in office, triggered a wave of editorials and cartoons about "begging." The very fact that polls taken in the wake of Operation Desert Storm would even ask questions about which country was economically stronger shows just how disorienting the collapse of the Soviet Union had been for Americans, after decades of political dialogue about containing communism and meeting the Communist challenge. Instead of a strong America negotiating with weaker countries, the popular image evolved into that of America "begging" for help from Japan. While Americans believed that they had better housing and health care than the Japanese, they believed that Japan had better schools, consumer products, and more advanced technology.[12]

The end of the Cold War, in other words, was changing the way Americans thought about the world and their own future in it. After the collapse of the Soviet Union and the election of non-Communist governments in Eastern Europe, a Cold War focus on military defense against communism was hardly salient. President Richard Nixon had electrified the country in 1971 when he announced he would visit "Red China," and his trip in early 1972 was followed attentively throughout the world, enhancing his standing. But twenty years later, in 1992, a comparable trip was a presidential mission seeking jobs and markets, rather than a mission for peace. For several years, a majority of Americans had said they were more concerned about future economic challenges from Japan than about military challenges, and the Bush trip was an attempt to show that he could deliver in the new arena.[13]

The trip was a failure both for the president and for the Republican party.

Immediately after its conclusion, 18 percent of the respondents in a CBS/ *New York Times* poll said they considered the trip a success, while 63 percent said it was a failure. This was more than just an embarrassment for the president; it was a political failure from which the Republicans would not recover all year.

For twelve years the Republican party had benefited from its image as the party better suited to deal with international military and defense issues. When President Reagan took office in 1981, after the Soviet invasion of Afghanistan and the Iranian hostage crisis, this was an important partisan advantage: 55 percent of Americans thought defense spending should be increased, and only 8 percent thought it should be decreased. Those figures had almost reversed by 1992: in January only 8 percent of Americans thought defense spending should be increased while 45 percent thought it should be decreased.[14]

As noted in chapter 3, the Republican party's presidential success rested heavily on its perceived advantage in managing the national defense and controlling inflation. The shift of the party to Ronald Reagan during the 1980 primaries was issue-driven, based on commitments to control inflation by cutting government spending and to build a more aggressive and capable national defense. The crisis of 1992 for the Republicans was how to convince voters that they were as adept at post–Cold War economics as they had been at controlling inflation and fighting communism.

Despite an anemic economy, until President Bush's trip to Japan the Republicans had maintained their advantage over the Democrats. When pollsters asked people what they thought the most important problem facing the country was, and which party would be better at dealing with it, the Republican party came out ahead of the Democrats throughout the first three years of the Bush presidency.[15] As the economy faltered, however, the gap narrowed and the parties were virtually even. Immediately after the president's trip to Japan, however, the gap on "better able to handle the country's most important problem" widened to the biggest Democratic advantage in more than a decade—42 to 29, a 13-point spread. This was as great as the lead the Republicans had held in 1980, when inflation was in double digits, the Soviets were in Afghanistan, and the hostages still in Teheran!

That a single calamitous trip could affect so many voters indicates how much was at stake in 1992, and how pervasive was a sense—as the primaries began—that something was deeply wrong with the country.

Read My Lips

Every campaign discussed in this book was framed by the voters' perceptions of the country and its place in the world. What was new in 1992 was
that the campaign was framed not only by the state of the economy and the
collapse of the Soviet Union but also by the 1988 campaign. If the GOP
team that had helped George Bush win in 1988 was unable to recycle him
in 1992, it was because voters remembered elements of that campaign so
clearly and, in many cases, so bitterly. At the end of that campaign, voters
were noticeably less satisfied than usual. Whereas in 1980 and 1984, half
of all registered voters had said they were satisfied with the choice of candidates, in 1988 the percentage who said they were satisfied dropped to 33.[16]

Thus, in 1992 many voters were looking for the public debate they had
found lacking in 1988. The 1988 campaign came at a time when a large
percentage of the electorate was concerned about the future of the country.[17] During his first term, President Reagan had successfully stemmed
inflation and strengthened the country's military defenses. However, the
public's unease about the future had increased dramatically during his
second term. There was widespread concern about governmental services,
particularly education, and about the increase in social problems such as
drug addiction and homelessness. There was also a general opposition to
tax increases to cover the mounting federal deficit.

When he accepted his party's nomination for president in 1988, George
Bush could not and did not promise "four more years" of the same policies.
Recognizing the public's fears about the future, their demands for better
education, and for solutions to the nation's social problems, as well as their
concerns about the harsher side of the 1980s, he promised "a kinder, gentler nation," a nation in which local civic and religious organizations of
concerned citizens would provide "a thousand points of light." "America
needs change and I am that change," he declared, vowing to be "the education president." He also made one of the strongest, starkest, and most
memorable promises of any recent presidential campaign. With no quali-
fiers, disclaimers, or "wiggle room" of any sort, he said:

> My opponent won't rule out raising taxes. But I will and the
> Congress will push me to raise taxes, and I'll say no, and
> they'll push, and I'll say no, and they'll push again. And all I
> can say to them is read my lips: No new taxes.[18]

Because Michael Dukakis reacted so weakly to the Willie Horton commercials, and in general did such a poor job of responding to Bush, the

debate over whether social problems could be addressed without cutting entitlement programs such as Social Security or cutting defense spending or raising taxes was never effectively joined.

In 1990, just two years after making his pledge, President Bush signed the largest single tax increase in the country's history. Faced with the growing federal deficit and a Democratic Congress unwilling to cut into entitlements and social programs, he agreed to a compromise that both surprised and infuriated many voters. After months of charges and countercharges between congressional Democrats and the president, a budget compromise was achieved: it enacted a large tax increase to help pay the costs of bailing out the failing savings and loan association banks (S&Ls) without making major cuts in programs favored by the Democrats or in popular entitlement programs.

As noted in chapter 4, voters are generally averse to making trade-offs, and they reacted with anger when the need for a compromise was forced upon them by the constraints of the growing federal budget deficit.[19] The ratings of both the president and Congress dropped precipitously in the polls. Only 29 percent of the public thought the budget agreement had been fair, and there was an even split between those who thought the deficit could be reduced solely with spending cuts and those who thought both cuts and new taxes were needed. The proportion of registered voters who thought the country was "run by a few big interests" jumped from 57 percent in 1988 to 77 percent in 1990.[20] The average vote for incumbent members of Congress in both parties in 1990 dropped for the first time in any election since World War II, and three-quarters of all incumbents received fewer votes than in 1988.[21]

The public stalemate between Congress and the president was detrimental to both sides. The political and theoretical implication of this is clear: there are no white knights once the dirt hits the fan. That is, when two groups engage in a long series of charges and countercharges, most people lose track of the issues or principles behind the skirmishes; what might have started as good guys versus bad guys soon becomes nothing more than a mudslinging free-for-all in which everyone looks bad. Just as Watergate left many voters disillusioned after successive waves of complicated charges, many in 1990 saw the debate over the federal budget as a pointless cacophony rather than a sustained rally between two principled opponents. Thus, concerns about the future of the country and pessimism about the economy were joined by a bitterness about the performance of both President Bush and Congress during the 1990 budget negotiations.

The disillusionment with Washington did not abate after the budget battle had ended. In the summer of 1991, the Senate confirmation hearings on the nomination of Judge Clarence Thomas to the United States Supreme Court fueled yet another round of anger and disgust. For days, millions listened to a debate they considered embarrassing and unseemly over whether Judge Thomas had sexually harassed a former associate of his, Anita Hill. This was followed in the autumn with the explosion of public anger over revelations that many members of the House of Representatives had consistently overdrawn their accounts in the House-run bank. Although no public funds were involved—because overdrawn checks were covered by the deposits of fellow Representatives—the practice became a focus for public resentment of members of Congress as people with special privileges unwarranted by their collective performance. Incumbents who had written hundreds of bad checks were particularly liable to challenges in the primaries and in the general election. So acrimonious was the atmosphere that the largest number of members of Congress since the Depression chose to retire rather than risk another campaign.[22]

Operation Desert Storm was but a brief interlude in the battle between the Democrats and Republicans about what approach to take in dealing with the federal budget deficit and the public's concerns over education, medical care, jobs, and the economy. The president continued to insist that the programs already in place were adequate to meet the challenge. But by April of 1992 fully 58 percent of the registered voters, including a plurality of Republicans, said the Bush administration was drifting without clear plans, and only 29 percent said the administration was moving carefully to develop its plans. Three years earlier, in April of 1989, these figures had been reversed; then, 61 percent thought the administration was moving carefully and only 31 percent believed it was drifting.

Throughout the primary season, public pessimism continued to grow. By May, Richard Wirthlin found that there was more concern about the direction in which the country was heading than at any time since 1980.[23] In the first Reagan administration, unemployment averaged higher than 9.5 percent for two years, and during 1982 the gross domestic product dropped by more than two percentage points. By contrast, in late 1991 and throughout 1992, unemployment was substantially lower, averaging near 7 percent, and the rate of growth rose to 2.2 percent from nearly zero in 1982.

In running for a second term, George Bush was in far deeper trouble than President Reagan had been when he ran for a second term, even though the downturn during President Bush's first term was far less severe than the downturn under President Reagan. By 1992 many voters had lost confidence in the Republican approach to the economy; in 1984, however, voters still thought the party's approach might work. During his first term, George Bush had not been the change he had promised: his tax increase had not led to a smaller federal deficit or to a more prosperous country, and he had not demonstrated that his international Cold War skills could create jobs in America by opening markets in Japan.

Read My Plan

George Bush paid a price in 1992 for his inability to correct the failures and inequities of Reaganomics, and for his reversal on tax increases. Similarly, Democrats paid a price for the low poll ratings of Congress and popular concern about taxes and deficits. The anger over congressional pay raises, banking scandals, the Clarence Thomas-Anita Hill hearings, and legislative gridlock confronted every candidate in every state. In other words, public faith in Reaganomics and George Bush collapsed at a time when there was no reservoir of faith in the Democrats, either.

The movements throughout the country for congressional term limitations were but one manifestation of the public's frustration with the performance of the national government. In April, after the names of members of Congress who had overdrawn their accounts at the House bank were released, only 15 percent of the electorate thought the political system needed only "minor changes"; 57 percent thought "fundamental changes" were needed, while 29 percent thought the system should be "completely rebuilt."

In 1976, many voters in the primaries had distrusted Democratic insiders because of the Democrats' support for busing and because the taint of Watergate affected everyone in Washington. In 1992, Democrats had to convince voters that they were not traditional "tax and spend" liberals from Washington who would raise taxes to start social programs of dubious potential at a time when the public was concerned about the slow but real decline in net wages.[24] In sum, the focus on wages and jobs accentuated voters' concern over whether Democrats could address the economy and not simply tackle social problems such as education and medical care.

The loss of faith in Reaganomics did not revive the voters' faith in liberalism, and the weaknesses of the Democratic party's establishment, so manifest in 1976 and 1984, were not obscured by the failures of Presidents Reagan and Bush. Throughout 1992, voters said their single greatest economic fear about a second term for George Bush was "gridlock" and "economic decline"; their greatest fear about a potential Democratic administration was increased taxes.[25]

Democratic primary voters angry about gridlock, broken promises, and privileged politicians looked to cold economic plans rather than to angry candidates like Jerry Brown or to traditional liberals. The debate in New Hampshire and subsequent primaries was dominated by Paul Tsongas, a former senator from Massachusetts who had resigned from the Senate because of cancer, and Bill Clinton, the governor of Arkansas. In New Hampshire these two candidates garnered 60 percent of the vote, with Tsongas winning by 35 percent to Clinton's 26 percent. What distinguished them from the others was their ability to focus on concrete steps for dealing with the economy, to the point of publishing actual plans for voters to read. Few voters believed that candidates such as Senator Tom Harkin of Iowa, Senator Robert Kerrey of Nebraska, or former Governor Edmund ("Jerry") Brown, Jr., of California had credible approaches to the economy. Harkin, for example, emphasized that the traditional liberalism of the past would still work; but votes for him, combined with the write-in votes for New York's Governor Mario Cuomo and consumer advocate Ralph Nader amounted to fewer than one-fifth of all the votes cast in New Hampshire.

Thousands of voters in New Hampshire obtained copies of the Tsongas and Clinton economic plans, and thousands more actually went to public libraries to read them. The Clinton plan was released, along with a television commercial promoting the plan, during the first week of January; in the next week Clinton moved from 16 percent and fourth place to 33 percent and first place in the polls. In the next six weeks, eighteen thousand people in New Hampshire telephoned Clinton headquarters to request a copy of the plan—the equivalent of more than 10 percent of the primary electorate.[26] This demonstrates, first, that some voters, some of the time, will take the time to read serious proposals. Second, and even more important, the attention paid to these plans, and the importance that Clinton's plan assumed during his general election campaign against George Bush and Ross Perot, tells us something significant about the kinds of cues voters use when they seek to assess a politician's policies.

The experience of the 1992 campaign suggests that whenever a candidate makes a clear and confident offer such as "Read my plan" or "Call my 800 number," voters perceive it as an important cue. A candidate who is willing to have his or her program examined, and thus expose him- or herself before the electorate, is giving people a chance to see his or her flaws. Furthermore, voters need not personally read the plan in order to believe in its content; they can assume that its meaning will emerge from public debate, as the candidate rebuts attacks on it by the other candidates and their surrogates. If voters reasoned that what they had not read was credible, it was largely because other candidates seemed not to find fatal flaws in the plan.

The Clinton and Tsongas economic plans both focused on the need for more jobs in the private sector. The Tsongas plan emphasized the need to help businesses expand to create jobs; it included tax incentives and capital gains tax cuts to spur investment. The Clinton plan stressed the need to upgrade the training and skills of the work force; it focused on apprenticeship programs, education, and the need to keep jobs in the United States.

Blue-collar, high school–educated voters and white-collar, college-educated voters evaluated these plans differently. Blue-collar workers, who as a group had experienced a decline in wages and jobs during the course of the 1980s, were attracted to an emphasis on investment in human capital; white-collar workers were drawn to an emphasis on making more capital available to businesses. In every primary, Tsongas's support was much stronger among college graduates and professionals, and Clinton's was much stronger among blue-collar, high school–educated voters. In New Hampshire, for example, Tsongas beat Clinton 43 percent to 22 percent among college graduates, while Clinton carried high school graduates, 31 percent to 29 percent. In Maryland, Tsongas beat Clinton better than two to one among college graduates, while Clinton won among whites who had not attended college. In Florida, Clinton defeated Tsongas among high school–educated whites by three to one, while Tsongas beat Clinton, again, among college graduates.

The Tsongas-Clinton divide was demographically similar to the Hart-Mondale divide in 1984, but the debate also showed the extent to which voters had changed their reasoning about both politics and policy. By contrast to 1984, in 1992 the candidate who most attracted working-class and less-educated voters was a man who was not warmly supported by unions, who emphasized the importance of skills and the creation of jobs rather than increased spending on welfare and transfer payments, and who emphasized personal responsibility rather than government obligations.

"Slick Willie"

In the final months of 1991 and in January of 1992, Clinton moved well ahead of the other candidates in the New Hampshire polls. By late January he was almost at 40 percent in most polls, with Tsongas in the low 20s. At that point, Clinton was hit with a barrage of news stories about his alleged marital infidelity and his actions during the Vietnam War. For the remainder of the primary season, and throughout the general election campaign, there was a succession of stories questioning his personal ethics, his drug use, and his marital fidelity: in short, his character.

On January 26, 1992—Super Bowl Sunday—Bill and Hillary Clinton appeared on *60 Minutes* to rebut charges that the Arkansas governor had had an affair with Gennifer Flowers. Clinton denied any affair with Flowers, but said that his marriage had weathered some troubles, and that people would "get the drift" of what he meant by that. The next week, a *Wall Street Journal* story said he had avoided serving in Vietnam by promising to join a Reserve Officers Training Corps (ROTC) unit, which he never joined. One week later, a letter he had written in 1969 to Colonel Eugene Holmes, who had been in charge of the unit he did not join, was released to the press. In the letter, Clinton thanked the colonel for "saving him from the draft" and linked his decision not to openly resist the draft to a desire "to maintain my political viability within the system." Later, two days before the April 7 New York primary, there were news stories that Clinton had, indeed, received an induction notice—which contradicted earlier statements he had made about the draft.[27]

The week before the New York primary, Clinton, who had answered previous questions about marijuana use with denials that he had ever broken "any state's" drug laws, was asked if he had ever tried marijuana in England, while he had been at Oxford as a Rhodes Scholar. In his answer he replied: "I never broke a state law . . . but when I was in England I experimented with marijuana a time or two, and I didn't like it. I didn't inhale it, and never tried it again."[28] In addition there were stories about Clinton's use of corporate jets while he was governor, stories about campaign contributions from companies accused of polluting the state of Arkansas, personal investments by the Clintons with S&L owners, and charges that Mrs. Clinton's law firm had profited from work with the state government.

In New Hampshire, where Clinton had campaigned for months, fewer than 40 percent of registered Democrats thought he was telling the truth about his personal affairs.[29] After New Hampshire when Clinton began to pull ahead, his opponents began to argue that there might well be more revelations and that Clinton could not be trusted on his political programs any more than he could be believed about his personal life. A Tsongas television commercial in Illinois, for example, used the opening line, "Heard the latest?"; another said of Tsongas, "He tells the truth. He's no Bill Clinton, that's for sure." Referring to his own pro-choice position, Tsongas quipped "I want women—no, that's the other guy." He also alluded to the Republicans' propensity for negative advertising by asking ominously,

"How many people do you think the Republicans have out there investigating Bill Clinton?"[30] After the New York primary, which Clinton barely won after more draft charges and his "I didn't inhale" comment, Robert Casey, the Democratic governor of Pennsylvania, argued that the party needed to keep the convention open so that a better nominee could be found. Jerry Brown then urged voters to support him just to keep the nomination open until a new nominee could be found: "Voting for Clinton is like taking a ticket on the Titanic. . . . It sounds good. It looks good. The food is fine. But it's going under water."[31]

As a result of all the stories about Clinton's character, and the stories about his allegedly partial, incomplete, or lawyerly answers to the charges, Robin Toner wrote in the *New York Times* that Clinton had gone from "inevitable to impossible to inevitable but doomed." That is, his nomination seemed inevitable before the tabloid charges, impossible after they appeared, and then inevitable again although doomed after he defeated Tsongas because no one believed he could beat Bush.[32] Throughout the primaries, a majority of Democrats said, both in exit polls and national surveys, that they wanted to see new candidates in the race.[33] Even though Clinton had virtually clinched the nomination by late March, a majority of Democratic voters continued to want new candidates in the race. The only other remaining candidate, Jerry Brown, was so unpopular that his main argument was that people should vote for him to keep the nomination at the convention open.

Most voters did not believe that Clinton's all-but-admitted adultery and alleged evasion of the draft disqualified him from the presidency. While between 10 and 20 percent of voters thought the charges were serious, far more important was the inference by many more from the way he handled the charges that he was insincere and overly political.[34] At the end of the primaries, 62 percent thought he said "what he thinks voters want to hear," while only 28 percent of registered voters thought he was a person who "says what he believes most of the time."[35] Phrases such as "I didn't inhale" and "maintain my viability" were interpreted as evidence that he was an ambitious politician who would say anything and who could not be trusted personally.[36] When *Washington Post* reporters Dan Balz and David Broder conducted a focus group in Chicago, participants described Clinton with words such as "slick," "slimy," and "cunning." They also compared him to television evangelists Jimmy Swaggart and Jim Bakker.[37]

Typically, voters have particular concerns about the character of political consensus builders; they focus on whether they are sincere, on whether their support for a cause represents a genuine personal commitment or merely a campaign tactic.[38] When a candidate is both a consensus builder and a person whose character is being questioned, the concern becomes even more serious. As the 1992 campaign suggests, when there is anger and resentment at the entire political system, the voters' concerns with sincerity will be even more salient.

Voters had inferred (erroneously, as it happened) from the draft evasion stories that Clinton had led a life of privilege. His personal history—successful avoidance of the draft during the Vietnam War, a Rhodes Scholarship, attendance at Yale Law School—suggested that he had been born to a life of social connections and privilege. This misperception raised suspicions about whether he had any genuine concern for average people or whether he was just posturing.

The Man from Hope

When Bill Clinton formally clinched his party's nomination on June 2 with victories in five states, including California, Ohio, and New Jersey, he had been badly damaged by the primary process.[39] Even though he was the first Democratic candidate to win primaries in all ten of the largest states, his candidacy was considered doomed by many commentators. Jay Leno, for example, suggested that when Clinton had a call-in show, the number should be "Rescue 911."[40] The undeclared candidacy of Ross Perot was gaining momentum, and Clinton was third in most of the national polls behind Perot and Bush. In fact, in California he could not even carry his own party against Ross Perot: in the June 2 exit polls, he lost a trial heat to Perot among voters in the California Democratic primary.[41] In a *Newsweek/Gallup* poll, 30 percent of Democrats thought the Democratic convention should dump Clinton and find another candidate.[42]

When shown television commercials of Clinton discussing his programs, potential voters in focus groups reacted derisively and discounted most of what he said as slick propaganda.[43] Yet only six weeks later, Clinton was rising so quickly in the polls that Ross Perot dropped out of the race and attributed his decision, in part, to a revitalized Democratic party.

If Clinton won the nomination by talking about the economy, he overcame the damage he had sustained in the primaries by talking about himself, connecting the issues with which he was concerned to his own personal history. To counter the impression that many people had of him as a privileged, slick, adulterous draft dodger, albeit a smart one with a plan for the economy, he provided voters with a fuller portrait of himself by giving the public a sense of his past.

Clinton's comeback would have not been possible ten years earlier because it depended upon new television networks such as MTV, Fox, and CNN, and on specific types of programs and formats, particularly viewer call-in shows, that had only recently risen in prominence. In the 1980s, as the traditional network news programs were trimming politicians' statements to mere nine-second sound bites, and dropping on-air interviews with real citizens in favor of poll reports, talk shows burgeoned on both radio and television. Clinton made the most of these new outlets, thus giving potential voters a longer look at him, and a chance to go beyond their preconceptions and misconceptions about him.[44]

Immediately after he had secured the nomination Clinton began to make guest appearances not only on the traditional television programs on which politicians had been seen for decades, but also on entertainment shows. He appeared on the late-night *Arsenio Hall Show* wearing sunglasses and playing the saxophone; he appeared on the NBC *Today* show and *CBS This Morning* answering hours of questions called in by viewers. He appeared on CNN's *Larry King Live* and on an MTV "Rock the Vote" special program answering questions from its youthful host, Tabitha Soren, and an audience aged eighteen to twenty-five.

Most commentators saw this strategy as an act of desperation, and most unpresidential, as well. Many news analysts said that appearing on the talk shows was Clinton's way of avoiding hard questions from professional journalists, and they were even more caustic about his *Arsenio Hall* appearance. The *New York Times'* columnist Tom Wicker thought that appearance was exactly what a man considered to have been a swinger didn't need: "This is undignified. . . . The association with jazz music, the dark shades and the Arsenio Hall Show, I don't think that is an asset." David Gergen, a MacNeil-Lehrer commentator and editor-at-large for *US News and World Report*, was even more critical: "The difference in the gap between Arsenio Hall and talking to someone like [British Prime Minister] John Major, to me, is so dramatic, it suggests that he doesn't have a handle on what it takes to be President."[45]

Just as traditionalists thought it was unpresidential in 1948 when the Republican candidate, Harold Stassen, participated in a question-and-answer session during the Republican primaries and shook hands with the audience afterward, commentators such as Wicker and Gergen thought Clinton was making a serious mistake.[46] But by appearing on programs such as *Arsenio Hall* and MTV's "Rock the Vote," Clinton was simply going where the voters were, for many of them did not regularly watch evening newscasts or the Sunday morning interview programs. Indeed, it turned out that in 1992 nearly half the electorate watched call-in shows on television.[47] What was more important, these programs afforded Clinton a greater chance than traditional news outlets would have to discuss issues. On the call-in shows, more of the questions were about issues and fewer concerned personal charges than in the more traditional formats.[48]

Just as significantly for Clinton, the interview programs and call-ins gave him the opportunity to give longer answers. The focus groups organized by his own campaign had shown that short sound bites of Clinton speaking were insufficient to overcome the people's preexisting beliefs about him. However, viewers who saw him talking at length, as well as those who saw him in situations where traditional politicians had seldom appeared, often noticed that there was something more to Clinton than they had expected. In many cases, this led then to a reassessment of his qualifications as a candidate.

It was missing the point, then, to assume that by soliciting questions from call-in viewers Clinton was trying to duck harder questions from professional journalists. The radio and television call-in sessions were *not* a way to evade interviews with Dan Rather or Tom Brokaw or Peter Jennings. They gave people who were unable to assess a candidate on the basis of nine-second sound bites a more satisfying opportunity to learn about him. They also gave Clinton an alternative to "eating tamales," that is, to visiting people informally and being judged mainly on how comfortable he appeared to be while eating their ethnic foods. They gave viewers far more information about issues than such traditional campaign rituals—and more, in fact, than some of the interviews on the regular news programs.

After two weeks of talk show appearances, Clinton had made major progress. On May 30, when voters were asked whether each of the candidates was "telling enough about where he stands on the issues for you to judge what he might do if he won the presidential election," 33 percent thought Bush, who had no plan, was telling enough, 32 percent thought Clinton, who did have a plan, was telling enough, and 15 percent thought Perot, who said he would soon present a plan, was telling enough. Over the next three weeks, Clinton was ignored by the traditional networks, which devoted most of their coverage to Perot, who had just hired Ed Rollins, Ronald Reagan's 1984 campaign manager, and Hamilton Jordan, Jimmy Carter's campaign manager in 1976 and 1980, and thus become the center of a media firestorm. At the same time, however, using talk shows and alternative settings, Clinton made major strides in informing voters about his plan. In mid-June while 22 percent thought Perot was telling enough, and 32 percent thought Bush was telling enough, 43 percent now thought Bill Clinton was telling enough.[49]

On the evening of July 16 at the Democratic national convention, the biographical film shown about Clinton, "The Man from Hope," successfully brought forward an important part of Clinton's life story: he had been born poor in the small town of Hope, Arkansas, had an alcoholic stepfather and a brother who later had drug problems, and had attended college on scholarships. This film, and Clinton's subsequent acceptance speech, directly challenged inferences about him that voters had drawn from the earlier stories, which had erroneously led them to conclude that Clinton had led a life of privilege.

After the Democratic convention, 84 percent of the public said they thought Bill Clinton had worked his way up from humble origins, 62 percent said they thought he shared the values of most Americans, and approximately half said they thought he was telling them enough about his stands on issues for them to know what he would do in office.[50] With a more complete biographical picture of Clinton, people were more willing to listen to him talk about issues, more willing to decide whether his plans for the economy were better than the other candidates'.

Mud, as East Europeans learned under communism, makes good paint: once a person is smeared with it, it is hard to wash off, regardless of whether the charges are valid. Thus, new information did not actually erase old information about Clinton; after the convention, people did not forget the allegations of Clinton's draft evasion or adultery or "I didn't inhale." Throughout the campaign, more than half the public thought he was "telling people what he thought they wanted to hear, not what he believed." From March until October, a near-constant 20 percent said they were disturbed by his draft evasion, and by a margin of more than two to one, voters said they were not confident he had the experience to deal with a difficult international crisis.[51]

Still, people learned enough about Clinton from the campaign to judge him positively on the basis of his economic plan and his political character; they were able to move from the personal to the political. This evolution in voters' perceptions of Clinton suggests that the best way to fight charges or problems against a candidate's character during a campaign is to provide *additional* information about *other* aspects of his or her character, in order to give voters the fullest possible picture. Clinton did not do away with voters' concerns about his alleged adultery, draft evasion, or his tendency to try to please everyone. But he did convince many of them that he could nonetheless bring about change and that his plan was worth trying. Regardless of whether or not he had inhaled, he had a plan.

By the summer of 1992, 92 percent of those questioned by one CBS/*New*

York Times poll said they thought the country needed real change. During the course of the campaign, at least 40 percent thought Clinton would make the changes the country needed. The number who thought George Bush could do so was only 24 percent.[52]

A New Kind of Democrat

The Clinton campaign sought to convince voters that the most telling distinction between Clinton and Bush was "change versus 'more of the same.'" People felt major change was needed, and the Clinton campaign sought to remind voters that George Bush, who failed to make the changes he had promised in 1988, could only offer "more of the same." Indeed the much-cited sign on the wall of the "war room" in Clinton campaign headquarters had "change versus more of the same" as the top line, followed by "the economy, stupid" and "don't forget health care."

The distinction the Bush campaign sought to emphasize was "trust versus taxes." George Bush was a leader who could be trusted, while Bill Clinton would only raise taxes. This meant, in effect, that Bush had to convince the public that his second term would be different from his first term, when he had broken his "no new taxes pledge" and ignored domestic concerns. In short, he had to convince people that "this time I really mean it" and "now I really care." Given the difficulty of raising his own ratings, a good part of his campaign was devoted to lowering ratings of Clinton and the Democratic party.[53] As it turned out, twelve of the fifteen television commercials run by the Bush campaign were negative, and nine of those twelve were about Bill Clinton's character. By contrast, eleven of twenty-four commercials run by Clinton were negative, and eight of the eleven focused on the president's record and utilized news footage.[54]

Maintaining the focus on a simple, clear distinction between "change versus more of the same" was only possible because the Clinton campaign neutralized attacks by the Bush campaign that had attempted to turn the debate from economic plans and toward taxes or international affairs, or to character flaws that would discredit Clinton's ability to bring about change.

The Bush attack on Clinton borrowed heavily from the recent British election, in which the Conservative prime minister, John Major, had won an eleventh-hour, come-from-behind victory over the Labour party.[55] The Bush offensive focused on the argument that Clinton was radical, that the Democratic party was a party of minorities and losers, and thus that any changes the Democrats made would be the wrong changes for the majority of Americans.

The Democratic convention, and the selection of Senator Al Gore as vice presidential candidate, however, had convinced the public that Bill Clinton was a "new kind of Democrat," and the Republican campaign proved unable to change that impression. The week after the Democratic convention, when the CBS/*New York Times* poll asked potential voters whether Bill Clinton and Al Gore were "different from Democratic candidates in previous years" or were "typical Democrats," 44 percent thought Clinton and Gore were a "new kind of Democrat." After the Republican convention, the number dropped to 41 percent, but in October it was up to 48 percent. At no time during the election did a plurality of Independents and Republicans ever think of Clinton as another Mondale or Dukakis.

In September the Bush campaign resorted to implying that Clinton was a pawn of the former Soviet Union because he had visited Moscow while a Rhodes Scholar at Oxford; these attempts resulted in making Bush a target of some ridicule.[56] That these attacks on Clinton were viewed as necessary at all was a testament to the ability of the Clinton campaign to keep the focus clearly on the distinction they sought to emphasize: "change versus more of the same," by negating all the peripheral attacks designed to shift the focus to trust or taxes or personal character.

When Bush attacked Clinton as a draft dodger and a possible dupe of Moscow, Ronald Reagan's two-term head of the Joint Chiefs of Staff, Admiral William J. Crowe, endorsed Clinton and said that he was confident of Clinton's ability to defend the country and provide continuity in foreign policy. With the Cold War at an end, Admiral Crowe's endorsement on September 20 was enough to keep the issues of foreign policy, defense, and fitness to serve as Commander-in-Chief from becoming central during the rest of the campaign.

Clinton had an economic plan, and a large part of the electorate knew of it and believed that he had told them what he would do if elected. Campaign advertisements featured nine Nobel laureates in economics as well as hundreds of business executives from prominent corporations who also endorsed the plan. Moreover, these business executives were not "losers" but the heads of some of the most successful high-technology firms in the country, such as Apple Computers and Hewlett-Packard. The percentage of the population who thought the Clinton plan was worth trying did not decline.[57]

Most important, Clinton's campaign advertising featured the candidate's record on welfare reform. During his tenure as governor of Arkansas, Clinton had developed a training program for mothers on welfare that had succeeded in moving seventeen thousand women off the welfare roles and into jobs. Against millions of unemployed nationally, seventeen thousand was a minuscule number, but the fact that Clinton had promoted a successful welfare reform provided an important source of reassurance that he was a "new kind of Democrat."[58] A successful record on welfare reform and an often-stated philosophy that welfare was a second chance and not a way of life made it difficult for the Bush campaign to assert that Bill Clinton was out of touch with the middle class.[59]

Clinton's poll ratings began to rise even before the Democratic convention, when he selected Senator Albert Gore, Jr., of Tennessee as his running mate. Clinton's choice of Gore was a distinct departure from the usual practice of balancing a Northerner with a Southerner, a liberal with a moderate, a younger with an older person, or a Catholic with a Protestant. Clinton and Gore were both young, moderate, Baptist, and from border states. The powerful popular reaction to the two of them as young, intelligent, and vigorous, as well as the widespread stories about people driving hours to see their bus tour appearances, suggests an important cognitive explanation for Gore's importance to the ticket. A ticket of complementary, "balanced" candidates requires a difficult process of "averaging" to arrive at its expected value: What, after all, does a Bush plus a Quayle equal? Or a Kennedy plus a Johnson? Clinton and Gore, by contrast, were so similar that such a calculation was unnecessary; and the ticket psychologically easier to understand. Indeed, if this hypothesis is correct, the presence of Gore, who served in Vietnam, had a wife and four children, and was such a straight arrow that most of the press described him as positively square, may have lessened Clinton's problems of draft evasion and marital infidelity by concentrating the voters' attention on the common features of the two.

Ross Perot

Well before Bill Clinton had succeeded in reintroducing himself to the public through the alternative television media, Ross Perot had become a leading contender for the presidency through talk shows. Three days after the New Hampshire primary, at a time when the economy was sluggish, and more than half of all Americans said they did not have a favorable opinion of any of the candidates, Perot, a feisty, self-satisfied Texas billionaire, appeared on *Larry King Live*. In response to questions from King, Perot said he would consider running for President if volunteers placed his name on the ballot in all fifty states. He made this statement two weeks before the *New York Times* even reported it, and a month before it was mentioned in the *Washington Post*. But before these newspapers or any of the television networks gave Perot serious coverage, word of his offer to run for president had spread throughout the country as viewers who had seen the CNN interview gave their reactions to it on local-radio talk shows.[60]

The Perot phenomenon illustrates both the power of the new media and the pervasive unease the voters felt in 1992 with the two major political parties and with politics as usual. The initial enthusiasm for Perot is a classic example of low-information infatuation.[61] Perot excited interest because he engendered hope in people who were disenchanted with both Clinton and Bush. From the few bits of information they had about him, people could form an image that was a marked contrast with Bush or Clinton; Perot was a billionaire with plain tastes and a genius for common-sense aphorisms, who had led an effort to reform public education in Texas and who had pulled off a rescue of American employees from an Iranian prison—a feat that had been the subject of a best-selling book and a television miniseries.

By late March, Perot's vote shares were higher than 20 percent in national polls in hypothetical three-way races with Bush and Clinton. In June, Clinton was in third place in the CBS/*New York Times* preference poll and Perot was within one point of an incumbent president: the actual results were Bush, 34 percent; Perot, 33 percent; and Clinton, 26 percent.

Analyzing the support for Perot, Martin Wattenberg found that with the exception of African Americans, Perot's support was nearly uniform across demographic, attitudinal, and ideological groups. The single indicator that most predicted support for Perot was low attachment to either of the two major political parties: Perot attracted people unhappy with both Democrats and Republicans, including Democrats and Republicans unattracted to their party's actual candidates.[62]

In 1980, John Anderson had been the beneficiary of low-information infatuation after he announced his candidacy, but his national support never approached even half that of Perot's, and Anderson eventually ended the campaign with only 7 percent support. Perot suddenly withdrew in July, bewildering many of his supporters, and subsequently gave several different reasons for his decision. That he could reenter the race and finish as the preferred choice of 19 percent of the public is further testament to what President Bush called a "weird, weird" year. That millions of Americans willingly watched his thirty-minute "infomercials" (paid television appearances in which the candidate presented viewers with a blizzard of economic data in the form of charts, graphs, and statistical tables) is but one more piece of evidence of the degree to which Americans craved political solutions in 1992, and how much attention they were willing to give to even relatively dry political presentations.

An Engrossing Campaign

In 1992, Bill Clinton was slick; George Bush was distant, out of touch, and insensitive; and Ross Perot was bizarre. Yet voters were more engrossed in the election of 1992 than in any recent presidential election. Even the decline in voter turnout was reversed: after dropping steadily since 1960, it increased by almost 5 percent in 1992 over 1988.

The voters' level of attention to the campaign increased even more. Since 1980, every CBS/*New York Times* poll during election years has asked, "How much attention have you been able to pay to the presidential campaign—a lot, some, not much, or no attention so far?" The level of attentiveness, gauged by the percentage of respondents who said they were paying a lot of attention to the campaign, was higher in 1992 than in any of the earlier elections, and was higher in the summer of 1992 than in the last week of any of the other elections. In 1980, in a three-way election that ushered in the Reagan-Bush era and also gave control of the Senate to the Republicans, the percentage of the electorate that said it paid a lot of attention to the campaign stayed below 40 percent until the final week of the campaign, when it rose to 50 percent. In 1984 and 1988, the proportion paying a great deal of attention only passed 40 percent in the last week, when it peaked at 45 percent.

In 1992, throughout June, July, and August, the proportion of the electorate that said they were paying a lot of attention to the election was higher than 40 percent. In September it was above 50 percent, in October higher than 60 percent, and in the final week two out of every three registered voters were heedful of the election.[63] In short, voters paid as much attention to the 1992 election during the summer as they typically pay in the campaign's final weeks, and they paid more attention during the last month than they usually pay during the final days.

Clearly, some of this extra attention was stimulated by heavier campaign expenditures, since Ross Perot spent as much on his on-again-off-again campaign as did the other two candidates combined. But the voters' level of attentiveness was still higher than in other years when Perot dropped out on July 16, and when the Democratic presidential and vice presidential nominees went on a bus tour through America's small towns during July and August. Voters were more attentive in 1992 than they had been in any

election year since at least 1980, when CBS began collecting this data, because they were so concerned about the future of their country.

There were three presidential debates and one vice presidential debate in
1992, and these also attracted unusually large audiences. Moreover, while
in previous years the audience was smaller for the final debate, in 1992 the
size of the audience increased for each successive presidential debate—
even though the last one began at 4 P.M. on the West Coast. CBS did not
broadcast the final debate because of a prior commitment to air one of the
games of the major league baseball playoffs and even then, the debate out-
drew the playoff games, resulting in CBS coming in third behind ABC and
NBC in audience share for that time slot.[64]

Finally, it should be noted that this attentiveness increased without campaign reforms that might have limited negative advertising, because voters,
recalling 1988 and seeking more serious discussion than had occurred four
years earlier, were willing to devote an unprecedented amount of time to
following the presidential campaign of 1992.

Conclusion

Campaigns do make a difference. As Vice President Quayle said of Bill
Clinton in his concession speech, "If he runs the country as well as he ran
his campaign, we'll be all right."[65] Bill Clinton overcame voters' doubts
about his personal character by giving them sufficient reasons to judge him
instead by his political character. He won the Democratic primary by convincing a majority of Democrats that his plan offered them more than did
Paul Tsongas's, and forced the issue by challenging Tsongas to explain how
his plan would move the country beyond its current economic crisis,
which, despite his personal credibility, Tsongas could not do.[66] He then
used the Democratic convention movingly to tell his extraordinary life story and to overcome the misperception that he had been born to privilege.
In his choice for a running mate, he demonstrated that he *was* indeed a new
kind of Democrat. He used his record of commitment to welfare reform to
rebut charges that he was just another "tax and spend" Democrat.

What may be most striking about the presidential campaign of 1992,
however, is how different it was from the campaign of 1976. In the aftermath of Watergate, nearly half of all Americans responding to one poll said
that they thought the problems in Washington could best be solved by a
morally upright candidate who would restore moral values to government, rather than by enacting new programs.[67] Sixteen years later,
American voters were so concerned about economic and social conditions
in the country, and so angry with "politics as usual," that they were ready

to listen to a person with a detailed plan despite their serious doubts about his character and his evasiveness. And they were so troubled by the two major political parties that they were willing to give a chance to a man who had never worked a day in government and who had made five billion dollars in the private sector mainly from government contracts.

That voters in 1992 listened to so many debates, "infomercials," and discussions of plans proves they will reason about the content of governmental policies even at a time when their dominant emotion is anger. In addition to anger and a positive desire to throw the bums out—as evidenced by the public response to the House of Representatives' bank scandal, or by the millions of wet tea bags the voters sent their Representatives to protest the congressional pay raise—in the end voters did not vote for the angriest candidates, Jerry Brown and Pat Buchanan. They moved beyond their anger and their thirst for retribution and thought, instead, about the future of their country.

Notes

Prologue

1. President Ford made this comment to the White House press corps in the third week after the election; it was published in the pool report but not in the official transcript. Personal communication to Virginia Moseley, CBS News Elections Unit, from Bob Barrett, press secretary to President Ford.

2. *New York Times*, Apr. 10, 1976, p. 1.

3. Reeves, "McGovern, Nixon, and the Jewish Vote," p. 26.

4. Ibid.

5. Somewhere in the multitude of personal cues there is probably the sensibility equivalent of a social distance scale.

6. Germond and Witcover, *Whose Broad Stripes and Bright Stars?* pp. 349–50.

7. Quoted in Diamond, *The Spot*, p. 350.

8. Patrick Caddell, in "The Democratic Strategy and Its Electoral Consequences," pp. 267–303, examines the 1980 campaign and presents data on the rapidly increasing pessimism in the last days of the campaign concerning America's position in the world and the release of the hostages. In opposition to a campaign and surge for Reagan, Richard Wirthlin, Reagan's pollster, argued that there was no shift in votes at the end of the campaign—that Reagan had been ahead by 10 points well before the last weekend. However, Warren Mitofsky has shown that Wirthlin's poll methodology overstated the Republican vote by as much as 10 points. (Mitofsky, "The 1980 Pre-Election Polls," pp. 47–52.) Wirthlin later disclosed that his polling actually showed Reagan ahead by 17 points the day before the election. Further, in a Virginia election the next year, Wirthlin's polls showed the Republican candidate for governor doing 10 points better than he actually finished and than other polls showed he would do. (Kaiser, "White-House Pulse-Taking," p. A1.) While I believe the evidence for a last-minute surge is very strong, more analysis will be needed to defend the argument that the last-minute change was due to the news of the hostage crisis. Iyengar and Kinder, in *News That Matters*, pp. 106–11, also provide experimental evidence consistent with arguments about the effect of the sudden increase of coverage of the hostage crisis. The last-minute surge is also discussed in Ladd, "The Brittle Mandate."

9. Ford's approval ratings in the next Gallup poll, however, rose 12 points. April 18–21, 1976: 39 percent approved, 46 percent disapproved, and 15 percent were undecided about his performance as president; May 30: 51 percent approved, 33 percent disapproved, and 16 percent were undecided.

10. Aldrich, *Before the Convention*, p. 179.

11. Fenno, *Home Style*, p. 242.

266 *Notes to Pages 7–23*

1. The Reasoning Voter

1. Himmelweit et al., *How Voters Decide*, pp. 11–12.

2. Aristotle, *Rhetoric and Poetics*, p. 21.

3. Risk refers to decisions where the odds of the different possible outcomes are known. Playing dice involves risk; evaluating whether to give aid to Gorbachev, or whether to buy earthquake insurance, involves uncertainty.

4. Lazarsfeld, Berelson, and Gaudet, *The People's Choice;* Berelson, Lazarsfeld, and McPhee, *Voting.*

5. Berelson et al., *Voting*, p. 316; emphasis in original.

6. Campbell, Converse, Stokes, and Miller, *The American Voter*, is the most important Michigan work.

7. My critique of its theories is contained in Popkin, Gorman, Smith, and Phillips, "Toward an Investment Theory of Voting Behavior," pp. 779–805. The most important recent critique of the empirical data and psychological theories underlying the Michigan work is E. Smith, *The Unchanging American Voter.*

8. Downs, *An Economic Theory of Democracy.*

9. Ibid., pp. 90–91, n. 6.

10. Fiorina, *Retrospective Voting in American National Elections*, is the most important development of Downs's insights about parties.

11. Ibid., p. 37.

12. Discussing advances in psychology, Robyn Dawes notes that much of the early research in psychology did not regard individuals as "decision-making units that weighed the consequences of various courses of action and then chose from among them." Many results in cognitive psychology, however, cannot be explained "without hypothesizing an active, hypothesis-testing mind." Because of these results, Dawes notes, "it is now legitimate for psychologists to talk about thinking, choice, mental representations, plans, goals, mental hypothesis testing, and 'cognitive' biases." Dawes, *Rational Choice in an Uncertain World*, p. 19.

13. Lau and Sears use the notion of "default values" in "Social Cognition and Political Cognition," pp. 347–66, esp. p. 352.

14. Quoted without reference in Nisbett and Ross, *Human Inference*, p. 43.

15. I am not suggesting, however, that more sophisticated Bayesian models, consistent with the findings of cognitive psychology, cannot be developed. Indeed, I hope and assume that by pointing out the discrepancies between elemental Bayesian ideas and the cognitive findings, I contribute to the stimulating of the next round of developments in decision theory and formal modeling of voting.

16. Nisbett et al., "Popular Induction," p. 116.

17. Tversky, Sattah, and Slovic, "Contingent Weighting in Judgment and Choice," p. 371.

18. Martin Wattenberg refers to the current period as a candidate-centered age in *The Decline of American Political Parties.* Popkin et al., in "Toward an Investment Theory of Voting Behavior," show the increasing importance of candidates relative to parties in voting from 1952 through 1972.

2. Acquiring Data

1. Downs, *An Economic Theory of Democracy,* p. 220.

2. The stock ownership data is from a CBS News/*New York Times* poll, November 1987. The other numbers are from Cambridge Survey Research polls nos. 455 and 560. These Cambridge numbers are from 1975 and 1976, but there is no reason to believe they are not representative of today's electorate as well. The number of people looking for work, of course, fluctuates more than the other numbers.

3. CBS News/*New York Times* poll, April 1978.

4. CBS News/*New York Times* polls, April 1983 and January 1985.

5. CBS News/*New York Times* poll, April 1980.

6. CBS News/*New York Times* polls, April 1977 and March 1977.

7. CBS News/*New York Times* poll, April 1980.

8. CBS News/*New York Times* poll, September 1989.

9. CBS News/*New York Times* polls: Japan poll, July 1987 (crime victim) and June 1981.

10. Cambridge Survey Research poll no. 560, 1976. In the mid-1970s, the proportion of adults who knew what cholesterol is, for example, was over 70 percent, and when asked whether animal or vegetable fat is healthier, nearly 60 percent of all adults answered vegetable fat, and less than 5 percent said animal fat. Further, the proportion of adults who read the labels on food products in any given week is greater than the number who know their congressional representative's name!

11. *New York Times* national health survey, May 1982.

12. Cambridge Survey Research poll no. 455, 1975. There is no reason to think these numbers are any lower today.

13. CBS News/*New York Times* poll, July 1977.

14. CBS Evening News poll, May 1983.

15. Gary Cox, in *The Efficient Secret,* develops the concept of a demand for public reputation.

16. Quoted in *Los Angeles Times,* Oct. 20, 1989, p. A3.

17. These numbers come from CBS News/*New York Times* polls of, respectively, March 1980, March 1979, and November 1979.

18. CBS News/*New York Times* poll, July 1985.

19. CBS News/*New York Times* Israel poll, April 1987; there was a special national oversample of Jews so that there were more than five hundred Jews in the sample.

20. Schuman, Ludwig, and Krosnick, "The Perceived Threat of Nuclear War," pp. 521–22.

21. Iyengar and Kinder, *News That Matters,* pp. 26–33.

22. Krosnick, "Government Policy and Citizen Passion," p. 83.

23. Converse, "The Nature of Belief Systems in Mass Publics," p. 245.

24. Iyengar, "Shortcuts to Political Knowledge."

25. Campbell, "Voters and Elections," p. 752; emphasis added. In this article Campbell is referring back to *The American Voter.*

26. Campbell et al., *The American Voter,* pp. 172–73.

27. Campbell and Kahn, *The People Elect a President,* p. 56. People with positions for or against Taft-Hartley were more likely to have turned out than voters uncertain about Taft-Hartley or those who had not heard of Taft-Hartley.

28. Ibid., p. 52.

29. Campbell, Gurin, and Miller, *The Voter Decides,* p. 119.

30. Berelson et al., *Voting,* p. 74.

31. Ibid.

32. Zaller, "Measuring Individual Differences in Likelihood of News Reception."

33. Lazarsfeld et al., *The People's Choice,* pp. 27, 137–38.

34. Paul Lazarsfeld was European, and much more intimately familiar with European than American society. As the late Peter Natchez so astutely pointed out, Lazarsfeld's approach assumed "a fairly close correspondence between social and economic cleavages and the structure of primary groups." This assumption, as he said, is more suited to European than to American society and politics. Natchez, *Images of Voting/Visions of Democracy,* p. 252, n. 13.

In 1940, in Erie County, Ohio, the IPP worked extremely well: the cleavages between laborers and farmers, Protestants and Catholics, were sharp, and most people talked with like-minded people. When the IPP was tested in a national survey, however, the results were far less impressive, although there were still large voting differences between urban Catholic laborers and rural Protestant farmers. Janowitz and Miller, "The Index of Political Predisposition in the 1948 Election." Compared to the 1940 study, the turnout differences between people in consistent and cross-pressured social categories were minimal.

35. Fiorina, *Retrospective Voting*, p. 5.

36. Brody and Sniderman, "From Life Space to Polling Place," p. 358.

37. Kinder and Mebane, "Politics and Economics in Everyday Life," p. 148; emphasis in original. See also Feldman, "Economic Self-Interest and Political Behavior," and Feldman, "Economic Individualism and American Public Opinion."

38. Iyengar, "How Citizens Think about National Issues." Iyengar also analyzes how people reason about international terrorism. See also Young, Borgida, Sullivan, and Aldrich, "Personal Agendas and the Relationship between Self-Interest and Voting Behavior."

39. For example, Fiorina, "Short- and Long-Term Effects of Economic Conditions on Individual Voting Decisions," p. 90; Kinder, Adams, and Gronke, "Economics and Politics in the 1984 American Presidential Election," p. 511.

40. There are, of course, important exceptions, like farmers or workers affected by a dramatic presidential action such as the imposition of a grain embargo or the lifting of quotas on foreign-car imports.

41. Abramowitz, Lanoue, and Ramesh, "Economic Conditions, Causal Attributions, and Political Evaluations in the 1984 Presidential Election," p. 859.

42. Kinder and Mebane, "Politics and Economics in Everyday Life," p. 165.

43. Ibid., pp. 150–52.

44. Hibbs, "The Dynamics of Political Support for American Presidents among Occupational and Partisan Groups," p. 328. See also Kinder, Adams, and Gronke, "Economics and Politics," p. 511, for evidence about voters' use of cues about groups with which they identify.

45. Rosenstone, "Economic Adversity and Voter Turnout." See also Eisenberg and Lazarsfeld, "The Psychological Effects of Unemployment." I am indebted to Richard Brody for reminding me that one of the first studies of the political effects of unemployment was by Lazarsfeld.

46. Popkin, "Optimism, Pessimism and Policy," p. 52.

47. Converse, "Comment: The Status of Non-attitudes," p. 650.

48. Delli Carpini and Keeter, "Political Knowledge of the U.S. Public."

49. Ibid., p. 3.

50. Ibid., p. 5.

51. Ibid., passim. Since 1958, studies conducted by the University of Michigan's Survey Research Center have asked respondents to name their congressmen. The proportion of all adults who could do so has never been over 50 percent, and the proportion of actual voters who could do so has ranged from a high of 64 percent in 1968 to a low of 46 percent in 1980. These surveys are conducted immediately after elections; if a survey asks respondents for the names of their congressmen before a campaign, the numbers are much lower. In October 1977 and January 1978, the CBS News/*New York Times* polls asked respondents the names of their congressmen; less than one-third of the adults in the two polls, and only 49 percent of those who were college graduates, could do so. Since 1978 the name of each respondent's congressional representative has been included in a list, and the respondents have been asked if they recognize the name. The percentage recogniz-

ing the name of the representative (not necessarily *as* a representative, but as someone whose name they recognize) is over 90 percent.

52. CBS News/*New York Times* polls: postelection poll, November 1976; January 1977 and July 1985. The 1976 poll asked only registered voters for the names of the vice-presidential nominees, so the recall of names for the entire electorate would be even lower.

53. CBS News/*New York Times* polls, July 1985, April 1986, May 1988, and May 1989. However, in Japan, 80 percent of the public know the name of the American president, and slightly more Japanese than Americans know the name of the U.S. secretary of state. (Tokyo Broadcasting System poll of Japan conducted simultaneously with the CBS News/*New York Times* poll in July 1985.)

54. CBS News/*New York Times* polls, January 1979 and November 1979.

55. CBS News/*New York Times* polls, July 1987 and September 1987.

56. CBS News/*New York Times* poll, January 1985.

57. CBS Evening News poll, May 1983. Unless otherwise noted, all the media numbers come from this survey.

58. Obviously, the absolute differences in discussions of foreign and national news between levels of education will vary with the salience of particular national and international issues.

59. CBS News/*New York Times* poll, May 1989.

60. Education also broadens the electorate because educated people travel more. Polls taken between 1985 and 1989 show that although only one in five Americans has visited Europe, 43 percent of college graduates have done so; that while only one in five Americans has met a Russian citizen, 40 percent of college graduates have; and that while only one in three Americans knows an immigrant who has recently come to the United States, 60 percent of college graduates know such a person. CBS News/*New York Times* polls, May 1989, September 1985, and June 1986.

61. Lippmann, *Public Opinion*, p. 21.

62. Berelson et al., *Voting*, p. 231.

63. Ibid., p. 220.

64. Ibid., chap. 10, "Political Perception," pp. 215–33.

65. Ibid., p. 233.

66. It is important to note that the 1940 study did not ask about party identification, and assumed an equivalence between party identification and voting. I am making the modest assumption that if these relationships hold for all supporters of a candidate, then they certainly hold for partisan supporters of the candidate.

67. Lazarsfeld et al., *The People's Choice*, p. 38.

68. Ibid., pp. 29–30. It is my surmise that the depression and public reaction to Republican management of it are a source of the Republican defensiveness, because allusions to unemployment were still "traumatic" (p. 29).

69. It is not clear, however, that a pure information-centered model can explain all projection and rationalization; there also appears to be some "will to believe" among voters. Many Democrats are so committed to taking money from the defense budget for domestic programs that they deny any and all evidence of unprovoked Russian aggression. Many Republicans are so committed to believing that no new domestic spending is needed to strengthen the social safety net that they deny any evidence of abject poverty not due to personal character flaws or drug use.

70. Lazarsfeld et al., *The People's Choice*, p. 200.

71. Conover and Feldman, "Candidate Perception in an Ambiguous World," p. 935 (emphasis in original).

72. Krosnick, "Americans' Perceptions of Presidential Candidates."

73. Abramowitz, Lanoue, and Ramesh, "Economic Conditions, Causal Attributions, and Political Evaluations," p. 860.

74. Gerald Kramer, in "The Ecological Fallacy Revisited," argues that people will look only at government-induced change, but assumes that people will know what portions of their net changes will be due to government action.

75. Lazarsfeld et al., *The People's Choice*, p. 100.

76. The term *incompetent citizen* is from Delli Carpini and Keeter, "Political Knowledge of the U.S. Public," p. 2.

3. Going without Data

1. Downs, *An Economic Theory of Democracy*, pp. 13, 80.

2. Uncertainty occurs whenever the exact probabilities of future events are not known; it differs from risk in that risk refers to different possible outcomes, for each of which the probabilities *are* known. Playing dice involves risk; playing the stock market involves uncertainty.

3. The use of the focus group as a research tool demonstrates yet again just how prescient were the findings and ideas of the original Columbia studies, which provide the theoretical impetus for the research and the rationale for choosing the focus group over many other non-survey-based research techniques.

4. "How Bush Won: The Inside Story of Campaign '88," *Newsweek*, special election issue, Nov. 21, 1988, p. 100. Germond and Witcover, in *Whose Broad Stripes and Bright Stars?* pp. 154–65, have a detailed description of the research and strategic thinking within the Bush organization which culminated in the use of Willie Horton (as an example of Dukakis's furlough policy) as a campaign issue.

5. Lazarsfeld et al., *The People's Choice*, p. 41.

6. Ibid., pp. 150–51.

7. Katz and Lazarsfeld, *Personal Influence*, p. 32.

8. Berelson et al., *Voting*, pp. 195–97.

9. Downs, *An Economic Theory of Democracy*, p. 229: "Our *a priori* expectation is that rational citizens will seek to obtain their free political information from other persons if they can."

10. McCubbins and Schwartz, "Congressional Oversight Overlooked."

11. "Public's Knowledge of Civics Rises Only a Bit," *New York Times*, May 28, 1989, p. 31.

12. Brody and Shapiro, "A Reconsideration of the Rally Phenomenon in Public Opinion."

13. In 1988, when Vice President Bush attacked Michael Dukakis for being unpatriotic and not sufficiently defending the flag against "anti-American flag-burners," Senator John Glenn, a war hero and former astronaut, and Senator Sam Nunn, the most respected Democrat on defense issues (and a southerner), both offered to make commercials for Governor Dukakis. Glenn, in fact, had already made such commercials to defend—successfully—Senator Howard Metzenbaum against similar attacks. The Dukakis campaign declined the offers.

14. Witcover, *Marathon*, p. 302.

15. He relied on a two-step flow of information. Reverend Martin Luther King, Sr., Coretta Scott King, and Andrew Young all made statements on his behalf.

16. Iyengar and Kinder, *News That Matters*, pp. 52, 84–85.

17. Ibid., p. 361. Angus Campbell at Michigan wrote a monograph based on a 1948 survey which suggested party identification and association as an important topic for further research, but the 1948 questionnaire that Campbell used asked no similar question. Campbell and Kahn, *The People Elect a President*. A question like

the Columbia question was first suggested to the Michigan researchers by V. O. Key. Natchez, *Images of Voting/Visions of Democracy*, pp. 167–68; p. 267, n. 17. As early as 1937, however, the Gallup poll asked, "Do you regard yourself as a Republican, a Democrat, a Socialist, or an independent in politics?"; in 1940, the question was changed to "In politics, do you consider yourself a Democrat, independent, Socialist or Republican?" Since 1946 the Gallup question has been "In politics, as of today, do you consider yourself a Republican, a Democrat or Independent?"

18. Berelson et al., *Voting*, p. 17.

19. Ibid., p. 316.

20. Lazarsfeld et al., *The People's Choice*, p. 89.

21. Downs, *An Economic Theory of Democracy*, p. 28.

22. Ibid., p. 26.

23. Ibid., p. 96.

24. Ibid., p. 98.

25. Ibid.

26. Ibid., p. 101.

27. Geertz, "Ideology as a Cultural System."

28. Downs, *An Economic Theory of Democracy*, p. 85.

29. Ibid., p. 136.

30. Pierce and Rose, "Non-attitudes and American Public Opinion," esp. p. 632; Brody, "Change and Stability in Partisan Identification"; Fiorina, *Retrospective Voting*, pp. 86–88.

31. Fiorina, *Retrospective Voting*, esp. pp. 84–130. Because Fiorina did not have all the data necessary for a full testing of his theory, and because many important questions were not included on all the surveys, neither of us is able to do summary justice to his travails. He has conclusively proved that there is political feedback, but there is as yet no satisfactory statement of what kinds of problems and events are most likely to affect political identification.

32. Campbell et al. considered the possibility that voters choose party because of issues, but found it "hard to imagine this is common" (*The American Voter*, p. 185).

33. Most contemporary studies based on data from the University of Michigan's Center for Election Studies use a seven-point party scale. Democrats and Republicans are asked if they would call themselves strong or not very strong Democrats or Republicans, and are divided into strong and weak Democrats and Republicans. Independents are asked if they consider themselves closer to the Republican or Democratic party, and are divided into Democratic-leaning independents, pure independents, and Republican-leaning independents. Movement between points on these scales is especially sensitive to short-run changes in political attitudes, and use of the seven-point scale erroneously reduces the estimated effect of attitudes and issues in contemporary polling. The seven-point scale is, to use Fiorina's words, "hopelessly polluted" (Fiorina, *Retrospective Voting*, p. 97).

34. The simple bivariate correlation between changes in the percentage Democratic and changes in the percentage (reported) voting Democratic for Congress from 1956 through 1988 has an R^2 of .49. Gary Jacobson conceived this elegant test and did the calculation reported here. See also MacKuen, Erikson, and Stimson, "Macropartisanship."

35. Markus and Converse, "A Dynamic Simultaneous Equation Model of Electoral Choice." "Political scientists should reconsider the widely-held assumption that party identification is more stable over time and has more impact on political cognition than any other political attitude" (Krosnick and Berent, "The Impact of Verbal Labeling of Response Alternatives and Branching on Attitude Measurement Reliability in Surveys").

36. Campbell et al., *The American Voter,* p. 430.

37. Ibid.

38. "Controversies about issue voting versus party identification miss the point: the 'issues' are *in* party identification." Fiorina, *Retrospective Voting,* p. 200; emphasis in original. See also Charles Franklin, "Issue Preference, Socialization, and the Evolution of Party Identification."

39. Petrocik, "Divided Government"; Popkin, "Optimism, Pessimism, and Policy."

40. Fiorina, "Short- and Long-Term Effects," p. 95.

41. Hibbs, "Dynamics of Political Support," p. 328.

42. Stokes, Campbell, and Miller, "Components of Electoral Decision," esp. p. 373. Studies of party images using the SRC data evaluate images of the parties by using data from open-ended questions asking respondents what they like and dislike about the parties.

43. Ibid., p. 375.

44. R. Trilling, *Party Image and Electoral Behavior,* p. 204. The SRC surveys did not ask the kinds of party-heat questions asked by Gallup, CBS, and other pollsters. They did, however, ask open-ended questions about each party, asking the respondents to tell what they liked and disliked about each party. Trilling's analyses, as well as those of Stokes and Wattenberg, are based on these responses.

45. Ibid., chap. 5.

46. Pool, Abelson, and Popkin, *Candidates, Issues, and Strategies,* pp. 144–63. Popkin, "Multivariate Analyses of Trends in Public Opinion."

47. Rubin, *Party Dynamics,* chap. 4, "National Coalitions and Federal Linkages." Rubin's argument, although based on data from only one election, shows great prescience, for it was precisely Reagan's ability to moderate the "country club" image that helped so much in 1980.

48. Adrian, "Some General Characteristics of Nonpartisan Elections."

49. Bruner and Korchin, "The Boss and the Vote."

50. Campbell, Gurin, and Miller, *The Voter Decides,* p. 58.

51. Popkin et al., "Toward an Investment Theory of Voting Behavior," contains analysis of the effects of the Eagleton affair and the Democratic convention. Kinder and Kiewiet verify this proposition in "Sociotropic Politics: The American Case." See also Kinder and Abelson, "Appraising Presidential Candidates"; Page, *Choices and Echoes in Presidential Elections.*

52. Campbell and Kahn, *The People Elect a President,* p. 46.

53. In this section I am assuming that voters are interested in the demographics as a way of estimating policy benefits they will derive from government. There are also benefits that members of a group—and others—will derive from having a president from that particular group to help legitimate it. A black or woman president will give many benefits to blacks or women just by being in office. A president who eats spinach provides immediate benefits to many parents; a president who refuses to eat broccoli aids the cause of many children.

54. Stokes and Miller, "Party Government and the Saliency of Congress," p. 209. The other example they give of an "irrelevant" cue to voting is gender.

55. L. Trilling, *Sincerity and Authenticity,* p. 4.

56. Aristotle, *Rhetoric and Poetics,* p. 25.

57. Lazarsfeld et al., *The People's Choice,* p. 102.

58. Downs, *An Economic Theory of Democracy,* pp. 40, 46, 107.

59. Rose Garden strategies of course upset journalists, who have even complained that presidents who do not campaign undermine the American system. Crouse, *The Boys on the Bus,* pp. 116–17, 282–83. It may undermine newsmen with

a particular view of what is news when a president elects not to campaign, but a president's decision to let people judge him on his record is certainly a reasonable one, particularly if the challenger is making no progress and if the incumbent feels he benefits by the publicity given the challenger.

60. Transcript of a recording of a meeting between President Nixon and H. R. Haldeman on June 23, 1972; *New York Times,* Aug. 6, 1974, p. 15. The context, a discussion of Nixon's approval ratings, suggests that this is a summary of the views of Robert Teeter, Nixon's pollster.

61. As congressional campaigns become more extensive, the focus in congressional elections is also moving more toward the candidates, and incumbency has become more important as a voting focal point. Nearly 75 percent of cross-party voting in congressional races is voting for an incumbent. Jacobson, *The Politics of Congressional Elections;* Ferejohn, "On the Decline of Competition in Congressional Elections."

62. *Newsweek,* "How Bush Won," p. 100. However, it is not the case that ratings of incumbents or near-incumbents (like vice presidents) do not change during campaigns.

63. Jacobson, *The Politics of Congressional Elections.*

64. Michael Oreskes, "Republicans Show Gains in Loyalty," *New York Times,* Jan. 21, 1990, p. 15. Oreskes' article summarizes changes in party identification on CBS News/*New York Times* polls.

65. Jacobson, *The Electoral Origins of Divided Government.*

66. Jacobson, "The Persistence of Democratic House Majorities," p. 12.

67. Petrocik, "Divided Government," p. 9.

68. Rahn, "The Role of Partisan Stereotypes in Information Processing about Political Candidates."

69. Berelson et al., *Voting,* pp. 94–96.

70. I am basing this claim in part on inference, for there are no directly comparable national surveys from the 1940s and the 1980s. Still, I make this claim confidently. The generational and gender cleavages, and the data available on spouses who vote differently, are enough in and of themselves to guarantee that more people today are in politically heterogeneous social groups than in the 1940s. The declining gaps between Protestant and Catholic voters, and the breaking-up of older ethnic neighborhoods, also lend strong support to my claim that fewer people are in politically homogeneous social settings today than in 1948.

71. Wattenberg, in *The Decline of American Political Parties,* p. 20, gives data for 1952 and 1980.

4. Going beyond the Data

1. Quoted in Nisbett and Ross, *Human Inference,* p. 17.

2. See chap. 1, n. 13.

3. Bruner, *Actual Minds, Possible Worlds,* p. 51; emphasis in original.

4. See chap. 1, n. 15.

5. Kahneman and Miller, "Norm Theory," p. 136; Lakoff, *Women, Fire, and Dangerous Things,* pp. 12–57; Zaller, "Toward a Theory of the Survey Response"; Lodge, McGraw, and Stroh, "An Impression-Driven Model of Candidate Evaluation."

6. Kaplan, *The Conduct of Inquiry,* pp. 11, 17–18.

7. Kahneman and Tversky, "Subjective Probability," p. 451. For a summary of recent efforts by economists to deal with the "unsettling" experimental confirmations of representativeness, see Grether, "Testing Bayes Rule and the Representativeness Heuristic."

8. Kahneman and Miller, "Norm Theory," p. 147.

9. Kahneman and Tversky, "On the Psychology of Prediction."

10. Kahneman and Tversky, "Subjective Probability," p. 451.

11. Zukier and Pepitone, "Social Roles and Strategies in Prediction," p. 358.

12. Bruner, *Actual Minds, Possible Worlds,* pp. 51–52.

13. Tversky and Kahneman, "Extensional versus Intuitive Reasoning"; Tversky and Kahneman, "Judgments of and by Representativeness." The conjunction fallacy can also occur *without* representativeness (Robert Abelson, personal communication, November 1990).

14. Ross and Anderson, "Shortcomings in the Attribution Process."

15. Lapchick, "Pseudo-Scientific Prattle about Athletes."

16. Ross and Anderson, "Shortcomings in the Attribution Process," pp. 139–43.

17. Zukier and Pepitone, "Social Roles and Strategies in Prediction," p. 350.

18. Ronald Reagan fell 26 points in one month in the 1980 Iowa preprimary polls when he chose not to campaign in the state and skipped a debate with other candidates. I believe, and I believe the surveys support me, that this fall resulted from dominance of recent personal evidence for the active campaigners over past evidence about Reagan, not from any concern that he skipped the campaign because he was getting old, or from local resentment that he was downplaying Iowa.

19. Bruner, *Actual Minds, Possible Worlds,* p. 91.

20. Kahneman and Tversky, "On the Psychology of Prediction," pp. 241–42. I am substituting the phrase *background data* for their "knowledge of base rates."

21. Kahneman and Miller, "Norm Theory," p. 147.

22. Ibid.

23. Conover and Feldman, "Candidate Perception in an Ambiguous World," p. 923.

24. Tversky and Kahneman, "The Framing of Decisions and the Psychology of Choice," p. 453.

25. Zukier and Pepitone, in "Social Roles and Strategies in Prediction," use the phrase "judgmental orientation" for *frame.*

26. Evaluations and choices are susceptible to formulation effects, as Kahneman and Tversky note, "because of the nonlinearity of the value function and the tendency of people to evaluate options in relation to the reference point that is suggested or implied." Kahneman and Tversky, "Choices, Values, and Frames," esp. p. 346.

27. Aristotle, *Rhetoric and Poetics,* pp. 90–91.

28. Tversky and Kahneman, "The Framing of Decisions."

29. Lichtenstein and Slovic, "Response-Induced Reversals of Preference in Gambling." This is an example of the common consequences effect, a concept developed in MacCrimmon and Larson, "Utility Theory."

30. Krosnick and Schuman, "Attitude Intensity, Importance, and Certainty and Susceptibility to Response Effects."

31. The limits to framing are in part a consequence of ways that people consciously guard against framing effects by organizing their lives to counter them. Simon, "The Theory of Binding Commitments Simplified and Extended."

32. Iyengar, "How Citizens Think about National Issues."

33. This is elaborated in Iyengar, *Framing Effects in Politics.*

34. Iyengar and Kinder, *News That Matters.*

35. I expect that many journalists, pollsters, and scholars will react to this pathbreaking book by saying that they knew it all already, that Iyengar and Kinder have done nothing but affirm the obvious. I have two replies to that. First, much of what scholars, pollsters, and journalists already "know" is confused and contradictory and has never been verified; what they will know after reading *News That*

Matters will be based on careful, creative testing and research. Second, when a phenomenon is properly highlighted and specified, the knowledge of it becomes clearer and more usable.

36. Ibid., pp. 16–33.

37. Ibid., pp. 67, 85. This doubling of weights assumes that the problem is generally within the president's purview but has not been featured recently.

38. Krosnick, "Attitude Importance and Attitude Accessibility."

39. Nisbett and Ross, *Human Inference*, p. 22.

40. Ford was president in 1976, but he had been *appointed* president and so had never had the legitimation that comes from winning a primary and being acclaimed by his party.

41. See also the discussion of reasoning from results in chapter 5.

42. Aldrich, Sullivan, and Borgida, "Foreign Affairs and Issue Voting."

43. Lakoff, in *Women, Fire, and Dangerous Things*, p. 89, uses the phrase "cognitive reference point."

44. CBS News/*New York Times* survey, New Hampshire, 1980. This was a panel survey; this example is based on 390 registered Democrats, 29 percent of whom said they had been contacted by the Carter campaign.

45. Rubin, *Press, Party, and Presidency*, pp. 151–56. Wattenberg, in *The Decline of American Political Parties*, chap. 6, "The Role of the Media," pp. 90–112, shows that the more money—which means the more media—spent in congressional races, the more candidate factors dominate party factors in voting.

46. Weaver, "Is Television News Biased?" The day American fighter planes forced down in Italy an Egyptian plane carrying the four terrorists who had hijacked the cruise ship *Achille Lauro*, the first paragraph of Lesley Stahl's report on the CBS Evening News with Dan Rather, October 11, 1985, reported that "White House aides called it 'hitting the jackpot in Sicily, the best two days the President has had in a long time.' "

47. Pool, "TV: A New Dimension in Politics."

48. Lubell, "Personalities versus Issues."

49. Weaver, "Is Television News Biased?"

50. Keeter, "The Illusion of Intimacy." My informed hunch is that the potent effect of television is not seeing alone, but listening while seeing. I base this argument on Schudson, "Telemythology and American Politics."

51. Lau and Sears, "Social Cognition and Political Cognition," p. 353. Furthermore, party identification provides accessible information that can counter framing effects of television and campaigns. Since there has been a decline in partisanship, the possibilities for framing changes from television and campaigns are increased.

52. Kahneman and Tversky, "On the Psychology of Prediction," p. 249.

53. Truman Bewley notes that this is one of the implications of the Ellsberg Paradox. Bewley, "Knightian Decision Theory."

54. Kahneman and Tversky, "On the Psychology of Prediction," p. 249.

55. Kahneman and Miller, "Norm Theory," p. 142.

56. Kahneman and Tversky, "On the Psychology of Prediction," p. 249.

57. Ibid.

58. I am particularly indebted to Robert Abelson for help with this section.

59. Dawes, "The Robust Beauty of Improper Linear Models in Decision Making," p. 574.

60. Tversky, Sattah, and Slovic, "Contingent Weighting in Judgment and Choice," p. 372.

61. Kahneman and Miller, "Norm Theory," pp. 141, 144.

62. Drew, *Campaign Journal*, pp. 353, 412, 419.

63. Candidates do not think it is bad to actually be ahead, just that it is bad to be *labeled* as ahead, or as the probable winner.

64. M. Kramer, "Should Anderson Quit?" Anderson is also a classic example of Gresham's law of information. Although he had introduced a constitutional amendment three times which would require that all officeholders either be Christians or acknowledge Christian supremacy, he received much favorable support from civil libertarians and Jews who were impressed by his arguments for a new politics and his willingness to act like Daniel in the lion's den—arguing for gun control in front of the NRA, for example.

5. Attributable Benefits and Political Symbols

1. Allen, "A Brief, Yet Helpful, Guide to Civil Disobedience," p. 107.

2. Fenno, *Home Style*, p. 56.

3. This example is discussed at length in chapter 7.

4. Verba and Schlozman's "Unemployment, Class Consciousness, and Radical Politics" is a demonstration of the connection between political reasoning and policy preferences. It demonstrates how beliefs about society and self interact in the formation of political opinions. Whereas Verba and Schlozman were the first to demonstrate the importance of complex political reasoning about policy, Shanto Iyengar, in his forthcoming *Framing Effects in Politics*, is the first person to show the depth and range of political reasoning in the mass public and how and when the types of reasoning that people do can be affected by television.

5. CBS News/*New York Times* poll, April 1980.

6. Gallucci, *Neither Peace nor Honor*, p. 53. "A large part of the ongoing story of the air war . . . turns on the necessity for the civilian leadership to demonstrate that air power was being used to the maximum desirable degree, and that its failure to end the war justified the constant increase in troop commitments."

7. Fiorina, *Retrospective Voting*. Fiorina discusses the concerns of the electorate in terms of results versus instruments. See also the discussion of "easy" issues in Edward Carmines and James Stimson, "The Two Faces of Issue Voting."

8. See chap. 3, n. 60.

9. October 7, 1975, Colony Theater, Cleveland, Ohio. Quoted in *Cleveland Plain Dealer*, Oct. 8, 1975.

10. Witcover, *Marathon*, p. 180n.

11. I believe it is no coincidence that, shortly thereafter, Mrs. Reagan began to spend more time with drug rehabilitation centers and less time with fashion designers.

12. Stokes, "Spatial Models of Party Competition." Stokes calls these issues "valence issues" and uses them to argue against economic theories of voting as expressed in the work of Downs. Although Stokes does point out that issues which *"might"* allow for political competition are behind these valence issues, the whole thrust of the argument is that the prevalence of symbols, or valences, is evidence of irrational and nonideological voting, and evidence against Downs, although only one aspect of Downs is discussed (pp. 172–73; emphasis in original). Despite the many pieces of wisdom in this article, the effect of the discussion of valence issues has been to confuse and mislead most researchers into worries about whether the presence of common symbols, or valence issues, in elections is a sign of lack of concern with policy and government performance. In contrast, see the illuminating discussion of common symbols, or consensus issues, in Himmelweit et al., *How Voters Decide*, pp. 105–11.

13. Luker, *Abortion and the Politics of Motherhood*.

14. Tocqueville, *Selected Letters*, pp. 46–47; emphasis in original.

15. When Clifford Geertz described ideology as a cultural system, his observations were relevant to electoral mobilization. I have been stimulated in particular by Geertz's "Ideology as a Cultural System."

16. Herken, *The Winning Weapon*.

17. There is an excellent summary of the role of Henry Luce and the missionary spirit in China, and the belief that China was America's, and was then lost, in Halberstam, *The Powers That Be*, pp. 84–133. Ironically, the same cry of "Who lost China?" was echoing through the Kremlin. Although the United States took it for granted that all Communists were united, Stalin felt as betrayed by the victory of an independent-minded Communist party he did not control as the United States did by the victory of any Communist.

18. Cambridge Reports nos. 480, 560, and 717.

19. McCarthy, "The Selling of the President," p. 67.

20. Berelson et al., *Voting*, p. 198.

21. Ibid., p. 200.

22. Even in 1940, when campaign effects were small compared to 1948, "insofar as the mass media led to conversion at all, it was through a redefinition of the issues. . . . In this way, political communications occasionally broke down traditional party loyalties." Lazarsfeld et al., *The People's Choice*, p. 98.

23. Ford's pardon of Nixon was also an important consideration for many voters in 1976. Fiorina, in *Retrospective Voting*, also found the pardon to be an important stimulus to changes in party identification away from the Republican party.

24. Kahneman and Miller, "Norm Theory," p. 137.

25. Bolles, *Remembering and Forgetting*. See also Loftus, *Eyewitness Testimony*, for discussions of the ways that postevent information such as labels, as well as wishes and desires, can affect memories.

26. Darnton, "Marxed Men," p. 15.

27. As Larry Bartels explains Kennedy's drop in support: "The dramatic reversal of fortunes began in a disastrous nationally televised interview with Roger Mudd, in which Kennedy could neither explain coherently why he wanted to be president nor dispel the perception he was holding back on Chappaquiddick." Bartels, *Presidential Primaries*, p. 220. See also J. Moore, *The Campaign for President*, pp. x, xiv, 48–49, and Abramson, Aldrich, and Rohde, *Change and Continuity in the 1980 Elections*, p. 22.

28. *Playboy* first offered a transcript to James Wooten of the *New York Times*. When Wooten declined, *Playboy* offered it to NBC's "Today" show; it was on the "Today" show the morning of September 20 and was carried by the network news shows the same day. Thus the "lust in my heart" story ran for three days before the debates, while Carter had been dropping in the polls for a month.

6. Expectations and Reassessments

1. Drew, *American Journal*, p. 4.

2. Aldrich, *Before the Convention;* Bartels, "Expectations and Preferences in Presidential Nominating Conventions"; Bartels, "Candidate Choice and the Dynamics of the Presidential Nominating Process"; Bartels, *Presidential Primaries;* Brady and Johnston, "What's the Primary Message."

3. Bartels, *Presidential Primaries*, p. 26. This definition highlights the difference, discussed below, between gaining additional votes because a candidate gets more coverage and becomes better known, and gaining more votes because voters and contributors have higher expectations for the candidate.

4. Quoted in Witcover, *Marathon*, pp. 692–93.

5. Zolberg, "Moments of Madness."

6. Ann Lewis, quoted in *Congressional Quarterly*, Dec. 20, 1975, p. 2804.

7. Lance Tarrance, quoted in *Congressional Quarterly*, Feb. 2, 1980, p. 281.

8. Polsby, *Consequences of Party Reform*, pp. 66–69. As the title implies, the main emphasis of this book is a (trenchant) critique of the *consequences* of primaries.

9. The level of attentiveness is strongly related to education. At the beginning of the primary season, before the first primaries, about two-thirds of registered voters who have been to college or are college graduates are paying some attention to primary campaigns in the news; by the end of the primary season, the proportion has risen to nearly 90 percent. Among voters who have not been to college, about half are paying some attention at the beginning of the primary season; by the end of the nomination campaign the proportion has risen to about 70 percent. There are slight differences between parties due to small differences in the average educational level of the parties. Independents, particularly educated independents, pay somewhat less attention to primaries. The one survey from 1976 that asks about attention to the campaign, taken between the Iowa and New Hampshire primaries, shows that attention to the campaign was substantially reduced, presumably by Watergate, at every educational level except college graduate.

10. All numbers are from CBS News/*New York Times* polls for February of the election year. I am simply adding the proportions with favorable and unfavorable ratings of the candidate.

11. CBS News/*New York Times* poll, March 21–24, 1984.

12. CBS News/*New York Times* poll, February 21–25, 1984. The rest of the respondents said they did not know who had won. The correct answer was given by 80 percent of college graduates, 70 percent of those with some college, 68 percent of high school graduates, and 56 percent with less than a high school degree.

13. CBS News/*New York Times* New Hampshire poll, February 9–15, 1988. Voters whose candidate fares poorly do not say that their candidate won, but they are less likely to remember who did win.

14. Beniger, "Winning the Presidential Nomination."

15. The 1976 poll results are based on all Democrats and all Republicans; the 1980 figures on only registered Democrats or Republicans, and the 1984 figures on registered Democrats and independents intending to vote in the Democratic primaries that year. In 1988 there was no CBS News/*New York Times* poll between Iowa and New Hampshire, so I have used the CNN/*USA Today* polls. All of the pre–New Hampshire polls were taken after the Iowa caucuses.

16. Quoted in Broder et al., *The Pursuit of the Presidency 1980*, p. 129.

17. There was no CBS News/*New York Times* poll in 1976 before Iowa. From other polls in late 1975, Carter was at about 3 points (or less), giving him a jump of 9 after Iowa. Including Carter, the average for Iowa since 1976 would be 13 points.

18. Henry Brady presented a formal mathematical model of this process in "Knowledge, Strategy, and Momentum."

19. Bartels, in *Presidential Primaries*, chap. 6, examines information levels and preferences in 1984.

20. Brady and Johnston, "What's the Primary Message," pp. 178–80. However, contrast with Bartels, *Presidential Primaries*, table A.17, p. 347.

21. Kennamer and Chaffee, "Communication of Political Information during Early Presidential Primaries."

22. Brady, "Is Iowa News?" p. 115.

23. Brady and Johnston, "What's the Primary Message," pp. 178–80.

24. Brady, "Chances, Utilities, and Voting in Presidential Primaries," p. 21.

25. Marsh, "Back on the Bandwagon."

26. Bruner, *Actual Minds, Possible Worlds*, p. 46.

27. Kahneman and Miller, "Norm Theory."

28. Bruner, "On the Perception of Incongruity," p. 208. In keeping with current usage, I have changed Bruner's terms "expectancy" and "organism" to *expectation* and *individual.*

29. Gollob et al., "Social Inference."

30. Drew, in *Campaign Journal,* p. 427, notes that the 1984 Hart campaign kept secret the data showing that they were likely to win in Ohio and Indiana, in order to maximize the impact of the victories.

31. NBC exit polls in all primaries asked voters to assess the likelihood that their candidate could win. Additionally, in Illinois and Connecticut, Jackson voters were asked whether they voted for Jackson because they thought he could win or because they wanted to show support for a black candidate.

32. In the rush to get on the momentum bandwagon, many scholars have ignored the equally plausible possibility of support for underdogs, although Herbert Simon, William McPhee, and Paul Lazarsfeld all considered underdog effects as likely as bandwagon effects.

33. The Jackson percentage is an average of the percentage of the black vote in the ABC/*Washington Post,* CBS News/*New York Times,* and NBC exit polls. The post–Super Tuesday data are based on Illinois, New York, Pennsylvania, Indiana, Maryland, North Carolina, Ohio, California, and New Jersey. There was no CBS News/*New York Times* poll in Florida, and no ABC/*Washington Post* polls in Indiana, Maryland, and North Carolina. I have omitted states with small black populations, such as Nebraska, Massachusetts, and Wisconsin. Later, after Super Tuesday, Jackson received 84 percent of the black vote in North Carolina at a time when Mondale was ahead of Hart.

34. CBS News/*New York Times* exit polls. Voters were not asked who was more likely to beat the Democrats but were asked to assess the chances of each candidate separately. I include only voters who placed Ford's chances in a higher likelihood category than Reagan's. Not every exit poll had all the questions necessary to establish whom the voter preferred, and who was thought to have a better chance against the Democrats, but there are enough questions on enough different polls to suggest that in many states more than 10 percent of Ford's voters preferred Reagan, but voted for Ford in order to maximize chances against Carter. (There were also Republicans who preferred Reagan, but voted for Ford because they thought it was wrong to go against a Republican president.)

35. CBS News/*New York Times* exit poll.

36. While the University of Michigan's Center for Election Studies interviews for 1984 do contain extensive information about expectations, there are generally only about forty interviews every week of the primary with Democrats.

37. CBS News/*New York Times* poll, March 21–24, 1984. This poll was after Hart had peaked, but was within the three-week period for which Bartels says the Hart bubble lasted. At the time of this poll, Hart's favorability rating among Democratic primary voters was 40 percent to 12 percent; a week after New Hampshire it had been 49 percent to 4 percent.

38. CBS News/*New York Times* poll, March 1984. The panel included 185 Mondale voters, 52 voters who moved to Hart from Mondale, and 85 who moved to Hart from other candidates, or didn't have a preference in February. While these are not large numbers, note that Bartels had an average of 38 primary voters per week in his ongoing twenty-three-week sample.

39. The differences in the distribution of expectations among the reinterviewed voters and the new sample of voters illustrate the effect of the prior interview on the attentiveness of the interviewees. In the panel survey, there were 65 voters who

moved to Hart from Mondale, 85 who moved to Hart from other candidates, and 85 other Hart voters.

40. The best examples are in Schelling, "Bargaining, Communication, and Limited War."

41. Bartels, "Candidate Choice," p. 8.

42. *Newsweek*, June 4, 1984, p. 21.

43. CBS Political Report 1987, Feb. 23, 1987, p. 3. George Bush and Robert Dole tied when the journalists were asked to predict the Republican winner.

44. For another typology, see Bartels, *Presidential Primaries*, chap. 7.

45. Brody, Sniderman, and Kuklinski, "Policy Reasoning in Political Issues," esp. p. 92. See also Brady and Sniderman, "Attitude Attribution."

46. Drew, *Campaign Journal*, pp. 374–75. Henry Brady and Richard Johnston found that liking a candidate leads to more optimistic assessments of the candidate, which Brady calls "wish fulfillment." Brady and Johnston, "What's the Primary Message," pp. 178–80. See also Bartels, *Presidential Primaries*, table A.8, p. 337.

47. Bruner, *In Search of Mind*, pp. 219, 227, 229.

48. Bartels, *Presidential Primaries*, p. 83. Kennamer and Chaffee, in "Communication of Political Information," also found that people obtained information about issue positions, personal qualities, and style.

49. Norman, *The Design of Everyday Things*, pp. 56–57.

50. CBS News/*New York Times* Illinois exit poll; only 5 percent of the voters thought Byrne had endorsed Kennedy.

51. This data, discussed at length in chapter 9, is from the CBS News/*New York Times* poll "March84." There were 573 registered Democrats or independents who said they were Democratic primary voters in the sample; 38 percent were favorable to the AFL-CIO and 28 percent were unfavorable.

52. Drew, *Campaign Journal*, p. 360.

53. Brady and Johnston, "What's the Primary Message," p. 170.

54. Brady, "Is Iowa News?"

55. This is not a case of a new frame in which to judge whether he was lying, but a new frame in which to judge whether it *mattered* that he was lying. I am grateful to Larry Bartels for helping to clarify this distinction.

56. CBS News figures from CBS News Elections Unit, Research Department. The categories "mentioned on the news" and "spoke on the news" are distinct; the 139 times he was shown in footage overlaps these other two categories and does not include still photos.

57. In July 1979, a CBS News/*New York Times* poll asked respondents whether they remembered Chappaquiddick. At that time, in the middle of summer, when political interest was low and there had been very little public discussion of Chappaquiddick, 84 percent of all Democrats remembered the incident, including 94 percent of those Democrats who had been to college.

58. CBS News/*New York Times* polls, July 1979 and March 1980.

59. CBS News/*New York Times* polls for November 1979 and January 1980; in February 1980, the proportion was 30 percent. All figures are for registered Democrats. The proportion who said Chappaquiddick made it more likely that they would vote for Kennedy was 3 percent. These polls also showed that the proportion of Democrats who thought Kennedy was lying about Chappaquiddick doubled. When asked, "Are you satisfied that Edward Kennedy is telling the truth about Chappaquiddick, or do you think that he has been lying, or aren't you sure what to believe?" the percentage who believed he was telling the truth dropped from 30 percent in November to 22 percent in January and 16 percent in February; the

percentage who believed he was lying rose from 12 percent in November to 15 percent in January and 24 percent in February.

60. A senator viewed as antidefense was not helped by an air of crisis; nor as a proponent of social programs was he helped by inflation.

61. Drew, *Portrait of an Election*, p. 50.

62. CBS News/*New York Times* polls for June 1983, September 1983, and January 1984. Glenn's June ratings: 53 percent were favorable, 11 percent were unfavorable, 6 percent were undecided, and 30 percent did not know enough to rate him. In January the figures were 31 percent favorable, 15 percent unfavorable, 29 percent undecided, and 25 percent didn't know.

63. Drew, *Campaign Journal*, p. 180. Richard Fenno, in *The Presidential Odyssey of John Glenn*, examines the Glenn campaign and Glenn's inability to communicate to primary voters or the media a political persona.

64. CBS News/*New York Times* poll, Iowa, 1984. In contrast, 75 percent of Iowa Democrats who favored Walter Mondale thought he cared about them a great deal.

65. Germond and Witcover, *Blue Smoke and Mirrors*, pp. 101–2.

66. Quoted in Broder et al., *The Pursuit of the Presidency 1980*, p. 121.

67. Senator Glenn also fell flat in Iowa and New Hampshire, even after the national drops that occurred before the primaries began in earnest in these two states. There is a CBS News/*New York Times* poll from Iowa which sheds light on the Glenn failure and again illustrates the importance to voters of personal qualifications. The January 1984 poll in that state showed that he was known to half of Iowa's Democrats, and that he also scored highly on ability to handle a crisis and on leadership. But like Connally, he failed to convince voters that he cared about them—that he was the kind of person who would keep them in mind in the White House.

68. CBS News/*New York Times* polls from Iowa and New Hampshire in January 1988. I will deal with this case at greater length in a forthcoming monograph about Iowa and New Hampshire.

69. Gary Hart at a presidential primary debate in Des Moines, Iowa, January 15, 1988, quoted in the *Los Angeles Times*, Jan. 16, 1988, pp. 1, 15.

70. Personal communication, July 1989.

71. I am grateful to Peter Hart for making this data available to me. The first of the polls on March 9 and 10 included 501 registered likely primary voters; the second, 500.

72. The first poll was little publicized.

73. CBS News/*New York Times* southern primaries composite exit poll containing 9,001 voters, 3,152 of whom were whites born in the South and 3,180 of whom were whites who were not born in the South. This difference stands when controlling for education and (liberal/moderate/conservative) ideology as well.

74. CBS News/*New York Times* 1988 poll of Super Tuesday states. There were 790 likely Democratic primary voters in the poll; among the 300 who could rate Senator Gore either favorably or unfavorably, 90 had seen commercials and 210 had not seen commercials.

75. As noted, nearly half of the blacks who voted for Jackson in 1984 voted for him in order to show their support for a black candidate.

7. The Democratic Primaries of 1976

1. Gallup Poll survey no. 924-K, February 28–March 3, 1975.

2. CBS News/*New York Times* poll, February 1976, containing 589 Democrats.

3. Witcover, *Marathon*, p. 239.

4. Ibid., p. 242.

5. Cambridge Report survey no. 871, July 1976. There were also polls in 1975 with similar percentages.

6. CBS News/*New York Times* poll, April 1976. The responses for Democrats were slightly less anti-Washington than for all voters, but the same relationships between education and a Washington background, and the widespread belief that an outside background was better, held for Republicans, independents, and Democrats.

7. Cambridge Survey Research poll no. 488, January 1976. This was a telephone poll of four hundred registered Democrats.

8. Incidentally, the difference between educated and uneducated voters was far wider among Democrats than among Republicans or independents.

9. Quoted in Drew, *American Journal*, pp. 37, 44.

10. This excludes voters who did not answer that question on the exit poll. Because the lists change, and because the number of qualities that voters are asked to select from the list also changes, no exact comparisons are available between 1976, 1980, 1984, and 1988. The concern with honesty in 1976, however, is clearly no artifact. It was also clearly not due to Carter's emphasis on his honesty; 63 percent of Republican primary voters and 48 percent of Democratic voters said honesty was the most important characteristic of their candidate.

11. Cambridge Survey Research poll no. 546. This was a telephone poll, taken in April 1976, of four hundred registered voters likely to vote in the Democratic primary. Other surveys from this period, however, make it clear that the findings are generally applicable in other states and for all voters, not just Democratic primary voters.

12. The ideas for these questions came directly from the research reported in Popkin et al., "Toward an Investment Theory of Voting Behavior." I remind readers, for the sake of full disclosure, that I worked on polling for the Carter campaign in both 1975–76 and 1979–80.

13. CBS News/*New York Times* New Hampshire exit poll. I am using the terms *blue-collar* and *non-college-educated* interchangeably because many surveys do not ask occupation, but all of them ask education.

14. Drew, *American Journal*, pp. 141–42.

15. The second poll is a telephone reinterview of three hundred people from an initial field poll of eight hundred people in 1975.

16. Time and again during the primaries, Udall tried to argue at joint appearances with Carter and other candidates that his racial policies were "not really that different" from Carter's.

17. "We suspect that perceptions of Carter on the social issues of abortion and particularly busing may have been influenced by his identification as a 'Southerner.' " Conover and Feldman, "Candidate Perception in an Ambiguous World," p. 926.

18. CBS News/*New York Times* exit poll for Pennsylvania.

19. Religion was not asked on the CBS News/*New York Times* Wisconsin exit poll.

20. CBS News/*New York Times* exit poll for New York, containing 1,074 voters. Among white Protestants, Carter's vote was 44 percent.

21. CBS News/*New York Times* exit poll for Michigan, containing 221 UAW members. It is possible that these results reflect the fact that so many white autoworkers come from West Virginia and Kentucky and have religious backgrounds similar to Carter's.

22. This is the religious equivalent of the analyses that Sidney Verba and Kay Schlozman have done on attitudes about the future, self-identity, and policy choices during the depression. Verba and Schlozman, "Unemployment, Class Consciousness, and Radical Politics."

23. Interview with Tom Quinn, August 1976. I also confirmed this with Governor Brown in 1982.

8. The Republican Primaries of 1980

1. If the respondents were not aware that Ford was "considering" running, this is an even more interesting story, for it means that they came up with Ford as an alternative to Reagan with even less external prompting.

2. CBS News/*New York Times* poll, June 1976. It is usually the case that the supporters of primary losers understate their vote for the primary winner, because much of the divisiveness is healed before November. However, these numbers are high even by postprimary standards.

3. CBS News/*New York Times* New Hampshire preelection survey, February 22–24, 1980. Forty-one percent of New Hampshire Ford supporters rated Reagan unfavorably, and only 46 percent were favorable. There were 1,307 respondents in this poll, 566 of whom were possible Republican primary voters. The follow-up survey contacted 1,042 of these respondents, including 456 of the 566 interviewed about the Republican election. Of the 456 reinterviewed, 281 actually voted in the primary.

4. Quoted in Drew, *Portrait of an Election,* p. 90.

5. It is clearly the case that some of the other candidates knew that Bush was being undermined by the secret change in plans. While taking part in the changed arrangements meant helping Reagan to defeat his closest challenger, it also gave these challengers a better chance to catch up with Bush and stay in the race.

6. Broder et al., *The Pursuit of the Presidency 1980,* pp. 141–42.

7. I am indebted to Kathleen Frankovic for informing me about Reagan's use of Tracy's script.

8. CBS News/*New York Times* Iowa poll, January 1980.

9. Campbell, "Interpreting the Presidential Victory," p. 269.

9. The Fight to Redirect the Democratic Coalition in 1984

1. Drew, *Campaign Journal,* p. 40.

2. The generational difference in interest in new ideas for government was not just based on a more negative response to the Carter administration by younger Democrats; there was little age difference in attitudes about the Carter administration. Carter's performance rating was 57 percent approval and 40 percent disapproval for Democrats under the age of forty-five, and 56 percent approval and 38 percent disapproval for Democrats over forty-five. CBS News/*New York Times* poll, March 1984.

3. Drew, *Campaign Journal,* p. 353.

4. CBS News/*New York Times* poll, September 1983.

5. Drew, *Campaign Journal,* p. 183. *Hellcats of the Navy* was a World War II film starring Ronald Reagan and Nancy Davis. This was the closest Reagan ever got to actual combat. It was also the only film he made with Davis, who later became his second wife.

6. Ibid., pp. 180, 185.

7. Ibid., p. 180.

8. Ibid., pp. 33, 188.

9. Some of these respondents would have seen clips of the debate on newscasts in addition to viewing the debate; some of the respondents who said they watched some of the debate probably only saw clips on the news.

10. For any conceivable measure of political activation, Hart scores higher and Glenn lower among the activated. For example, if we take only the Democrats con-

tacted by the Mondale campaign (132), those who saw the debate rated Hart much higher than those who did not. Glenn also scores lower and Hart higher among those paying a lot of attention to the campaign.

11. Hickman, "Presidential Election Debates." Hickman is comparing primary debates and general-election debates, and does not discuss the effect of the debate on preferences. While the effects of debates on preferences in general elections are clearly minimal, it is also clearly the case that the debates do matter in primaries. There is no plausible way that the very large difference in the vote for John Glenn between viewers and nonviewers could be due to a markedly lower propensity of Glenn voters to watch the debate.

12. CBS News/*New York Times* exit poll for Iowa.

13. D. Moore, "The Death of Politics in New Hampshire."

14. I discuss the Iowa and New Hampshire primaries at greater length in Popkin, "The Iowa and New Hampshire Primaries."

15. In the first March 1984 CBS News/*New York Times* survey, 37 percent were confident of Hart's ability to deal with the Soviet Union and 28 percent were uneasy; for Mondale, 38 percent were confident and 36 percent uneasy.

16. Drew, *Campaign Journal,* p. 374.

17. Henry Brady has raised the question of how long it takes to learn about the candidates in "Is Iowa News?"

18. Similar arguments have been made in Frankovic, "The Democratic Nomination Campaign." This chapter has benefited from a number of insights from Dr. Frankovic.

19. Quoted in Drew, *Campaign Journal,* pp. 387 and 366, respectively.

20. Ibid., p. 382.

21. Ibid., p. 383.

22. When reconstructing Mondale's past support using two questions, a question about current preference and a question which asks whether the respondent had supported anyone else earlier, 43 percent of the respondents are classified as past Mondale supporters. This is what his support was *before* Iowa.

23. The national survey taken after the New Hampshire primary contained 244 registered potential Democratic primary voters who said they had supported Mondale earlier in the year; 60 of them had moved to Hart after New Hampshire. The panel survey reinterviewing respondents from February after Super Tuesday reinterviewed 366 of the 467 original registered potential Democratic primary voters; 209 of these respondents had been for Mondale after Iowa, and 52 of them were supporting Hart after Super Tuesday.

24. One hundred eleven people who supported Mondale after Iowa said helping the poor was more important; 79 percent were still supporting Mondale in the second interview, and 15 percent had moved to Hart. Sixty-two people who supported Mondale after Iowa placed more emphasis on cutting deficits; 50 percent had stayed with Mondale and 43 percent had moved to Hart.

25. Among voters unfavorable to the AFL-CIO, it did not matter whether they knew of the actual endorsement.

26. Clymer, "The 1984 National Primary."

27. The entire change in support for new ideas came from voters over forty-five. Younger voters were favorable 52 percent to 42 percent in 1983 and 52 percent to 40 percent in 1984; older voters were favorable 34 percent to 45 percent in 1983 and 44 percent to 33 percent in 1984. It may be, therefore, that the stimulus to support for change was Mondale's defense of traditional ideas, not Hart's advocacy of new ideas.

28. These divisions are not an artifact of age differences in the vote because younger Democrats were more tolerant of union endorsements than older voters, whether they were pro- or anti-union.

29. In April, 35 percent in union households agreed that unions have too much political power in America, and 57 percent disagreed. The poll showed further that white-collar union members were far more critical of union political involvement. Among all other Democrats, the figures were 57 percent agree and 32 percent disagree, which are the same figures as for the rest of the electorate. Nonunion Democrats, then, are no more supportive of union political involvement than Republicans and independents. CBS News/*New York Times* poll, April 1984. Note that this is strong resentment of union political influence, which is not the same as resentment of unions. Americans are much more supportive of the economic role of unions than of their political role.

30. Mondale had a list of significant issues on which he had, in fact, differed from the AFL-CIO, but he personally did not believe in discussing the differences, despite the entreaties of his aides and union officials. Personal communication, William Galston, 1984.

31. The percentages saying "says what he believes" and "says what the public wants to hear": 63 percent to 28 percent for Hart favorables; 47 percent to 44 percent for Mondale favorables; and 58 percent to 35 percent for those favorable to both the AFL-CIO and Mondale. (Those unfavorable to both Mondale and the AFL-CIO were 37 percent to 52 percent!)

32. While it is the firm recollection of top Hart strategists, such as his pollster Dottie Lynch, that Hart began to go down when Mondale confronted him and tied together all the little personal doubts and questions about signature, name changes, and age, the strength of their belief says more about their foreboding at the time than it does about the actual changes in preference. (Interviews with Lynch in 1986 and 1989.)

33. The night of Super Tuesday, Dan Rather asked during the CBS News "whether Mondale has won enough in the primary states to keep his hopes for the nomination *alive.*" That same night during a CBS News Special Report, Rather asked Mondale, "Doesn't that indicate to you that if your candidacy is still alive, it's hanging on the ropes?"

34. Drew, *Campaign Journal,* pp. 404–7.

35. Percentages from the March 5–8 CBS News/*New York Times* poll are based on 573 interviews; percentages from the second poll are based on 411 interviews, 235 on the first two days and 176 on the last two days. Some of the interviews in the last two days are with people who were sampled but could not be reached on the first two days; eliminating these interviews makes no difference.

36. The rise in Mondale's favorability does, however, suggest an effect of expectations on favorability.

10. Conclusion

1. Quoted in Will, *Men at Work,* p. 30.

2. See also the discussion in Houston, "Walter Lippmann."

3. Kinder and Mebane, "Politics and Economics in Everyday Life," p. 146.

4. Ibid., pp. 27–28, 30; the phrase "disinterested interest" is Kinder and Mebane's.

5. Berelson et al., *Voting,* p. 183.

6. My appreciation for the interaction of the media and personal sides of mobilization has been particularly enriched by my research into the origins and

development of the Hoa Hao religion in Vietnam. See Popkin, *The Rational Peasant,* pp. 202–13.

7. There are few people we ever come to know as well as our parents, yet many people are deeply ambivalent and subject to changes of opinion about their parents.

8. Kaplan, *The Conduct of Inquiry,* pp. 17–18.

9. Polsby, *Consequences of Party Reform.*

10. Frances Fitzgerald, in "A Critic at Large (Memoirs of the Reagan Era)," reconstructs the inner workings of the Reagan White House from the memoirs. Joan Didion, in "Life at Court," also reviews and integrates several of the memoirs.

11. Burnham, *The Current Crisis in American Politics,* esp. chap. 3, "The Appearance and Disappearance of the American Voter."

12. Ibid., p. 169, and Powell, "American Voter Turnout in Comparative Perspective," p. 27.

13. Wolfinger and Rosenstone's *Who Votes?* is the starting point for all discussions of turnout and registration in the United States.

14. Wattenberg, *The Decline of American Political Parties,* pp. 79–81, and Wattenberg, "The 1988 and 1960 Elections Compared."

15. Although no primary candidates would mention it directly, some of them would run ads showing themselves "pumping iron" or jogging, and the less fit would talk about the rigors of negotiating with Russians or Japanese.

16. Ross, *The Loneliest Campaign,* p. 48.

17. Henry Brady first raises the question of whether voters learn about candidates' character and competence in Brady, "Is Iowa News?" and Brady and Johnston, "What's the Primary Message." Brady is looking only at national data, so his estimate of how long it takes to learn about candidates is greater than mine. Larry Bartels has also found, with different methodologies and foci, that "the most intense uncritical form" of the demonstration effects of victories is no more than two or three weeks. Bartels is referring, I believe, to the kinds of projection from personal data to office that are most worrisome. Bartels, *Presidential Primaries,* p. 290.

18. Wolfinger and Rosenstone, *Who Votes?* p. 44.

19. Strate et al., "Life Span Civic Development and Voting Participation."

20. Quattrone and Tversky, in "Causal versus Diagnostic Contingencies," develop the concept of the voter's illusion. Voters' illusions and the "links in a chain" arguments of political organizers are based on the same logic. See Popkin, *The Rational Peasant,* p. 259.

21. Popkin, "The Iowa and New Hampshire Primaries."

22. Penniman, "U.S. Elections: Really a Bargain?"

23. C. Smith, "Captives of Cash"; David Sanger, "Will Japan Scandal Force Changes in the System?" *New York Times,* Apr. 27, 1989. When told how much more is spent in Japan, many people appear to instantly change their opinions about the lavishness of campaign spending in the United States; this says much about perceptions of America's status.

24. Note further that the Japanese money is all spent on contributions, funeral wreaths, organizations, and the like, because there is no television advertising by candidates.

25. Berelson et al., *Voting,* p. 95.

26. See chap. 3, n. 70.

27. Hallin, "Sound Bite News."

28. "Noonan Q & A: What She Said at the University," *New York Times,* Aug. 5, 1990, p. E5.

29. Weaver, "Is Television News Biased?" p. 69. See also the discussion in the conclusion of Iyengar and Kinder, *News That Matters*, pp. 112–33.

30. Witcover, *Marathon*, p. 446.

31. Germond and Witcover, *Blue Smoke and Mirrors*, p. 215.

32. In President Carter's 1980 surveys, most Catholics, for example, had no idea what the Moral Majority was. By 1984, they rated the Moral Majority negatively by over five to one in the March CBS News/*New York Times* poll.

33. CBS News/*New York Times* polls, October 1984.

34. Schudson, "Telemythology and American Politics."

35. The inside cover for Joe McGinniss's *Selling of the President,* chronicling Richard Nixon's 1968 campaign, included Alastair Cooke's praise of McGinniss, "His frankness would be brutal if his perceptions of the inherent fraud were not so acute," and Murray Kempton's comment that Nixon's staff talked to McGinniss "with the candor possible only to persons who have no idea how disgusting they are." McGinniss, *The Selling of the President.*

36. The term *stop and think effects* is from Zaller, "Political Competition and Public Opinion." Ultimately, I believe, Zaller's work on the effects of one-sided and two-sided communications will make it possible to ascertain just how much of the decline in turnout is due to a decline in media stimulation, and how much is due to a decline in interpersonal use of political information.

37. Several of the initial studies of the turnout rates of SRC respondents are reported in Kinder and Sears, "Public Opinion and Political Action," p. 703. Verified turnout among survey respondents has been higher than for the rest of the country in every election since verification began in 1964. Barbara A. Anderson, Brian D. Silver, and Paul R. Abramson, in "The Effects of Race of the Interviewer on Measures of Electoral Participation by Blacks," have also found that the turnout boost, ceteris paribus, is higher for blacks interviewed by blacks than for blacks interviewed by whites.

38. Kinder and Sears, "Public Opinion and Political Action."

39. "Noonan Q & A," p. E5.

40. Ibid.

41. The term *genteel populists* is from Simon Lazarus, *The Genteel Populists,* a prescient analysis of their effects upon party politics.

11. The Election of 1992

1. CBS/*New York Times* poll, March 1991. This poll was taken in the week immediately following the hundred-hour war against Iraq.

2. Evans and Novak are quoted in *The Hotline,* March 1, 1991; *Newsweek,* March 18, 1991, p. 40.

3. Gramm was quoted by Paul West in the *Baltimore Sun,* March 1, 1991, and reported that day in *The Hotline.*

4. CBS/*New York Times* polls February through June 1992. These polls pose the favorability question in a more restrictive fashion than most other polls. Instead of only asking respondents whether they generally have a favorable or unfavorable opinion of a candidate, they ask, "Is your opinion of [Bill Clinton] favorable, unfavorable, undecided or haven't you heard enough about [Bill Clinton] to have an opinion?" Clinton's ratings plummeted as low as 15 percent favorable and 40 percent unfavorable, with 32 percent saying they had not yet heard enough and 15 percent undecided. This format gives lower favorability ratings, particularly for new candidates, because it gives respondents the additional option of saying they do not yet know enough to form an opinion.

5. The model of Yale economist Ray Fair, which was based only upon economic

variables, predicted that Bush would win 57 percent. Other models based upon various combinations of economic data and public opinion data proved more accurate, and the divergence between the models with and those without opinion data emphasizes that it is assessments of the president's economic efforts and not simply the actual economy that matters to voters. Fair's model is described in Ray C. Fair, "The Effect of Economic Events on Votes for President: 1984 Update," *Political Behavior* 10:2 (1988): 168–79. For a summary of 1992 predictions, see Jay P. Greene, "Forewarned before Forecast: Presidential Election Forecasting Models and the 1992 Election," *PS* 26:1 (March 1993): 17–21. For a summary of the major models, including those incorporating economic data and opinion data, see Michael S. Lewis-Beck and Tom W. Rice, *Forecasting Elections,* Washington, D.C.: Congressional Quarterly Press, 1992.

6. CBS/*New York Times* poll, March 4–6, 1991.

7. Operation Desert Storm, in fact, did not even increase the percentage of Americans who considered themselves patriotic. In June 1991, 55 percent of the respondents in a CBS News/*New York Times* poll said they were "very patriotic" and 37 percent said they were "somewhat patriotic"; in November 1983, the respective figures were 53 percent and 37 percent.

8. See also chapter 2, p. 33.

9. Similar analyses of the changed relation between consumer confidence and aggregate economic activity were presented to the New England Economic Project by Roger Brinner of Data Resources Incorporated and Mark Zandi of Regional Financial Associates. The finding of a 1990 "gap" between confidence and aggregate economic activity is a robust finding holding for both Conference Board and Michigan measures of consumer confidence and a wide range of aggregate measures of current employment, growth, and inflation measures. Personal communications with Mark Zandi and John Gorman, November, 1993.

10. Since the CBS News/*New York Times* began asking this question in 1989, a plurality of Americans has thought that Japan would surpass the U.S. economically. Operation Desert Storm made only a modest dent in the Japanese lead; after Operation Desert Storm, there were more Americans who thought the United States would be number one in the next century than there were in 1990, but still fewer than in 1989.

11. *The Tonight Show,* NBC, January 9, 1993. Transcript excerpted from *The Hotline,* January 10, 1993.

12. CBS/*New York Times* polls June 1990 and March 1991.

13. By June of 1990, even before the Soviet Union finally collapsed, when respondents in the CBS News/*New York Times* poll were asked whether the greatest "threat to America" was the Soviet military threat or the Japanese economic threat, respondents by more than two to one (58 percent to 26 percent) believed that the Japanese economy was the greater threat.

14. CBS/*New York Times* polls, April 1981 and January 1992.

15. In October 1991 the Republicans had a one-point lead. Just before the president's trip in 1992 a CBS/*New York Times* poll asked, "Who do you think can do a better job of handling the problem you just mentioned, President Bush or the Democrats?" That variant showed the same results as the previous October.

16. CBS/*New York Times* polls for October 1980, 1984, and 1988.

17. Popkin, "Optimism, Pessimism and Policy."

18. The genesis of the speech is described by Peggy Noonan, who wrote the speech, in "A Thousand Points of Light," pp. 298–317 of *What I Saw at the Revolution* (New York: Random House, 1990). The complete text of the speech is in the *New York Times,* August 19, 1988, p. 14. "What are you doing?" Congressman Dan

Rostenkowski, chairman of the House Ways and Means Committee, asked James Baker after Bush made his pledge. Baker's answer was "We're going to elect a President of the United States. We'll talk about *that* after he's elected." Sidney Blumenthal, "The Sorcerer's Apprentices," *The New Yorker* 69, July 19, 1993, pp. 29–31, quotation on p. 31.

19. See, especially, p. 92.

20. CBS/*New York Times* poll, October 1990.

21. Gary C. Jacobson "Deficit Politics and the 1990 Elections," 1992, American Political Science Association, Chicago, Sept. 3–6, 1992.

22. Gary C. Jacobson and Michael A. Dimock, "Checking Out: The Effects of Bank Overdrafts on the 1992 House Elections." Delivered at the Annual Meeting of the Midwest Political Science Association, Chicago, Illinois, April 15–17, 1993.

23. Robin Toner, "Anxious Days for Bush's Campaign as G.O.P. Heads into a 3-Way Race," *New York Times,* May 21, 1992, p. 1.

24. The classic study of changes in the wage structure since 1945, and particularly of the declining fortunes of recent cohorts, is Frank Levy's *Dollars and Dreams: The Changing American Income Distribution* (New York: Russell Sage Foundation, 1987).

25. On four of the Clinton surveys, voters were asked to express their worries about a second Bush term and about a Clinton presidency. The two most common answers for Bush were gridlock and decline, while for Clinton they were inexperience and taxes.

26. Thomas Rosenstiel, *Strange Bedfellows: How Television and the Presidential Candidates Changed American Politics, 1992* (New York: Hyperion, 1993), pp. 54–55.

27. The *Wall Street Journal* story appeared on February 6; the letter to Colonel Holmes was printed in the *New York Times* on February 13, and the stories about his induction notice appeared there on April 5.

28. The *New York Times,* March 30, p. A15.

29. Surveys by Opinion Dynamics Corporation for WCVB-TV, Boston.

30. The Tsongas quotations and advertising copy were reported in *The Hotline,* March 12, 1992.

31. Brown's comments were made on WTAE-AM in Pittsburgh, April 26; they were reported in *The Hotline,* April 27, 1992.

32. Robin Toner, *New York Times,* April 21, 1992.

33. Exit polls for CNN, ABC, CBS, and NBC were conducted jointly by VRS. The two choices presented to respondents were "I am satisfied with my party's candidates for President" or "I would like to see someone else enter the race." A similar question was asked on the CBS/*New York Times* polls; at the end of March, 67 percent of registered Democrats said they wanted to see another candidate enter the race. The stories also increased the problems that Clinton had, as a Southerner and Baptist, with Catholic voters. For example, among whites, in the VRS Florida exit poll, Clinton beat Tsongas 52 percent to 33 percent among Protestants and Tsongas beat Clinton 43 percent to 41 percent among Catholics.

34. In ABC polls in New Hampshire, for example, only 11 percent of the respondents thought the information on Clinton's marriage was relevant, while 80 percent thought the press was wrong to discuss the charges. Rosenstiel, *Strange Bedfellows,* p. 70. National polls showed similar figures, while the number of voters thinking the draft charges were relevant was generally around 20 percent. However, only 24 percent of respondents in the April CBS/*New York Times* poll said they thought Clinton had more integrity than most people in public life.

35. CBS/*New York Times* poll, June 1992. These figures had been relatively stable since March.

36. The Clinton campaign's research, including surveys and focus groups, about the "character problem" is described in "How He Won," *Newsweek* Special Election Issue, November/December 1992, pp. 40–41.

37. *Washington Post*, March 20, 1992. See also Rosenstiel, *Strange Bedfellows*, p. 143.

38. See pp. 63–65.

39. So far, the focus of this chapter has been on primaries, as in the rest of the book. In the rest of this chapter, I analyze the 1992 general election and begin to demonstrate the relevance of low information rationality and the themes developed in this book for general elections as well as for primaries.

40. NBC *Tonight Show*, June 9, 1992. Text from *The Hotline*, June 10, 1992.

41. VRS exit polls as reported in *The Hotline*.

42. *Newsweek*, June 15, 1992, cited in *The Hotline*, June 16, 1992.

43. *Newsweek*, "How He Won," p. 41.

44. Rosenstiel, *Strange Bedfellows*.

45. Wicker's comments appeared on the ABC News program *The Brinkley Report*, and Gergen's on the *MacNeil-Lehrer News Hour*. The texts of their remarks appeared in *The Hotline*, June 8, 1992.

46. Stassen was criticized for behaving in a manner more appropriate for an election for sheriff. See chapter 10, p. 224.

47. CBS/*New York Times* polls, April 1992 and June 17–20, 1992

48. Rosenstiel, *Strange Bedfellows*, p. 183.

49. CBS/*New York Times* polls, May 27–30, 1992 and June 17–20.

50. The last two questions are from CBS/*New York Times* polls for July and August 1992. The first question was from a poll conducted for the Clinton campaign by Greenberg-Lake Research.

51. CBS/*New York Times* polls for March, June, July, August and October 1992.

52. The first statistic is from CBS/*New York Times* poll for August 14, 1992; the questions about Bush and Clinton are from the CBS/*New York Times* poll for October 2–4, 1992.

53. See page 66 for a discussion between H. R. Haldeman and Richard Nixon. When Haldeman explained to Richard Nixon in 1972 that it would be easier to raise George McGovern's negatives than to raise Nixon's positives, he was summarizing the views of the Republican pollster Robert Teeter, who would give much the same advice to George Bush twenty years later.

54. Rosenstiel, *Strange Bedfellows*, p. 289.

55. Sidney Blumenthal, "The Order of the Boot," *The New Yorker* 68, December 7, 1992, pp. 55–63, describes the attempts by the Bush campaign to imitate the successful campaign by the British Conservative party.

56. *Newsweek*, "How He Won," pp. 83–85.

57. It is worth noting that campaign research showed that the endorsement of Nobel laureates was more credible to the public than the endorsement of the CEOs. I remind readers, for the sake of full disclosure, that I worked with the Clinton campaign on polling and targeting in 1992.

58. In campaign surveys, after pollsters read to respondents the Republican attacks on Clinton as a "tax and spend" Democrat and then told them about his accomplishments as governor, the welfare reform program was the most reassuring element of his record as rebuttal to Republican charges against him. Welfare reform was even more reassuring than eleven consecutive balanced budgets, an Arkansas growth rate twice the national average, and a rate of creating manufacturing jobs in Arkansas which was ten times the national average.

59. Rosenstiel, *Strange Bedfellows,* pp. 281–82, also discusses the campaign research on welfare reform.

60. Rosenstiel, *Strange Bedfellows,* pp. 163–97. Rosenstiel's analysis of the media in 1992 describes how decentralized the media are and how very different they have become from the days of pack journalism described by Timothy Crouse in *The Boys on the Bus.*

61. See pp. 130–32.

62. Martin P. Wattenberg, "The 1992 Election: Ross Perot and the Independent Voter," forthcoming as chapter 10 of *The Decline of American Political Parties.* In an appearance at the annual convention of the National Association for the Advancement of Colored People, Perot had used the phrase "you people" referring to his audience, which many African Americans interpreted as a sign of Perot's racial insensitivity and social insularity.

63. See also the discussion in chapter 6, pp. 118–20. All poll figures are from CBS/*New York Times* polls. The change in levels of political attentiveness in 1992 was first noted by Kathleen Frankovic in "Public Opinion in the 1992 Campaign," pp. 110–31 of Gerald Pomper, ed., *The Election of 1992: Reports and Interpretations* (Chatham, N.J.: Chatham House, 1993).

64. *Washington Post,* Style Section, p. 1, October 21, 1992.

65. Quoted in *New York Times,* November 4, 1992, p. B5.

66. Perhaps the greatest irony of the 1992 campaign was that the man regarded as the epitome of integrity for telling hard, unvarnished truths misled the public about his health. Tsongas told reporters that he had been cancer-free since his treatments in 1984 when he had, in fact, suffered a relapse; "Tsongas Says He Mishandled Issue of His Cancer," Lawrence K. Altman, *New York Times,* December 1, 1992, p. A:1.

67. See chapter 7, esp. pp. 164–65.

Bibliography

Abelson, Robert P. "Script Processing in Attitude Formation and Decision Making." In *Cognition and Social Behavior*, edited by J. S. Carroll and J. W. Payne. Hillsdale, N.J.: Lawrence Erlbaum Associates, 1976.

————. "Social Psychology's Rational Man." In *The Concept of Rationality in the Social Sciences*, edited by G. W. Mortimore and S. I. Benn. London: Routledge & Kegan Paul, 1976.

Abelson, Robert P., Donald R. Kinder, and Mark D. Peters. "Affective and Semantic Components in Political Person Perception." *Journal of Personality and Social Psychology* 42:4 (1982): 619–30.

Abramowitz, Alan I., David J. Lanoue, and Subha Ramesh. "Economic Conditions, Causal Attributions, and Political Evaluations in the 1984 Presidential Election." *Journal of Politics* 50:4 (November 1988): 848–63.

Abramowitz, Alan I., and Walter J. Stone. *Nomination Politics: Party Activists and Presidential Choice*. New York: Praeger, 1984.

Abramson, Paul R., John H. Aldrich, and David W. Rohde. *Change and Continuity in the 1980 Elections*. Washington, D.C.: Congressional Quarterly Press, 1982.

Adrian, Charles. "Some General Characteristics of Nonpartisan Elections." *American Political Science Review* 46:3 (September 1952): 766–76.

Akerloff, George A. "The Economics of Caste and of the Rat Race and Other Woeful Tales." *Quarterly Journal of Economics* 90 (November 1976): 599–617.

Akerloff, George A., and William T. Dickens. *The Economic Consequences of Cognitive Dissonance*. Berkeley, Calif.: University of California at Berkeley, Institute of Industrial Relations (Reprint no. 451), 1982.

Aldrich, John H. *Before the Convention*. Chicago: University of Chicago Press, 1980.

Aldrich, John H., John L. Sullivan, and Eugene Borgida. "Foreign Affairs and Issue Voting: Do Presidential Candidates 'Waltz before a Blind Audience'?" *American Political Science Review* 83:1 (March 1989): 123–42.

Allen, Woody. "A Brief, Yet Helpful, Guide to Civil Disobedience." *Without Feathers*. New York: Random House. 1975.

Anderson, Barbara A., Brian D. Silver, and Paul R. Abramson. "The Effects of Race of the Interviewer on Measures of Electoral Participation by Blacks in SRC National Election Studies." *Public Opinion Quarterly* 52 (1988): 53–83.

————. "The Effects of Race of the Interviewer on Race-related Attitudes of Black Respondents in SRC/CPS National Election Studies." *Public Opinion Quarterly* 52 (1988): 289–324.

Aristotle. *The Rhetoric and Poetics of Aristotle*. New York: Random House, 1954.

Arlen, Michael J. *Living Room War.* New York: Penguin, 1982.

Atwood, L. Erwin, and Keith R. Sanders. "Information Sources and Voting in a Primary and General Election." *Journal of Broadcasting* 20:3 (Summer 1976): 291–300.

Bartels, Larry M. "Candidate Choice and the Dynamics of the Presidential Nominating Process." *American Journal of Political Science* 31:1 (1987): 1–30.

———. "Expectations and Preferences in Presidential Nominating Conventions." *American Political Science Review* 79:3 (September 1985): 804–15.

———. "Issue Voting under Uncertainty: An Empirical Test." *American Journal of Political Science* 30:4 (1986): 709–28.

———. *Presidential Primaries and the Dynamics of Public Choice.* Princeton, N.J.: Princeton University Press, 1988.

Beck, Nathaniel. "Presidents, the Economy, and Elections: A Principal-Agent Perspective." In *The Presidency in American Politics,* edited by Paul Brace, Christine Harrington, and Gary King. New York: New York University Press, 1989.

Becker, Gary. "The Economic Approach to Human Behavior." In *Rational Choice,* edited by Jon Elster. New York: New York University Press, 1986.

Becker, Lee B., and Maxwell E. McCombs. "The Role of the Press in Determining Voter Reactions to Presidential Primaries." *Human Communication Research* 4 (1977): 301–7.

Beer, Samuel H. "Two Models of Public Opinion: Bacon's 'New Logic' and Diotima's 'Tale of Love.'" *Political Theory* 2:2 (May 1974): 163–80.

Beniger, James. "Winning the Presidential Nomination: National Polls and State Primary Elections, 1936–1972." *Public Opinion Quarterly* (Spring 1976): 22–38.

Berelson, Bernard, Paul Lazarsfeld, and William McPhee. *Voting: A Study of Opinion Formation in a Presidential Campaign.* Chicago: University of Chicago Press, 1954.

Bereton, Charles. *First in the Nation: New Hampshire and the Premier Presidential Primary.* Portsmouth, N.H.: Peter E. Randall, 1987.

Bewley, Truman F. "Knightian Decision Theory: Part 1." *Cowles Foundation Discussion Paper no. 807.* New Haven: Yale University, 1986.

Boller, Paul F., Jr. *Presidential Campaigns.* New York: Oxford University Press, 1984.

Bolles, Edmund Blair. *Remembering and Forgetting: Inquiries into the Nature of Memory.* New York: Walker, 1988.

Brady, Henry E. "Chances, Utilities, and Voting in Presidential Primaries." Manuscript, 1985.

———. "Do Voters Choose What They Prefer?" Manuscript, 1987.

———. "Is Iowa News?" In *The Iowa Caucus and the Presidential Nominating Process,* edited by Peverill Squire. Boulder: Westview Press, 1989.

———. "Knowledge, Strategy, and Momentum." Paper presented at the California Institute of Technology, February 1984; revised 1989.

Brady, Henry E., and Stephen Ansolabehere. "The Nature of Utility Functions in Mass Publics." *American Political Science Review* 83:1 (1989): 143–63.

———. "Rational Choice, Knowledge, and Preferences for Presidential Candidates." *American Political Science Review,* forthcoming.

Brady, Henry E., and Michael G. Hagen. "The 'Horse-Race' or the Issues? What Do Voters Learn from Presidential Primaries?" Paper presented at the annual meeting of the American Political Science Association, Washington, D.C., August 1986.

Brady, Henry E., and Richard Johnston. "What's the Primary Message: Horse Race or Issue Journalism?" In *Media and Momentum,* edited by Gary Orren and Nelson Polsby. Chatham, N.J.: Chatham House, 1987.

Brady, Henry E., and Paul Sniderman. "Attitude Attribution: A Group Basis for Political Reasoning." *American Political Science Review* 79:4 (1985): 1061–78.

Broder, David, Lou Cannon, Haynes Johnson, Martin Schram, and Richard Harwood. *The Pursuit of the Presidency 1980.* New York: Berkeley, 1980.

Brody, Richard A. "Candidate Evaluations and the Vote: Some Considerations Affecting the Application of Cognitive Psychology to Voting Behavior." In *Political Cognition,* edited by Richard R. Lau and David O. Sears. Hillsdale, N.J.: Lawrence Erlbaum Associates, 1986.

————. "Change and Stability in Partisan Identification: A Note of Caution." Manuscript, 1975.

————. "International Crises: A Rallying Point for the President." *Public Opinion* 6:6 (December–January 1983–84): 41–43, 60.

————. "Vote Choice in the 1988 South Carolina Republican Primary: Issues, Religious Fundamentalism, and the Stability of the Republican Coalition." Manuscript, 1988.

Brody, Richard A., and Bernard Grofman. "Stimulus Differentiation versus Stimulus Complexity as Factors Affecting Turnout in Two-Candidate and Multicandidate Races." *Political Behavior* 4:1 (1982): 83–92.

Brody, Richard A., and Catherine R. Shapiro. "Policy Failure and Public Support: The Iran-Contra Affair and Public Assessment of President Reagan." *Political Behavior* 11:4 (1989): 353–69.

————. "A Reconsideration of the Rally Phenomenon in Public Opinion." In *Political Behavior Annual,* vol. 2, edited by S. Long. Denver: Westview Press, 1989.

Brody, Richard A., and Paul M. Sniderman. "From Life Space to Polling Place: The Relevance of Personal Concerns for Voting Behavior." *British Journal of Political Science* 7 (1977): 337–60.

Brody, Richard A., Paul M. Sniderman, and James Kuklinski. "Policy Reasoning in Political Issues: The Problem of Racial Equality." *American Journal of Political Science* 28 (1984): 75–94.

Brown, R. "Schizophrenia, Language, and Reality." *American Psychologist* 28:5 (1973): 395–403.

Bruner, Jerome. *Acts of Meaning.* Cambridge: Harvard University Press, 1990.

————. *Actual Minds, Possible Worlds.* Cambridge: Harvard University Press, 1986.

————. *In Search of Mind.* New York: Harper Colophon, 1984.

————. *On Knowing.* Cambridge: Harvard University Press, 1962.

————. "On the Perception of Incongruity: A Paradigm." *Journal of Personality* 18 (1949): 206–23.

Bruner, Jerome, and Sheldon Korchin. "The Boss and the Vote: A Case Study in City Politics." *Public Opinion Quarterly* 10 (1946): 1–23.

Bryce, James. *The American Commonwealth.* New York: Macmillan, 1893.

Burnham, Walter Dean. *The Current Crisis in American Politics.* New York: Oxford University Press, 1982.

Caddell, Patrick H. "The Democratic Strategy and Its Electoral Consequences." In *Party Coalitions in the 1980s,* edited by Seymour Martin Lipset. New Brunswick: Transaction Books, 1981.

Cain, Bruce E., I. A. Lewis, and Douglas Rivers. "Strategy and Choice in the 1988 Presidential Primaries." Paper presented at the annual meeting of the American Political Science Association, Washington, D.C., September 1988.

Callaway, John D., Judith A. Mayotte, and Elizabeth Altick-McCarthy. *Campaigning on Cue.* Chicago: William Benton Fellowships Program in Broadcast Journalism, University of Chicago, 1988.

Calvo, Maria Antonia, and Steven J. Rosenstone. "The Re-Framing of the Abortion Debate." Manuscript, 1990.

Campbell, Angus. "Interpreting the Presidential Victory." In *The National Election of 1964,* edited by Milton C. Cummings, Jr. Washington, D.C.: Brookings, 1966.

———. "Voters and Elections: Past and Present." *Journal of Politics* 26 (November 1964): 745–57.

Campbell, Angus, Philip Converse, Donald Stokes, and Warren Miller. *The American Voter.* New York: John Wiley, 1960.

Campbell, Angus, Gerald Gurin, and Warren Miller. *The Voter Decides.* Evanston, Ill.: Peterson, 1954.

Campbell, Angus, and Robert Kahn. *The People Elect a President.* Ann Arbor: Survey Research Center, 1952.

Campbell, Angus, and Donald Stokes. "Partisan Attitudes and the Presidential Vote." In *American Voting Behavior,* edited by Eugene Burdick and Arthur J. Brodbeck. Glencoe, Ill.: Free Press, 1959.

Carmines, Edward G., and James H. Kuklinski. "Incentives, Opportunities, and the Logic of Public Opinion in American Political Representation." In *Information and Democratic Processes,* edited by John A. Ferejohn and James H. Kuklinski. Chicago: University of Illinois Press, 1990.

Carmines, Edward G., and James A. Stimson. "The Two Faces of Issue Voting." *American Political Science Review* 74 (1980): 78–91.

Chaffee, Steven H., and Sun Yuel Choe. "Time of Decision and Media Use during the Ford-Carter Campaign." *Public Opinion Quarterly* 44 (1980): 53–69.

Chaffee, Steven H., and Yuko Miyo. "Selective Exposure and the Reinforcement Hypothesis: An Intergenerational Panel Study of the 1980 Presidential Campaign." *Communication Research* 10:1 (1983): 3–36.

Cheney, Richard B. "The 1976 Presidential Debates: A Republican Perspective." In *The Past and Future of Presidential Debates,* edited by Austin Ranney. Washington, D.C.: American Enterprise Institute for Public Policy Research, 1979.

Clarke, Peter, and Eric Fredin. "Newspapers, Television, and Political Reasoning." *Public Opinion Quarterly* 42 (1978): 143–60.

Clymer, Adam. "The Economic Basis for 'Throwing the Bums Out' in the 1980 and 1982 American Elections." Paper presented at the annual meeting of the American Political Science Association, Chicago, Illinois, September 4, 1983.

———. "The 1984 National Primary." *Public Opinion* (August–September 1984): 52–53.

Conover, Pamela Johnston, and Stanley Feldman. "Candidate Perception in an Ambiguous World: Campaigns, Cues, and Inference Processes." *American Journal of Political Science* 33:4 (November 1989): 912–39.

———. "Projection and the Perceptions of Candidates' Issue Positions." *Western Political Quarterly* 35:2 (1982): 228–44.

Converse, Philip E. "Comment: The Status of Non-attitudes." *American Political Science Review* 68 (June 1974): 650–60.

————. "The Nature of Belief Systems in Mass Publics." In *Ideology and Discontent*, edited by David Apter. Glencoe, Ill.: Free Press, 1964.

————. "Popular Representation and the Distribution of Information." In *Information and Democratic Processes*, edited by John A. Ferejohn and James H. Kuklinski. Chicago: University of Illinois Press, 1990.

————. "Public Opinion and Voting Behavior." In *NonGovernmental Politics*, vol. 4, edited by Nelson Polsby and Fred Greenstein. Menlo Park, Calif.: Addison-Wesley, 1975.

Converse, Philip E., and Georges Dupeux. "Politicization of the Electorate in France and the United States." *Public Opinion Quarterly* 26 (1962): 1–23.

Converse, Philip E., and Michael W. Traugott. "Assessing the Accuracy of Polls and Surveys." *Science* 234 (November 1986): 1094–98.

Conway, M., and M. Ross. "Getting What You Want by Revising What You Had." *Journal of Personality and Social Psychology* 47 (1984): 738–48.

Cox, Gary W. *The Efficient Secret*. Cambridge: Cambridge University Press, 1988.

Cox, Gary W., and Charles H. Franklin. "The Dynamics of Public Support in Presidential Nominating Campaigns." Manuscript, 1986.

Crouse, Timothy. *The Boys on the Bus: Riding with the Campaign Press Corps*. New York: Ballantine, 1974.

Darnton, Robert. "Marxed Men." *New Republic* (January 1, 1990): 12–15.

Dawes, Robyn. *Rational Choice in an Uncertain World*. San Diego: Harcourt, Brace, Jovanovich, 1988.

————. "The Robust Beauty of Improper Linear Models in Decision Making." *American Psychologist* 34:7 (1979): 571–82.

————. "Shallow Psychology." In *Cognition and Social Behavior*, edited by J. S. Carroll and J. W. Payne. Hillsdale, N.J.: Lawrence Erlbaum Associates, 1976.

Delli Carpini, Michael X., and Scott Keeter. "Political Knowledge of the U.S. Public: Results from a National Survey." Paper presented at the annual meeting of the American Association for Public Opinion Research, St. Petersburg, Florida, May 18–21, 1989.

Devlin, L. Patrick. "Contrasts in Presidential Campaign Commercials of 1980." *Political Communication Review* 7 (1982): 1–38.

Diamond, Edwin. *The Spot: The Rise of Political Advertising on Television*. Cambridge, Mass.: MIT Press, 1984.

Didion, Joan. "Life at Court." *New York Review of Books* (December 21, 1989): 3–10.

Divine, Robert A. "The Cold War and the Election of 1948." *Journal of American History* 59 (June 1972): 90–110.

Downs, Anthony. *An Economic Theory of Democracy*. New York: Harper & Row, 1957.

Drew, Elizabeth. *American Journal*. New York: Random House, 1977.

————. *Campaign Journal: The Political Events of 1983–1984*. New York: Macmillan, 1985.

————. *Portrait of an Election: The 1980 Presidential Campaign*. New York: Simon & Schuster, 1981.

Einhorn, H. J., and R. M. Hogarth. "Confidence in Judgment: Persistence of the Illusion of Validity." *Psychological Review* 85 (1978): 395–416.

Eisenberg, Phillip, and Paul Lazarsfeld. "The Psychological Effects of Unemployment." *Psychological Bulletin* 35 (June 1938): 358–90.

Elster, Jon, and Aanund Hylland. *Foundations of Social Choice Theory*. Cambridge: Cambridge University Press, 1986.

Erbring, Lutz, Edie N. Goldberg, and Arthur H. Miller. "Front-Page News and Real World Cues: A New Look at Agenda-Setting by the Media." *American Journal of Political Science* 24:1 (1980): 17–49.

Eubank, Robert B., and David John Gow. "The Pro-Incumbent Bias in the 1978 and 1980 National Election Studies." *American Journal of Political Science* 27:1 (February 1983): 122–39.

Feldman, Stanley. "Economic Individualism and American Public Opinion." *American Politics Quarterly* 11:1 (January 1983): 3–29.

———. "Economic Self-Interest and Political Behavior." *American Journal of Political Science* 26:3 (August 1982): 446–65.

Feldman, Stanley, and Pamela Johnston Conover. "Candidates, Issues, and Voters: The Role of Inference in Political Perception." *Journal of Politics* 45 (1983): 810–39.

Fenno, Richard F., Jr. *Home Style: House Members in Their Districts.* Boston: Little, Brown, 1978.

———. *The Presidential Odyssey of John Glenn.* Washington, D.C.: Congressional Quarterly Press, 1990.

Ferejohn, John A. "Information and the Electoral Process." In *Information and Democratic Processes,* edited by John A. Ferejohn and James H. Kuklinski. Chicago: University of Illinois Press, 1990.

———. "On the Decline of Competition in Congressional Elections." *American Political Science Review* 71 (1977): 177–81.

Ferejohn, John A., and Randall L. Calvert. "Presidential Coattails in Historical Perspective." *American Journal of Political Science* 28:1 (February 1984): 127–46.

Fiorina, Morris P. "Information and Rationality in Elections." In *Information and Democratic Processes,* edited by John A. Ferejohn and James H. Kuklinski. Chicago: University of Illinois Press, 1990.

———. *Retrospective Voting in American National Elections.* New Haven: Yale University Press, 1979.

———. "Short- and Long-Term Effects of Economic Conditions on Individual Voting Decisions." In *Contemporary Political Economy,* edited by D. A. Hibbs, Jr., and H. Fassbender. Amsterdam: North-Holland, 1981.

Fiorina, Morris P., and Kenneth A. Shepsle. "Is Negative Voting an Artifact?" Occasional Paper no. 87-2, Center for American Political Studies, Harvard University, Cambridge, Massachusetts.

———. "Negative Voting: An Explanation Based on Principal-Agent Theory." In *Information and Democratic Processes,* edited by John A. Ferejohn and James H. Kuklinski. Chicago: University of Illinois Press, 1990.

Fischhoff, B. "For Those Condemned to Study the Past: Reflections on Historical Judgment." In *New Directions for Methodology of Behavioral Science: Fallible Judgments in Behavioral Research,* edited by R. Schweder and D. W. Fiske. San Francisco: Jossey-Bass, 1980.

Fiske, Susan T., and Donald R. Kinder. "Involvement, Expertise, and Schema Use: Evidence from Political Cognition." In *Personality, Cognition, and Social Interaction,* edited by N. Cantor and J. F. Kihlsttom. Hillsdale, N.J.: Lawrence Erlbaum Associates, 1981.

Fitzgerald, Frances. "A Critic at Large (Memoirs of the Reagan Era)." *New Yorker* (January 16, 1989): 71–94.

Franklin, Charles H. "Issue Preference, Socialization, and the Evolution of Party Identification." *American Journal of Political Science* 28 (1984): 459–78.

Franklin, Mark N. *The Decline of Class Voting in Britain: Changes in the Basis of Electoral Choice, 1964–1983.* New York: Oxford University Press, 1985.

Frankovic, Kathleen A. "The Democratic Nomination Campaign: Voter Rationality and Instability in a Changing Campaign Environment." In *Elections in America*, edited by Kay Schlozman. Boston: Allan & Unwin, 1987.

Frohlich, Norman, Joe A. Oppenheimer, Jeffrey Smith, and Oran R. Young. "A Test of Downsian Voter Rationality: 1964 Presidential Voting." *American Political Science Review* 72:1 (March 1978): 178–97.

Gallucci, Robert. *Neither Peace nor Honor: The Politics of American Military Policy in VietNam.* Baltimore: Johns Hopkins University Press, 1975.

Gant, Michael M., and Norman R. Luttbeg. "The Cognitive Utility of Partisanship." *Western Political Quarterly* (September 1987): 499–517.

Gardner, Howard. *The Mind's New Science: A History of the Cognitive Revolution.* New York: Basic Books, 1985.

Garramone, Gina M. "Issue versus Image Orientation and Effects of Political Advertising." *Communication Research* 10:1 (January 1983): 59–76.

Geertz, Clifford. "Ideology as a Cultural System." In *Ideology and Discontent*, edited by David Apter. Glencoe, Ill.: Free Press, 1964.

Germond, Jack W., and Jules Witcover. *Blue Smoke and Mirrors: How Reagan Won and Why Carter Lost the Election of 1980.* New York: Viking Press, 1981.

———. *Whose Broad Stripes and Bright Stars?* New York: Warner Books, 1989.

Gollob, H. R., B. B. Rossman, and R. P. Abelson. "Social Inference as a Function of the Number of Instances and Consistency of the Information Presented." *Journal of Personality and Social Psychology* 27:1 (1973): 19–33.

Green, Donald Philip. "On the Dimensionality of Public Sentiment toward Partisan and Ideological Groups." *American Journal of Political Science* 32:3 (August 1988): 758–80.

Grether, David M. "Testing Bayes Rule and the Representativeness Heuristic: Some Experimental Evidence." Social Science Working Paper no. 724, California Institute of Technology, 1990.

Grossman, Michael Baruch, and Martha Joynt Kumar. *Portraying the President.* Baltimore: Johns Hopkins University Press, 1981.

Grossman, Michael Baruch, and Francis E. Rourke. "The Media and the Presidency: An Exchange Analysis." Paper presented at the annual meeting of the American Political Science Association, San Francisco, California, September 1975.

Guth, James L. "The New Christian Right." In *The New Christian Right*, edited by Liebman and Wuthnow. Hawthorne, N.Y.: Aldine, 1983.

———. "Southern Baptist Clergy: Vanguard of the Christian Right?" In *The New Christian Right*, edited by Liebman and Wuthnow. Hawthorne, N.Y.: Aldine, 1983.

Halberstam, David. *The Powers That Be.* New York: Alfred A. Knopf, 1979.

Hallin, Daniel C. "Sound Bite News." In *Blurring the Lines*, edited by Gary Orren. New York: Free Press, forthcoming.

Hamill, R., T. D. Wilson, and R. E. Nisbett. "Insensitivity to Sample Bias: Generalizing from Atypical Cases." *Journal of Personality and Social Psychology* 39:4 (1980): 578–89.

Hardin, Russell. *Collective Action.* Baltimore: Johns Hopkins University Press, 1982.

———. "Difficulties in the Notion of Economic Rationality." *Social Science Information* 23 (1984): 453–67.

———. "Game Theory and the Nature of Man." Paper presented at the annual meeting of the American Political Science Association, New York City, September 1978.

———. "Rational Choice Theories." In Terence Ball, ed., *Idioms of Inquiry: Critique and Renewal in Political Science.* New York: State University of New York Press, 1987.

———. "Rationality, Irrationality, and Functionalist Explanation." *Social Science Information* 19 (1980): 755–72.

Harsanyi, John C. "Advances in Understanding Rational Behavior." In *Rational Choice,* edited by Jon Elster. New York: New York University Press, 1986.

Hastie, Reid. "A Primer of Information-Processing Theory for the Political Scientist." In *Political Cognition,* edited by Richard Lau and David Sears. Hillsdale, N.J.: Lawrence Erlbaum Associates, 1986.

Hawley, Willis D. *Nonpartisan Elections and the Case for Party Politics.* New York: John Wiley & Sons, 1973.

Hedlund, Ronald D. "Cross-over Voting in a 1976 Open Presidential Primary." *Public Opinion Quarterly* 41:4 (Winter 1977–78): 498–514.

Heider, F. *The Psychology of Interpersonal Relations.* New York: Wiley, 1958.

Herken, Gregg. *The Winning Weapon: The Atomic Bomb in the Cold War, 1945–1950.* New York: Alfred A. Knopf, 1980.

Herstein, John A. "Keeping the Voter's Limits in Mind: A Cognitive Process Analysis of Decision Making in Voting." *Journal of Personality and Social Psychology* 40:5 (1981): 843–61.

Hibbs, Douglas A. "The Dynamics of Political Support for American Presidents among Occupational and Partisan Groups." *American Journal of Political Science* 26:2 (May 1982): 312–32.

Hickman, Harrison. "Presidential Election Debates: Do They Matter?" *Election Politics* 2:1 (Winter 1984–85): 10–14.

Himmelweit, Hilde T., Patrick Humphreys, Marianne Jaeger, and Michael Katz. *How Voters Decide: A Longitudinal Study of Political Attitudes and Voting Extending over Fifteen Years.* London: Academic Press, 1981.

Hirshleifer, J., and John G. Riley. "The Analytics of Uncertainty and Information— An Expository Survey." *Journal of Economic Literature* (December 1979): 1375–1421.

Houston, Alan. "Walter Lippmann: Public Opinion in the Great Society." Manuscript, 1984.

Hovland, Carl I., Irving L. Janis, and Harold H. Kelley. *Communication and Persuasion.* New Haven: Yale University Press, 1953.

Hovland, Carl I., Arthur A. Lumsdaine, and Fred D. Sheffield. *Experiments on Mass Communication.* New York: Science Editions, 1965.

Hughes, Michael. "The Fruits of Cultivation Analysis: A Reexamination of Some Effects of Television Watching." *Public Opinion Quarterly* 44 (1980): 288–302.

Hyman, Herbert H., and Paul B. Sheatsley. "Some Reasons Why Information Campaigns Fail." *Public Opinion Quarterly* 11 (1947): 412–23.

Iyengar, Shanto. *Framing Effects in Politics: Television and Political Responsibility.* Chicago: University of Chicago Press, forthcoming.

———. "How Citizens Think about National Issues: A Matter of Responsibility." *American Journal of Political Science* 33:4 (November 1989): 878–97.

———. "Shortcuts to Political Knowledge: Selective Attention and Accessibility." In *Information and Democratic Processes,* edited by John Ferejohn and James Kuklinski. Chicago: University of Illinois Press, 1990.

———. "Television News and Citizens' Explanations of National Affairs." *American Political Science Review* 81:3 (September 1987): 815–31.

Iyengar, Shanto, and Donald Kinder. *News That Matters: Television and American Opinion.* Chicago: University of Chicago Press, 1987.

Jackman, Robert W. "Political Institutions and Voter Turnout in the Industrial Democracies." *American Political Science Review* 81:2 (June 1987): 405–23.

Jacobitti, Suzanne Duvall. "Causes, Reasons, and Voting." *Political Theory* 7:3 (August 1979): 390–413.

Jacobson, Gary C. "The Effects of Campaign Spending on Voting Intentions: New Evidence from a Panel Study of the 1986 House Elections." Paper presented at the annual meeting of the Midwest Political Science Association, Chicago, Illinois, April 14–16, 1988.

———. *The Electoral Origins of Divided Government.* Boulder: Westview, 1990.

———. "Meager Patrimony: Republican Representation in Congress after Reagan." Paper presented at the Conference on the Legacy of the Reagan Presidency, University of California at Davis, May 24–26, 1988.

———. "The Persistence of Democratic House Majorities: Structure or Politics?" Paper presented at the Conference on Divided Government of the American Political Institutions Project and the Department of Political Science, University of California at San Diego, June 30, 1990.

———. *The Politics of Congressional Elections.* Boston: Little, Brown, 1983.

Jacoby, William G. "The Impact of Party Identification on Issue Attitudes." *American Journal of Political Science* 32:3 (August 1988): 643–61.

Jamieson, Kathleen Hall. *Packaging the Presidency.* New York: Oxford University Press, 1984.

Janowitz, Morris, and Warren E. Miller. "The Index of Political Predisposition in the 1948 Election." *Journal of Politics* 14 (November 1952): 710–27.

Jervis, Robert. "Representativeness in Foreign Policy Judgments." *Political Psychology* 7:3 (1986): 483–505.

Judd, Charles M., and Jon A. Krosnick. "The Structural Bases of Consistency among Political Attitudes: Effects of Political Expertise and Attitude Importance." In *Attitude Structure and Function,* edited by A. R. Pratkanis, S. J. Breckler, and A. G. Greenwald. Hillsdale, N.J.: Lawrence Erlbaum Associates, 1979.

Kahneman, Daniel, Jack L. Knetsch, and Richard Thaler. "Fairness as a Constraint on Profit Seeking: Entitlements in the Market." *American Economic Review* 76:4 (September 1986): 728–41.

Kahneman, Daniel, and Dale T. Miller. "Norm Theory: Comparing Reality to Its Alternatives." *Psychological Review* 93:2 (1986): 136–53.

Kahneman, Daniel, Paul Slovic, and Amos Tversky, eds. *Judgment under Uncertainty: Heuristics and Biases.* Cambridge: Cambridge University Press, 1982.

Kahneman, Daniel, and Amos Tversky. "Choices, Values, and Frames." *American Psychologist* 39:4 (April 1984): 341–50.

———. "On the Psychology of Prediction." *Psychological Review* 80:4 (July 1973): 237–51.

———. "Prospect Theory: An Analysis of Decision under Risk." *Econometrica* 47 (1979): 263–91.

———. "Subjective Probability: A Judgment of Representativeness." *Cognitive Psychology* 3 (1972): 430–54.

Kaiser, Robert G. "White-House Pulse-Taking: Pollster Wirthlin Reaps Spoils, Pain of Fame." *Washington Post* (February 24, 1982): A1.

Kaplan, Abraham. *The Conduct of Inquiry.* San Francisco: Chandler, 1964.

Katz, Elihu, and Paul Lazarsfeld. *Personal Influence.* Glencoe, Ill.: Free Press, 1955.

Keeter, Scott. "The Illusion of Intimacy: Television and the Role of Candidate Personal Qualities in Voter Choice." *Public Opinion Quarterly* 51 (1987): 344–58.

Keeter, Scott, and Cliff Zukin. *Uninformed Choice: The Failure of the New Presidential Nominating System,* edited by Gerald M. Pomper. New York: Praeger, 1983.

Kelley, Harold H. "The Process of Causal Attribution." *American Psychologist* 28:2 (February 1973): 107–28.

Kelley, Stanley, Jr. *Interpreting Elections.* Princeton, N.J.: Princeton University Press, 1983.

Kennamer, J. David, and Steven H. Chaffee. "Communication of Political Information during Early Presidential Primaries: Cognition, Affect, and Uncertainty." In *Communication Yearbook,* vol. 5, edited by M. Burgoon. New Brunswick: Transaction Books, 1985.

Key, V. O., Jr. "The Politically Relevant in Surveys." *Public Opinion Quarterly* 24:1 (Spring 1960): 54–61.

———. *Public Opinion and American Democracy.* New York: Alfred A. Knopf, 1961.

———. *The Responsible Electorate: Rationality in Presidential Voting, 1936–1960.* Cambridge: Harvard University Press, 1966.

Kiewiet, D. Roderick. *Macroeconomics and Micropolitics.* Chicago: University of Chicago Press, 1983.

Kiewiet, D. Roderick, and Douglas Rivers. "A Retrospective on Retrospective Voting." Social Science Working Paper no. 528, California Institute of Technology, 1984.

Kinder, Donald R. "Presidents, Prosperity, and Public Opinion." *Public Opinion Quarterly* 45 (1981): 1–21.

Kinder, Donald R., and Robert P. Abelson. "Appraising Presidential Candidate: Personality and Affect in the 1980 Campaign." Paper presented at the annual meeting of the American Political Science Association, New York, September 3–6, 1981.

Kinder, Donald R., Gordon S. Adams, and Paul W. Gronke. "Economics and Politics in the 1984 American Presidential Election." *American Journal of Political Science* 33:2 (May 1989): 491–515.

Kinder, Donald R., and D. Roderick Kiewiet. "Sociotropic Politics: The American Case." *British Journal of Political Science* 11 (1981): 129–61.

Kinder, Donald R., and Walter R. Mebane, Jr. "Politics and Economics in Everyday Life." In *The Political Process and Economic Change,* edited by Kristen R. Monroe. New York: Agathon Press, 1982.

Kinder, Donald R., and Lynn M. Sanders. "Pluralistic Foundation of American Opinion on Race." Paper presented at the annual meeting of the American Political Science Association, Chicago, Illinois, September 3–6, 1987.

Kinder, Donald R., and David O. Sears. "Public Opinion and Political Action." In *The Handbook of Social Psychology,* edited by Gardner Lindzey and Elliot Aronson. Hillsdale, N.J.: Random House, 1985.

Knight, Frank H. *Risk, Uncertainty, and Profit.* New York: Kelley & Millman, 1957.

Kramer, Gerald H. "The Ecological Fallacy Revisited: Aggregate- versus Individual-Level Findings on Economics and Elections, and Sociotropic Voting." *American Political Science Review* 77:1 (March 1983): 92–111.

Kramer, Michael. "Should Anderson Quit?" *New York* (October 13, 1980): 26.

Krassa, Michael A. "The Structure of Interaction and the Transmission of Political Influence and Information." In *Information and Democratic Processes,* edited by John A. Ferejohn and James H. Kuklinski. Chicago: University of Illinois Press, 1990.

Krause, Sidney, ed. *The Great Debates: Carter vs. Ford.* Bloomington: University of Indiana Press, 1979.

————, ed. *The Great Debates: Kennedy vs. Nixon.* Bloomington: University of Indiana Press, 1977.

Kreps, David M. *A Course in Microeconomic Theory.* Princeton, N.J.: Princeton University Press, 1990.

Krosnick, Jon A. "Americans' Perceptions of Presidential Candidates: A Test of the Projection Hypothesis." *Journal of Social Issues,* forthcoming.

————. "Attitude Importance and Attitude Accessibility." *Personality and Social Psychology Bulletin* 15:3 (1989): 297–308.

————. "Attitude Importance and Attitude Change." *Journal of Experimental Social Psychology* 24 (1988): 240–55.

————. "Government Policy and Citizen Passion: A Study of Issue Publics in Contemporary America." *Political Behavior* 12:1 (1990): 59–93.

————. "The Role of Attitude Importance in Social Evaluation: A Study of Policy Preferences, Presidential Candidate Evaluations, and Voting Behavior." *Journal of Personality and Social Behavior* 55:2 (1988): 196–210.

Krosnick, Jon A., and Duane F. Alwin. "Aging and Susceptibility to Attitude Change." *Journal of Personality and Social Psychology* 57:3 (1989): 416–25.

————. "An Evaluation of a Cognitive Theory of Response-Order Effects in Survey Measurement." *Public Opinion Quarterly* 51 (1987): 201–19.

————. "The Stability of Political Preferences: Comparisons of Symbolic and Non-Symbolic Attitudes." Manuscript, 1990.

————. "A Test of the Form-Resistant Correlation Hypothesis." *Public Opinion Quarterly* 52 (1988): 526–38.

Krosnick, Jon A., and Matthew K. Berent. "The Impact of Verbal Labeling of Response Alternatives and Branching on Attitude Measurement Reliability in Surveys." Manuscript, 1990.

Krosnick, Jon A., and Donald R. Kinder. "Altering the Foundations of Support for the President through Priming." *American Political Science Review* 84:2 (June 1990): 497–512.

Krosnick, Jon A., and Michael A. Milburn. "Psychological Determinants of Political Opinionation." *Serial Cognition,* forthcoming.

Krosnick, Jon A., and Howard Schuman. "Attitude Intensity, Importance, and Certainty and Susceptibility to Response Effects." *Journal of Personality and Social Psychology* 54:6 (1988): 940–52.

Kuklinski, James H. "Information and the Study of Politics." In *Information and Democratic Processes,* edited by John A. Ferejohn and James H. Kuklinski. Chicago: University of Illinois Press, 1990.

Ladd, Everett Carll. "The Brittle Mandate: Electoral Dealignment and the 1980 Presidential Election." *Political Science Quarterly* 96:1 (1981): 1–26.

Lakoff, George. *Women, Fire, and Dangerous Things.* Chicago: University of Chicago Press, 1987.

Lakoff, George, and Mark Johnson. *Metaphors We Live By.* Chicago: University of Chicago Press, 1980.

Lamis, Alexander P. *The Two-Party South.* New York: Oxford University Press, 1984.

Lang, Gladys Engel, and Kurt Lang. "The Formation of Public Opinion: Direct and Mediated Effects of the First Debate." In *The Presidential Debates: Media, Electoral, and Policy Perspectives,* edited by George F. Bishop, Robert G. Meadow, and Marilyn Jackson-Beeck. New York: Praeger, 1980.

Lapchick, Richard E. "Pseudo-Scientific Prattle about Athletes." *New York Times* (April 29, 1989): 15.

Lau, Richard, and David Sears. "Cognitive Links between Economic Grievances and Political Responses." *Political Behavior* 3:4 (1981): 279–302.

———. "Social Cognition and Political Cognition: The Past, the Present, and the Future." In *Political Cognition*, edited by Lau and Sears. Hillsdale, N.J.: Lawrence Erlbaum Associates, 1986.

Lazarsfeld, Paul, Bernard Berelson, and Helen Gaudet. *The People's Choice: How the Voter Makes Up His Mind in a Presidential Campaign*, 2d ed. New York: Columbia University Press, 1948.

Lazarus, Simon. *The Genteel Populists*. New York: Holt, Rinehart & Winston, 1974.

LeBon, Gustave. *The Crowd*. London: Ernest Benn, 1952.

Lesher, Stephen, with Patrick Caddell and Gerald Rafshoon. "Did the Debates Help Jimmy Carter?" In *The Past and Future of Presidential Debates*, edited by Austin Ranney. Washington, D.C.: American Enterprise Institute for Public Policy Research, 1979.

Lewin, Kurt. *Field Theory in Social Science*. New York: Harper & Brothers, 1951.

Lichtenstein, Sarah, and Paul Slovic. "Response-Induced Reversals of Preference in Gambling: An Extended Replication in Las Vegas." *Journal of Experimental Psychology* 101:1 (1973): 16–20.

———. "Reversals of Preference between Bids and Choices in Gambling Decisions." *Journal of Experimental Psychology* 89:1 (1971): 46–55.

Lichter, S. Robert, Daniel Amundson, and Richard Noyes. *The Video Campaign*. Washington, D.C.: American Enterprise Institute for Public Policy Research, Center for Media and Public Affairs, 1988.

Linsky, Martin. *Television and the Presidential Elections*. Lexington, Mass.: D. C. Heath, 1983.

Lippmann, Walter. *Public Opinion*. New York: Macmillan, 1961.

Lodge, Milton, Kathleen M. McGraw, and Patrick Stroh. "An Impression-Driven Model of Candidate Evaluation." *American Political Science Review* 83:2 (June 1989): 399–419.

Loftus, Elizabeth F. *Eyewitness Testimony*. Cambridge: Harvard University Press, 1979.

Lubell, Samuel. "Personalities vs. Issues." In *The Great Debates: Kennedy vs. Nixon*, edited by Sidney Krause. Bloomington: University of Indiana Press, 1977.

Luce, R. Duncan. "Analyzing the Social Process Underlying Group Voting Patterns." In *American Voting Behavior*, edited by Eugene Burdick and Arthur J. Brodbeck. Glencoe, Ill.: Free Press, 1959.

Luker, Kristin. *Abortion and the Politics of Motherhood*. Berkeley: University of California Press, 1984.

McCarthy, Larry. "The Selling of the President: An Interview with Roger Ailes." *Gannett Center Journal* 2 (Fall 1988): 67, as quoted in Martin Wattenberg, "The Elections of 1984 and 1988: Realignment without Revitalization," manuscript, 1989.

McClure, Robert D., and Thomas E. Patterson. "Television News and Political Advertising: The Impact of Exposure on Voter Beliefs." *Communication Research* 1:1 (January 1974): 3–31.

McCombs, Maxwell. "Reforming the News Media." Paper presented at "The Challenge of Creating an Informed Electorate," National Press Club, Washington, D.C., May 7, 1990.

MacCrimmon, Kenneth R., and Stig Larson. "Utility Theory: Axioms versus Paradoxes." In *Expected Utility Hypothesis and the Allais Paradox*, edited by Maurice Allais and Ole Hagen. Dordrecht, Holland: D. Reidel, 1979.

McCubbins, Matthew, and Thomas Schwartz. "Congressional Oversight Overlooked: Police Patrols versus Fire Alarms." *American Journal of Political Science* 2:1 (February 1984): 165–79.

McGinniss, Joe. *The Selling of the President.* New York: Pocket Books, 1974.

Machina, Mark J. "Choice under Uncertainty: Problems Solved and Unsolved." *Economic Perspectives* 1:1 (Summer 1987): 121–54.

———. "Decision-Making in the Presence of Risk." *Science* 236 (May 1987): 537–43.

MacKuen, Michael B. "Speaking of Politics: Individual Conversational Choice, Public Opinion, and the Prospects for Deliberative Democracy." In *Information and Democratic Processes,* edited by John A. Ferejohn and James H. Kuklinski. Chicago: University of Illinois Press, 1990.

MacKuen, Michael B., Robert S. Erikson, and James A. Stimson. "Macropartisanship." *American Political Science Review* 83:4 (December 1989): 1125–42.

Maital, Shlomo. *Minds, Markets, and Money.* New York: Basic Books, 1982.

Mansbridge, Jane. "Self-Interest in Political Life." *Political Theory* 18:1 (February 1990): 132–53.

Markus, Gregory B. "The Impact of Personal and National Economic Conditions on the Presidential Vote: A Pooled Cross-Sectional Analysis." *American Journal of Political Science* 32:1 (February 1988): 137–54.

———. "Stability and Change in Political Attitudes: Observed, Recalled, and 'Explained.'" *Political Behavior* 8:1 (1986): 21–44.

Markus, Gregory B., and Philip E. Converse. "A Dynamic Simultaneous Equation Model of Electoral Choice." *American Political Science Review* 73:4 (December 1979): 1055–70.

Marsh, Catherine. "Back on the Bandwagon: The Effect of Public Opinion Polls on Public Opinion." *British Journal of Political Science* 15:1 (1984): 51–74.

Martel, Miles. *Political Campaign Debates.* New York: Longman, 1983.

Meadow, Robert G., and Marilyn Jackson-Beeck. "A Comparative Perspective on Presidential Debates: Issue Evolution in 1960 and 1976." In *The Presidential Debates: Media, Electoral, and Policy Perspectives,* edited by George F. Bishop, Robert G. Meadow, and Marilyn Jackson-Beeck. New York: Praeger, 1980.

Meehl, P. E. "Causes and Effects of My Disturbing Little Book." *Journal of Personality Assessment* 50 (1986): 370–75.

Miller, Arthur H. "Policy and Performance Voting in the 1980 Election." Paper presented at the annual meeting of the American Political Science Association, New York, September 3–6, 1981.

Miller, Arthur H., and Michael B. MacKuen. "Learning about the Candidates: The 1976 Presidential Debates." *Public Opinion Quarterly* 43 (1979): 326–46.

Mitofsky, Warren. "The 1980 Pre-Election Polls: A Review of Disparate Methods and Results." Proceedings of the Survey Research Methods Section of the American Statistical Association (1982): 47–52.

———. "A Short History of Exit Polls." Manuscript, 1990.

Moore, David. "The Death of Politics in New Hampshire." In *The Mass Media in Campaign '84: Articles from Public Opinion Magazine,* edited by Michael J. Robinson and Austin Ranney. Washington, D.C.: American Enterprise Institute, 1985.

Moore, Jonathan. *The Campaign for President: 1980 in Retrospect.* Cambridge: Ballinger, 1981.

Moran, Jack, and Mark Fenster. "Voter Turnout in Presidential Primaries." *American Politics Quarterly* 10:4 (October 1982): 453–76.

Mueller, John E. *War, Presidents, and Public Opinion.* New York: John Wiley & Sons, 1973.

Natchez, Peter. *Images of Voting/Visions of Democracy.* New York: Basic Books, 1984.

Neuman, W. Russell. "The Threshold of Public Attention." *Public Opinion Quarterly* 54 (1990): 159–76.

Nisbett, Richard E., Eugene Borgida, Rick Crandall, and Harvey Reed. "Popular Induction: Information Is Not Necessarily Informative." In *Judgment under Uncertainty: Heuristics and Biases,* edited by Kahneman, Slovic, and Tversky. Cambridge: Cambridge University Press, 1982.

Nisbett, Richard E., and Lee Ross. *Human Inference: Strategies and Shortcomings of Social Judgment.* Englewood Cliffs, N.J.: Prentice Hall, 1980.

Norman, Donald. *The Design of Everyday Things.* New York: Doubleday, 1989.

Norrander, Barbara. "Correlates of Vote Choice in the 1980 Presidential Primaries." *Journal of Politics* 48:1 (1986): 156–66.

Norrander, Barbara, and Gregg W. Smith. "Type of Contest, Candidate Strategy, and Turnout in Presidential Primaries." *American Politics Quarterly* 13:1 (January 1985): 28–50.

Orren, Gary R. "Candidate Style and Voter Alignment in 1976." In *Emerging Coalitions in American Politics,* edited by Seymour Martin Lipset. San Francisco: Institute for Contemporary Studies, 1978.

Ottati, Victor C., M. Fishbein, and S. E. Middlestadt. "Determinants of Voters' Beliefs about the Candidates' Stands on the Issues: The Role of Evaluative Bias Heuristics and the Candidates' Expressed Message." *Journal of Personality and Social Psychology* 55:4 (1988): 517–29.

Ottati, Victor C., and Robert S. Wyer, Jr. "Affect and Political Judgment." Manuscript, 1990.

———. "The Cognitive Mediators of Political Choice: Toward a Comprehensive Model of Political Information Processing." In *Information and Democratic Processes,* edited by John A. Ferejohn and James H. Kuklinski. Chicago: University of Illinois Press, 1990.

Ottati, Victor C., Robert S. Wyer, Jr., Ellen J. Riggle, and Norbert Schwarz. "Cognitive and Affective Bases of Opinion Survey Responses." *Journal of Personality and Social Psychology* 57:3 (1989): 404–15.

Page, Benjamin I. *Choices and Echoes in Presidential Elections.* Chicago: University of Chicago Press, 1978.

Paletz, David L., and Richard J. Vinegar. "Presidents on Television: The Effects of Instant Analysis." *Public Opinion Quarterly* 41:4 (Winter 1977–78): 488–97.

Palmer, Paul. "The Concept of Public Opinion in Political Theory." In *Essays in History and Political Theory.* Cambridge: Harvard University Press, 1936.

Patterson, Thomas C. *The Mass Media Election: How Americans Choose Their President.* New York: Praeger, 1980.

———. "The Press and Candidate Images." *International Journal of Public Opinion Research* 1:2 (1989): 123–35.

Peffley, Mark, and John T. Williams. "Attributing Presidential Responsibility for National Economic Problems." *American Politics Quarterly* 13:4 (1985): 393–425.

Penniman, Howard R. "U.S. Elections: Really a Bargain?" In *The Mass Media in Campaign '84: Articles from Public Opinion Magazine,* edited by Michael J.

Robinson and Austin Ranney. Washington, D.C.: American Enterprise Institute, 1985.

Petrocik, John R. "Divided Government: Is It All in the Campaigns?" Paper presented at the Conference on Divided Government of the American Political Institutions Project, San Diego, California, June 29–July 1, 1990.

———. "The Theory of Issue Ownership: Issues, Agendas, and Electoral Coalitions in the 1988 Election." Paper presented at the annual meeting of the American Political Science Association, Atlanta, Georgia, August 31–September 3, 1989; revised 1990.

Pierce, John C., and Douglas D. Rose. "Non-attitudes and American Public Opinion: The Examination of a Thesis." *American Political Science Review* 68 (June 1974): 626–50.

Polsby, Nelson W. *Consequences of Party Reform.* Oxford: Oxford University Press, 1983.

Pool, Ithiel de Sola. *Technologies without Boundaries: On Telecommunications in a Global Age.* Cambridge: Harvard University Press, 1990.

———. "TV: A New Dimension in Politics." In *American Voting Behavior,* edited by Eugene Burdick and Arthur J. Brodbeck. Glencoe, Ill.: Free Press, 1959.

Pool, Ithiel de Sola, Robert P. Abelson, and Samuel L. Popkin. *Candidates, Issues, and Strategies: A Computer Simulation of the 1960 and 1964 Presidential Elections.* Cambridge: MIT Press, 1965.

Popkin, Samuel L. "The Iowa and New Hampshire Primaries: The Interaction of Wholesale and Retail Campaigning." Paper presented at the annual meeting of the American Political Science Association, San Francisco, California, September 1, 1990.

———. "Multivariate Analyses of Trends in Public Opinion." Senior thesis, Department of Political Science, Massachusetts Institute of Technology, 1963.

———. "Optimism, Pessimism, and Policy." *Public Opinion* 11:4 (November–December 1988): 51–55.

———. "Outlook on the Future and Presidential Voting: The 1988 Election and Concerns for the Next Generation." Paper presented at the annual meeting of the American Political Science Association, Washington, D.C., September 1988.

———. "Public Choice and Peasant Organization." In *Toward a Political Economy of Development,* edited by Robert Bates. Berkeley: University of California Press, 1988.

———. *The Rational Peasant: The Political Economy of Rural Society in Vietnam.* Berkeley: University of California Press, 1979.

Popkin, Samuel L., John Gorman, Jeffrey Smith, and Charles Phillips. "Comment: Toward an Investment Theory of Voting Behavior: What Have You Done for Me Lately?" *American Political Science Review* 70:3 (September 1976): 779–805.

Powell, G. Bingham, Jr. "American Voter Turnout in Comparative Perspective." *American Political Science Review* 80:1 (March 1986): 17–44.

Quattrone, George A., and Amos Tversky. "Causal versus Diagnostic Contingencies: On Self-Deception and the Voter's Illusion." *Journal of Personality and Social Psychology* 46 (1984): 237–48.

———. "Contrasting Rational and Psychological Analyses of Political Choice." *American Political Science Review* 82:3 (September 1988): 719–36.

Ragsdale, Lyn. "Campaigns for Campaigners: A Review Essay." *Western Political Quarterly* 40:4 (1987): 736–47.

Rahn, Wendy M. "The Role of Partisan Stereotypes in Information Processing about Political Candidates." Paper presented at the annual meeting of the American Political Science Association, Atlanta, Georgia, August 31–September 3, 1989.

Rahn, Wendy M., John H. Aldrich, Eugene Borgida, and John L. Sullivan. "A Social-Cognitive Model of Candidate Appraisal." In *Information and Democratic Processes*, edited by John A. Ferejohn and James H. Kuklinski. Chicago: University of Illinois Press, 1990.

Rahn, Wendy M., Eugene Borgida, John H. Aldrich, and Susan Klein. "The Process of Candidate Appraisal: An Experimental Investigation." Paper presented at the annual meeting of the American Political Science Association, Washington, D.C., September 1988.

Ranney, Austin. *Channels of Power.* New York: American Enterprise Institute/Basic Books, 1983.

Reed, Adolph L., Jr. *The Jesse Jackson Phenomenon.* New Haven: Yale University Press, 1986.

Reeves, Richard. "McGovern, Nixon, and the Jewish Vote." *New York* (August 14, 1972): 26.

Riecken, Henry W. "Primary Groups and Political Party Choice." In *American Voting Behavior,* edited by Eugene Burdick and Arthur J. Brodbeck. Glencoe, Ill.: Free Press, 1959.

Rivers, Douglas. "Microeconomics and Macropolitics: A Solution to the Kramer Problem." Manuscript, 1988.

Rosenstone, Steven J. "Economic Adversity and Voter Turnout." *American Journal of Political Science* 26:1 (February 1982): 25–46.

Ross, Irwin. *The Loneliest Campaign: The Truman Victory of 1948.* New York: Signet/New American Library, 1968.

Ross, Lee, and Craig A. Anderson. "Shortcomings in the Attribution Process: On the Origins and Maintenance of Erroneous Assessments." In *Judgment under Uncertainty: Heuristics and Biases,* edited by Daniel Kahneman, Paul Slovic, and Amos Tversky. Cambridge: Cambridge University Press, 1982.

Rossi, Peter H. "Four Landmarks in Voting Research." In *American Voting Behavior,* edited by Eugene Burdick and Arthur J. Brodbeck. Glencoe, Ill.: Free Press, 1959.

Rothenberg, Lawrence S., and Richard A. Brody. "Participation in Presidential Primaries." *Western Political Quarterly* 41 (1988): 253–71.

Rubin, Richard. *Party Dynamics: The Democratic Coalition and the Politics of Change.* New York: Oxford University Press, 1976.

———. *Press, Party, and Presidency.* New York: W. W. Norton, 1981.

Sabato, Larry J. *Campaigns and Elections: A Reader in Modern American Politics.* Glenview, Ill.: Scott, Foresman, 1989.

Schelling, Thomas C. "Bargaining, Communication, and Limited War." *Journal of Conflict Resolution* 1 (1957): 19–36.

———. *Choice and Consequence: Perspectives of an Errant Economist.* Cambridge: Harvard University Press, 1984.

Schlozman, Kay Lehman, and Sidney Verba. *Injury to Insult: Unemployment, Class, and Political Response.* Cambridge: Harvard University Press, 1979.

Schneider, William. "Democrats and Republicans, Liberals and Conservatives." In *Emerging Coalitions in American Politics,* edited by Seymour Martin Lipset. San Francisco: Institute for Contemporary Studies, 1978.

Schoemaker, Paul J. H. "The Expected Utility Model: Its Variants, Purposes, Evidence, and Limitations." *Journal of Economic Literature* (June 1982): 529–63.

Schoenberger, Robert A. "Campaign Strategy and Party Loyalty: The Electoral Relevance of Candidate Decision-Making in the 1964 Congressional Elections." *American Political Science Review* 63 (1969): 515–20.

Schram, Martin. "The Making of Willie Horton." *New Republic* (May 28, 1990): 17–19.

Schudson, Michael. *Discovering the News*. New York: Basic Books, 1978.

———. "Telemythology and American Politics." Manuscript, 1990.

Schuman, Howard, Jacob Ludwig, and Jon A. Krosnick. "The Perceived Threat of Nuclear War, Salience, and Open Questions." *Public Opinion Quarterly* 50 (1986): 519–36.

Sears, David O., and Steven H. Chaffee. "Uses and Effects of the 1976 Debates: An Overview of Empirical Studies." In *The Great Debates: Carter vs. Ford*, edited by Sidney Krause. Bloomington: Indiana University Press, 1979.

Sears, David O., and Richard R. Lau. "Inducing Apparently Self-Interested Political Preferences." *American Journal of Political Science* 27:2 (1983): 223–52.

Sen, Amartya. "Behaviour and the Concept of Preference." In *Rational Choice*, edited by Jon Elster. New York: New York University Press, 1986.

Simon, Julian L. "The Theory of Binding Commitments Simplified and Extended, with Generalization to Interpersonal Allocation." *Rationality and Society* 2:3 (July 1990): 287–309.

Slovic, Paul, and Sarah Lichtenstein. "Relative Importance of Probabilities and Payoffs in Risk Taking." *Journal of Experimental Psychology* 78:3 (November 1968): 1–18.

Slovic, Paul, and Amos Tversky. "Who Accepts Savage's Axiom?" *Behavioral Science* 19 (1974): 368–73.

Smith, Charles. "Captives of Cash." *Far Eastern Economic Review* (March 9, 1989): 16–21.

Smith, Eric R. A. N. *The Unchanging American Voter*. Berkeley: University of California Press, 1989.

Smith, Jeffrey A. *American Presidential Elections, Trust, and the Rational Voter*. New York: Praeger, 1980.

Smith, M. Brewster, Jerome Bruner, and Robert W. White. *Opinions and Personality*. New York: John Wiley, 1956.

Smith, Tom. "America's Most Important Problem—A Trend Analysis, 1946–1976." *Public Opinion Quarterly* 44 (1980): 164–80.

Sniderman, Paul M., Richard A. Brody, and James H. Kuklinski. "Policy Reasoning and Political Values: The Problem of Racial Equality." *American Journal of Political Science* 28:1 (February 1984): 75–94.

Sniderman, Paul M., James M. Glaser, and Robert Griffin. "Information and Electoral Choice." In *Information and Democratic Processes*, edited by John A. Ferejohn and James H. Kuklinski. Chicago: University of Illinois Press, 1990.

Squire, Peverill, Raymond E. Wolfinger, and David P. Glass. "Residential Mobility and Voter Turnout." *American Political Science Review* 81:1 (March 1987): 45–65.

Steeper, Frederick T. "Public Response to Gerald Ford's Statements on Eastern Europe in the Second Debate." In *The Presidential Debates: Media, Electoral, and*

Policy Perspectives, edited by George F. Bishop, Robert G. Meadow, and Marilyn Jackson-Beeck. New York: Praeger, 1980.

Stephens, Mitchell. *A History of News: From the Drum to the Satellites*. New York: Viking, 1988.

Stimson, James A. "A Macro Theory of Information Flow." In *Information and Democratic Processes*, edited by John A. Ferejohn and James H. Kuklinski. Chicago: University of Illinois Press, 1990.

Stokes, Donald E. "Spatial Models of Party Competition." In *Elections and the Political Order*, edited by Angus Campbell. New York: Wiley, 1966.

Stokes, Donald E., Angus Campbell, and Warren E. Miller. "Components of Electoral Decision." *American Political Science Review* 52 (June 1958): 367–87.

Stokes, Donald E., and Warren E. Miller. "Party Government and the Saliency of Congress." In *Elections and the Political Order*, edited by Angus Campbell. New York: Wiley, 1966.

Stone, Walter J. "Prenomination Candidate Choice and General Election Behavior: Iowa Presidential Activists in 1980." *American Journal of Political Science* 28:2 (May 1984): 361–78.

Strate, John M., Charles J. Parrish, Charles D. Elder, and Coit Ford III. "Life Span Civic Development and Voting Participation." *American Political Science Review* 83:2 (June 1989): 443–64.

Texeira, Ruy A. *Why Americans Don't Vote: Turnout Decline in the United States, 1960–1984*. Westport, Conn.: Greenwood Press, 1987.

Thompson, Dennis. *The Democratic Citizen*. Cambridge: Cambridge University Press, 1970.

Tocqueville, Alexis de. *Selected Letters on Politics and Society*, edited by Roger Boesche. Berkeley: University of California Press, 1985.

Trilling, Lionel. *Sincerity and Authenticity*. New York: Harcourt Brace Jovanovich, 1971.

Trilling, Richard. *Party Image and Electoral Behavior*. New York: John Wiley, 1976.

Tversky, Amos. "Elimination by Aspects: A Theory of Choice." *Psychological Review* 79 (1972): 281–99.

Tversky, Amos, and Daniel Kahneman. "Availability: A Heuristic for Judging Frequency and Probability." *Cognitive Psychology* 5 (1973): 207–32.

———. "Belief in the Law of Small Numbers." *Psychological Bulletin* 76:2 (1971): 105–10.

———. "Causal Schemas in Judgments under Uncertainty." In *Progress in Social Psychology*, vol. 1, edited by Martin Fishbein. Hillsdale, N.J.: Lawrence Erlbaum Associates, 1980.

———. "Extensional versus Intuitive Reasoning: The Conjunction Fallacy in Probability Judgment." *Psychological Review* 90:4 (October 1983): 293–315.

———. "The Framing of Decisions and the Psychology of Choice." *Science* 211 (January 1981): 453–58.

———. "Judgments of and by Representativeness." In *Judgment under Uncertainty: Heuristics and Biases*, edited by Daniel Kahneman, Paul Slovic, and Amos Tversky. Cambridge: Cambridge University Press, 1982.

———. "Rational Choice and the Framing of Decisions." *Journal of Business* 59:4 (1986): 251–78.

Tversky, Amos, Shmuel Sattah, and Paul Slovic. "Contingent Weighting in Judgment and Choice." *Psychological Review* 95:3 (1988): 371–84.

Verba, Sidney, and Kay Schlozman. "Unemployment, Class Consciousness, and Radical Politics." *Journal of Politics* 39 (May 1977): 299–324.

Wainer, Howard. "Estimating Coefficients in Linear Models: It Don't Make No Nevermind." *Psychological Bulletin* 83 (1976): 312–17.

Wattenberg, Martin P. *The Decline of American Political Parties.* Cambridge: Harvard University Press, 1984.

————. "The Elections of 1984 and 1988: Realignment without Revitalization." Forthcoming in third edition of Wattenberg, *The Decline of American Political Parties: 1952–1988.* Cambridge: Harvard University Press, 1990.

————. "The Hollow Realignment: Partisan Change in a Candidate-Centered Era." Paper presented at the annual meeting of the American Political Science Association, New Orleans, August 29–September 1, 1985.

————. "The 1988 and 1960 Elections Compared: What a Difference Candidate-Centered Politics Makes." Paper presented at the annual meeting of the American Political Science Association, Washington, D.C., September 1–4, 1988.

————. "The Reagan Polarization Phenomenon and the Continuing Downward Slide in Presidential Candidate Popularity." *American Politics Quarterly* 14 (1986): 219–45.

————. "The Republican Presidential Advantage in the Age of Party Disunity." Paper presented at the Conference on Divided Government, University of California at San Diego, June 29–July 1, 1990.

Wattier, Mark J. "Ideological Voting in 1980 Republican Presidential Primaries." *Journal of Politics* 45:4 (November 1983): 1016–26.

————. "The Simple Act of Voting in 1980 Democratic Presidential Primaries." *American Politics Quarterly* 11:3 (July 1983): 267–91.

Weatherford, M. Stephen. "Parties and Classes in the Political Response to Economic Conditions." In *The Political Process and Economic Change,* edited by Kristen R. Monroe. New York: Agathon Press, 1982.

Weaver, Paul. "Is Television News Biased?" *Public Interest* (Winter 1972): 57–74.

Weisberg, Herbert F. "The Demographics of a New Voting Gap: Marital Differences in American Voting." *Public Opinion Quarterly* 51 (1987): 335–43.

Wides, Jeffrey W. "Perceived Economic Competency and the Ford/Carter Election." *Public Opinion Quarterly* 43 (1979): 535–43.

Wikler, Norma Juliet. "Sexism in the Classroom." Paper presented at the American Sociological Association meetings, New York, September 1976.

Will, George. *Men at Work.* New York: Macmillan, 1990.

Williams, Daniel C., Stephen J. Weber, Gordon A. Haaland, Ronald H. Mueller, and Robert E. Craig. "Voter Decisionmaking in a Primary Election: An Evaluation of Three Models of Choice." *American Journal of Political Science* 20:1 (1976): 37–49.

Witcover, Jules. *Marathon: The Pursuit of the Presidency, 1972–1976.* New York: Viking, 1977.

Wolfinger, Raymond E., and Steven J. Rosenstone. *Who Votes?* New Haven: Yale University Press, 1980.

Wright, Gerald C., Jr. "Constituency Response to Congressional Behavior: The Impact of the House Judiciary Committee Impeachment Votes." *Western Political Quarterly* 30 (1977): 401–10.

Wyer, Robert S., Jr., and Victor C. Ottati. "Political Information Processing." In *Current Approaches to Political Psychology.* Urbana: University of Illinois Press, forthcoming.

Young, Jason, Eugene Borgida, John Sullivan, and John Aldrich. "Personal Agendas and the Relationship between Self-Interest and Voting Behavior." *Social Psychology Quarterly* 50 (1987): 64–71.

Zaller, John. "Measuring Individual Differences in Likelihood of News Reception." Paper presented at the annual meeting of the American Political Science Association, San Francisco, California, 1990.

———. "Political Competition and Public Opinion." Manuscript, UCLA Department of Political Science, 1990.

———. "Toward a Theory of the Survey Response." Paper presented at the annual meeting of the American Political Science Association, Washington, D.C., September 1, 1984.

Zaller, John, and Vincent Price. "In One Ear and Out the Other: Learning and Forgetting the News." Paper presented at the annual meeting of the Midwest Political Science Association, Chicago, Illinois, 1990.

Zolberg, Aristide. "Moments of Madness." *Politics and Society* 2:2 (Winter 1972): 182–207.

Zukier, Henri, and Albert Pepitone. "Social Roles and Strategies in Prediction: Some Determinants of the Use of Base-Rate Information." *Journal of Personality and Social Psychology* 47:2 (1984): 349–60.

Index

An entry with a т designates a table (e.g., 45т indicates a table on page 45).